BRITISH MILITARY
LAND ROVERS

BRITISH MILITARY LAND ROVERS

By
JAMES TAYLOR AND GEOFF FLETCHER

Herridge & Sons

Published in 2015 by
Herridge & Sons Ltd
Lower Forda, Shebbear
Devon EX21 5SY

Design by Ray Leaning, MUSE Fine Art & Design

ISBN 978-1-906133-65-8
Printed in China

CONTENTS

INTRODUCTION

This book really came together by a happy accident. We were working together on a different project and realised that, between us, we had enough information about Land Rovers in British military service to create a credible history. Geoff had approached the subject from the military side and had been gathering information for a number of years; James had approached it from the Land Rover side and had done much the same. Our sources differed, and so we had complementary information.

It became clear early on that we had enough information for a very sizeable book on the subject, and so we made it more manageable by focussing this volume on leaf-sprung Land Rovers and leaving the later coil-sprung vehicles for a future volume. Even though Range Rovers entered military service during the "leaf-sprung" period, we decided to save these for a later volume, too.

Even so, we certainly did not have all the information that is now in this book. It took several months of comparing notes and filling in gaps before we felt that we had a worthwhile record of what happened. We are very conscious of the fact that there are still gaps in the information about both RAF and Royal Navy vehicles. Early RAF contract records appear no longer to exist, and as far as we are able to discover, no complete records exist for RN vehicles. We have made a Freedom of Information request to MoD and have consulted the RN Museum at Portsmouth, but neither avenue of research proved fruitful. The information on RN vehicles is the result of research in the Land Rover despatch records at BMIHT Gaydon and a number of sources that gave data on individual vehicles. The RN Museum at Portsmouth holds a number of record cards for vehicles that left service in the 1980s and 1990s, and these also yielded some information.

It proved difficult in some cases to find photographs to illustrate this book. Official sources do not contain everything we wanted (or, if they do, we have been unable to find them), and in some cases we have had to rely on photographs taken by enthusiasts or photographs which were taken more to record an individual's time in service than to record the vehicle. Wherever possible, we have acknowledged our sources in the captions, but in some cases the provenance is in doubt or has been lost.

Both of us have gathered information over the years from a wide variety of sources and from a wide variety of individuals, and we are grateful to everybody who has contributed material, often unwittingly, to this book. We cannot acknowledge all of them, but our thanks are no less sincere.

ACKNOWLEDGEMENTS

I n particular, we are pleased to acknowledge the assistance of the following organisations:

British Motor Industry Heritage Trust, Gaydon (BMIHT)
The REME Museum, Arborfield
D&ES Policy Secretariat
The Dunsfold Collection, Dunsfold
Freelance Military Writers (FMW)
The RAF Museum, Hendon
The RLC Museum, Deepcut (RLC)
The Tank Museum, Bovington (TMB)
The Ex-Military Land Rover Association (EMLRA) and its members
101FC Club and Register (101 FCC&R)

and of the following individuals:

Les Adams
Brian Baxter
Keith Brooker (KB)
Roger Conway
John Craddock
Roger Crathorne
R Dawson
Richard De Roos
Dave Eason of Census Branch at Chilwell
Clive Elliott (CE)
Aidan Fisher
Paul Hancox (PH)
Paul Hazell
Gordon Leith of the RAF Museum
John Mastrangelo
Gareth Mears
Darren Parsons
Andrew Passmore
Dave Shephard
Steve Shirley
Gordon Smith
Andrew Stevens
Robert Swan
Garth Teagle
Ken Twist
Pat Ware (PW)
RE Smith Collection (RES)

Photographs have been credited to the authors using their initials (JT and GF) or to others using the initials in brackets above. Other sources are credited in full where known. We are grateful to all those who have provided photographs.

We have tried to present the book in a useful format dealing with what the services called a "Mark" in each Chapter. Each "Mark" (Mk) corresponded to a particular phase of Land Rover production and also normally referred to the wheelbase length. To enable enthusiasts to find particular vehicles we have included tables of information at the end of each chapter listing those delivered to each service. These tables list batches of serials and the associated contract with the chassis numbers – usually but not invariably of the first and last vehicle in that batch. Note that we have shown chassis numbers with a hyphen between the chassis code prefix and the serial number (eg 241-00535A). This is to aid clarity only; the hyphen does not appear on the chassis plate or in the vehicle documentation.

Chapter 13 is deliberately designed as a "catch-all" to sweep up vehicles that for one reason or another do not fit into the preceding chapters, such as one-off purchases, inter-service transfers, and so on. We also have an appendix that provides information on Army purchases under contract by Financial Year.

We plan to continue research on this topic and hope to be able to produce a companion volume at some point in the future. In the mean time, we would be pleased to hear from individuals who can add to (or contradict) the information here.

James Taylor and Geoff Fletcher
March 2015

CHAPTER 1:

THE MARK 1 AND MARK 2 (80-INCH)

Nowhere in early Land Rover sales material is there any indication at all that the vehicle might be suitable for military use. Nor in fact is there any discussion of the possibility in the Minutes of the Rover Board for 1947 and 1948, when the design was being turned into prototypes. This is rather odd, in view of the vehicle's obvious military potential, although it could be explained by

the fact that WW2 had ended just a couple of years earlier. Nobody was in any mood to discuss military matters any more, and there may have been an element of "don't mention the war" in the polite discussions in the Rover Boardroom. The same went for showroom sales literature, where the new vehicle was described as "For the Farmer, the Countryman, and General Industrial Use".

Nevertheless, there is absolutely no doubt that the Rover Board knew its new Land Rover might be of use to military authorities. Arthur Goddard, who was Chief Engineer on the Land Rover project and whose job at the time was to get the vehicle into production, was quite convinced of the fact. As he remembered it more than half a century later in 2010, "They were designed as a military or agricultural vehicle – that's what they were supposed to do." He also pointed out that his boss, Rover's Chief Engineer Maurice Wilks, would have known exactly what he was doing in creating the new vehicle. There is evidence buried in the Board minutes, too. On 23 March 1948, the Board learned that Rover had received an enquiry about the Land Rover from the Indian Army. At that stage, the new model had not even been announced in public, so somebody must have told the Indian Army that it was coming – and who more likely to have told them than a Rover representative touting for possible sales?

A similar trail of evidence leads to the British War Office's first interest in the Land Rover, although in this case the military could have learned about the new vehicle from media announcements in April and May. Towards the end of June, they took two of the pre-production vehicles on loan for evaluation – although it is not clear whether they had asked or had been invited by Rover to take a look. One way or the other, one RHD vehicle (R30) and one LHD example (L29) went to Chobham for trials.

The Wheeled Vehicle Experimental Establishment (WVEE) Trials report on those two vehicles should be in the National Archives at Kew in the WO/194 series but so far it has not been traced. However, the trial must have been a success as a contract (6/Veh/2854) was placed on 25 October 1948 for 20 further RHD examples as "Car, 5cwt, 4x4" – the same as its predecessor the Jeep. A well-known picture shows uniformed Army representatives collecting the batch from Rover's Solihull factory in December 1948. All of the Land Rovers had serial numbers painted on their bonnets, and these numbers were from the series that had been used prior to and during

In 1948, FVDE evaluated two pre-production Land Rovers, of which one had left-hand drive. This had chassis number L29. Nevertheless, no LHD chassis were ordered until several years later. (PW)

The first 20 Land Rovers ordered by the British Army were delivered in December 1948. Here they are, lined up ready for collection at Rover's Solihull factory. Note the M-prefix serial numbers painted on their bonnets that were among the last under the system used from the 1920s until 1949. (BMIHT)

WW2. The allocations were M6279781 to M6279800 and the vehicles' chassis numbers ran from 86-0751 to 86-0770 – so started with the 751st production Land Rover. The original contract card shows that 18 vehicles of this batch had the standard-issue 6.00 x 16 tyres, but two were delivered with the wider 7.00 x 16 tyres that were an option on the civilian models.

Particularly interesting is that Rover were already prepared to deviate from their standard production model to meet military requirements. Although the vehicles were essentially the same as civilian-pattern Land Rovers (and there are more details on p18), all 20 vehicles were delivered in the Deep Bronze Green paint on which the War Office had standardised for its "home" fleet of vehicles since the mid-1930s. At the time, and for another few months yet, the only available civilian colour was the very different light green that Rover called "No. 2 Green".

These early orders have to be seen in the correct context. The War Department was acutely aware that it would need something to replace the American Jeeps on which it had come to depend so heavily during the war years. Although there were still unused stocks of Jeeps, the earliest examples were coming up for five years old, and at that age vehicles in their class were routinely replaced. Perhaps the Government was concerned about the long-term spares position; or perhaps it was anxious to provide work for British car manufacturers. One way or the other, in the late 1940s the Ministry of Supply (MoS) became involved in developing its own ¼ ton vehicle which would eventually become the Austin Champ, although it would not enter service until 1952.

Why was the Ministry of Supply therefore interested in the Land Rover? The answer is really twofold. First of all the Land Rover could fulfil an interim role until the new Austin Champ vehicle was developed and ready to replace the ageing and well-worn Jeeps from WW2. Secondly the Land Rover fulfilled the Commercial (CL) ¼ ton role while the Austin Champ was seen as a Combat (CT) type. Commercial (CL) vehicles were intended to fulfil adminis-

11 BC 57 was typical of the first large batch order. Just one windscreen wiper was fitted, and there were semaphore turn indicators on the windscreen pillars. The door-mounted mirror is a military addition, and the bumper and galvanised body cappings, all unpainted on civilian models, have been painted over. The grille is as delivered; in service, many grilles had sections cut away in front of the headlights. The grid on the windscreen suggests that the photograph was taken at Feltham (2VG) and also shows the vehicle's code 6039-10-192 identifying a "Truck, 1/4 ton, GS, 4x4, Rover (1.6-litre Engine)". (Unknown, via Land Rover)

THE MILITARY TRIALS ORGANISATION

The very first trials vehicles were ordered by the Ministry of Supply , which at the time was responsible for acquisition of all vehicles for both Government and military users. They were sent to FVDE (the Fighting Vehicles Design Establishment), which was based at Chertsey in Surrey.

FVDE was itself re-organised shortly afterwards, becoming FVRDE (Fighting Vehicles Research and Development Establishment) during 1948 when it amalgamated with the wartime Fighting Vehicles Proving Establishment, Department of Tank Design and Department TT2 of the Ministry of Supply. The new organisation was responsible for the research, design and development of tracked and wheeled vehicles to meet the requirements of the Services and certain other Government Departments.

FVRDE carried out development trials to prove both the technical and user aspects of designs, and subsequently offered vehicles (or equipment, as appropriate) to the relevant Service Departments for formal acceptance. The organisation retained an active interest in vehicles and equipment through their service lives, and would produce designs for modification or improvement as required by all three services.

FVRDE carried out laboratory and static tests as appropriate in its Engineering Test Laboratory. Vehicle testing was carried out on the natural courses at Bagshot and Long Valley, which provided severe conditions for the assessment of reliability and durability. In addition, there were basic performance test facilities and man-made obstacles around the Main Test Track at Longcross, near Chertsey.

A later reorganisation on 1 April 1970 saw FVRDE merge with MEXE (the Military Engineering Experimental Establishment at Christchurch) to form MVEE (the Military Vehicle Engineering Establishment).

trative roles in units well back from the front line while Combat (CT) types were intended for use by frontline units alongside tanks and other armoured vehicles. Equally CL vehicles were so named as they were purchased direct from the manufacturer and entered service with a minimum of modification, while CT types were designed from inception as military vehicles and were not necessarily expected to be suitable for any other work.

Further Army deliveries

The Army's evaluation batch seems to have met the CL requirement, and by the end of March 1949 the Rover Board knew that an order for 1800 vehicles was in prospect. They also knew that it would be accompanied by a special allocation of steel through the Ministry of Supply, which was still rationing raw materials according to manufacturers' performance. By 3 May, the Board knew it would be for 1878 vehicles, and contract 6/Veh/3659 of 18 July 1949 was for exactly that number. The first 150 were drawn from 1949 production (866-series chassis) and were delivered in July and August; the rest were 0610-series 1950 models, and were delivered between August 1949 and February 1950. Rover clearly had some trouble accommodating such a large order, and the vehicles were built in batches, fitted around orders to meet civilian demand from home and abroad.

By this stage, two things had happened. The first was that Rover had decided to standardise on Deep Bronze Green paint for all its civilian deliveries as well as those for the

Army (the change seems to have been made in June 1949) – a clear indication of how important it thought Army contracts might become. The second was that the Army had changed its serial numbering system. So the 1878 Land Rovers ordered in 1949 became 00 BC 01 to 18 BC 78; they were the first Army "B" vehicles (i.e. transport types) in the new system, BA and BB serials being reserved for armour. At some point in 1949 (or possibly later), the 20 evaluation vehicles were also re-numbered in the new system, acquiring serials in the range 90 YJ 00 to 90 YJ 26; the YJ serials were one of the sequences reserved for re-numbered vehicles.

A little later, contract 6/Veh/3659 was amended to add 33 further vehicles (under what became "Item 2" of the contract). These gained serials 39 BC 02 to 39 BC 34 and replaced those vehicles from the 1878 in the first order that had been modified, apparently as test-beds for the Rolls-Royce B40 engine which would be fitted to the Champ. The 33 Land Rovers to be modified had been picked from the War Office Depot at Feltham in Middlesex and handed to Hudson Motors based in West London for the conversion work under contract 6/Veh/4679. Stocks held in depot were never stored in serial number order, and an apparently random group of vehicles was selected for conversion. Their serial numbers are shown in the accompanying panel.

11 BC 98 had led a hard life by the time these pictures were taken at Solihull; the vehicle may have been returned so that the Rover engineers could see how the typical Land Rover stood up to military service. Note how the grille has been cut away around the headlights. This vehicle was one of the 33 converted to run the Rolls-Royce B40 engine, although the only outward sign is the wedge under the bonnet side.

THE B40-ENGINED CONVERSIONS

In the late 1940s, the British Army was keen to use a common range of engines within its fleet of CT vehicles, and was planning to order the various types with variants of the Rolls-Royce B-series engine range. This consisted of four-cylinder, six-cylinder and eight-cylinder types which used a high proportion of common components.

A plan was drawn up to use a batch of Land Rovers for field trials of the 2.8-litre four-cylinder B40 engine, the variant earmarked as the power unit of the forthcoming Austin Champ. Whether there were also thoughts of fitting future military Land Rovers with the Rolls-Royce engine is simply not clear. It looks as if a first Land Rover was converted as an assessment vehicle for WVEE with the assistance of Rolls-Royce, and took the civilian registration number KXW 66. Once the concept had been approved, 33 of the 1878-strong 1949-1950 batch of Land Rovers went to Hudson Motors Ltd of Chiswick, London, to be fitted with the B40 engine. (The Hudson Essex Motor Company was formed in 1922 from the Essex Motor Company and both were subsidiaries of Hudson Motors of the USA. In 1926 the company moved to Chiswick from Acton Vale, and the company dropped "Essex" from its name in 1932.)

A lot of work was needed to fit the Rolls-Royce engine. It included relocation of the rear axle an inch further back, which is why these vehicles are often known as 81-inch models. As the engine sat higher in the chassis than the original Rover unit, the 81-inch models could always be recognised easily by the higher mounting of the front bumper (which carried the cut-out for the starting handle) and by the rubber blocks between bonnet and wings which gave extra clearance in the engine bay. Less visibly, all the converted vehicles carried a brass plate in the engine bay that bore witness to Hudson Motors' work.

The Rolls-Royce engine was a B40 Mk IIB type, with a swept volume of 2838cc, a bore of 88.9mm and a stroke of 114.3mm. With a 6.4:1 compression ratio, it developed 82bhp. The carburettor was a Solex side-draught type and there were overhead inlet and side exhaust valves, as in the Rover engine. There were important differences between this version of the engine and the version fitted to the Champ, which was a Mk IIA type.

Comparative trials at Chobham in spring 1950 are said to have demonstrated that the engine was actually not as good as the standard Rover 1.6-litre type. Nevertheless, the vehicles were issued to units, and most of them served overseas with the Far East Land Forces (FARELF), the Middle East Land Forces (MELF) and with the British Army of the Rhine (BAOR). Ten remained in the UK, seven being used in troop trials while one each went to the Army Driving School, MTDE (the Maintenance Technical Development Establishment), and to 5 Training Regiment, Royal Corps of Signals.

The 33 vehicles converted under contract 6/Veh/4679 seem to have been drawn from stocks at random and were:

10 BC 71	11 BC 85	12 BC 03	12 BC 10	12 BC 16	12 BC 27
11 BC 50	11 BC 90	12 BC 04	12 BC 11	12 BC 17	12 BC 29
11 BC 65	11 BC 96	12 BC 05	12 BC 12	12 BC 19	12 BC 33
11 BC 75	11 BC 98	12 BC 07	12 BC 13	12 BC 22	
11 BC 77	12 BC 00	12 BC 08	12 BC 14	12 BC 23	
11 BC 80	12 BC 02	12 BC 09	12 BC 15	12 BC 25	

Most were withdrawn by the end of the 1950s although two (11 BC 75 and 12 BC 05) were retained "for Royal Use". Both had been turned into review platforms, and had probably been chosen for the job because of their non-standard specification. They were cast much later; 11 BC 75 was passed to the Imperial War Museum in August 1981 and then to the Army Museum of Transport at Beverley. 12 BC 05 was also retained for some time.

During 1950, the Ministry of Supply invited the Rover Company to tender for the production of 15,000 Austin Champs. Rover did so, and the company's Chairman SB Wilks also "told the Ministry that he was prepared to supply a modified version of the Land Rover at a net overall saving to the Ministry of approximately 4½ to 5 million pounds on the Contract" according to the minutes of the Rover Board meeting held on 11 July 1950. There is a good possibility that this modified version of the Land Rover would have been a B40-engined model. However, the MoS did not take the bait, and did not award the Champ contract to Rover either, eventually going to Austin for the job.

A further trials vehicle

In October 1948, Rover announced a new Station Wagon variant of the Land Rover, with bodywork coachbuilt in the traditional way by the Salmons-Tickford company of Newport Pagnell, having aluminium panels nailed to a wooden framework. On the face of it, this vehicle had limited military potential, but FVDE at Chobham nevertheless borrowed an example for evaluation in or about September 1949.

The vehicle itself was a LHD example with chassis number L867-0031. So far no report on its evaluation has come to light, although it is possible that FVDE were looking at its potential as a commander's vehicle. About a year after it had been returned to Rover (it was re-despatched to Karachi in Pakistan in May 1950), a prototype "staff car" or commander's vehicle was constructed at Solihull and was subsequently sent to FVRDE for evaluation. There is more about this unique vehicle later.

Royal Navy deliveries

A Rover photograph taken at the factory in February 1949 shows a Land Rover apparently destined for the Royal Navy

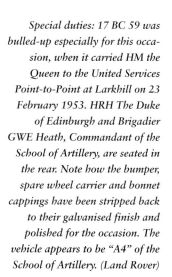

Special duties: 17 BC 59 was bulled-up especially for this occasion, when it carried HM the Queen to the United Services Point-to-Point at Larkhill on 23 February 1953. HRH The Duke of Edinburgh and Brigadier GWE Heath, Commandant of the School of Artillery, are seated in the rear. Note how the bumper, spare wheel carrier and bonnet cappings have been stripped back to their galvanised finish and polished for the occasion. The vehicle appears to be "A4" of the School of Artillery. (Land Rover)

The number-plate reads RN 79154, and the picture dates from February 1949. This may have been the first Land Rover for the Royal Navy, although it would be some time before any more were ordered. This one has the original silver-painted chassis and its bodywork was probably dark blue. (BMIHT)

and carrying serial number RN 79154. Although the photograph is in black-and-white, it strongly suggests that the vehicle was painted in the Royal Navy's dark blue livery. It has not so far been possible to identify this vehicle positively from the Rover despatch records, or to find any Royal Navy contract details. It therefore seems very likely that the vehicle was mocked-up for some kind of demonstration to Royal Navy representatives and was not in fact taken on to the RN strength. If it did enter Royal Navy service, it would not have retained that registration number for long because vehicles were given new serials after 1949 in the range 101 RN to

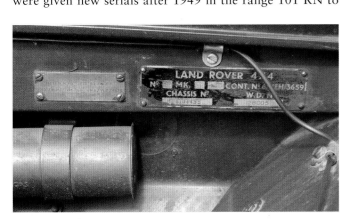

This is 12 BC 05 again, showing the WD plate and the brass plate bearing witness to the engine conversion by Hudson Motors. Both plates had been painted over at some stage. (JT)

The B40 engine was a tight fit within the engine bay of an 80in Land Rover. (JT)

12 BC 05, seen here in preservation with a civilian number-plate, was one of two B40-engined vehicles converted into review platforms (JT)

The repositioned radiator sat higher when the Rolls-Royce engine was fitted, and so a hole was cut into the bonnet for the filler cap. The flagstaff was part of the "review" specification of 12 BC 05. (JT)

34 BD 94 shows the "1951" specification, with larger headlamps and apertures for them in the grille. This example is shown serving with the Women's Royal Army Corps in a "Provost" (Military Police) role. (PW)

Vehicles are seen here in store in an Army depot. The likelihood is that this picture was specially posed to show all three types of light 4x4 in service in the early 1950s. At the top of the stack is a Willys Jeep, below it a Land Rover (11 BH 90), and at the bottom one of the new Austin Champs. (PW)

9999 RN or 00 RN 01 to 99 RN 99.

One way or the other, the Royal Navy did not take any more Land Rovers until 1950, and the Rover despatch records show that 16 vehicles were delivered in August that year to the Royal Navy vehicle depot at Clayton, near Newcastle-under-Lyme. All left the factory painted yellow, a high-visibility colour which strongly suggests that these Land Rovers were destined for RNAS stations. No other 1.6-litre models were delivered directly to the Royal Navy.

RAF deliveries

The RAF issued a contract for its first 100 Land Rovers (6/Veh/5040) in 1950, and these were delivered between May and July that year. They were all painted in the RAF's favoured grey-blue livery. A second contract (6/Veh/5798) for 24 vehicles (30 AA 47 to 30 AA 70) followed in December 1950 and was fulfilled with vehicles that were painted green. A third RAF contract (6/Veh/7188) then called for no fewer than 622 vehicles, although only 150 of these were delivered as 1.6-litre types and the remaining 472 had the later 2-litre engine. All of the initial 150, which became 33 AA 71 to 35 AA 20, were also delivered in green paint. (Note that the details of these early contracts no longer seem to exist in RAF records.)

Many of the vehicles in these last two contracts were later designated "Car, Airfield Crash Rescue, Land Rover", which shows that they were being purchased for Fire Sections on RAF Airfields – although it was not long before many reverted to "Car, 5 cwt, 4x4" with the firefighting equipment removed. The firefighting equipment seems to have been somewhat rudimentary, consisting of a couple of CO_2 extinguishers, axes and a ladder, although other tools may also have been carried. It seems that the Land Rovers were used as first-response vehicles capable of reaching the scene quickly to extract the aircrew; heavier firefighting trucks would arrive later to deal with any fires and associated risks.

Evolution

The basic design of the Land Rover had meanwhile been evolving, and the specification of the British military deliveries reflected this. From the time of the switch to Deep Bronze Green as standard on the production lines, all chassis frames were also painted this colour (the first 20 British military deliveries and the trials vehicles had silver chassis). Towards the end of 1949, there was a taller third gear in the main gearbox, and a lever with distinctive yellow knob replaced the ring-pull that had earlier controlled the freewheel system. From March 1950 or thereabouts the seat backs changed from the original "spade" shape to a more solid-looking "shovel" design, and in autumn that year a selectable four-wheel-drive system (with front axle disconnect) replaced the permanent four-wheel drive with freewheel. Vehicles delivered from about May 1951 had

THE STAFF CAR PROTOTYPE

Possibly following up FVRDE interest in a Station Wagon model during 1949, Rover developed a special Staff Car in mid-1951. Pictured for the Rover archives in early July that year, it was trialled at FVRDE during 1952 against a mock-up heavy utility vehicle on the Humber 1-ton chassis, according to research by Pat Ware. It carried a "civilian" FVRDE registration number, LYN 67. Nothing more came of the design, although John Mastrangelo notes that the trials vehicle was still listed in 1964 as a Rover Mk 1 Station Wagon GS 4x4, with asset code 1150-0750.

Surviving pictures strongly suggest that this vehicle had an 86-inch wheelbase rather than the 80-inch size then in production. If so, that would make it the very first 86-inch Land Rover, as it pre-dated the first prototypes by about a year. Possibly built on a modified 80-inch chassis, it combined the 1951-season "lights-through" grille with a Tickford station-wagon style bulkhead and single-piece windscreen.

The body was a very boxy affair with a built-in roof

rack, and the extra six inches in the wheelbase were very necessary to make room for two doors on either side. A single side-hinged tail door carried an enormous map box on the outside, and gave access to the rear of the vehicle, where a removable map table could be fitted in one corner. The fuel tank had also been relocated at the rear of the chassis, although the reason for this is not clear.

There were six seats, but the accommodation must have been very cramped indeed. The two front seats were more substantial than the standard Land Rover type, and there were two inward-facing seats in the back. The other two seating positions were on a rear-facing bench seat behind the driving compartment. The backrest of this seat was arranged so that it could be swung across the squab to make a forward-facing seat.

The 1951 Staff Car prototype had a boxy body on what was probably an extended-wheel-base chassis. It seems not to have progressed beyond a single prototype. (BMIHT)

More valuable happy snaps taken in-period: 12 BH 75 was one of large numbers of vehicles delivered in Light Stone paint for use in appropriate conditions. This one was probably pictured with an Infantry Battalion in Cyprus in the late 1950s. The first picture shows the rear-mounted aerial used with a W88 infantry radio; the second picture shows the vehicle with a trailer-mounted MOBAT anti-tank gun. (GF)

wider front road springs, and a new front-end design with larger-diameter headlamps that were now framed within the grille instead of hidden behind it.

The second Army contract, 6/Veh/7008, was placed on 3 March 1951 for 600 vehicles (32 BD 05 to 38 BD 04). Production of this contract straddled the changeover from the original 1.6-litre engine to the later 2-litre type (see below). As a result only the first 400 vehicles delivered under this contract had the 1.6-litre engine.

A few more 1.6-litre models did enter British military service, however. Around 20 vehicles were transferred to British stocks from the Malay Regiment, when the battalions of the Federated Malay States came under control of the British Army in about 1952 as the communist insurgency grew. These vehicles had been acquired by the Malay Regiment in small numbers between 1948 and 1952. They were given various serials in the ZC range as each battalion's complement of vehicles was numbered in the British Army series.

The first ten ex-Malayan vehicles were given serial numbers in the sequence 40 ZC 12 to 40 ZC 21. The remaining ten were allocated serials as and when they arrived, becoming 40 ZC 98, 41 ZC 81, 41 ZC 98, 42 ZC 49, 43 ZC 41, 44 ZC 50, 46 ZC 65, 46 ZC 84, 47 ZC 00 and 47 ZC 03. The handover of these vehicles can clearly be seen in the Key Cards, which shows that each unit's fleet of vehicles was renumbered in to the ZC series one unit at a time. The Key Cards are held at RLC Museum, Deepcut.

THE 2-LITRE OR MK 2 LAND ROVERS

Rover stopped production of the original 1.6-litre (1595cc) Land Rover engine over the summer of 1951, and replaced it with a 2-litre (1997cc) type which was essentially a big-bore version of the earlier engine. The new engine delivered an insignificant extra 2bhp but the torque was increased by around 25% to 101 lb ft, at a lower engine speed. The larger bores had resulted in the loss of some water passages, and these engines have always been known as the Siamese-bore types.

Introduction of the new engine occurred mid-way through deliveries of two contracts, one for the Army (6/Veh/7008) and one for the RAF (6/Veh/7188). Both services took the change in their stride, and simply referred to the 2-litre models which Rover supplied to meet the contracts after autumn 1951 as Mk 2 models. In all other important respects, they were after all the same as the earlier 1.6-litre types, which inevitably now became Mk 1s in retrospect. There were other detail changes between the two types, however; notable were the addition of chromed exterior door handles and the relocation of the front sidelights, which were now located on the wing fronts instead of the bulkhead. The Army took all of the first 200 2-litre models built to Home Market specification – an indication of the high priority that

Rover was then giving to orders for the British military.

The next 2-litre Army Land Rovers were delivered under contract 6/Veh/7711 which was placed on 13 June 1951 for 1900 vehicles. These were given serials 00 BH 01 to 19 BH 00 and at the time the contract was placed were anticipated to arrive at the rate of 300 per month, commencing in October 1951. The price per unit was £512 11s 6d and chassis numbers ran from 2610-1191 to 2610-4942. At the time the contract was placed, it was anticipated that some would be delivered with the 1.6-litre engine, but in practice all were 2-litre 1952 models. At this stage the vehicles were still designated "Car, 5cwt, 4x4" just like the Jeeps, although later they became "Truck, GS, ¼ ton, 4x4, Rover Mark 2".

RAF Mk 2 deliveries

The RAF put in a repeat order for Land Rovers during 1952, calling for nearly 500 more under contract under contract 6/Veh/10185. These became 42 AA 23 to 47 AA 24. Just under 360 of these were delivered in RAF Blue, but the remainder came in the standard Bronze Green. Some of them seem to have been intended for Fire Section tasks on airfields at home, but others served with Mountain Rescue teams, the RAF Provost services and the RAF Regiment.

John Mastrangelo has said that some of these vehicles, and probably some Mk 1 types as well, were fitted with a winch in the late 1950s for glider retrieval work. The Mk 2s so equipped were coded as 16A/1390/1404/2483.

This was what the 80-inch Land Rover looked like under the skin. 17 BH 65 became a REME instructional unit, and still survived in the military vehicle collection at Bordon at the time of writing. (JT)

Specially equipped as a crash tender at a Royal Naval Air Station.

Photographs of RNAS crash tenders are hard to find, but this heavily airbrushed one was used in Land Rover sales literature. Note the tools carried at the front, the ladder-rack at the rear and the searchlight. The vehicle was probably painted bright yellow or orange; whether the serial number is real or not is simply not clear. (Land Rover)

Royal Navy Mk 2 deliveries

The Rover Company's despatch records show that a total of 37 Mk 2 models were delivered direct to the Royal Navy. There were 34 in September 1951 and a further three in May 1952. These may match up with contracts thought to have been numbered as 6/Veh/9302 and 6/Veh/12227, although no Royal Navy documents have been found to confirm this suggestion.

It is likely that the vehicles from the larger batch were kept on board warships and were used for official duties on land when a vessel was in dock; all were painted in the blue associated with the Royal Navy. Of the other three, one is recorded as having orange paint; the other two are shown as green, although the Rover despatch records did not always record the colour accurately. It may therefore be that these two were also painted orange. The suggestion is that all three vehicles were therefore destined for RNAS stations as airfield crash rescue tenders.

Any other Mk 2 models in RN service would probably have been transferred from the Army.

A MILESTONE VEHICLE

The Rover Company built its 50,000th Land Rover in January 1952, and the vehicle was one of the large batch for the British Army that was then going through production to fulfil contract 6/Veh/7711. Registered 11 BH 22, it had chassis number 2610-3384 and was one of the 850 vehicles from that contract delivered with Light Stone paint for service in the Middle East. It left the production lines after a special ceremony on 15 January 1952 and entered service on 28 January. It was struck off in Cyprus (by Middle East Land Forces Command) on 31 May 1957 and was probably sold locally.

This is another valuable private picture, taken by the adjutant of the RAF Regiment stationed at RAF Woodvale in Lancashire around 1950. The picture was probably taken because it was the first new Land Rover anybody on the station had seen. 23 AA 88 was from the first batch of 100 RAF Land Rovers. (Garth Teagle)

FEATURES OF THE MK 1 AND MK 2 MODELS

Although the 1.6-litre Mk 1 and 2-litre Mk 2 models were essentially adapted civilian vehicles, their specification was by no means identical to that of a typical vehicle sold on the domestic civilian market.

From the beginning, most vehicles for the Army were painted by the Rover Company in Deep Bronze Green. Nevertheless, this colour was far from universal, and 850 vehicles of the 1900 ordered under contract 6/Veh/7711 in 1951 were delivered with Light Stone paint, presumably for service in Middle Eastern and Far Eastern theatres. The RAF took many vehicles in its favoured blue-grey livery but also took vehicles in the standard Deep Bronze Green. Many Royal Navy vehicles were meanwhile delivered in bright yellow or orange for high-visibility work.

Basic specification

The Mk 1 models were all fitted with the windscreen ventilator flap that was an optional extra on civilian models. According to John Mastrangelo, "the reason given was that with the back of hood open, the use of the vent would prevent dust from being sucked in". They also had the optional bonnet mounting for the spare wheel.

Like their civilian counterparts, they were delivered with a single Lucas CW1 wiper motor on the driver's side, although

a second motor was sometimes fitted in service. The majority, probably beginning with 866-7261 (00 BC 01) came with inward-facing folding bench seats in the rear, capable of seating an extra four occupants. These were accompanied by guard rails to prevent the occupants falling out. The seats were otherwise available only for export; the grab rail was an optional extra on civilian models.

All vehicles were delivered with a full-length canvas hood in the standard civilian colour of khaki. A few vehicles were fitted with a metal hardtop in service, another standard Rover option that became available from February 1950.

It is commonly assumed that all these early Land Rover purchases were fitted with split-rim wheels, but they were not. Photographs suggest that the majority probably had standard one-piece road wheels for most of their service life. Rover did list a split-rim wheel in a 4.50E x 16 size, and it appears that some vehicles were fitted with these during service; possibly some were so fitted from new. The Army, at least, settled on 6.50 x 16 cross-country tyres, which were not a civilian option, although some vehicles may also have worn the standard civilian size of 6.00 x 16.

Electrical and lighting

Generally speaking, the electrical system on the Rover Mk 1 was to factory civilian standard, although heavy-duty items were fitted where they were available on civilian production.

All the Mk 1 and Mk 2 models seem to have been delivered with standard civilian-pattern lights, although FV-pattern headlights were fitted during service to some vehicles. According to the User Handbook, the headlights were behind the grille up to chassis number 0611-2000, which would

Now beautifully restored (the flashing indicator lights between wings and bumper are not original), 43 AA 83 is a 1953-model 2-litre 80-inch from RAF contract number 6/Veh/10185. (GF)

have been one of the Mk 1 vehicles registered in BD. Photographic evidence suggests that some of these grilles were modified in service, having sections of the grille cut away in front of the headlights. This was probably to improve access to the lights as much as to improve the light they cast ahead of the vehicle.

The User Handbook also notes that vehicles from 0611-2001 to 1610-0722 had a grille with circular cut-outs around larger-diameter headlights. From chassis 1610-0723, Lucas lights were then fitted. On civilian models, the exposed headlights had been introduced at the start of 1610-series (1951-season) production. According to John Mastrangelo, "a few early Rover Mk 1 with lights behind grille were modified by fitting the later grille and lights". Note that these changeover points do not match with the dates of corresponding changes on civilian-production Land Rovers.

The front sidelights were mounted on the bulkhead on all the Mk 1 models, as was the civilian production standard. However, some had their sidelights moved to the wings during service because the bulkhead-mounted lights reflected in wing mirrors. Mk 1 models were delivered with standard production type wing mirrors, but these were often replaced in service. Rear lights were standard civilian production D-lamps by Lucas, and in service REME fitted large circular rear reflectors to many vehicles, either on the tailgate or on brackets bolted to the rear cross-member. The reflectors were standard Rover parts, introduced to meet new UK lighting regulations introduced in 1954, and were mainly fitted on vehicles serving in the UK and in BAOR. Many vehicles – though perhaps not all – were delivered with the Lucas SE62 semaphore trafficators that were an extra-cost option on

civilian vehicles. However, these were removed in some theatres of operation for obvious reasons.

Some vehicles were modified by REME during service with a convoy light. This light was mounted on a bracket behind the rear cross-member and shone onto the rear face of the differential, which was painted white. The idea was that a following driver could see the vehicle ahead even when the main lights were off during blackout conditions. The switch for the convoy light was mounted to the dash or, in some cases, to the rear cross-member. The white face of the differential was sometimes painted with identifying numbers in black, either to identify the vehicle's parent unit or to show the type of oil to be used in servicing.

Unique military extras

All Mk 1 models were fitted with a rectangular brass plate on the left-hand side of the bulkhead in the engine bay. This showed the contract number, chassis number and the serial number. After a major repair or Base Overhaul (shown as

Pictures of the early RAF crash tenders are very rare, and the name of the photographer who recorded this one is unknown. 42 AA 34 was a 1953 model with the 2-litre engine. The equipment carried is distinctly rudimentary.

Posed picture this may be, but it
shows an RAF Aircraft Crash
Rescue tender on the late 80-inch
chassis. 41 AA 74 was from a
large number of Mk2 models
delivered under contract
6/Veh/7188. The ambulance on
the right is an Austin of the type
in service in the early 1950s.
(Royal Air Force)

Posed picture this may be, but it shows an RAF Aircraft Crash Rescue tender on the late 80-inch chassis. 41 AA 74 was from a large number of Mk2 models delivered under contract 6/Veh/7188. The ambulance on the right is an Austin of the type in service in the early 1950s. (Royal Air Force)

Base O/H) a second and larger brass Ministry Of Supply plate was usually fitted to the inner wing in the engine bay. This plate had spaces for the same details as the first – although these were not always filled in – and also had spaces for a record of repairs, major maintenance and the workshop responsible.

A brass Pyrene fire extinguisher was fitted to the bulkhead inside the vehicle, on a Rover-supplied bracket that was a civilian option. The extinguisher body carried WD identification and a date, and was usually painted to match the vehicle's exterior.

All Mk 1 models had a towing jaw assembly on the rear cross-member, drawn from the standard civilian options list. In the early days, the trailers used with Mk 1 and Mk 2 models were usually either wartime or early post-war two-wheel types. A two-pin civilian-type trailer socket with adaptor was fitted to the right-hand side of the rear cross-member. In later service, and particularly after 1956, some Mk 1 and Mk 2 vehicles had a Warner socket fitted so that they could tow the newer military-specification two-wheel trailers made by Brockhouse and Sankey.

In service, a Bridge Plate was sometimes painted on to the front of either wing. Some vehicles carried a metal bridge plate that was actually supplied by Rover (part number 206818 was unsurprisingly not listed in civilian catalogues) and was fitted to the front of the wing or to the bumper. If a number was painted onto this, it was in black and, according to John Mastrangelo, was usually a 2 but could be a 3 if the vehicle was towing a trailer.

When the spare wheel was carried on the bonnet, its carrier at the front of the back body could be used as a jerrycan holder. This was achieved by using a clamping plate kit that was provided by Rover.

The serial numbers of the 1948 evaluation batch vehicles were painted on the bonnet sides and tailgate in white. Later vehicles typically had the number on vertical rectangular plates, with its three elements stacked vertically. The rear plate was typically mounted to the right-hand tail panel. The front plate was sometimes carried ahead of the right-hand front wing, but was later more commonly seen on the left-hand wing to make room for a bridge plate on the right.

AN ARMOURED RAILCAR

In Kenya, where the British Army was engaged in assisting the local government against the threat of Mau-Mau terrorist activity, the REME workshops developed an armoured Land Rover to act as an escort for trains operating out of Nairobi. This conversion, of vehicle 16 BH 59 from contract 6/Veh/7711, was probably a one-off and was described in Soldier magazine for July 1954. It had chassis number 2610-4521.

The basic concept was similar to that of Jeep railcars used during World War II. The road wheels were replaced by flanged railway wheels and a "hardtop" body was created from light armoured panels. A machine gun with 360-degree traverse was mounted in the rear. The vehicle was designed to carry a crew of four, could reach 130km/h (81mph) on the tracks, and had twin fuel tanks to give a range of 1500km (932 miles). The crew also maintained radio contact with the guard of the following train. There was obviously no steering wheel, and acceleration was controlled by a hand throttle.

The absence of Royal Navy records makes it impossible to identify this vehicle completely, but it is clearly a Mk 2 80inch model. Note the RN marking on the door. (Unknown source, via Land Rover)

THE MK 1 AND MK 2 LAND ROVERS IN SERVICE

The Army used its Land Rovers largely to replace wartime Jeeps, which were now being withdrawn in large quantities, but the vehicles often also had to stand in for the anticipated Austin Champs. Production of these did not begin until autumn 1951 and deliveries to field units began in 1952. Meanwhile, Britain had become involved in the Korean War as part of the United Nations contingent in 1951, and of necessity the British Army took with it whatever vehicles it had. Although Austin Champs did serve in Korea in the later stages of the conflict, it has often been said that the Land Rovers demonstrated their full value and versatility in Korea, with the ability to do around 80% of the tasks that the Champ was designed to perform. The Champs, meanwhile, showed that they had limited use beyond the narrowly defined CT role for which they had been designed. It also appears that British troops generally preferred their Land Rovers.

The early Army Land Rovers were used all over the world where the British had military commitments. They saw service in the Middle East (Aden, Canal Zone, Libya), the Far East (Hong Kong, Malaya, Singapore) and Africa (Kenya), although the Austin Champ was predominant in BAOR with front- line units. Some of course remained in the UK, and John Mastrangelo has said that the Mk 1 and Mk 2 models here mostly served with Territorial Army units. Most of the Mk 1 and Mk 2 models in Army service were cast between 1959 and 1962, although a few remained in service after that.

What is quite striking about these early orders is the fact that none of them were for LHD examples, even though the

Army still had major commitments in countries that used LHD vehicles, and even though LHD types had been tested at Chobham. A possible explanation is that the Jeeps which remained in service all had LHD, and that the armed services believed these would be best suited for use in countries where LHD was the norm until the requirement for RHD vehicles had been met by new Land Rovers. However, no clear evidence for this supposition has yet been found.

45 AA 77 would have been nearly new when it was converted into a temporary review vehicle for a visit by the Queen and the Duke of Edinburgh during the Commonwealth Tour of 1953-1954. The picture was taken in Aden in April 1954. (Land Rover)

Some early Royal Navy Land Rovers were used by fire crews of the RNAS. This one was pictured during a training session at RNAS Ford (now HM Prison Ford). All airfields had (and still have) a decommissioned hulk that is used for this kind of training.
(Unknown source, probably RNAS)

SUMMARY OF 80-INCH MODEL DELIVERIES, 1948-1953

ARMY

(a) Mk 1, 1.6-litre

Serials	Contract	Chassis Nos	Total	Remarks
M6279781 to M6279800	6/Veh/2854	R860-751 to R860-770	20	Later re-registered in series 90 YJ 00 to 90 YJ 26.
00 BC 01 to 18 BC 78	6/Veh/3659	R866-7261 to R866-7807 and 0610-0091 to 0610-7434	1878	Dated 18 July 1949.
39 BC 02 to 39 BC 34	6/Veh/3659	0610-7647 to 0610-7679	33	33 vehicles from first batch were converted to B40 engine; contract amended to add 33 replacements, making grand total 1911.
10 BC 71 to 12 BC 33 (range)	6/Veh/4679	See range above	33	Converted from vehicles ordered under 6/Veh/3659.
32 BD 05 to 36 BD 04	6/Veh/7008	1610-3018 to 1610-3881	400	Contract for 600 vehicles was fulfilled with 200 2-litre types. Dated 6 March 1951.
			Total 2331	

(b) Mk 2, 2.0-litre

Serials	Contract	Chassis Nos	Total	Remarks
36 BD 05 to 38 BD 04	6/Veh/7008	2610-0001 to 2610-0200	200	Second part of order for Mk1 models.
00 BH 01 to 19 BH 00	6/Veh/7711	2610-1191 to 2610-4942	1900	Dated 13 June 1951.
			Total 2100	

RAF

(a) Mk 1, 1.6-litre

Serials	Contract	Chassis Nos	Total	Remarks
23 AA 06 to 24 AA 05	6/Veh/5040	0611-1901 to 0611-2000	100	
30 AA 47 to 30 AA 70	6/Veh/5798	1610-1046 to 1610-1069	24	These were built as Airfield Crash Rescue vehicles, according to John Mastrangelo.
33 AA 71 to 35 AA 20	6/Veh/7188	1610-3263 to 1610-3769	150	Contract called for 622 vehicles; balance of 472 were delivered as 2.0-litre models. These were built as Airfield Crash Rescue vehicles, according to John Mastrangelo.
			Total 274	

(b) Mk 2, 2.0-litre

Serials	Contract	Chassis Nos	Total	Remarks
35 AA 21 to 37 AA 70	6/Veh/7188	2610-0520 to 2610-1031	250	Airfield Rescue.
40 AA 01 to 42 AA 22	6/Veh/7188	2610-1032 to 2610-4027	222	Balance of earlier order for Mk 1 models.
42 AA 23 to 47 AA 24	6/Veh/10185	3610-0819 to 3610-3109	502	Only 497 traced in despatch records.
			Total 974	Possibly only 969; see note above.

ROYAL NAVY
(a) Mk 1, 1.6-litre

Serials	Contract	Chassis Nos	Total	Remarks
RN series	6/Veh/6818	0611-5334, 0611-5381 to 0611-5385,		
		0611-5409 to 611-5418	16	
			Total 16	

Notes:

*The vehicle with serial number RN 79154 that may have been a demonstration mock-up is likely to have been on chassis number 86-0795
and to have been built in January 1949.*
*Various WD sales catalogues list the registration numbers 1101 RN, 1158 RN, 1873 RN, 2015 RN and 2217 RN as 80-inch Land Rovers. Another source
gives 1003 RN as having chassis number 1616-3146; this would have been a RHD export model and might have been acquired as a second-hand vehicle.*

(b) Mk 2, 2.0-litre

Serials	Contract	Chassis Nos	Total	Remarks
RN series	6/Veh/9302	n/a	n/a	
RN series	6/Veh/12227	n/a	n/a	
n/a	n/a	2610-0538 to 2610-0551 and		
		2610-0564 to 2610-0583	34	All delivered in September 1951, painted Blue.
n/a	n/a	2610-5160 to 2610-5162	3	All delivered in May 1952; 5160 was painted orange and the other two may have been; they probably all became RNAS crash rescue tenders.
			Total n/a	**(At least 37)**

Notes:

*Serial numbers known from other sources (mostly photographic) are 5982 RN, 6182 to 6186 RN, and 21 RN 81. 50 RN 73 had chassis number 2610-3577
and was transferred to the Royal Navy from the Army.*

LAND ROVER CHASSIS CODES FOR 80IN MODELS, 1948-1953

The Land Rover chassis numbering system gradually evolved in the early part of this period as annual production increased. The 1948 models had a three-digit prefix followed by a four-digit serial number; the 1949 models had a four-digit prefix followed by a four-digit serial number, and the 1950 models had a five-digit prefix followed by a four-digit serial number. From 1951, a four-digit prefix was standardised. On the 1948-1950 models, the first digit was a letter R (for RHD) or L (for LHD).

The 1951 and later four-digit identifying prefix indicated the model type, the model-year (not calendar-year) of manufacture, the steering position and other factors. The ones relevant to the Mk 1 and Mk 2 models are shown below. The four-figure prefix was followed by a four-figure serial number that began at 0001 for each separate sequence.

Note that the Land Rover model-year began in September and continued until the end of the following July, leaving August clear for the works' annual holiday and for preparing the assembly lines to take new models. A Land Rover built in the 1951 model-year could therefore have been built at any time between September 1950 and July 1951.

R86	1948 RHD
R866	1949 RHD
R0610	1950 RHD
R0611	1950 RHD (extension series)
1610	1951 RHD (Mk 1)
2610	1952 RHD (Mk 2)
3610	1953 RHD

TECHNICAL SPECIFICATIONS, MK 1 AND MK 2 (80-INCH) MODELS

ENGINES:
1948-1951 models:
1595cc (69.5mm x 105mm) four-cylinder with overhead inlet and side exhaust valves; single Solex 32 PBI-2 carburettor. 6.8:1 compression ratio. 50bhp at 4000rpm and 80 lb ft at 2000rpm.

1952-1953 models:
1997cc (77.8mm x 105mm) four-cylinder with overhead inlet and side exhaust valves; single Solex 32 PBI-2 carburettor. 6.8:1 compression ratio. 52bhp at 4000rpm and 101 lb ft at 1500rpm.

SUSPENSION, STEERING AND BRAKES:
Semi-elliptic leaf springs all round.
Recirculating-ball steering with 15:1 ratio.
Drum brakes (10in x 1.5in) on all four wheels; separate drum-type transmission parking brake

ELECTRICAL SYSTEM:
12-volt with dynamo

UNLADEN WEIGHT:
2594 lb (1177kg)

TRANSMISSION:
1948-1951 models:
Permanent four-wheel drive with freewheel.
Four-speed main gearbox with synchromesh on 3rd and 4th gears only; ratios 3.00:1, 2.04:1, 1.47:1, 1.00:1, reverse 2.54:1.
Two-speed transfer gearbox; ratios 1.148:1 (High) and 2.89:1 (Low)
Axle ratio: 4.7:1

1952-1953 models:
Selectable four-wheel drive.
Four-speed main gearbox with synchromesh on 3rd and 4th gears only; ratios 3.00:1, 2.04:1, 1.38:1, 1.00:1, reverse 2.54:1.
Two-speed transfer gearbox; ratios 1.148:1 (High) and 2.89:1 (Low)
Axle ratio: 4.7:1

PERFORMANCE
(with 1.6-litre engine):

0-40mph:	18secs
Maximum:	50mph approx (80.4km/h)
Fuel consumption:	24mpg approx

(with 2-litre engine):

0-50mph:	20.5secs
Maximum:	52mph approx (84km/h)
Fuel consumption:	24mpg approx

ARMY SERIAL NUMBERS

The serial numbers allocated by the Army gave a clue to the date of the vehicle, although those issued by the RAF and Royal Navy did not. In this period, two consecutive systems were used.

When the first Land Rovers were procured in 1948, the Army was still using its wartime numbering system. Vehicles were allocated a seven-figure serial number preceded by M, and a typical example was M6279781, numerically the first Army Land Rover.

From 01 January 1949, a new system was introduced. Existing vehicles were renumbered in this new system, where an identifying letter pair was sandwiched between the two halves of a four-digit serial number. The 1948 Land Rovers were re-numbered in the YJ sequence otherwise allocated to Jeeps. A typical number was 90 YJ 00, which indicated the 9000th vehicle in the YJ series.

From 01 April 1950, a new series of serial letters was allocated, reflecting both vehicle class and the financial year in which the vehicle was purchased (which is not necessarily the same as the calendar year in which it was delivered). Those relevant to the Mk 1 and Mk 2 models are shown below.

As had been the case for the YJ series, the new sequences began at 0001 (eg 00 BC 01) and ran to 9999 (eg 99 BC 99). There was not necessarily any correlation between chassis number order and military serial number within batches.

BC	1950-1951
BD	1951-1952
BH	1953-1954

ASSET CODES

At the end of WW2, the first codes appeared in the "B Vehicle Nomenclature 1945" and their purpose was explained in paragraph 4 of that document's opening page:

"The object of the Code ... is to enable all overseas theatres who are using a mechanically operated punched-card census, to adopt uniformity.

"The Code is built up as follows:

(a)   The first figure denotes the War Office ordnance provision branch;
(b)   The next three figures denote the general vehicle class;
(c)   The final two figures – following the "oblique" sign – denote any subdivision of (b) above."

The Jeep was designated "Car, 5cwt, 4x4" and given code 6038/00. However this original coding system failed to identify the manufacturer and so a further suffix was added around 1947. When the Land Rover was introduced it was designated "Car, 2 seater, 4x4" and coded 6011-01-192 (192 indicated Land Rover as manufacturer) although this was changed on 6 January 1948 to "Car, 5cwt, 4x4" and the code became 6039-10-192. Around 1954 the designations became "Truck, ¼ ton, GS, 4x4".

So by 1954 the codes and designations were:

6011-10-192	Car, 2 seater, 4x4, 'Land Rover'
6039-10-192	Truck, GS, ¼ ton, 4x4, Rover (1.6-litre Engine)
6039-11-192	Truck, GS, ¼ ton, 4x4, Rover (2.0-litre Engine)

CHAPTER 2:

THE MARK 3 (86-INCH) AND MARK 5 (88-INCH)

This was one of the large batch of Mk 3 models delivered in 1954-1955 under contract 6/Veh/16223. The vehicle is towing a 25-pounder field gun, and the gun crew are sitting, probably somewhat uncomfortably, on the inward-facing rear seats. (GF)

Feedback from both military and civilian users revealed quite early on that one major flaw with the Land Rover was its size: its cargo area was too small for the demands being placed on it. By mid-1950, the Rover Company was already experimenting with bigger Land Rovers, and in due course took the decision to tackle the problem by introducing two new models to replace the existing 80-inch type. The direct replacement for that would have an 86-inch wheelbase and an extra nine inches of overhang behind the rear wheels to create a larger load area within dimensions not much greater than before. Rover claimed a 25% increase in carrying capacity. Completely new would be a long-wheelbase model with 107 inches between the axle centres and a load-bed that was a full six feet long. Both became available in autumn 1953.

All three branches of the British armed forces took to the 86-inch model, after a precautionary trial of one at Chertsey in late 1953 or early 1954. It was simply an improved version of the Land Rovers they already used in quantity. Nevertheless, it was almost three years after the previous contract (6/Veh/7711) that a further contract was placed with the Rover Company, and by the time deliveries began to fulfil it there had been a key production modification.

The first 2-litre engines in Land Rovers had all been essentially overbored versions of the original 1.6-litre four-cylinder engine, the larger bores resulting in a lack of water passages between the outer two pairs of cylinders. From summer 1954, a redesigned version of the engine was introduced, with the same bore and stroke dimensions as before but with the bores repositioned in the block to give water passages between all of them. This was known to Rover as the "spread-bore" engine. It is worth noting that the redesign did not reflect any failings in the earlier 2-litre engines; it resulted from manufacturing rationalisation when the Rover six-cylinder car engines took on the newer cylinder block design.

Although the 86-inch models purchased by the War

From the next large Mk 3 contract, 6/Veh/18599, this is 93 BP 73. The special FV-pattern headlamps are in evidence here. The exact location is unknown – possibly Aden, in view of the uniform worn by one of the soldiers standing in the back. The British soldiers are probably mostly National Servicemen, having a bit of fun after getting their Land Rover stuck in the water. Note the large tow hook just in front of the vehicle! (PW)

Department were still essentially adapted civilian vehicles, they were now delivered with a special soft top which had presumably been requested by the armed services. The military-pattern soft top had extra straps to enable the sides to be rolled up when required. It had Rover part number 304014 and was accompanied by a special rear curtain numbered 304015. Neither was available to civilian buyers.

Army Mk 3 deliveries

The first military contract for 86-inch Land Rovers materialised as 6/Veh/16223 on 26 May 1954 and called for 1174 vehicles, which became 36 BP 85 to 48 BP 58. The contract was first amended to request "250 vehicles to be fitted with Standard Tread Tyres" and shortly afterwards to amend the quantity to 2700; the extra vehicles became 60 BP 37 to 74 BP 62.

The new dimensions of the 86-inch Land Rover did affect the military designation of the vehicles resulting from the contract. This started out as "Truck, ¼ ton, GS, 4x4, Mark 2, Land Rover", was amended to "Truck, ¼ ton, GS, 4x4, Mark 3, Land Rover" on 8 October 1954, and then on 26 October 1955 included reference to the change in wheelbase and became "Truck, ¼ ton, GS, 4x4, 86" WB, Mark 3, Land Rover". The Asset Code was also amended to reflect the vehicle delivered and it became 6039-13-192. A "Fighting Vehicle" Number – FV18001 – was now allocated for the first time, showing that the vehicle was the General Service (GS) vehicle in the ¼ ton class; the Austin Champ (FV1800 series) was of course the Combat (CT) vehicle.

Deliveries were to commence in September 1954 with a

From the last batch of Mk 3 models, delivered in 1956, 79 BR 45 is looking particularly smart with a polished front bumper and light-coloured seat covers. Its markings suggest it is from HQ 28 Commonwealth Brigade. (PW)

68 BP 13 was pictured in Libya in 1962, when it was the OC's vehicle of 2 RTR who were based in Tripoli. This was one of many vehicles delivered with the Light Stone paint used in desert conditions. (KB)

43 BR 33 was a Mk 3 sacrificed in the interests of science during the Operation Buffalo nuclear tests at Maralinga in Australia, September 1956. The vehicle was located 600 yards from the centre of the explosion of the Red Beard device (codenamed One Tree for this test), equivalent to 12.9 kilotonnes of TNT. Note the yellow band painted around it to identify it as one of the test vehicles. The sacrificial vehicles were buried on-site after the tests (Source not known)

quantity of 100 followed by 400 a month suggesting that deliveries would not be complete until May 1955. In fact the first vehicle was not delivered until 13 October 1954 and the last arrived in May 1955. The military serials were allocated in two separate batches (36 BP 85 to 48 BP 58 and 60 BP 37 to 74 BP 62). Although the chassis numbers were drawn from a range of over 4000, the last of the first batch and the first of the second batch had sequential chassis numbers (48 BP 58 was 5710-2342 and 60 BP 37 was 5710-2343).

A single LHD vehicle (92 BP 07, Chassis Number 5713-2638) was ordered under contract 6/Veh/18421 dated 10 January 1955. This is the first known LHD Land Rover in British military service – although a LHD model had been evaluated in 1948 (see Chapter 1). Although this also had an 86-inch wheelbase, there are various suggestions on the contract card that it was not a soft top version. It has a pencil designation of "Car, GS, Utility, Heavy" and was formally designated "Car, GS, Light Utility, 4x4, Rover LHD", all of which suggests that it could have been one of the new seven-seat Station Wagon models. It was delivered to Vehicle Depot Feltham in late March 1955 and was probably intended for a Military Attaché.

A further contract (6/Veh/18599) was placed in the same financial year for 1500 further Mk 3 vehicles. Deliveries were planned as 1050 by 22 January 1955 with a further 450 following by 25 July 1955 to make the total of 1500. These vehicles were given serials 92 BP 59 to 07 BR 59 (excepting 00 BR 00). The following Financial Year (1955/56) brought a further contract for 1000 vehicles, which became 42 BR 45 to 52 BR 44. All of these bar one were RHD. The LHD vehicle was 48 BR 74 (1736-02105) and its arrival signalled the Army's intention to buy LHD vehicles for BAOR in the future.

The final Army contract for the Mk 3 86-inch was 6/Veh/22633, which was for 1500 vehicles and was later amended to 2000. In fact only the first 545 (77 BR 30 to 82 BR 74) were delivered as 86-inch models, the rest being delivered as 88-inch Mk 5 types.

RAF Mk 3 deliveries

The RAF continued to take quite large quantities of Land Rovers in 1954-1955, under several different contracts. Several hundred Mk 3 examples were delivered to the RAF Regiment, and the Rover Company was sufficiently proud of this to photograph some being collected by RAF personnel during February 1955.

The RAF also created its own special Mk 3 variant, of which just 18 appear to have been delivered against contract 6/Veh/21227. This was an airfield lighting maintenance van (or Truck, 10cwt, 4x4, Airfield Lighting Maintenance, Rover Mk 3) that attracted the type code FV18003. These vehicles appear to have been fitted with the standard civilian-option alloy hardtop cover for the cargo area, with a top-hinged flap complementing the drop-down tailgate.

The airfield lighting vehicles were crewed by either three or four people, and when a fourth was carried he used a folding seat that was normally mounted on the right-hand wheel arch but could be swapped to the other side if necessary. The rest of the body contained stores and tools, and there was a rack on the roof to carry a two-section wooden ladder with a length of 2.3 metres (7ft 6in approximately).

These vehicles from the same large batch are wearing cross-country tyres. They were pictured in February 1955, when RAF personnel collected a large quantity from Rover's Solihull factory. These examples were destined for the RAF Regiment. (BMIHT)

This collection of vehicles was part of a batch of Mk 3 models delivered to the RAF in 1954-1955. Note that all are wearing road tyres and that only some have the spare wheel mounted on the bonnet. (CE)

A fairly rare variant was the FV18003 airfield lighting maintenance vehicle, operated by the RAF. This official picture, probably airbrushed from a photograph, shows that it had what Land Rover called a hardtop body. The light areas of paint may have been in yellow to aid visibility. Note again that road tyres are fitted. (Unknown source)

Royal Navy Mk 3 deliveries

Our knowledge of the Mk 3 in Royal Navy service is hampered by the absence of contract information. However, only small numbers of short-wheelbase Land Rovers entered service in this period, and it very much looks as if the Royal Navy relied for a time on vehicles transferred from the Army. Just three small contracts are known. The first was 6/Veh/15462, which seems to have called for six vehicles, and the second was 6/Veh/15619, which appears to have called for three vehicles with the new Station Wagon body. The third contract was 6/Veh/22178, which embraced both Mk 4

The Royal Navy kept Land Rovers aboard some of its capital ships, and used them for duties ashore. The aircraft carrier HMS Albion had two, and one of them was converted temporarily to a review vehicle when the Queen and the Duke of Edinburgh reviewed the Home Fleet at Invergordon on 28 May 1957. Sadly, the lack of information about RN vehicles makes it impossible to be certain what 18 RN 65 is; the date of the photograph makes it too early for the Mk 5 deliveries, so this is probably a Mk 3. (Land Rover)

107-inch models (see Chapter 3) and Mk 3 86-inch types, although there were just three of the smaller vehicles. There may have been others.

55 AA 89 is a Mk 3 model that was modified immediately after delivery in 1954 to a review platform. It still survives, and was pictured in the RAF Museum at Cosford. The deep sills are a unit modification, and the rear hubcaps were also special – although why none were fitted to the front wheels is a mystery. Note the plated and polished bumpers and door hinges. (JT)

AN RAF REVIEW PLATFORM

One of the 86-inch Mk 3 models delivered to the RAF under contract 6/Veh/16499 was converted to Review Platform immediately after delivery in November 1954. 55 AA 89 (chassis number 5710-0976) was delivered in the standard RAF Blue-Grey livery. It was modified at 30 Maintenance Unit (MU) to act as a Royal viewing vehicle and was ready for its new role by 20 January 1955.

Over the next 12 years, it was issued just 14 times on short-term loans to various RAF Commands as required for reviews and parades. After three years in storage at RAF Cosford, it was then donated to the RAF Museum at RAF Henlow in Bedfordshire, and in 1976 was refurbished for an exhibition at RAF Museum Hendon to mark the Queen's Silver Jubilee Year in 1977. It has since become the property of RAF Museum Cosford, where it is on permanent display.

This is the rear of the same vehicle. The steps could be folded up if necessary. (Andrew Passmore)

80 BR 06 was pictured when doing duty with UN forces in Cyprus (UNFICYP). It was painted in UN white at that time. (KB)

Wider horizons

The additional carrying capacity seems to have led to an increase in activity providing special versions of the vehicle for the Army, and various trials and experiments began at FVRDE. This was the start of much conversion work on the Land Rover as many special versions were built for the Army – most numerous being the 24-volt FFW (Fitted for Wireless) versions. These were not the same as the later FFR (Fitted for Radio) types: the FFW specification came with only basic radio fitting, and workshop action was required before the set could be fitted.

Field Ambulance

A Field Ambulance using a "Carter Frame" similar to that used on Jeeps and also on Austin Champs was developed on 95 BP 95. The work began in 1956 and trials began in January 1958. Although two types of stretcher frame were developed, neither was described by FVRDE as wholly satisfactory and the project seems to have proceeded no further at this stage.

Light Recovery Vehicle

REME created a light recovery variant of the Land Rover by mounting a tubular steel A-frame to the rear cross-member, with steel cables to restrain and steady it. A portable hand-operated winch provided a means of lifting the vehicle to be recovered, and a simple lightweight dolly was used as a towing ambulance. The first example may have been built from 99 BP 78 (from contract 6/Veh/18599), as that vehicle was recorded on photographs by REME. These were for a long time the only recovery vehicles available to parachute units.

FEATURES OF THE MK 3 MODELS

The Mk 3 models differed in a number of other respects from earlier British military types. External recognition was simple: they had sturdy door handles recessed into the door panels, straight instead of angled rear edges to the doors, twin ventilators below the windscreen instead of one large one, and a different design of front wing with a horizontal seam below the inset side light. Inside, there were two large instrument dials in the centre, where earlier models had a much smaller instrument panel. Less visibly, both front and rear road springs differed from earlier types, and there was no well for the spare wheel at the front of the cargo area. Nevertheless there was still a mounting bracket for the wheel on the bulkhead behind the seats, and this bracket could be used to hold a jerrycan when the spare wheel was mounted on the bonnet. A Warner electric towing socket was also a standard fit on the rear cross-member.

In the mid-1950s, there were attempts to create a Field Ambulance from the Mk 3 by fitting a stretcher frame. This was one version: as the picture makes clear, the stretcher hung out over the rear of the vehicle. (PW)

This Mk 3 was converted to line-laying duties after entering service. It is shown in service with the School of Artillery, Larkhill around July 1960. (GF Collection)

Line Layer

Some Land Rovers were fitted with a Line-laying kit to serve with Line Troops of the Royal Corps of Signals (RCS). As this was a kit, it could be fitted to any suitable vehicle, and the individual kits seem to have lasted a long time, being transferred later to 109-inch Series IIIs and Lightweights.

The advantage of communicating over wires as opposed to radio is that interception is more difficult when the line is laid well to the rear of the front line. Radio for short range communication near the front line is inevitably broadcast across the front and the enemy can listen in. Sometimes the wires were laid underground, although this took time and required specialised equipment for cutting the necessary narrow trench – unless cables were laid over-ground hanging from posts or through trees, as often happened. "Crooksticks" were used to lay the cable in the correct position.

On the Line-laying vehicles, a tubular frame was fitted to the front bumper, the sides of the bulkhead and the rear bumper. The sloping section over the cargo area could carry ladders, the crooksticks and poles, whilst two tool bins at the rear were used for carrying various working tools. The early version fitted to the Land Rover 86-inch (Mk 3) involved some drilling but the later version fitted to the 88-inch (Mk 5) was mounted using existing holes for the door hinges and tilt frames.

The kit also had a basket around the spare wheel on the bonnet, and the racks to hold four dispenser packs of wire on each side could also be attached to this frame. In total, 11 miles of cable could be carried in the vehicle. This front frame seems often to have been omitted by users of the kit. The rear part of the frame was supported by two curved hoops which ran from the rear of the front doors. At the rear top of the frame were two boxes that prevented the ladders or poles slipping off the back of the frame as the vehicle travelled. In the rear load bed was mounted an Apparatus Cable Laying (ACL), and cable could be dispensed slowly at the rear as the vehicle moved forward.

BAT and MOBAT platforms

Some Land Rovers were used as a mount for the M40 recoilless rifle introduced in 1955 primarily for anti-tank use. This in turn had been developed from the under-developed US-made M27 recoilless rifle introduced during the Korean War. The M40 shared the M27's 105mm calibre, but was generally known as the 106mm type to avoid confusion with the earlier weapon, whose ammunition was incompatible with it. It was mounted on a tripod on which the front leg had a wheel for mobility. This front leg entered the portee vehicle while the two rear legs were propped on the rear platform or (later) bumperettes.

In 1953 the L1 120mm BAT (Battalion Anti-Tank gun) was introduced and was intended to replace the 17-pounder anti-tank gun. However, despite efforts to provide a lighter weapon the BAT L1 turned out to weigh almost as much as the weapon it was intended to replace because of its shield and transport wheels.

The L1 did enter service but proved too heavy to be used by airborne infantry. A lighter weapon was quickly put under development and this became L4 MOBAT (Mobile BAT), which entered service around 1958. Some L4 MOBAT were later fitted with a .50 spotting rifle and were known as L7 CONBAT (CONverted BAT). MOBAT was later was replaced by WOMBAT (Weapon of Magnesium BAT), which is covered in Chapter 5.

Later, there was a purpose-designed MOBAT towing vehicle (FV18009, based on the Mk 5 Land Rover), but Pat Ware has noted that several other Series I Land Rovers were converted to MOBAT portees with the MOBAT mounted in the cargo area. In what may have been a local modification, the windscreen was removed and a blast shield was mounted on the bonnet.

SAS version

From 1955, various short-wheelbase Land Rovers were converted for use by the Special Air Service (SAS). The majority were probably Mk 3 86-inch models. These vehicles followed the style of the Jeeps that had been used in the Western Desert by predecessors of 22 SAS Regiment. The vehicle had its doors, windscreens and canvas top and frame removed. To increase the range, a large additional fuel tank was fitted in the cargo bay, and a rear-facing gunner sat on top of this tank with a pintle-mounted Browning .30 calibre machine gun. The passenger seat was raised so that twin drum-fed general-purpose machine guns mounted on a rail over the scuttle could be fired forwards. These vehicles were used in SAS operations in support of the Sultan of Oman's forces battling an insurrection from November 1958.

Winch equipped

There is photographic evidence of a vehicle from the large order for 1500 vehicles (contract 6/Veh/18599, vehicle 07 BR 09) after modification to carry a front-mounted drum winch. The modification had been carried out by 13 Infantry Workshop REME, and the winch was capable of hauling one ton.

INDEPENDENT SUSPENSION EXPERIMENTS

Rover probably embarked on experiments with independent front suspension (IFS) on a Land Rover in anticipation of the need to protect its military contracts. The Austin Champ with its all-round independent suspension had entered Army service, and either Rover, or the Army, or both wanted to see how independent suspension would work on the cheaper vehicle.

A first "mule" prototype was based on an 86-inch model with chassis number 5710-3355, and was probably constructed during 1955. This ran on trade plates during its life as an experimental vehicle, but was registered as 7763 AC in mid-1959. During 1956, it was tested by FVRDE against a standard Land Rover and an Austin Champ at Chertsey, but it did not shine. The major drawback of the IFS system was that the differential would ground out all too easily if one of the front wheels was on full bump.

The installation was quite complicated. In front of the bulkhead, the chassis side-members were modified to rise up about three inches higher than on a standard 86-inch, to make room for the IFS hardware underneath. The front cross-member was reinforced and bolted to that was a massive cast-iron differential casing. Fabricated unequal-length upper and lower wishbones pivoted from that differential casing, and the drive-shafts had universal joints at their ends instead of the characteristic ball swivels of the production Land Rover. The rear suspension was modified to use dual-rate springs.

Springing was by laminated torsion bars, a system later investigated for the Road-Rover (eventually aborted) and the Rover 3-litre saloon (introduced in 1958). These were firmly anchored to a reinforced gearbox cross-member. There was a larger steering box with chassis-mounted relay and an idler on the opposite side. Sticky steering proved to be a problem during development, but this was cured by fitting needle roller king pin bushes instead of the standard bronze type.

Despite the drawbacks of the design, Rover tried it out again on a batch of experimental Series IIs when the Austin Gipsy looked like presenting a threat to civilian Land Rover sales.

07 BR 09 was a late Mk 3 model (unusually described on the placard as a Mk III), and was being used for trials of a drum winch when photographed. (Unknown source)

SUMMARY OF 86-INCH (MK 3) MODEL DELIVERIES, 1954-1957

ARMY

Serials	Contract	Chassis Nos	Total	Remarks
36 BP 85 to 48 BP 58 and 60 BP 37 to 74 BP62	6/Veh/16223	5710-0282 to 5710-2342 and 5710-2343 to 5710-4375	2600	Contract dated 26 May 1954.
92 BP 07	6/Veh/18421	5713-2638	1	Contract dated 10 January 1955. LHD, Station Wagon.
92 BP 59 to 99 BP 99 and 00 BR 01 to 07 BR 59	6/Veh/18599	5710-4381 to 5710-8014	1500	Contract dated 22 January 1955.
42 BR 45 to 52 BR 44	6/Veh/20244	1706-01003 to 1706-03724 and 1736-02105	1000	Contract dated 27 October 1955. 48 BR 74 was LHD.
77 BR 30 to 82 BR 74	6/Veh/22633	1706-03843 to 1706-04807	545	Contract dated 23 February 1956; 445 vehicles were required by 28 April 1956. John Mastrangelo notes that the contract was amended four times (3 July 1956, 10 July 1956, 15 January 1957 and 9 May 1957) to add 1038, 17, 400 and 100 respectively making a total of 2000. 1455 of these were delivered as Mk 5s.
			Total 5646	

RAF Vehicles are listed in serial number order. This did not always reflect the order in which contracts were issued.

Serials	Contract	Chassis Nos	Total	Remarks
37 AA 71 to 37 AA 88	6/Veh/21227	1706-02915 to 1706-02914	18	Airfield Lighting.
48 AA 81 to 50 AA 01	6/Veh/13840	4710-0849 to 4710-1015	121	Total vehicles in contract not confirmed.
50 AA 02 to 52 AA 47	6/Veh/13921	4710-1016 to 4710-1550	246	Total vehicles in contract not confirmed.
52 AA 48 to 54 AA 24	n/a	4710-1551 to 4710-1928	177	
55 AA 43 to 56 AA 92	6/Veh/16499	5710-00489 to 5710-01986	150	
65 AA 60 to 65 AA 94	n/a	5710-7335 to 1706-04660	35	
60 AA 15 to 62 AA 88	6/Veh/19982	1706-00888 to 1706-01442	274	
63 AA 14 to 63 AA 38	6/Veh/22529	1706-03718 to 1706-03836	25	Contract also included Mk 3 86s and Mk 4 107s for RAF. NB: chassis numbers overlap with other contracts.
			Total 1046	(Subject to confirmation of individual contract totals.)

Note: *55 AA 89 became a Royal Review Vehicle, as explained in the main text.*

ROYAL NAVY

Serials	Contract	Chassis Nos	Total	Remarks
25 RN 08 to 25 RN 13	6/Veh/15462	4710 series	6	Probably in chassis range 4710-2259 to 4710-2270, delivered April-May 1954.
36 RN 82 to 36 RN 84	6/Veh/15619	4710 series	3	Station Wagons. Probably in chassis range 4710-2259 to 4710-2270, delivered April-May 1954.
n/a	n/a	5710-00760	1	Green paint.
43 RN 13 to 43 RN 15	6/Veh/22178	1706-03751 to 1706-03753	3	Contract also included Mk 4 107 models; see below
			Total 13	Plus at least 3; see Note below.

Notes: *All 12 chassis numbered from 4710-2259 to 4710-2270 were delivered to the Royal Navy, according to Rover despatch records held by BMIHT; only 9 are accounted for the in the table above.*
Photographs show that 18 RN 65 was allocated to the aircraft carrier HMS Albion. The vehicle was in service by May 1957 and was therefore too early for the Mk 5 models known to have been delivered to the Royal Navy. It is not inconceivable that it had been transferred from Army stocks.

TECHNICAL SPECIFICATIONS, 86-INCH MK 3 MODELS

ENGINE:

1997cc (77.8mm x 105mm) four-cylinder with over-head inlet and side exhaust valves; single Solex 32 PBI-2 carburettor. 6.8:1 compression ratio. 52bhp at 4000rpm and 101 lb ft at 1500rpm.

SUSPENSION, STEERING AND BRAKES:

Semi-elliptic leaf springs all round.
Recirculating-ball steering with 15:1 ratio.
Drum brakes (10in x 1.5in) on all four wheels; separate drum-type transmission parking brake.

TRANSMISSION:

Selectable four-wheel drive.
Four-speed main gearbox with synchromesh on 3rd and 4th gears only; ratios 3.00:1, 2.04:1, 1.38:1, 1.00:1, reverse 2.54:1.
Two-speed transfer gearbox; ratios 1.148:1 (High) and 2.89:1 (Low)
Axle ratio: 4.7:1

ELECTRICAL SYSTEM:

12-volt with dynamo.

UNLADEN WEIGHT:

2702 lb (1226kg)

PERFORMANCE

0-50mph:	25secs
Maximum:	60mph approx (96.6km/h)
Fuel consumption:	23mpg approx

DIMENSIONS:

Overall length:	132in (3353mm)
Overall length:	140.7in (3574mm)
Wheelbase:	86in (2184mm)
Overall width:	62.6in (1590mm)
Unladen height:	76in (1930mm) with hood up
Track:	50in (1270mm)

LAND ROVER CHASSIS CODES FOR 86-INCH AND 88-INCH MODELS, 1954-1958

All Land Rovers in this period had a four-digit identifying prefix in the chassis code, which indicated the model type, the model-year (not calendar-year) of manufacture, the steering position and other factors. The ones relevant to the Mk 3 and Mk 5 models are shown below. The four-figure prefix was followed by a four-figure (1954-1955) or five-figure (1956 on) serial number that began at 0001 or 00001 for each separate sequence (although the serial numbers for the 88 models followed on from those for the 86 types).

Note that the Land Rover model-year began in September and continued until the end of the following July, leaving August clear for the works' annual holiday and for preparing the assembly lines to take new models. A Land Rover built in the 1956 model-year could therefore have been built at any time between September 1955 and July 1956.

1116	1956 RHD 88in
1117	1957 RHD 88in
1118	1958 RHD 88in
1147	1957 LHD 88in
1706	1956 RHD 86in
1736	1956 LHD 86in
4710	1954 RHD 86in
5710	1955 RHD 86in

ARMY SERIAL NUMBERS

The serial numbers allocated by the Army gave a clue to the date of the vehicle, although those issued by the RAF and Royal Navy did not. In this period, serial letters indicated the financial year in which the vehicle was purchased (which is not necessarily the same as the calendar year in which it was delivered). Those relevant to the Mk 3 and Mk 5 models are shown below.

As before, serial sequences began at 0001 (eg 00 BP 01) and ran to 9999 (eg 99 BP 99). There was not necessarily any correlation between chassis number order and military serial number within batches.

BP	1955-1956
BR	1955-1956
BS	1956-1957
CE	1957-1958

THE ROVER MK 5 (1957-1958)

Market demand had led Land Rover to design a diesel engine as an option for the Land Rover, and this became available in June 1957. The new diesel engine shared its basic architecture with the planned replacement for the 2-litre petrol engine, which would not become available until autumn 1958. Both of these new OHV engines were an extremely tight fit in the Land Rover's engine bay, and in some circumstances the front axle could foul the sump and the cooling fan could foul the radiator. So Rover played for safety by moving the front cross-member and the radiator mounted on it forwards by an inch, and moving the front axle forwards by two inches. This created another new wheelbase of 88 inches, which became standard for the short-wheelbase Land Rovers. The British armed forces responded by describing these revised models as Rover Mk 5 (FV18001) types, the Mk 4 designation having already gone to the long-wheelbase models described in Chapter 3.

FEATURES OF THE MK 5 MODELS

The Mk 5 models carried on from where the Mk 3 types had left off, and to the casual onlooker there was no discernible difference between them. However, an easy recognition point of these models was the larger gap between the front wing mounting bolt and the trailing edge of the front wheelarch; the grille support panel also had only three holes and was made of steel, whereas that on the Mk 3 86-inch was made of alloy and had five holes.

Less visibly, the chassis frame differed at the front with its relocated cross-member, the steering linkages were different, a longer front propshaft was needed, and the horn was relocated to a bracket under the bonnet panel because the revisions left no room for it in its original position on the front cross-member. Difficult to spot was that the front wings were actually different pressings, with the wheelarch cutout positioned further forwards and less metal ahead of it than on the Mk 3 or 86-inch type.

The Mk 5 88-inch Land Rovers were normally delivered to the British armed services with inward-facing bench rear seats and a grab handle on either side of the tailgate. John Mastrangelo has noted that flashing turn indicators were fitted to the last 40 delivered under contract 6/Veh/22633, and to all of those delivered under contracts 6/Veh/24950 and 6/Veh/26222.

MK 5 VARIANTS

4x2 models

A particularly interesting variant of the Mk 5 Land Rover appeared in 1957. By this stage, the War Department had begun to standardise on the Land Rover as its front-line light utility vehicle, and it made perfect sense in logistical terms to consider using a version of it to replace the elderly and miscellaneous fleet of car-derived vans and utilities ("tillies").

However, the vehicles due for replacement were two-wheel drive (4x2) types, and the military procurement people insisted that they should be replaced by more 4x2 types, not by 4x4s. So they asked the Rover Company to build a special 4x2 derivative of the Land Rover. It looks as if this request was preceded by the conversion of an 86-inch Mk 3 model (39 BP 30, on chassis number 5710-0696) to show what was needed.

Rover readily agreed: there was a large contract at stake. The engineering was in any case straightforward enough. The propshaft to the front axle was omitted, and the axle itself was replaced by a simple tubular type with no differential and with the hub carriers welded to its ends. The transfer box front output housing was blanked off, low range was locked out by means of sleeves on the selector shaft, and no transfer box lever was fitted. These alterations actually made the 4x2 Land Rover more expensive than the standard 4x4 type, but

83 BR 50 was from the first batch of Mk 5 models and was pictured here in November 1957 during an exhibition at the Rover factory in Solihull. The configuration of the rear body differs from the Mk 3 line-layer shown above. It bears the markings of 2 Training Regiment, Royal Corps of Signals. (BMIHT)

Those 675 vehicles were built at Solihull between January and March 1958, in the chassis range between 1118-00962 and 1118-01911. They were registered within the sequences of 01 CE 89 to 08 CE 43 (pick-ups) and 08 CE 44 to 08 CE 63 (Station Wagons), and were distributed to a variety of Army installations. Some served as camp runabouts, some as school vehicles, and some were probably used on recruitment and driver training duties. Some may have been used by Territorial Army detachments, and a small number were lent to the RAF in Hong Kong during 1960, where they were equipped for use by Dog Patrols.

Military policy was to dispose of cars – and the 4x2s were classified as such – after five years, and so most of these Land Rovers were sold off in 1963, although a few remained in service until 1967. Around 500 (the exact figure is not known) were bought by the Ministry of Public Buildings and Works (MPBW), who re-registered them on civilian plates in the reversed FUV series. They served a further five to seven years with the MPBW, the last ones probably being withdrawn around 1970. Most were probably used as general runabouts and tender vehicles at historic buildings and sites of the type now run by English Heritage and the National Trust. When they were eventually sold off to the public, many of their new owners converted them to standard 4x4 configuration.

Now in preservation and wearing a civilian registration plate, this is 07 CE 55, one of a large batch of Mk 5 models delivered with a 4x2 drive configuration. The trailer is a more modern military Sankey type. (GF)

in view of the perceived benefits this was of no concern to the military. Among the real benefits was a 10% reduction in fuel consumption, from 18mpg to 20mpg.

Ministry of Supply contract number 6/Veh/26222 was placed on 1 November 1957 and called for 655 4x2 Mk 5 Land Rovers, all with canvas tilts and right-hand drive. This order was swiftly followed by a second, placed on 20 December, which called for 20 Station Wagon variants of the 4x2 Rover Mk 5 and made the total up to 675 vehicles in all.

MOBAT tractor
Pat Ware notes that six 88-inch Mk 5 models were converted to tow and support the 120mm MOBAT (Mobile Battalion Anti-Tank) gun, and that these were re-classified as FV 18009 types.

Twenty of the 4x2 models were delivered with Station Wagon bodies, although the Army knew them as Utilities. 08 CE 55 was here being used as the tractor unit for a recruiting caravan for HQ West Midlands District. (PW)

66 BS 09 was one of probably eight Mk 5 models modified to SAS specification. It was pictured here at Rover's Solihull factory in November 1957, almost certainly before it had seen any active service. Note how the observer's seat has been raised. (BMIHT)

SAS version

After the Malayan Emergency of the early 1950s had effectively been neutralised by a ceasefire, there were still pockets of guerrillas operating in the jungle. So, although the main British military force was withdrawn, the SAS squadrons which had been operating in Malaya stayed behind to carry out what are euphemistically called "mopping-up" operations. It seems likely that this was the reason why the Regiment developed its own special version of the short-wheelbase Land Rover in the first half of 1956.

The prototype was converted by the Regiment's own workshops, and was based on a Mk 3 86-inch model with right-hand drive, 43 BR 70 from contract 6/Veh/20244. This first vehicle – perhaps surprisingly for one destined to be used in clandestine operations – was displayed at the annual exhibition jointly hosted by the Society of Motor Manufacturers and Traders (SMMT) and FVRDE at Chertsey in 1956, and was illustrated in the catalogue as well. However, it seems to have remained unique because Rover production was just about to switch to the 88-inch or Mk 5 model.

66 BS 09 was another one of the SAS conversions, and this view shows it from the rear.

The tall box on the right of the SAS vehicle's back body contained a radio set. This one is shown in a carefully restored example. (JT)

The best sources suggest that eight more vehicles were converted to the SAS specification, and that these were all drawn from the first batch of Mk 5 models, 6/Veh/24950, that was delivered in 1957. Those so far identified are 66 BS 03, which appears in official photographs, 66 BS 09, which was shown at a special NATO display held at Rover's Solihull factory in November 1957, and 66 BS 14, which survives in a private collection.

The SAS Mk 5 Land Rovers carried their own special designation of FV18006. Uprated front and rear springs allowed them to carry extra weight, and the spare wheel was mounted on the front bumper, jutting out ahead of the vehicle and leaving the grille aperture clear so that cooling was not impaired. A jerrycan was mounted ahead of each front wing, one for water and the other for petrol, and so the sidelight positions were blanked off and standard FV-pattern side-lamps were attached to the outer edge of each wing. The Equipment Schedule for the FV18006 lists an auxiliary fuel tank fitted beneath the passenger seat, but neither 66 BS 09 nor 66 BS 14 had this.

The doors and windscreen were removed, and a swivelling searchlight was mounted on the driver's side of the front bulkhead. The observer's (passenger's) seat was raised on a wooden platform, and twin Vickers K.303 machine guns were fitted to a swivel mount in front of him. Even though there was no centre seat – between the two front seats were angled tubes where ammunition could be stored – there was a bench front seat back on the observer's side that may have been intended to prevent material being thrown from the back of the vehicle into the front. The seat back itself was actually from the De Luxe trim option available for civilian long-wheelbase truck cab models.

The vehicles were configured for a three-man crew of driver, observer and radio operator, who also acted as the rear gunner. This third man had his own rearward-facing seat, elevated to provide a better field of vision, and he had a heavy machine gun mounted on a pedestal in the rear cargo area. Typically, this was a .30 or .50-calibre Browning. A third weapon was normally stowed in a vertical holster on the end of the bulkhead, beside the driver's right hand. In the back, a rocket launcher was carried on the floor of the cargo area, encased in its protective tubular carrying-case.

A sun compass was fitted to the middle of the front bulk-head where both driver and observer could see it. In the back body, mounted on the right-hand wheelbox, was a tactical radio set, and there was an antenna for this on the right-hand front wing. The Equipment Schedule also listed a camo net, four Lee Enfield rifles, a signal pistol, 10 magazines for the twin Vickers guns, an ammo box for the rear Browning gun, an oil can, a tow rope, and a large First Aid kit. In practice, however, each patrol would select the kit it needed before embarking on a mission, and so this list is necessarily "typical" rather than definitive.

RAF Mk 5 deliveries

The RAF continued to take Land Rovers in Mk 5 form. Just three contracts are known, calling for 151 vehicles in all: these were 6/Veh/24271, 6/Veh/24587 and 6/Veh/25266. All were fulfilled with 1957-model 88-inch Mk 5s.

Royal Navy deliveries

Royal Navy deliveries of the Mk 5 models appear to have been minimal, although our knowledge is once again hampered by a lack of records. Contract 6/Veh/25662 called for a single vehicle with left-hand drive. There were very probably others, and some are said to have been delivered with the new diesel engine, although there is no evidence of this in the Rover despatch records.

ASSET CODES

6039-13-192	Truck, Utility, 1/4 ton, 4x4, Rover 86" WB

A new Asset Code system was introduced in 1956. The initial six digits indicated the vehicle's rôle and the next two indicated both the steering position (RHD or LHD) and the version. The final three digits not only indicated the manufacturer but also the chassis type. The codes allocated to the Mk 5 vehicles were:

207040-00-906	Car, CL, Utility, Light, 4x2, Rover Mk 5
207041-00-906	Car, CL, Utility, Light, (Station Wagon), 4x2, Rover Mk5
304010-41-906	Truck, Utility, 1/4 ton, 4x4, Rover Mk 5 88" WB FV18007 LHD
304010-61-906	Truck, Utility, 1/4 ton, 4x4, Rover Mk 5 88" WB FV18007 RHD
307040-00-906	Truck, CL, Utility, Light, 4x2, Rover Mk 5

SUMMARY OF 88-INCH (MK 5) MODEL DELIVERIES, 1956-1958

ARMY

Serials	Contract	Chassis Nos		Total	Remarks
82 BR 75 to 92 BR 29	6/Veh/22633	1116-04808 to 1117-01736	S	1055	For first part of contract for Mk 3 86-inch, see above.
25 BS 36 to 29 BS 35	6/Veh/22633	1117-01748 to 1117-02926	S	400	
65 BS 87 to 66 BS 82	6/Veh/24950	1117-02927 to 1117-03105	S	96	Contract dated 18 December 1956.
66 BS 83 to 66 BS 86	6/Veh/24950	1147-02764 to 1147-02767	C	4	LHD.
01 CE 89 to 08 CE 43	6/Veh/26222	1118-00962 to 1118-01892	S	655	Mk 5 4x2 CL; contract dated 4 October 1957.
08 CE 44 to 08 CE 63	6/Veh/26222	1118-01726 to 1118-01817	S	20	Mk 5 4x2 Utility.
				Total 2230	

RAF

Serials	Contract	Chassis Nos	Total
63 AA 99 to 64 AA 29 and			
64 AA 31 to 64 AA 60	6/Veh/24271	1117-00001 to 1117-00390	61
64 AA 61 to 65 AA 30	6/Veh/24587	1117-01909 to 1117-02177	70
65 AA 31 to 65 AA 50	6/Veh/25266	1117-03147 to 1117-03202	20
			Total 151

ROYAL NAVY

Serials	Contract	Chassis Nos	Total	Remarks
n/a	6/Veh/25662	1147-04291	1	LHD.
n/a	n/a	1118-0218 to 1118-0766	30	Five batches of six each delivered between October 1957 and February 1958; all in Royal Blue.
			Total 31	

Note: *50 RN 68 has been reported as a diesel-engined short-wheelbase model, and must therefore have been a Mk 5 88-inch.*

TECHNICAL SPECIFICATIONS, 88-INCH MK 5 MODELS

As for 86-inch Mk 3, except:

DIMENSIONS:
Overall length: 140.75in (3580mm)
Wheelbase: 88in (2235mm)
Overall width: 62.6in (1590mm)
Unladen height: 76in (1930mm) with hood up
Track: 50in (1270mm)

UNLADEN WEIGHT
2740lb (1243kg)

CHAPTER 3:
THE MARK 4 (107-INCH AND 109-INCH)

A s Chapter 2 explains, the long-wheelbase 107-inch Land Rover was developed as part of the Rover Company's plan to provide greater carrying capacity for the vehicle. It was introduced alongside the new 86-inch Land Rover in autumn 1953. Despite its greater capacity, the 107-inch had the same mechanical underpinnings as the smaller vehicles.

Unexplained is the purpose of this box-bodied Mk 4 with left-hand drive that passed through FVRDE. It seems to have remained unique, and may not have been intended for military service. (TMB)

Nowadays it is difficult to imagine that the War Department did not immediately purchase large numbers of long-wheelbase Land Rovers, but in fact it took some time for the new vehicle to be seen as meeting a requirement. In the early 1950s the Army had no need of a ¾ ton load and personnel carrier because many rôles, in particular infantry section vehicles, were being met by recently purchased vehicles in the 1-ton Class – Humber (CT), Morris (GS) and Austin (GS) – as well as 15 cwt vehicles from WW2 that had been re-rated as 1-ton Class vehicles – Bedford MW (CL) and Ford WOT2 (CL). Both the Austin 1-ton GS and Humber 1-ton CT trucks were also available in FFW form to carry out many of the command rôles in infantry battalions, Royal Artillery Regiments and other units.

Although the Army saw no use for the long-wheelbase Land Rover at the start, it did examine a single example specially fitted with a tall box body on a LHD chassis. This was ordered for unknown purposes, probably in 1955, and appears never to have carried a military serial number. The RAF and Royal Navy, meanwhile, both took examples of the 107-inch model for special duties.

In the meantime, the Rover Company had seen the potential for a Station Wagon derivative of the new long-wheelbase Land Rover. Unfortunately, the realisation came a little too late, and it quickly became apparent that the chassis signed-off for production needed considerable modification if it were to suit a Station Wagon body. First, the upsweep in the side-members had to be eliminated to make a flat floor possible; and secondly, the rear suspension had to be modified in order to prevent excessive body roll. Rover did this by mounting the rear springs further outboard, on outriggers. All this additional development took time, and the 107-inch Station Wagon was not ready until the autumn of 1955. Despite early enthusiasm from the Army, these Station Wagons were never numerous in British military service.

In fact, no version of the 107-inch Land Rover was ever ordered in large quantities by the War Department. It looks

This early 107-inch pick-up was evaluated at FVRDE, and the features in the photograph suggest that it dates from around 1954. Note the road tyres, as supplied on early examples of what the manufacturer described as the Land-Rover 4-wheel-drive Pick-up Truck. Although the Army did not take to this variant, it was ordered in small quantities by the RAF and Royal Navy. (TMB)

as if fewer than 160 entered service between 1955 and 1957, even with the inclusion of those vehicles running on civil registrations allocated to War Office and Air Ministry establishments. Both pick-up and Station Wagon derivatives were known as Rover Mk 4 types, although there were different FV numbers for the different varieties.

Army deliveries

FVRDE looked at a prototype Station Wagon (which carried Rover identity LRSW/2) probably in late 1954, and as a result the Army was very quick off the mark in placing an order. Contract 6/Veh/19981 was placed on 23 May 1955 – some seven months before any production examples were built at Solihull – and called for 20 vehicles. It was subsequently amended so that one of the batch was delivered with left-hand drive. Each vehicle was priced at £890.

The 107-inch Station Wagon was far from appealing to the eye because it had been built as far as possible from the Land Rover parts box. In military guise, what was classified as an FV18004 offered seating for seven personnel, although the civilian model was a 10-seater. In civilian form it also attracted Purchase Tax, but this did not trouble Government Departments. The Army seems to have bought these Station Wagons largely for evaluation as a replacement for the Humber "Box" designated "Car, GS, Utility, Heavy, 4x4". There were around 2000 of these, and by the early 1950s many were being struck off. However, no more Mk 4 Station Wagons were ordered, so it looks as if the experiment was a failure.

The FV18004s had FV-pattern headlights and were specified as FFW vehicles with the special electrical system that went with that designation. The idea that they became "radio command cars" is a persistent one, although they could have been issued to many types of unit. The photographic evidence suggests that at least one went to a Royal Engineers Postal Unit in the Middle East, a couple went to FVRDE and a couple went to Malta. As for the solitary LHD example (42 BR 44), it was issued to the Military Attaché in Poland who was based in Warsaw. During the Cold War, the Military Attaché would have been involved in some serious intelligence gathering on the strength of Warsaw Pact forces and their troop movements. The vehicle survived for over 20 years and was finally struck off in Poland in June 1977!

One other Station Wagon deserves mention, and that is a production model that was evaluated by FVRDE in late 1955 or early 1956. Unfortunately, it has been impossible to iden-

42 BR 29 was one of just 19 Mk 4 "Utility" models purchased. These were Station Wagons on the 107-inch chassis, and were fitted out as FFW vehicles. However, some were later used for other duties; one well-known picture shows one delivering the mail at an overseas post! (RES)

On civilian plates 353 EXE, this vehicle belonged to Proof & Experimental Establishment, Lavington – although the crest on the door suggests that it might have found its way into GPO service! Note the ladder rack on the roof and that, unlike the Army deliveries in the BR series, this vehicle retains its unpainted body cappings. (RES)

tify the vehicle precisely, although it may have been one of the early deliveries in the batch of 20. While at FVRDE, it ran on civilian plates PLF 502, and had FVRDE Wing Number 4876. A number of other 107-inch Station Wagons are known to have run on civilian registrations even though they served with War Office and Air Ministry establishments: among these are PGK 624, RGX 616, 340 EXE, 353 EXE and 213 GXC.

RAF deliveries

The RAF took a batch of 60 Mk 4 pick-up models in 1956, converting some of them to airfield crash rescue vehicles later. However, it also recognised the potential of the long-wheelbase Land Rover as the basis of an ambulance for its Mountain Rescue service (originally set up to rescue downed pilots but in practice increasingly playing a rôle in civilian mountain rescue operations as well), and ordered a first batch some time around July 1955. These were fitted with tall and ungainly ambulance bodies that were constructed by Bonallack & Sons, a commercial body builder based at Basildon in Essex. The prototype was evaluated at FVRDE with the civilian registration number RGX 6, but may have been given an RAF serial number when it entered service.

That tall and top-heavy body must have created handling problems, because the RAF order for Mountain Rescue ambulances was fulfilled by examples of the 107-inch Station Wagon chassis with its outrigged rear springs that reduced body roll. With two-stretcher bodies, these ambulances were FV18005 types, and with four-stretcher bodies they were FV18008 types. Some questions still remain over how many of these were taken into service; the Rover despatch records show 11 Station Wagon chassis delivered

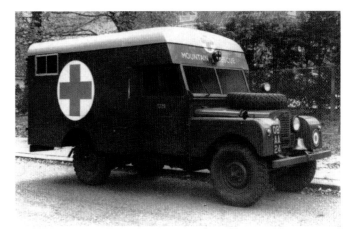

The RAF Mountain Rescue ambulances had a specially-designed body constructed by Bonallack. 08 AA 24 was the example that was evaluated at FVRDE. (Top: TMB; above: PW)

directly to Bonallack (1317-0023 to 0025 and 0031 to 0037), a quantity which is hard to reconcile with the known contract details.

Royal Navy deliveries

The Royal Navy took its first Mk 4 Land Rovers in 1956, and went on to order around 50 in all. Most were Station Wagons, delivered in Royal Blue livery; there were also three pick-up models in Green that year. The greater carrying capacity of the long-wheelbase chassis made this well suited to the airfield crash tender rôle (which was then being filled by Mk 1 short-wheelbase models), and an order was also placed for 15 such vehicles for the Royal Naval Air Service. Royal Navy deliveries were made to the RN Motor Transport Depot at Clayton, near Newcastle-under-Lyme.

63 AA 46 was one of many Mk 4 pick-ups that the RAF converted to Airfield Crash Rescue tenders. It was pictured here in 1961 at RAF Gaydon, the airfield which is now the Jaguar Land Rover test track and engineering centre. (BMIHT)

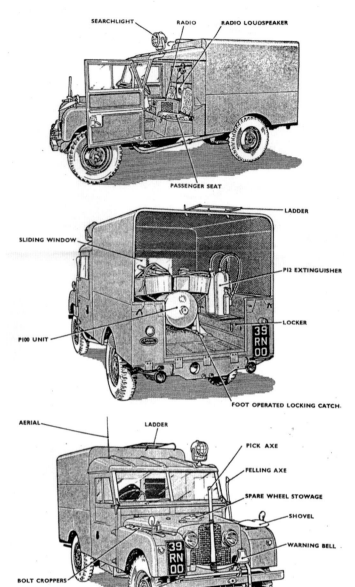

SEARCHLIGHT · RADIO · RADIO LOUDSPEAKER

PASSENGER SEAT

LADDER

SLIDING WINDOW

P12 EXTINGUISHER

P100 UNIT

LOCKER

39 RN 00

FOOT OPERATED LOCKING CATCH.

AERIAL · LADDER

PICK AXE

FELLING AXE

SPARE WHEEL STOWAGE

SHOVEL

39 RN 00

WARNING BELL

BOLT CROPPERS

PINCH BAR

NOTEBOOK DIAGRAM
S.R./1435/N.B.
ADMIRALTY A.D

RESCUE VEHICLE

The Royal Navy also used Mk 4 pick-ups as crash rescue vehicles at RNAS stations. Although the serial number 39 RN 00 is thought to be a fake, these drawings from an RN handbook give a good idea of how the vehicle was equipped. The tall hardtop seen here was not available as a civilian option. (WD publication)

RNAS rescue vehicles

Most of the Mk 4 107-inch pick-up models delivered to the Royal Navy were equipped as Pilot Rescue Vehicles for the RNAS. These carried serials 39 RN 10 to 39 RN 24, were delivered under contract 6/Veh/20676 and entered service in November 1955. They were painted red. (Although an offi-

cial drawing of 39 RN 00 exists, the serial number is assumed to be fake),

These vehicles were fitted by Royal Navy workshops with a tall canopy over the pick-up body, and a ladder was carried in a rack on top of this. The back body contained a large P100 dry-powder fire extinguisher retained by a foot-operated locking catch, and a pair of smaller P12 (dry powder) fire extinguishers that were carried on top of the right-hand wheelbox. Some equipment was carried in one or both of the wheelbox lockers. A radio was mounted between the seats, with a loudspeaker on the bulkhead behind it and an aerial on the cab roof. The cab roof also carried a searchlight on a rotating mount, and there was a warning bell on a bracket above the bumper on the left.

Items of rescue equipment were carried on the outside of the vehicle at the front. There was a long pinch bar behind the front bumper and a pickaxe was carried vertically ahead of the radiator. There were bolt croppers on the right-hand front wing and a shovel on the left-hand front wing, and a felling axle was mounted on the left-hand front wing next to the windscreen pillar.

A SPECIAL STATION WAGON

In 1955 or early 1956, the War Department purchased a single special-bodied Land Rover on a RHD 107-inch chassis under contract number 6/Veh/19031. Pictures reveal that the body was built by Jones Bros, a commercial body-builder in Willesden, London. The shape of the rear cross-member and the position of the rear spring hangers both suggest that it was built on a pick-up rather than Station Wagon chassis, and it was probably on chassis 5720-0410, which was delivered in February 1955 to Jones Bros. The vehicle carried civilian registration number RXN 368, no doubt from the batches allocated to FVRDE.

The tall and rather angular estate-type body could well have come from the same drawing board as the 1951 Staff Car (see Chapter 1). It had no galvanised cappings, and incorporated a two-piece windscreen and side-hung double doors at the rear with fixed glazing. All four side doors had sliding windows and bright-metal coachbuilder's door handles, and a step running below them on each side eased entry and exit. The roof had external bracing around what was probably a built-in luggage rack.

A pair of very similar bodies were later ordered by the Post Office Engineering Department, which regularly had special bodies constructed by Jones Bros.

This special-bodied Mk4 remained unique. The identity of the body builder is unknown, but the vehicle has some similarities to special bodies built by Jones Bros of Willesden for the Post Office at about the same time. (Jones Bros)

SUMMARY OF 107-INCH (MK 4) MODEL DELIVERIES, 1955-1957

ARMY

Serials	Contract	Chassis Nos	Total	Remarks
42 BR 25 to 42 BR 43	6/Veh/19981	8706-0010 to 8706-0055	19	Contract dated 23 May 1955. FFW Utility models with FV headlights and, towing rings; they were RHD export- specification Station Wagons.
42 BR 44	6/Veh/19981	8736-00392	1	LHD Utility, FFW; but otherwise as above.
			Total 20	

RAF

Serials	Contract	Chassis Nos	Total	Remarks
08 AA 17 to 08 AA 25	6/Veh/20841	8706-0013 to 8706-0022	10	Contract dated 5 December 1955 for 9 vehicles; linked to 6/Veh/21105, presumably for Bonallack bodies. These were "Mk 4 Ambulance" types on 1956-model Station Wagon chassis.
63 AA 39 to 63 AA 98	6/Veh/22529	2706-00823 to 2706-00884	60	1956-model pick-ups; many converted to Airfield Crash Rescue later.
08 AA 35 to 08 AA 41	6/Veh/24584	1317-00023 to 1317-00035	7	Contract dated 7 November 1956; body contract 6/Veh/24818 dated 29 January 1957. These were Mk 4 Ambulance types on 1957-model Station Wagon chassis.
			Total 77	

Note: *Pat Ware lists 6/Veh/25878 (1317-00053) as a single Mk 4 ambulance.*

ROYAL NAVY

Serials	Contract	Chassis Nos	Total	Remarks
39 RN 10 to 39 RN 24	6/Veh/20676	2706-00576 to 2706-00591(less 0580)	15	RNAS crash tenders ("Rescue Vehicles"); 39 RN 00 assumed fake.
42 RN 43 and 42 RN 44 plus one unidentified	6/Veh/21173	2706-00614 and 2706-00616	3	Pick-ups, delivered in Green.
43 RN 10 to 43 RN 12	6/Veh/22178	2706-00818 to 2706-0820	3	Contract also included Mk 3 86-inch models; see Chapter 2; delivered in Royal Blue.
45 RN 72 to 45 RN 77	6/Veh/23039	8706-0056 to 8706-0061	6	Station Wagons in Royal Blue.
57 RN 42 to 57 RN 63	6/Veh/25959	1318-00007 to 1318-00039 (less 13-14, 25-33 and 38)	24	Station Wagons.
			Total 51	

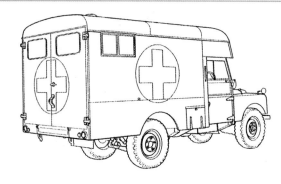
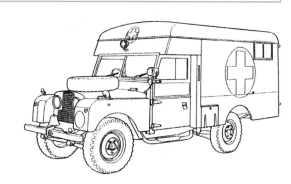

The Bonallack-bodied RAF ambulances were never numerous, and good pictures are hard to find. These were the illustrations provided in the user's handbook as an aid to recognition of the type. (WD publication)

THE MK 4
109-INCH MODELS

On the Rover production lines, the 107-inch chassis gave way to a 109-inch chassis in June 1957 for exactly the same reasons as the 86-inch gave way to the 88-inch type. In this case, however, there was an exception: the special 107-inch Station Wagon chassis remained in production until it was replaced by a Series II model in mid-1958, and there were no Station Wagon versions of the 109-inch type. There were therefore 107-inch and 109-inch models in production together for a period of around a year.

The War Department took the change to the 109-inch chassis in its stride, as it had with the change to the 88-inch. However, where the 88-inch had merited a new (Rover Mk 5) designation, the 109-inch model appears to have retained the Mk 4 designation that had been used for the 107-inch models. The rationale behind this is far from clear!

The short production period of the 109-inch models ensured that these would be among the rarest of all Land Rovers in British military service. There appear to have been fewer than 50 in all.

SUMMARY OF 109-INCH (MK 4) MODEL DELIVERIES, 1956-1958

ARMY

Serials	Contract	Chassis Nos	Total	Remarks
n/a	6/Veh/25505		1	109 pick-up with Turner L60 diesel engine; contract 6/Veh/25447 with Turner for engine
			Total 1	

Note: *This vehicle may well have been a prototype with a civilian (perhaps FVRDE) registration and would therefore not have been "on census".*

RAF

Serials	Contract	Chassis Nos	Total	Remarks
65 AA 51 to 65 AA 52	6/Veh/25443	1217-00580 to 1217-00581	2	This contract may originally have been intended for Army.
			Total 2	

ROYAL NAVY

Serials	Contract	Chassis Nos	Total	Remarks
n/a	6/Veh/23942	1216-1212 to 1216-1226	15	Delivered in Royal Blue, to RN MT Depots at Clayton and Kidbrooke.
n/a	6/Veh/25957	1218-0077 to 1218-0226 (batches)	23	First part of contract was for Mk 5 88-inch models; these were pick-ups, painted Royal Blue.
n/a	6/Veh/26322	1218-0227 to 1218-0255	10	Chassis numbers continue from previous contract; delivered to RN Clayton in February 1958.
			Total 48	

MOS

Serials	Contract	Chassis Nos	Total	Remarks
n/a	6/Veh/25505	1217-00515	1	A single military contract is recorded for a 109-inch model that was destined for the Ministry of Supply.
			Total 1	

TECHNICAL SPECIFICATIONS, 107-INCH AND 109-INCH MODELS

ENGINE:
1997cc (77.8mm x 105mm) four-cylinder with overhead inlet and side exhaust valves; single Solex 32 PBI-2 carburettor. 6.8:1 compression ratio. 52bhp at 4000rpm and 101 lb ft at 1500rpm.

TRANSMISSION:
Selectable four-wheel drive.
Four-speed main gearbox with synchromesh on 3rd and 4th gears only; ratios 3.00:1, 2.04:1, 1.38:1, 1.00:1, reverse 2.54:1.
Two-speed transfer gearbox; ratios 1.148:1 (High) and 2.89:1 (Low)
Axle ratio: 4.7:1

SUSPENSION, STEERING AND BRAKES:
Semi-elliptic leaf springs all round.
Recirculating-ball steering with 15:1 ratio.
Drum brakes (10in x 1.5in) on all four wheels; 11in x 1.5in brakes from April 1954; separate drum-type transmission parking brake.

UNLADEN WEIGHT:
3031 lb (1375kg) for 107-inch pick-up;
3080 lb (1397kg) for 109-inch pick-up;
3444 lb (1562kg) for 107-inch Station Wagon.

ELECTRICAL SYSTEM:
12-volt with dynamo.

PERFORMANCE:
0-50mph:	29secs
Maximum:	58mph approx (93.3km/h)
Fuel consumption:	19 mpg approx

DIMENSIONS:
Overall length:	173.5in (4407mm) for both variants
Wheelbase:	107in (2718mm), or 109in (2768mm)
Overall width:	62.6in (1590mm)
Unladen height:	83.5in (2121mm) with hood up, for both variants; 78in (1981mm) for 107-inch Station Wagon
Track:	50in (1270mm)

ASSET CODES

6019-10-192   Car, GS, Utility, Heavy, 4x4,
                          107" WB, Rover Mk 4
6019-12-192   Car, GS, Utility, Heavy, 4x4,
                          107" WB, Rover Mk 4 LHD

Note that no code was allocated for a GS Cargo Truck at this stage.

From 1957 new codes were allocated as follows:
204030-01-905   Car, Utility, Heavy, GS, 4x4,
                          Rover Mk 4 (107" WB)
204030-51-905   Car, Utility, Heavy, GS, 4x4,
                          Rover Mk 4 (107" WB) LHD
304015-01-901   Truck, ½ ton, Cargo, 4x4,
                          Rover Mk 1 FV18041

From 1962 new codes were again allocated as follows:
1150-0755   Car, Utility, ¼ ton, 4x4,
                       Rover Mk 4
1150-5755   Car, Utility, ¼ ton, 4x4, LHD,
                       Rover Mk 4
1710-0755   Truck, General Service, ¾ ton, 4x4,
                       Rover Mk 4

LAND ROVER CHASSIS CODES FOR 107-INCH AND 109-INCH MODELS, 1954-1958

All Land Rovers in this period had a four-digit identifying prefix in the chassis code, which indicated the model type, the model-year (not calendar-year) of manufacture, the steering position and other factors. The ones relevant to the Mk 4 models are shown below. The four-figure prefix was followed by a four-figure (1954-1955) or five-figure (1956 on) serial number that began at 0001 or 00001 for each separate sequence (although the serial numbers for the 109-inch models followed on from those for the 107-inch types).

Note that the Land Rover model-year (MY) began in September and continued until the end of the following July, leaving August clear for the works' annual holiday and for preparing the assembly lines to take new models. A Land Rover built in the 1956 model-year could therefore have been built at any time between September 1955 and July 1956.

1216	1956 RHD 109in
1217	1957 RHD 109in
1218	1958 RHD 109in
1317	1957 RHD 107in Station Wagon chassis
1318	1958 RHD 107in Station Wagon chassis
2706	1956 RHD 107in pick-up chassis
2736	1956 LHD 107in pick-up chassis
5726	1955 RHD 107in pick-up (export specification)*
8706	1956 RHD 107in Station Wagon chassis

* The export specification sequence was often used for vehicles that deviated in some way from the normal RHD specification but were not necessarily destined for export.

CHAPTER 4:

THE MARK 6 (SERIES II 88-INCH) AND MARK 7 (SERIES II 109-INCH)

This early Mk 6 model carries FVRDE identification, and is seen here as vehicle number 41 in a 1959 comparative trial conducted by the French armed forces. YUE 402 belonged to the Rover Company, and was used as an experimental vehicle for all kinds of conversions. Although the vehicle has FV-pattern headlights, the lights on the front wing have the horizontal civilian arrangement. (Ken Twist)

Land Rover's Series II models were announced in April 1958, a date chosen because it was exactly 10 years after the introduction of the first models. It was at this stage that all the earlier types (Mk 1 to Mk 5 military types) became known as Series I models.

By this stage, the War Department was firmly wedded to further purchases of Land Rovers. Since 1956, it seems to have been policy to standardise as far as possible on Land Rovers in their relevant weight classes and so the switch to Series II models presented no major problems for any of the three services. The new short-wheelbase types became known as Mk 6 models and their long-wheelbase equivalents as Mk 7 models.

The Series IIs were very much a continuation of what had gone before – and their base specification may well have been influenced by discussions between the War Department and Rover top management that took place in 1956. The most obvious difference was that the body had been deliberately styled for the first time, with a more rounded shape that incorporated a distinctive "shoulder" in the panels at waist level. This was partly a way of concealing wider axle tracks, which were introduced to give greater stability, but the new appearance was also a determined attempt to match the anticipated threat from a new rival vehicle – the Austin Gipsy that was also introduced in 1958. A further change was to a more powerful petrol engine, now a new OHV four-cylinder with a swept volume of 2286cc (always described as 2¼ litres). The first few months' production of Series II 88-inch models actually had the old 2-litre engine, but the only examples of these supplied to the War Department were a small batch for the RAF.

The Series II Land Rovers purchased by the War Department were still very much adapted civilian vehicles, without major differences from their standard production equivalents. However, it was during the Series II era that the War Department made progress towards a more deliberate military specification, and so some late deliveries had elements of the full military specification that would become standard on the Series IIA (Mk 8 and long-wheelbase Mk 9) models in the early 1960s. Most of the Series IIs delivered to the War Department were RHD petrol models with full canvas tilts, although the RAF took a number of Mk 6 models with the optional 2-litre diesel engine; the Army also took a further quantity with a 4x2 drivetrain, as pioneered on late Mk 5

(Series I 88-inch) chassis.

The Mk 6 and Mk 7 models were not very numerous in War Department service. One reason was their short production life of just three years (1958-1961), but another was that this period coincided with a round of cutbacks in military spending and so fewer vehicles were ordered. John Mastrangelo has noted that by 1963 the Mk 6 and Mk 7 models were no longer mentioned in some War Office manuals and were simply listed with the later Rover Mk 8 and Mk 9 models as if there were no important differences.

THE MK 6 (88-INCH) MODELS

The Army was by far the largest user of the Rover Mk 6 among the three services, but there were examples for the RAF and Royal Navy too.

Army Mk 6 deliveries

All the Mk 6 Land Rovers for the Army were delivered with a 12-volt positive earth electrical system like that on their civilian equivalents, although a few may have been converted to 24-volt AC negative earth during service to suit radio installations, probably beginning in January 1961. All were fitted with a Warner trailer socket; none at this stage had the later NATO type. They had a single 10-gallon tank (now with a filler in the body side instead of under the seat), and the spare wheel bracket in the back body could be adapted for use as a jerrycan holder. All had a spare wheel carrier on the bonnet, and all were delivered with WD-type split-rim wheels.

The Mk 6 models also came with FV-pattern headlights, a bridge plate on the front wing and a convoy light behind the rear cross-member, although all these features were absent from the 4x2 CL variants for the Army. The convoy light illuminated the rear face of the differential which was normally painted white, and permitted vehicles to follow one another at night without other lighting. A Pyrene fire extinguisher carried in a bracket on the dashboard was a standard feature on all varieties. Running changes on the Rover production lines also affected the detail specification of these vehicles. In October 1960, the red ignition and green oil pressure warning lights swapped places, and the horn button moved from an arm on the steering column to the centre of the steering wheel. Early models had a white turn signal switch on the dash, but from May 1961 approximately, military deliveries came with the new civilian option of a stalk control on the steering column.

As noted above, some of the later vehicles had modifications that anticipated the full military specification seen on Mk 8 deliveries. These changes were probably introduced

from late 1960 or early 1961, but may not all have appeared at the same time. Late models had an FV design of ignition switch, which was also differently located from the early type, and they had FV-pattern side and tail lights with screw-cap lenses to simplify bulb changing in the field. At the front, these lights were now located one above the other in the wings, and not next to each other as on the civilian models; this arrangement gave more room for the "portrait" number-plates favoured by the Army, and for unit markings as well. (Bridge plates were most often attached to the grille when unit markings took up the wing fronts.)

Rear reflectors were relocated below the tail lights, although early models had them in the same position as the Mk 1 to Mk 5 Land Rovers. Late Mk 6 models also had a NATO-pattern rotating tow hitch instead of the earlier WD towing hook, and some may have had towing rings front and rear. A further change was the introduction of an oil cooler on very late models. Some Mk 6 models had a hand throttle on the dashboard, but this was probably only on those that were converted to a 24-volt electrical system, where the engine had to be run with the vehicle stationary in order to keep the batteries charged when radios were in use.

There were several in-service modifications, too. A mortar-carrier conversion was authorised from September 1960, the 24-volt conversion from approximately January 1961, and a waterproofed ignition switch could be added from April 1964 (John Mastrangelo linked this to contract KL/H/0934). A front-mounted winch became available from July 1963 (and on FFR models from August 1964), an eight-blade fan to the latest military standard arrived in November 1964, and a modified fan cowl shroud from March 1965. Some vehicles gained protective screening "for internal security duties" (again according to John Mastrangelo) from March 1967, and others appear to have been fitted with mine protection plates from August 1970. By this stage, however, many Mk 6 Land Rovers had already been withdrawn from service and those remaining did not have many years to go.

The 4x2 models

Contract 6/Veh/27756 called for a further 275 4x2 models (17 CL 48 to 20 CL 22), making the Army's total up to 950 when the Mk 5 models are added into the equation. These Mk 6 models were nevertheless the last of their kind, and a change of policy meant that there would be no more War Department orders for two-wheel-drive Land Rovers. Their successors in the "Utility, 4x2" rôles would be estate models of passenger cars – initially the Ford Escort and later the Hillman Husky.

All these vehicles were delivered as Soft Top types, and were essentially the same as other Mk 6 Land Rovers except that they were modified to eliminate drive to the front axle in the same way as the Mk 5 types had been (see Chapter 2). They had civilian-pattern headlights, no bridge plate on the front wing, no jerrycan holder in the back body, and no convoy light. Nevertheless, they did have a WD-pattern towing hook, a Warner towing socket, military-pattern rear reflectors, a Pyrene fire extinguisher in its bracket on the front bulkhead, and of course a Ministry of Supply identity plate on the bulkhead as well.

Thirty of these vehicles were transferred to the Ministry of Public Buildings and Works (MPBW) in 1963 and were re-registered with civilian numbers in the reversed FUV series. This date reflects the formation of the MPBW which took over the management of the Defence Estate from the War Office; the vehicles which had been allocated to the various branches of the Defence Land Agent were transferred to civil registrations under MPBW. The 30 vehicles in this transfer were:

17 CL 69	17 CL 94	18 CL 08	19 CL 06	19 CL 88
17 CL 74	17 CL 95	18 CL 32	19 CL 14	19 CL 95
17 CL 77	17 CL 97	18 CL 49	19 CL 27	19 CL 99
17 CL 86	17 CL 98	18 CL 52	19 CL 39	20 CL 01
17 CL 87	18 CL 00	18 CL 82	19 CL 73	20 CL 12
17 CL 88	18 CL 06	19 CL 03	19 CL 85	20 CL 14

Multi-fuel experiments

By 1957, NATO had recognised that the need for three different types of fuel at the battlefront – diesel, petrol and aviation kerosene – was an unwelcome complication. So the idea arose that motor transport should be able to use what-ever fuel happened to be available. What NATO wanted was a multi-fuel engine.

The idea of multi-fuel vehicle engines never did become a formal requirement. However, the Land Rover engineers got on with preparing a multi-fuel Land Rover engine right away. Unfortunately, experiments with single-cylinder test engines using the bore and stroke dimensions of the Land Rover 2-litre diesel produced unimpressive projections about power output.

So by 1959 the larger bore of the forthcoming 2.25-litre diesel was in the programme, and two multi-fuel 88-inch Land Rovers were built. They were festooned with extra fuel tanks so that they could be demonstrated switching from one type of fuel to another. They worked – although design of their fuel distribution pumps was problematical. An FVRDE Symposium on Multi-Fuel Engines held in November also thought their engines lacked power.

In due course Land Rover also lengthened the engine's

14 AA 84 was a Mk 6 short-wheelbase model that served with the RAF. This picture shows the window soft-top configuration (not available on civilian models for the UK) and the striking combination of RAF Blue with a yellow bonnet – the latter for better visibility on airfields. (Land Rover)

The multi-fuel experiments were carried out in 1959. This is an early prototype, showing the massive fuel distribution pump required to cope with three different fuels. (BMIHT)

The double bumpers visible on this vehicle mean that it could be either a very late Mk 6 or a Mk 8: it is impossible to tell from the photograph. The RAF equipped a number of both types as helicopter servicing platforms. This one was pictured on duty in Singapore with the ANZUK Force; the helicopter is a Westland Whirlwind. (MoD PR)

stroke to give a 2.5-litre capacity. They had an engine ready by 1961 and by the end of 1963 had made it develop 67bhp – enough for WD thinking. Even so, the WD said they would like to look at a turbocharged derivative and set a target output of 85bhp! This appears never to have been achieved before interest in multi-fuel engines died in early 1964, and the Land Rover project came to an end.

RAF Mk 6 deliveries

The RAF took more than 1100 Rover Mk 6 models. Although the majority were delivered in the service's Blue-Grey livery, there were also examples in Bronze Green as early as 1959. The first contract (6/Veh/27387) was met by 88-inch models with the "spread-bore" 2-litre engine associated with the Mk 3 and Mk 5 models – an expedient on the assembly lines at Rover between April and about September 1958 while production of the new 2.25-litre engine built up. Diesels were also ordered, and the first examples were delivered in May 1960; these were presumably chosen for duties where a spark-ignition engine might present an unacceptable hazard. Some vehicles were fitted out for the Airfield Lighting rôle, and there was also a small number of Cuthbertson tracked conversions.

Cuthbertson conversions

In May 1962, six of the Mk 6 models delivered under contract KL/H/01270 were sent to James A Cuthbertson Ltd of Biggar in Scotland to be fitted with tracks. The six vehicles

were 76 AA 42, 76 AA 62, 76 AA 65, 76 AA 70, 76 AA 72 and 76 AA 75. They returned from conversion in September 1962 and were issued in November to the Explosive Ordnance Disposal teams working at the bombing ranges of Holbeach, Orford Ness and other places.

The Cuthbertson tracked conversion had been developed in the late 1950s in order to create a Land Rover with extremely low ground pressure that enabled it to cross very marshy ground. The conversion was available on the civilian market, but was not common. It involved fitting a sub-frame with

Just six Mk 6 models were fitted with Cuthbertson tracks for use by the RAF's ordnance disposal teams. 76 AA 75 was already several years old when lent back to Land Rover for a display. The main bodywork was in RAF Blue, and the wings were in red, as seen on the picture of 76 AA 42, which was pictured at a military display. (BMIHT)

76 AA 42 was numerically the first of the Cuthbertson tracked conversions based on a Mk 6 and destined for the RAF. The combination of the RAF Blue-Grey paint with the red wings identifying an EOD vehicle made for a particularly striking appearance. (Paul Hancox)

four sets of bogies – one set under each wheel station of the Land Rover above. The road wheels were removed from the Land Rover and a toothed driving wheel was bolted in place of each one. This drove rubber tracks that ran over the driving sprocket and the twin road wheels of the bogie. Power-assisted steering was needed to overcome the weight of the bogies, and a radiator overflow tank was added to deal with the effects of slow running.

The vehicles had enormous ground clearance, which was perhaps another important factor in their purchase. The design also allowed the vehicles to be refitted with ordinary road wheels if required, but this seems never to have been done in RAF use. An interesting feature was that the RAF conversions had the later military front lighting configuration (with FV headlights and vertically stacked sidelamps and turn signals) but with civilian-pattern lenses for the sidelamps and turn signals.

As far as can be understood from remaining records, the Cuthbertson conversions were issued to RAF Bomb Disposal units in pairs. It is known that 76 AA 42 and 76 AA 72 were issued to RAF Bicester and 76 AA 62 and 76 AA75 went to RAF Leconfield. The other two either went to another Bomb Disposal Flight which was later disbanded or were retained as spares – records do not detail their use. In 1967 the unit at Bicester became 71 Maintenance Unit Explosive Ordnance Disposal Flight (71 MU EOD Flight) and the one at Leconfield became 60 Maintenance Unit Explosive Ordnance Disposal Flight (60 MU EOD Flight).

The longest post war EOD clearance operation, and also the biggest, took place in the disused slate quarries at RAF Llanberis in North Wales. RAF Llanberis opened as a storage depot in 1941 under the control of 31 Maintenance Unit and comprised a 70-acre site of old quarries and interlinking tunnels. In 1942 a quarry collapsed and buried over 8000 tons of bombs, not all of which could be removed. In 1969 the decision was made to clear the site of explosives and 71 MU EOD Flight were tasked with the job. The unit slowly cleared the quarry pits surrounding the disused depot, uncovering incendiary bombs, High Explosive bomb detonators and a large number of bomb fuses. Many of the pits were difficult to access, so 38 Engineer Regiment, Royal Engineers was called in to lay roads to them. It took 71 MU until 1975 to clear the last of the explosives from the area.

60 MU EOD Flight was meanwhile responsible for clearing bombing ranges on the east coast of spent ammunition and undoubtedly had much reason to be grateful for the low ground pressure of the Cuthbertson.

By 1975 the Series II Cuthbertsons were at the end of their life, and they were replaced by four Lightweights converted to use the Cuthbertson track system (see Chapter 10).

Royal Navy Mk 6 deliveries

The Royal Navy took 56 Rover Mk 6 models in standard pick-up form, plus one as a domestic fire tender for the barracks in Plymouth. The pick-ups were probably all destined to be kept aboard the Navy's capital ships, for use on official duties ashore. Of those 56 vehicles, 14 were delivered with diesel engines, beginning in autumn 1960. This is generally interpreted as recognition that spark-free diesel engines presented fewer fire hazards on board ship than a spark-ignition petrol engine.

THE MK 7 (109-INCH) MODELS

The long-wheelbase models had still not caught the military imagination by the time of the Mk 7 models, although the War Department was actively looking at new ways of using them while the Mk 7s were in production. Nevertheless, examples were delivered to all three branches of the armed forces.

Army Mk 7 deliveries

The Army ordered relatively few Mk 7s in General Service pick-up form with full-length canvas tilts, but there were some purchases of Station Wagons and of Ambulances, the latter inaugurating a type which was ordered regularly right through until the early 1970s. There was a single fire tender, too.

Notable was the start of work on the Air-Portable General Purpose (APGP) "floating" models, which began right at the end of the Series II era but was realised more fully in the Rover Mk 9 (Series IIA) era covered in Chapter 5. It is also likely, although not proven, that some Rover Mk 7 GS models were among the earliest long-wheelbase Land Rovers converted to desert patrol vehicles by the SAS. Their design ultimately led to the legendary Pink Panthers of the later 1960s.

Ambulances

Contract KL/H/0390 was placed in 1959 and called for 10 two-stretcher ambulances (05 DE 35 to 05 DE 44) based on the Rover Mk 7 chassis. These were the first of a new breed of ambulance, specially designed to meet military requirements and with bodies designed and built by Mickleover Transport of Park Royal in London. They were delivered in 1960. Like the earlier Mountain Rescue ambulances for the RAF based on Mk 4 107-inch vehicles, they used Station Wagon chassis. They were, however, the only examples of the new ambulance to do so, and later orders were based on standard military-specification long-wheelbase chassis.

These ambulances were initially configured as a two-stretcher design but were later (possibly in 1964) converted

05 DE 37 was an early example of the new ambulance on the long-wheelbase Mk 7 chassis. The first bodies were built by Mickleover, but the design was later passed over to Marshalls of Cambridge. The angled lower rear body was so designed to prevent the long rear overhang grounding on aircraft or landing-ship loading ramps. Here it is as it was shown at the British Military Vehicles display at FVRDE Chertsey in September 1962. (RES)

to take four stretchers. Their bodywork had been carefully designed with a low roof height that not only lowered their centre of gravity but also made it possible to load them into RAF transport aircraft. The rear overhang – extended beyond the rearmost chassis cross-member to give enough room for the stretchers – had an angled cutaway underside to ensure that the body would not foul the ground when the vehicle was using the steep ramps associated with both transport aircraft and landing craft.

Station Wagons

Some Station Wagons (25 CL 50 to 25 CL 99) were bought with an FFW specification, under contract 6/Veh/28020 dated 11 November 1958. However, others were bought with a specification closer to the civilian 10-seater standard. These were designated "Car, Utility, Heavy, GS, Land Rover Mk 7 109" WB" and had Asset Code 204030-01-908.

WOMBAT portees

At least three Mk 7 vehicles were used for WOMBAT trials at Fort Halstead and were later transferred to the SP registra-

tion series (see Chapter 13). 18 DE 75 and 18 DE 82 became 00 SP 28 and 00 SP 29 respectively, and a third specially-purchased vehicle joined them. This was 15 BT 18, later 00 SP 27. WOMBAT would eventually replace MOBAT, and the

Several Mk 7 models were converted as portees for the WOMBAT anti-tank gun. 18 DE 93, from the 1960-1961 deliveries, shows the gun in its travelling position. (RES)

The WOMBAT weapon could be removed from the vehicle for firing, or could be fired from within the vehicle. These pictures both show 18 DE 94. (Land Rover)

25 CL 74 was one of 50 Mk 7 Station Wagons ordered with an FFW specification. The standard rear-mounted fuel tank was replaced by twin underseat tanks to meet military requirements. This preserved vehicle has been fitted with freewheeling front hubs that would not have been fitted in service.

mounted on the cab roof.

Fire-fighting equipment included a ladder rack over an open rear body; in service, some examples were later given a canopy over the ladder frame. There were two large dry-powder "kettles", each with a nitrogen cylinder to pressurise it and force the powder through canvas hoses that were fitted with special nozzles or "branches". The back body also contained racking for the hoses, air cylinders to power cutting tools, a crash axe, and bolt croppers.

There were 75 of these vehicles on Rover Mk 7 chassis, spread between two contracts. A further 103 examples were built on Rover Mk 9 chassis between 1961 and 1970 (see Chapter 5).

Royal Navy Mk 7 deliveries
The Royal Navy took 156 Rover Mk 7 models, of which 20 were Station Wagons. These were probably used as crew buses for the Navy's diving teams. The remainder were pick-ups destined for use as cargo vehicles.

name derived from its description as a Weapon Of AluminiuM – Battalion Anti-Tank; it was an infantry anti-tank weapon which had its own wheels but could not be towed. The WOMBAT portee Land Rover would become more common during the Rover Mk 9 era (see Chapter 5).

RAF Mk 7 deliveries
The RAF took small numbers of Rover Mk 7s, and these included some Station Wagons (of which some had left-hand drive), a single GS pick-up and four crash-rescue ambulances. However, the majority were a new type known as the Airfield Crash Rescue Tender (ACRT).

ACRT
The ACRT was the RAF's first purpose-designed vehicle of its type. Development work was carried out by FVRDE, to meet Air Ministry Operational Requirement 6231, and a first prototype was built on Rover Mk 7 chassis in late 1960. The contractor was Foamite, of Feltham in Middlesex, and testing of that prototype led to only detail changes on the production vehicles.

The basic vehicle was a 109-inch Land Rover with truck cab, and all of them were fitted with what the RAF called a brush guard – a large steel construction mounted on the front bumper which was designed to protect the vehicle if it had to burst through airfield "crash gates" on its way to an emergency. There were distinctive lockers in the body sides, headlight shades (to prevent the lights dazzling aircraft), and a double-skin "tropical" roof for the cab because these vehicles were intended to serve at RAF stations all round the world. In this roof was a round hatch, through which a crew member could operate the large Harley searchlight, also

LAND ROVER CHASSIS CODES
All Land Rovers in this period had a four-digit identifying prefix in the chassis code, which indicated the model type, the model-year (not calendar-year) of manufacture, the steering position and other factors. The ones relevant to the Mk 6 and Mk 7 models are shown below. The four-figure prefix was followed by a five-figure serial number that began at 00001 for each separate sequence.

Note that the Land Rover model-year began in September and continued until the end of the following July, leaving August clear for the works' annual holiday and for preparing the assembly lines to take new models. A Land Rover built in the 1960 model-year could therefore have been built at any time between September 1959 and July 1960.

1410	1960 RHD 88in
1411	1961 RHD 88in
1418	1959 RHD 88in (with 2-litre engine)
1419	1959 RHD 88in
1441	1961 LHD 88in
1460	1960 RHD 88in diesel
1461	1961 RHD 88in diesel
1510	1960 RHD 109in
1511	1961 RHD 109in
1519	1959 RHD 109in
1610	1960 RHD 109in Station Wagon
1611	1961 RHD 109in Station Wagon
1619	1959 RHD 109in Station Wagon
1649	1959 LHD 109in Station Wagon

SERIES II ROVER MK 6 AND MK 7

The earliest Mk 6 and Mk 7 contracts were numbered in the old 6/Veh series for "B" vehicles. However, the file code for military vehicle contracts changed in 1959, and the later contracts had a KL/H prefix.

ARMY
(a) Mk 6 (88inch)

Serials	Contract	Chassis Nos	Total	Remarks
17 CL 48 to 20 CL 22	6/Veh/27756	1419-01445 to 1419-02210	275	Contract dated 10 September 1958; RHD Cargo CL 4x2.
03 DL 35 to 07 DL 94	KL/H/0934	1411-00963 to 1411-02172	460	Contract dated 11 May 1961; RHD GS.
08 DL 93 to 10 DL 12	KL/H/0934	1411-02173 to 144102720	120	Contract dated 29 September 1960. 09 DL 98 and 10 DL 07 were RHD Station Wagons.
10 DL 23	KL/H/01077	1411-02523	1	Contract dated 2 December 1960. RHD Station Wagon.
10 DL 24 to 10 DL 27	KL/H/01077	1441-03027 to 1441-03030	4	Contract dated 2 December 1960. LHD Station Wagon.
			Total 860	

ARMY SERIAL NUMBERS

The serial numbers allocated by the Army gave a clue to the date of the vehicle, although those issued by the RAF and Royal Navy did not. In this period, serial letters indicated the financial year in which the vehicle was purchased (which is not necessarily the same as the calendar year in which it was delivered). Those relevant to the Mk 6 and Mk 7 models are shown below.

As before, serial sequences began at 0001 (e.g. 00 BP 01) and ran to 9999 (e.g. 99 BP 99). There was not necessarily any correlation between chassis number order and military serial number within batches.

CL	1958-1959
DE	1959-1960
DL	1960-1961

RAF
(a) Mk 6 (88inch)

Serials	Contract	Chassis Nos	Total	Remarks
65 AA 95 to 66 AA 04	6/Veh/27387	1428-00540 to 1428-00194	10	RHD Cargo; 2-litre engine.
66 AA 07 to 66 AA 26	KL/H/012	1419-02792 to 1419-02855	20	RHD Airfield Lighting.
66 AA 27 to 66 AA 36	KL/H/0252	1410-00049 to 1410-00058	10	RHD Airfield Lighting.
66 AA 37 to 66 AA 47	KL/H/0252	1410-00392 to 1410-00402	11	RHD GS.
71 AA 49 to 71 AA 86	KL/H/0330	1460-00736 to 1460-01131	38	RHD GS Diesel.
66 AA 49 to 70 AA 06	KL/H/0385	1410-00590 to 1410-01648	358	RHD GS.
70 AA 07 to 70 AA 48	KL/H/0385	1440-02487 to 144002572	42	LHD GS.
28 AA 22 to 28 AA 31	KL/H/0578	1410-03072 to 1410-03063	10	RHD Airfield Lighting.
30 AA 71 to 30 AA 94	KL/H/01120	1461-01069 to 1461-01092	24	RHD GS Diesel.
37 AA 89 to 37 AA 99	KL/H/0578	1410-03140 to 1410-03150	11	RHD Airfield Lighting.
70 AA 49 to 70 AA 96	KL/H/0628	1440-05151 to 1440-05525	48	RHD Cargo.
71 AA 87 to 74 AA 21	KL/H/0628	1410-03670 to 1410-04249	235	RHD Cargo.
14 AA 82 to 15 AA 03	KL/H/0628	1410-04270 to 141004330	22	RHD Cargo.
74 AA 22 to 76 AA 80	KL/H/01276	1411-03446 to 1411-04446	259	RHD Cargo.
76 AA 81 to 77 AA 20	KL/H/01276	1441-05316 to 1441-05602	40	LHD Cargo.
			Total 1138	

ROYAL NAVY (a) Mk 6 (88inch)

No Royal Navy purchase records have been found. The list below is therefore derived from the Land Rover despatch records held by the Heritage Motor Centre at Gaydon, which can be considered accurate. All vehicles were painted in Royal Blue unless otherwise noted.

Serials	Contract	Chassis Nos	Total	Remarks
n/a	n/a	1418-00592	1	RHD fire tender for RN Barracks, Plymouth, delivered December 1958; red.
n/a	n/a	1419-01230 to 1419-01233 and 1419-01234 to 1419-01235	6	Delivered January and February 1959.
n/a	n/a	1410-01855 to 1410-01860, 1410-01971 to 1410-01972 and 1410-01980-01983	12	Delivered February 1960.
n/a	n/a	1410-03134 to 1410-03139	6	Delivered July 1960.
n/a	n/a	1460-01995 to 1460-02002	8	Delivered September-October 1960; diesel engines.
n/a	n/a	1411-01256 to 1411-01261 and 1411-01273 to 1411-01278	12	Delivered January 1961.
n/a	n/a	1411-03245 to 1411-03250	6	Delivered June 1961.
n/a	n/a	1461-01133 to 1461-01138	6	Delivered June 1961; diesel engines.
			Total 57	

ARMY (b) Mk 7 (109-inch)

Serials	Contract	Chassis Nos	Total	Remarks
25 CL 50 to 25 CL 99	6/Veh/28020	1619-00005 to 1619-00068	50	Contract dated 12 November 1958. RHD FFW Station Wagon.
35 CL 21 to 35 CL 40	KL/H/0100	1519-00907 to 1519-00948	20	Contract dated 25 February 1959. GS 4x4 Cargo with full-length tilt.
01 DE 31	KL/H/0180	1649-00687	1	Contract dated 15 April 1959. LHD Station Wagon, probably for a Military Attaché.
01 DE 32	KL/H/0221	1619-00094	1	Contract dated 8 May 1959. RHD Station Wagon, probably for a Military Attaché.
03 DE 29 to 03 DE 30	KL/H/0375	1510-00439 to 1510-00430	2	Contract dated 27 October 1959. RHD GS; converted to WOMBAT portee.
05 DE 35 to 05 DE 44	KL/H/0390	1610-00037 to 1610-00047 (range)	10	Contract dated 21 August 1959. Ambulance 2/4 stretcher; Station Wagon chassis; NB 11 numbers in chassis range!
18 DE 74 to 19 DE 01	KL/H/0638	1510-01061 to 1510-01308 (range)	28	Contract dated 31 October 1960. RHD GS, FV18041. 18 DE 74 was 1510-01302; 19 DE 01 was 1510-01061.
11 DL 63 to 11 DL 68	KL/H/01130	1511-00181 to 1511-00548	6	Contract dated 20 January 1961. RHD GS.
			Total 118	

ASSET CODES

1055-0758	Ambulance, 4 stretcher, 4x4, Rover 7	
1150-0757	Car, Utility, ¼ ton, 4x4, Rover 6	
1150-0758	Car, Utility, ¼ ton, 4x4, Rover 7 [109" WB]	
1150-5757	Car, Utility, ¼ ton, 4x4, LHD, Rover 6	
1150-5758	Car, Utility, ¼ ton, 4x4, LHD, Rover 7 [109" WB]	
1610-0757	Truck, Firefighting, ¼ ton, 4x4, Rover 6	
1618-2757	Truck, Utility, ¼ ton, 4x4, 24v, Helicopter Starting, Rover 6	
1620-0757	Truck, General Service, ¼ ton, 4x4, Rover 6	
1620-1757	Truck, General Service, ¼ ton, 4x4, Rover 6	
1620-2757	Truck, Utility, ¼ ton, 4x4, 24v, Helicopter Starting, Rover 6	
1620-5757	Truck, General Service, ¼ ton, 4x4, LHD, Rover 6	
1620-6757	Truck, General Service, ¼ ton, 4x4, LHD, Anti-spark, Rover 6 Diesel Engine	
1710-0758	Truck, General Service, ¾ ton, 4x4, Rover 7	
1710-1758	Truck, General Service, ¾ ton, 4x4, 750/900 tyres, Rover 7	

RAF (b) Mk 7 (109-inch)

Serials	Contract	Chassis Nos	Total	Remarks
70 AA 97	KM/G/0140	1510-01337	1	RHD ACRT Prototype; Foamite bodywork.
39 AA 00 to 39 AA 33	KM/G/0140	1511-00213 to 1511-00246	34	RHD ACRT.
39 AA 34 to 39 AA 73	KM/G/0262	1511-01010 to 1511-01083	40	RHD ACRT.
40 AA 00	n/a	1540-00397	1	GS RHD.
77 AA 21	KL/H/0803	1641-01084	1	LHD Station Wagon; possibly for Oman.
77 AA 22 to 77 AA 26	n/a	1611-00088 to 1611-00092	5	RHD Station Wagon; possibly for Oman.
30 AA 95 to 30 AA 98	KL/J/0391	1611-00131 to 1611-00134	4	RHD Crash Rescue Ambulance; Light Stone.
15 AA 04 to 15 AA 05	n/a	1641-00051 to 1641-00052	2	LHD Station Wagon.
			Total 88	

ROYAL NAVY (b) Mk 7 (109-inch)

No Royal Navy purchase records have been found. The list below is therefore derived from the Land Rover despatch records held by the Heritage Motor Centre at Gaydon, which can be considered accurate. All vehicles were painted in Royal Blue (occasionally recorded as BSC 106).

Serials	Contract	Chassis Nos	Total	Remarks
n/a	n/a	1519-00409 to 1519-00470	62	Delivered January-February 1959.
n/a	n/a	1619-00020 and 1619-0023 to 1619-0027	6	Delivered May 1959; Station Wagons.
96 RN 82 to 96 RN 87 and others	KL/H/043 covered six vehicles	1519-00856 to 1519-00867	12	Delivered July 1959.
n/a	n/a	1610-0009 to 1610-00012 and 1610-00020 to 1610-00023	8	Delivered December 1959.
n/a	n/a	1510-00732 to 1510-00734	3	Delivered February 1960.
n/a	n/a	1510-01137 to 1510-01139, 1510-01160 to 1510-01162, 1510-01202 to 1510-01207 and 1510-01243 to 1510-01248	18	Delivered July-September 1960.
n/a	n/a	1610-00071 to 1610-00076	6	Delivered August 1960; Station Wagons.
n/a	n/a	1511-00458 to 1511-00466 and 1511-00473 to 1511-00475	12	Delivered January 1961.
n/a	n/a	1611-00025 to 1611-00029	5	Delivered January 1961; Station Wagons.
n/a	n/a	1511-01110 to 1511-01113, 1511-01117 to 1511-01125 and 1511-01127 to 1511-01134	21	Delivered June-July 1961.
n/a	n/a	1611-00093 to 1611-00095	3	Delivered July 1961; Station Wagons.
			Total 156	

Note: *Known serials include 69 RN 04 (pick-up), 70 RN 02, 71 RN 85, 76 RN 78 and 76 RN 79 (all Station Wagons).*

CHAPTER 5:

THE MARK 8 (SERIES IIA 88-INCH) AND MARK 9 (SERIES IIA 109-INCH)

The long-wheelbase models came into their own in the early 1960s, as the Mk 9 models. 49 DM 35 was pictured towing a 25-pounder field gun on the test course at Long Valley and wears the markings of 25 Field Regiment of 51 Gurkha Brigade. (Ken Twist)

54 EN 62 shows the characteristic profile of the Rover Mk 9. Although aerial tuners are mounted on the wings, this one does not have the special grille associated with the FFR models. It is serving with Headquarters 24 (Airportable) Brigade in March 1970 during an exercise on Westward Ho beach. (RES)

The Duncan Sandys Defence Review of 1957 had a significant effect on the British Army and also, in its way, on the rôle of the Land Rover. The British Army was to be reduced in size and reorganised to reflect the ending of National Service and the change to a voluntary army, and to "keep the Army abreast of changing circumstances, policies, weapons and techniques of war". By 1962 the Army had been re-structured to undertake Britain's remaining overseas responsibilities on the basis of a Strategic Reserve principally based in the UK.

This Strategic Reserve was designed to be transported rapidly by air or by sea to any trouble spot to support local garrisons, which were being reduced. Transport would rely on the ageing Beverley aircraft as around 50 new Armstrong Whitworth AW660 Argosies entered service by 1964. The capacity of the Argosy was limited and hence the Beverley would remain in service for some years. In terms of sea transport, by 1959 HMS Bulwark had been converted from an aircraft carrier to a commando carrier (capable of carrying a Commando Group) and HMS Albion followed in 1962. Orders for the Assault Landing Ships HMS Fearless and HMS Intrepid were commissioned in 1965 and 1967 respectively and six new logistic vessels were launched between 1963 and 1967.

These methods of transport put pressure on infantry battalions to use lighter vehicles and the Land Rover 109 was adopted to replace the Austin K9 1 ton GS Cargo vehicle. Radios were becoming smaller and the Larkspur range had begun to enter service in the mid-1950s. Initially the Larkspur equipment was only issued to the Royal Armoured Corps and the Royal Artillery. By 1962 there was a plan named "Larkspur" to issue it on an all-arms basis. This meant it was now possible to mount the radios needed to command an infantry company or battalion in a Land Rover 88 or Land Rover 109 rather than one of the Austin K9s. (Note that battalions in Germany had used the Humber 1 ton CT vehicles for many years.) The only heavy vehicles that a Strategic Reserve infantry battalion would have were up to 10 3 ton Bedford RL cargo vehicles to carry the unit's heavier equipment such as tents, ablutions and cooking facilities.

Thus the first half of the 1960s saw a huge influx of Land Rovers into the British services, with a particular focus on the 109-inch models, which were rated as ¾-ton types. A number of military-specific modifications to the base commercial

"Pusher bumpers" were introduced on the last of the Mk 6 and Mk 7 models, and became standard on the Mk 8 and Mk 9. The idea was that one vehicle could push-start another – even at an angle – without causing bodywork damage. (BMIHT)

vehicles had already begun to arrive with the last of the Mk 6 and Mk 7 models in early 1961, such as "pusher" bumpers, drop-shackle springs, twin fuel tanks and a 24-volt FFR electrical system for some vehicles. Electrical system apart, these all became part of the standard British specification for the Mk 8 and Mk 9 models which began to arrive in late 1961.

The new Mk 8 and Mk 9 identifications were often expressed simply as Rover 8 and Rover 9. They did not relate to these military specification changes, but rather to a change from Series II to Series IIA models of the basic vehicle. On the civilian models, the change mainly reflected a new chassis numbering system that now incorporated a suffix letter (see the panel on p83). There was also a new diesel engine but other changes were mainly minor and cosmetic. The diesel engine did have some attraction for the RAF but the Army continued to purchase both the 88-inch and 109-inch with the 2¼-litre petrol engine.

ARMY ROVER 8 AND 9 DELIVERIES

By the time of the 1962 British Military Vehicles show sponsored by FVRDE and SMMT, Land Rover was able to display 88-inch Rover 8 and 109-inch Rover 9 vehicles in both General Service and FFR form. These vehicles subsequently formed the backbone of most "light rôle" units in the Strategic Reserve as well as support vehicles for the units of the armoured battlegroups in BAOR. They served in the

overseas garrisons and with the brigades deployed to those theatres. Rover 8s and Rover 9s were purchased in large numbers in both RHD and LHD form until the introduction of the Rover 10 and Rover 11 in 1967.

The very first Series IIA vehicles were supplied with commercial differentials and half-shafts although these were uprated from March 1964. The plan was that deliveries after this date would become Rover Mk 8/1 and Rover Mk 9/1, and earlier models without the upgrade would be Rover Mk 8/2 and Mk 9/2. However, for unknown reasons the early batches of IIA 88 were designated "Truck, General Service, (FFR) ¼ ton, 4x4, Rover 8/2" but the 109s were all "Truck,

This picture taken in March 1968 shows Mk 6 FFR Land Rovers of the Duke of Wellington's Regiment bearing UN markings in Cyprus. (Land Rover)

A special grille became standard on FFR models, giving protection to the additional electrical equipment mounted at the front of the vehicle. The standard oil cooler can also be seen through the grille bars on 30 DM 79. (BMIHT)

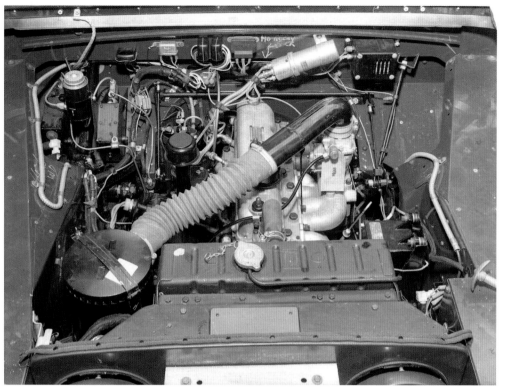

Rover Mk 8 10 ER 98 shows a camouflage scheme typical of the mid-1960s. The additional water cans and headlamp covers were unit modifications. The parent unit is probably 1st Battalion The Prince of Wales's Own Regiment of Yorkshire, part of 19 Brigade. (Land Rover)

This was the under-bonnet layout of an FFR model, with the screened coil and its filter (the ventilated box on the right) visible on the bulkhead, plus additional cabling. The radiator cap on military models was attached by a chain – not a feature of civilian Land Rovers. (BMIHT)

General Service, (FFR), ¾ ton, 4x4, Rover 9/1". The first contracts were placed in April 1961 and resulted in batches of Mk 8/2 as follows: 00 DM 06 to 02 DM 05 (FFR), 13 DM 83 to 17 DM 82 (FFR), and 20 DM 28 to 29 DM 27 (GS). The Mk 9/1 batches were 02 DM 06 to 03 DM 35 (GS), 18 DM 01 to 20 DM 27 (GS) and 30 DM 79 to 32 DM 31 (FFR).

By early 1962 three new contracts (WV32, WV33 and WV34) were placed for the revised version of the 88-inch with the strengthened half-shafts and differentials as well as

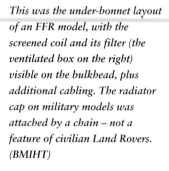

In complete contrast is this EP-series 88, painted in Light Stone. The workshops attached to its parent unit clearly had a different idea of how to attach jerrycans to the front. (Land Rover)

Somewhat dwarfed by the Scammell recovery tractor next to it, this 88 FFR shows the special FFR grille and the side-mounted aerials. The bumpers remained unpainted on vehicles retained in the UK; this one also carries the markings of the Royal School of Artillery and fleet number '28' on the grille. (GF)

Some Mk 8 short-wheelbase models were again employed as line-layers. One is seen here at an exhibition, carrying a board showing that it belonged to the Line Troop of 57 Signal Squadron (V). The rear views of two others are shown. (Above and below – GF. Right – Land Rover)

Pictured in August 1974, 06 EM 49 was by then attached to 12 Driver Training Regiment, RCT at Aldershot. (MoD PR)

more 109-inch models. These were designated Rover 8 and 9 (rather than 8/1 and 9/1) and purchases continued until the introduction of the Rover 10 and 11 in 1967. However, most of the Station Wagons (designated 'Car, Utility, ¾ ton, 4x4') purchased were supplied with commercial differentials and half-shafts as Rover 9/2, the exception being 20 EL 17 which was a 'Rover 9' and was an army prototype for FVRDE that was struck off to 00 SP 26. The "Car, Utility, ¾ ton, 4x4, Rover 9/2" was purchased in small quantities and mainly in LHD form to meet the needs of Military Attachés, some based in Warsaw Pact countries, and BRIXMIS. One might guess that the reason for this was that Military Attachés were involved in similar activities to BRIXMIS! It was not until 1964 that a batch of this type was purchased for more

14 ET 25 was a Mk 9 Station Wagon, in this case used by an EOD unit. The red front wings are clear in this photograph. The long pole on the roof was part of an experimental ordnance handling device that was on trial at the time. (TMB)

Rover Mk 8 FFR 89 EN 18 was pictured here in restored condition, showing the correct disposition of pioneer tools on the tailgate. The yellow frame around the rear number-plate is the edge of the civilian number-plate that has been covered over for display purposes. (JT)

There was special signage on the seat box of FFR models. (JT)

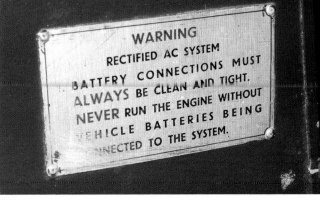

WARNING
RECTIFIED AC SYSTEM
BATTERY CONNECTIONS MUST
ALWAYS BE CLEAN AND TIGHT.
NEVER RUN THE ENGINE WITHOUT
VEHICLE BATTERIES BEING
CONNECTED TO THE SYSTEM.

This version of the Mk 9 entered service in 1965 and was configured to carry Vigilant anti-tank missiles. The vehicle shown was on trial at FVRDE for a time. (TMB)

general issue within the Army.

From about mid-1964 small numbers of these Land Rovers painted in Light Stone were ordered for the Army. The first such was 11 EM 11, delivered to Vehicle Depot Irvine, Scotland in late 1964; the vehicles saw service in the Middle East (Cyprus, Malta, Aden) and Far East (Singapore, Malaya, Hong Kong). They were often overpainted with black or green irregular patches to achieve a camouflage scheme and many were subsequently given mine protection (in the form of roll-over bars and additional blast protection).

The introduction of the Series IIA represented a significant change in the use of the Land Rover in the British Army, and new rôles for the vehicle began to proliferate. Some of the major special rôles are discussed below.

The APGP

The new emphasis on combined operations led inevitably to the idea that Army vehicles should meet air transport requirements and should be capable of crossing stretches of water under their own power. FVRDE seems to have suggested collaborating with Rover to develop a long-wheelbase Land Rover that could be stacked two-high inside aircraft for transportation, and could also float. The prospect of orders for several thousand vehicles no doubt persuaded the company to agree. Had they not done so, FVRDE would have sought collaboration elsewhere, and the end result would have been severe damage to Land Rover military sales.

The concept was developed as the Air Portable General Purpose (APGP) Land Rover, and later took on the code of FV18051. At Rover, it was also known as the Scheme A Amphibian; a Scheme B model was designed but was built only in mock-up form. A first prototype of the APGP was ready by August 1961 – some nine months before the formal

The APGP was an experimental derivative of the Rover Mk 9 that progressed as far as troop trials but was not ordered in quantity. In order to cross rivers, it had a specially waterproofed body and carried floatation bags that were inflated from the exhaust. The first design of bags is seen here on 641 ELM, an FVRDE test vehicle, as it emerges from the water tank. The second design, known as "mattress" bags, is seen on test at an inland lake. The final design, using "cigar" bags, is seen on dry land. (Above, above right and right – TMB)

01 ER 01 certainly suggests a royal connection, but the number was not original to this Mk 8 that was converted to a review vehicle. (John Craddock)

War Office Statement of Requirement was issued in June 1962. That called for a vehicle which could perform all the rôles of the existing long-wheelbase military Land Rover, including that of emergency stretcher-carrier. Ideally, it would be powered by a multi-fuel engine, and FVRDE even hoped that the crew and cargo could be protected against nuclear thermal flash!

The basic design, which came from FVRDE, involved attaching rubber flotation bags to the vehicle and inflating them from the exhaust. Propulsion in the water was achieved by a demountable propellor on the propshaft, and the vehicle's own steering gave limited directional control. Rover developed the APGP from the existing 109-inch model with 2¼-litre petrol engine, adding larger 9.00 x 16 tyres and uprating components as necessary to give a 1 ton payload (existing 109s were rated as ¾ ton types).

The body widened out behind the bulkhead to give a more boat-like shape, and the cab had fixed side panels instead of doors. These blended into a low platform-type back body. Under the floor of this were stowage lockers for the flotation gear, the removable windscreen and other items, and inward-facing bench seats also folded down into the floor. There was a short rear overhang; there was of course no tailgate; and rails running below the body sides acted as steps for troops to

The "rails" seen here could be removed when required. One occasion when this was necessary was when the vehicles were stacked, two-high, for transport inside an aircraft. The wooden pole is a measuring stick, to check that the two vehicles do not exceed the height available in the aircraft. (BMIHT)

enter and leave the vehicle. The low rear platform allowed the vehicles to be stacked two-high, nose-to-tail, for air transportation; this idea was not new, having been tried earlier with pre-production examples of the Mini Moke, which could be stacked three-high. Some of the closed body sections were filled with Ozonote foam to aid buoyancy in the water.

FVRDE ordered three trials vehicles, under contract KL/H/01426 in September 1961. Their identities are not clear, but they were probably registered within the group of six that FVRDE eventually had; these were 636 ELM to 641 ELM, with the civilian registrations then typically allocated to trials vehicles by the Ministry of Supply. One of them, apparently equipped as an FFR model, was shown at the FVRDE-SMMT exhibition of military vehicles in Chertsey in summer 1962. Trials led to an order for 12 more vehicles on 7 June 1962, under contract WV/579; the order was increased to 20 in October 1964 and winches were to be fitted to the additional eight. Meanwhile, deliveries of the first 12 examples had begun in July 1963. The 20 delivered under WV/579 took serial numbers 16 EK 01 to 16 EK 20.

Three different arrangements of the flotation bags were tried. The ELM-registered vehicles had just two "mattress" bags, one on either side. The production vehicles were delivered with a set of four bags – one each at the front and rear, and one on each side – and this arrangement was recorded in the military User Handbook. Then from some time in 1963 or 1964, a new twin-bag arrangement was introduced, this time using a cylindrical bag on each side of the vehicle. The original two-bag system was designed by RFD Limited, a

Godalming-based firm which was already making inflatable boats for the Armed Forces, although actual manufacture was sub-contracted to MFC Survival of mid-Glamorgan. The same arrangement may have applied to the four-bag system, but the final cylindrical bag system was manufactured by Avon, supposedly at lower cost.

The APGPs were issued for troop trials in 1963-1964 and were trialled with a penthouse tent erected to one side for command rôles, as WOMBAT portees, as tractors for the 105mm Pack Howitzer and as troop carriers. However, the project went no further. A total of 28 production vehicles had been built, of which six went to FVRDE, 20 went to the Army for troop trials, and two were retained by Rover. As this was a specifically military design, the vehicle had no future as a production model for the civilian market.

One reason for the APGP's failure may have been excessive weight, and former Rover employees remember an attempt to reduce this by fitting one of the two examples retained at Rover with a 2S/140 gas turbine engine and the two-speed automatic gearbox from a Chevrôlet Corvair! Another reason may have been that the flotation system was excessively cumbersome, while the availability of helicopters with greater lifting capacity from around 1965 may have focussed military thinking in a different direction. One way or the other, most of the APGPs were struck off at the end of 1966; three of the civilian-registered ELM batch, re-registered with military numbers, remained on the strength until approximately 1971. These were 637 ELM (latterly 59 EP 61), 640 ELM (02 SP 33) and 641 ELM (02 SP 32).

The Carmichael FT/6 was a commercially-available conversion of the Land Rover to a low-height forward-control fire tender. The Army Fire Service took on a number, giving them the Mk 9 classification used for the standard normal-control long-wheelbase Land Rover of the time. 78 EL 70 provided fire cover at Central Ammunition Depot, Kineton.

Carmichael FT/6 Redwing Fire Appliance

Carmichael was a specialist fire tender converter based in Gloucester, and enjoyed Land Rover "approval" as a manufacturer of fire tenders for the civilian market. From 1962, it manufactured a special forward-control conversion of the 109-inch Land Rover, known as the FT/6 version of its Redwing fire appliance series.

The FT/6 was based on a standard 109 chassis to which Carmichael's added a front extension. The driving position was relocated here, alongside and slightly ahead of the engine, and the original bulkhead formed a strengthening member in the middle of the new body, ahead of the rear seating compartment. The vehicle was designed to carry a crew of five, and its enclosed body combined standard and modified Land Rover body panels with specially-made GRP panels. Its advantage was large carrying capacity within a low overall height, which made the appliance ideal for confined spaces on factory sites. In Army service, these vehicles provided first-response fire cover at ammunition depots and other storage facilities.

A total of 15 examples entered British military service. The first group of five was delivered direct to the Army Fire Service in 1964 under contract WV2853, and took serials in the EL series. Six more, which included one example with LHD, were delivered to the Army Fire Service under contract WV3025 later in 1964 and gained serials in the EM series.

The remaining four were delivered to the Ministry of Supply, which still controlled the various experimental establishments that designed and tested equipment for the forces.

Originally run on civilian registration numbers CYY 686C to CYY 689C, they were transferred to the Army Fire Service under contract WV3170 shortly after delivery in 1965 when control of the experimental establishments passed to the newly-established Ministry of Defence. They were then re-serialled with EP numbers. (For further details of these four, please see Chapter 13.)

Field Ambulance

As Chapter 4 explains, the first examples of a new pattern of ambulance had entered Army service in 1960, on Rover Mk 7 chassis with bodies by Mickleover Transport. The new type was clearly a success, and a contract for exactly 200 more was placed in 1964. Many more of these ambulances would be delivered on various iterations of the 109-inch Land Rover chassis until a Field Ambulance based on the One-Tonne Land Rover began to replace the type in the second half of 1981.

For use as a field ambulance, the Army modified the original two-stretcher design to carry four stretchers, awarding the body contract to Marshall's of Cambridge. The actual modification involved fitting a second stretcher rack on each side directly above the existing stretcher positions; the additional stretchers themselves were normally carried on the roof under canvas covers. The original batch of ambulances was probably modified to four-stretcher type at about the same time as the first orders were placed with Marshall's.

The Rover 9 ambulances were delivered under two contracts. The first was WV3315 which was placed in 1964

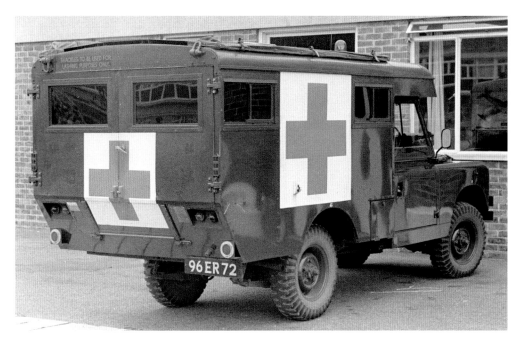

27 EK 36 was one of just 11 Sensitivity Test Vehicles on modified Station Wagon derivatives of the Rover Mk 9. These were used in conjunction with the Thunderbird 2 Air Defence missile. This one is shown with School of Electronic Engineering markings at Aldershot Army Show in June 1970. (RES)

24 EN 26 and 96 ER 72 were among the large numbers of ambulances procured on the Rover Mk 9 chassis. A four-stretcher interior became standard from about 1964, and the bodies were now built by Marshall's of Cambridge. (GF)

and was for 200 vehicles. These were delivered in three groups: 23 EN 83 to 24 EN 70 with RHD, 24 EN 71 to 24 EN 82 with RHD and Light Stone paint, and 24 EN 83 to 25 EN 82 with LHD. The second contract was WV4838, placed in 1966 and calling for 115 vehicles. Of these, only 106 were delivered as Rover 9 types and the balance arrived as Rover 11s. The Rover 9s all received ER serials (see the tables below); the Rover 11s would be given ET serials (see Chapter 6).

Various minor changes took place during the vehicles' service life. The rear number-plate was originally below the body on the right-hand side, but was later moved to a less vulnerable position on the panel above the doors. As delivered, the vehicles probably all had wing mirrors, but from 1971 door mirrors were fitted, on special top hinges. Anti-roll bars were added in 1973-1974, and some vehicles are

said to have been fitted with spring assisters as well. From 1974, an additional locker was also fitted into the body behind the left-hand rear wheel.

Some bodies were built with a single central air intake above the cab and others with two at the outer ends. The Rover 9s were FV18067, although the contract refers to them as FV18054 which was the Rover Mk 7 designation.

Sensitivity Test Vehicle

Initially codenamed "Green Flax" and later "Yellow Temple", the Thunderbird 2 Surface to Air Guided Weapon (SAGW) began to enter service with the Royal Artillery, although probably only for trials, in 1965. The missile was very different from Thunderbird 1 although appearing similar externally. A revised Sensitivity Test vehicle was developed, based on a Rover Mark 9 Station Wagon. The rear door and rear windows around the cargo area were replaced by plain panels, giving it a rather clandestine air. At the rear there was a hatch, and there was another on the offside rear where the cables were connected to the missile while doing checks. A total of 11 were purchased, and these served alongside the missile until 1977 when those remaining were struck off to the RAF.

Straussler wheels

As part of its investigations into how Land Rovers could be made to float, FVRDE tested two Mk 9 Land Rovers with Straussler wheels. These carried giant balloon tyres which provided buoyancy in the water. However, they were quite impractical for road use, and the experiment was abandoned. The two vehicles involved in the trials were 00 EM 56 and 45 ER 04. Nicolas Straussler was a Hungarian-born inventor who had become a naturalised Briton and had devised the Duplex Drive conversion that allowed Sherman tanks to "swim" during the D-Day landings in 1944.

Vehicle Protection Kits (VPKs)

In early 1971 a number of vehicles were attacked with Claymore-type mines in Northern Ireland. The C-in-C Northern Ireland, Major General Anthony Farrar-Hockley, requested HQ REME to develop suitable counter-measures.

At that time the 2IC REME in Northern Ireland was Major Reg Pearce, and he happened to be carrying out ballistic trials on some Glass Reinforced Plastic (GRP) Sheets. The sheets were effective against mine blast and splinters, and gave the impression that they might be a useful protective measure. Major Pearce then designed and produced drawings of a Vehicle Protection Kit (VPK) made from GRP panels and suitable to protect a Land Rover 88-inch.

Next, REME approached the Royal Navy, who had considerable experience of fabricating GRP, not least for making conning towers and other parts for submarines. The RN Dockyard at Chatham agreed to make up a prototype VPK from Major Pearce's drawings. This was made in around a week and was flown to Northern Ireland. It was fitted to a suitable vehicle, which was subjected to a series of attacks from Thompson Sub-Machine Gun, nail bombs and Claymore in front of an array of senior military and RUC officers. It passed its test with flying colours, and approval for the series production of VPKs followed.

RN Dockyards Chatham, Portsmouth and Plymouth began production of VPKs in early 1971. The work was given high priority and staff worked shifts of over 12 hours a day to get the kits completed quickly. RAF St Athan also became involved. The kits were then fitted to vehicles at 34 Central Workshop, REME in Donnington. Later, the fitting process was moved to 46 Command Workshop at Kinnegar in Northern Ireland.

The major components of the kit numbered some 20 to 30

As part of the Army's experiments with floating Land Rovers, 00 EM 56 was trialled by FVRDE with Straussler wheels. Though they seem to have worked, they were a distinctly cumbersome addition to this long-wheelbase Mk 9. (TMB)

In the early 1970s, many Land Rovers serving in Northern Ireland were equipped with a Vehicle Protection Kit of appliqué armour. 62 EN 52 was among them. The vehicle also has a front-mounted winch. (RLC)

pieces, depending on where they had been made, and the total weight of a VPK for a Land Rover was around ¼ ton. Four different kits were produced for the Series IIA 88-inch, the Lightweight, the 109 and the 109 Field Ambulance.

The exact process for moulding the panels was complex, involving several layers of glass fibre and generating small bubbles of air in layers between the strands of glass fibre. This was essential because solid sheets of GRP would just shatter when hit by a round; by contrast, the less dense sheet used in the VPK would absorb the shock layer by layer, each layer absorbing more and more energy from the round as it penetrated.

The armour is often referred to as Makrolon, but this is incorrect. Makrolon is the trade name for a clear polycarbonate sheet manufactured by Bayer AG. It is often used for riot shields, police helmet visors and the like. Nevertheless, Makrolon was used in the VPKs, to provide clear rear windows in the doors, in place of side windows, and sometimes as a protective shield covering the rear lights.

A major advantage of the VPK was that only standard hand tools were needed to fit one. It took about 32 to 35

man-hours to fit each kit, which was essentially bolted to the outside of the vehicle. If the VPK was no longer required, it was a simple job to remove it, and the vehicle was left with only a few extra holes as evidence that a VPK had been fitted. The only major modification required was the addition of Aeon spring assisters, a commercial product already available for use on Land Rovers. These were large rubber cylinders mounted between the axle and chassis. The bump stops were removed and a shoe plate was welded on top of the axle. In theory, the spring assisters were to be fitted to the rear of ¼ Ton, and the front of ½ Ton and ¾ Ton Land Rovers, but in practice they were often fitted on both axles.

Vehicles were painted in accordance with theatre instructions. This meant Deep Bronze Green until around 1973, and subsequently NATO Infra-Red Reflecting (IRR) Green. Contrary to popular belief, some VPK-equipped vehicles were painted with disruptive green and black. In the late 1980s, it became common practice to stencil on the body sides in yellow or red "CONFIDENTIAL TELEPHONE 0800 666999". As this task was carried out by units, the lettering was not to a consistent standard.

Surviving documents suggest that 752 kits were produced for ½ Tonne Lightweight Land Rovers, 611 for ¾ ton models, 11 for ¼ ton variants and just 8 for the Rover 9 Field Ambulance. The VPKs were also manufactured to suit other vehicles serving in the Northern Ireland theatre at the time.

Winches

A Turner horizontal drum winch was mounted behind the front bumper on some 109s and also a few 88-inch vehicles from the mid-1960s, the modification being made after delivery by REME Workshops. The winch was driven by a shaft from the front of the crankshaft and was engaged by a dog clutch. This gave such vehicles a self-recovery capability as well as enabling them to recover other similar light vehicles. In addition some 105mm Pack Howitzer tractors were so equipped as this also allowed the tractor to recover the gun from difficult ground without the need to enter that ground.

The winch-equipped vehicles were issued to the units of 16 Parachute Brigade in Aldershot and 5, 19 and 24 Airportable Brigades as well as some divisional troops of 3 Division and also to the infantry battalion attached to the recently formed ACE Mobile Force (AMF). Indeed by 1975 it seems half the gun tractors in a typical Light Battery of the Royal Artillery were equipped with winches and this led on to all 101 tractors for the Light Gun being winch-equipped. Some REME vehicles had rear-mounted gantries to give a limited lifting capability using the front-mounted winch.

WOMBAT portees

Some Rover 9s became WOMBAT portees. The WOMBAT anti-tank weapon is described more fully in Chapter 6.

Among the RAF transport aircraft of the mid-1960s was the Andover. One is seen here discharging an RAF Mk 8 Land Rover. The picture makes clear how limited space was inside the aircraft. (MoD PR)

RAF ROVER 8 AND 9 DELIVERIES

The RAF had its own special types of Land Rover although it used large numbers of the 88-inch Rover 8 in soft-top form. However, fewer 109s were purchased in soft-top form, and the RAF preferred the so-called Window Hardtop version with a fixed roof and a pair of windows in each side. This was a factory option normally available only for export, for tax reasons. It offered security when carrying valuable equipment as well as offering better weather protection on longer journeys and exposed airfields! In addition, there were specialist types for use by Mountain Rescue Teams including a "Mountain, Desert and Jungle Rescue" (MDJR) vehicle and a "Stretcher Carrier".

The RAF had an aversion to petrol-engined vehicles in certain rôles. The ignition systems of petrol engines could produce sparks, which were unwelcome around airfields in close proximity to fuelled-up aircraft and live bombs, and so "Anti-Spark" versions of both the 88-inch and 109-inch were purchased. These had standard Land Rover diesel engines and were often to be found serving with Aircraft armourers as they loaded and unloaded live munitions from fuelled-up aircraft.

The RAF also used large numbers of 24-volt Land Rovers,

Increasingly, RAF Regiment vehicles were appearing with the same camouflage schemes as Army Land Rovers. This group had matt black disruptive patches on IRR green paint and were photographed at RAF Catterick around 1970. (GF)

The RAF used a Window Hardtop variant of the Rover Mk 9 for their Mountain, Desert and Jungle Rescue teams. 13 AA 70 is typical of the breed. (TMB)

87 AA 74 was one of several Mk 9 ambulances delivered to the RAF. Their general specification was the same as the Army types, but the vehicles carried different equipment to suit their crash-rescue rôle. (JT)

The Tigercat missile launcher tractor tows the launch trailer and carries four missiles in the cargo bay. This missile system only ever equipped one squadron (48 Squadron) of the RAF Regiment.(TMB)

90 AA 35 was a Rover 9 pictured at FVRDE during trials with the radar trailer used with the Tigercat missile system.(TMB)

in a rôle very different from the FFR rôle normally associated with 24-volt Army vehicles. The 24-volt RAF vehicles were intended to provide ground power supply – mainly to helicopters. Their task was to provide up to 90 amps of current to the intended recipient.

In addition, the RAF had a succession of three different Airfield Crash Rescue Tenders based on the 109. Although painted red like the larger fire appliances, their primary purpose was as fast-response vehicles to rescue the crew from a crashed aircraft.

ACRT

The ACRT (Airfield Crash Rescue Tender) has already been described in Chapter 5. Five further contracts for the type, now on Rover 9 chassis, were placed between 1961 and 1970, and total production amounted to 178 vehicles. This was more than the total number of RAF stations, and some airfields were allocated two. Two batches, of just six vehicles, went to the Army Air Corps with serial numbers in EK and EN. All the early vehicles were built by Foamite, who had built the prototype, but later examples appear to have come from Merryweather. The Army later had a single Rover 11 ACRT – 47 FG 09.

This was the ACRT (Airfield Crash Rescue Truck), based on a Mk 9 chassis and used primarily by the RAF. (Land Rover)

The ACRT was also used by the Army Fire Service for similar duties on Army airfields. Even the RAF-pattern crash bar was the same. This one was based at Middle Wallop and photographed there in July 1969. (RES)

TAC-T

The TAC-T (Truck, Fire Fighting, Airfield Crash – Tactical) represented a completely different line of thinking and was designed for a special purpose. Although original plans dated from 1965 and the Rover 9 chassis were purchased shortly afterwards, these vehicles did not enter service until 1972.

The TAC-T was designed for the RAF Harrier squadrons, which were expected to operate from improvised temporary airfields and needed a dedicated crash tender among their support vehicles. As no mains water supply could be counted on, they also needed to carry a large first-aid supply of their own. However, a problem was that the RAF wanted to be

The TAC-T was a special RAF derivative, designed to be airportable and to operate at makeshift landing sites for the Harrier jump-jets. Although the towing vehicle was essentially a Rover Mk 9, it was very different indeed from the standard-issue Mk 9 models.

able to move these appliances into position by helicopter, and that no helicopter of the time was capable of lifting a full-size fire tender with a full water tank.

The solution was to break the appliance down into three loads. The body with all its fire-fighting equipment was made fully demountable so that it could be taken forward as a unit. The chassis and driving cab – initially planned without roof and upper panels, to save weight – would go forward separately, and the water trailer would make a third load. This trailer was also special: it was a powered-axle type developed by Scottorn in conjunction with Land Rover's Special Projects Department, and had been under evaluation by FVRDE when the RAF was drawing up its plans for the Harrier squadrons. Not only could it carry the water tank, but it also gave the combination a 6x6 capability, which was ideal for the sort of terrain where the Harriers might operate.

The Harrier entered operational service in late 1969. In the meantime, the RAF ordered the chassis for the 15 TAC-T vehicles it wanted. These were 24-volt military-specification Rover 9 types, and they were put into storage until the Harrier deliveries were imminent. The reason for the 24-volt specification is unclear, although it may have been intended for use with cutting gear that needed such an electrical supply. Most interesting is that the 24-volt specification had a negative earth, and that these vehicles were classified as Rover 11 types when they entered service, a negative-earth system being a characteristic of the Rover 11s.

The body contract was awarded to Pyrene, fire-fighting specialists based at Brentford in Middlesex, who completed the prototype in 1970. This went to FVRDE for trials. Unlike the "production" models, it had a fully open cab, following the original weight-saving plan. This prototype was acquired later by the RAF as 30 AG 15. The production models not only had a full truck cab, but also one-piece doors – a rarity generally confined to vehicles destined for extremely cold territories.

The TAC-Ts entered service in 1972 but were never really a success. Some may never have served with a Harrier squadron at all. One reason for their failure was that they were not equipped to handle the new AFFF fire-fighting foam that came into service in the mid-1970s, and many were stripped of their trailers and modified to handle AFFF. Some became ordinary first-response tenders on airfields and some went into store. By the early 1980s, they began to be sold off, generally after removal of the special fire-fighting body.

ROYAL NAVY ROVER 8 AND 9 DELIVERIES

Like the RAF, the Royal Navy chose diesel-engined Land Rovers for some jobs where the risk of sparks from a petrol engine's ignition system was unacceptable. Some of these vehicles were destined to be carried on ships.

An interesting oddity from this period is an unknown small quantity of specially modified Rover 8s, supposedly intended for use aboard an aircraft carrier and constructed in 1966-1967. These vehicles were specially shortened, probably by Royal Navy workshops, from 88-inch to 80-inch wheelbase

Pictured at FVRDE during evaluation trials, this is clearly a Mk 9 airfield crash tender intended for the RAF, but appears to have remained unique. Other pictures of the same vehicle show that it was primarily equipped as a foam tender. (Tank Museum)

This Royal Navy Mk 9 hardtop carries an aircraft towing dolly on its roof and was presumably attached to the RNAS in some capacity. (Unknown source)

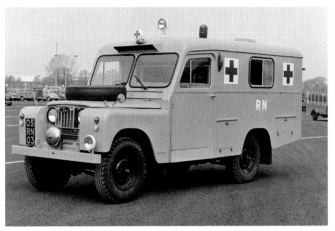

Although this was a staged publicity photograph, it does show how the Royal Navy used some of its Mk 9 Station Wagons. 03 RN 36 was clearly used to transport a diving team and its equipment. (Land Rover)

Pictured at RNAS Culdrose in July 1972, this Royal Navy 109 hardtop was classified as a Rescue Vehicle, and carried a Fireball and its associated equipment. The Fireball was a 300 lb dry powder extinguisher that was carried underslung by a helicopter. (Gordon Smith Collection)

The Royal Navy had its own type of ambulance on the Mk 9 chassis, with a commercial-pattern body by Lomas. 05 RN 03 was pictured when new; the other vehicle was pictured in preservation with a civilian number-plate, but shows how these ambulances looked with their bright yellow paint for high visibility at RNAS airfields. (BMIHT; JT)

(the dimension found on Rover Mk 1 and Mk 2 models). The shortened chassis is also reported to have been galvanised to improve durability.

The Royal Navy also chose not to use the Field Ambulance on Rover Mark 9 chassis that both the Army and RAF favoured. Instead, it bought an unknown quantity of rather elegant coachbuilt ambulances constructed by ambulance specialist Herbert Lomas on the Rover 9 chassis.

SERIES IIA ROVER 8 AND ROVER 9

Once again there was a change in the registry reference to vehicle contract files and most references changed from KL/H to WV (Wheeled Vehicle) in early 1962. The full reference prefix for such contracts was in fact A/CTS/WV, and this was followed by a number and sometimes by suffixes as well. These lists use the short form of the prefix, WV, which was used in most contemporary documentation.

Lists cover vehicles ordered under contracts, and do not include vehicles transferred in from other services or elsewhere. RAF vehicles allocated to NATO are not included.

ARMY

(a) Mk 8 (88inch)

Serials	Contract	Chassis Nos	Total	Remarks
00 DM 06 to 02 DM 05	KL/H/01291	241-00163A to 241-01318A	130	8/2 FFR RHD.
03 DM 49 to 08 DM 45	KL/H/01305	241-00001A to 241-00535A	497	8/2 GS RHD; dated 25 April 1961.
08 DM 46 to 08 DM 48	KL/H/01305	244-02770A to 244-03053A	3	8/2 Station Wagon LHD; 08 DM 46 to Military Attaché, Seoul; 08 DM 47 to Military Attaché, Moscow; 08 DM 48 to to Military Attaché, Vientiane; dated 25 April 1961.
13 DM 83 to 17 DM 82	KL/H/01291	241-01210A to 241-03683A	400	8/2 FFR RHD. Note overlap of chassis numbers with above.
20 DM 28 to 29 DM 27	KL/H/01305	241-01068A to 241-03694A	900	GS RHD; dated 25 April 1961.
40 DM 12 and 40 DM 13	KL/H/0803 R766	241-02988A and 241-03167A	2	Station Wagon RHD; 40 DM 12 to Military Attaché, Tokyo; 40 DM 13 Military Attaché Mogadishu; dated 29 December 1961.
40 DM 14	KL/H/0803 R766	244-03039A	1	Station Wagon LHD; Military Attaché, Amman; dated 29 December 1961.
40 DM 23	KL/H/0803 R776	244-03040A	1	Station Wagon LHD; Military Attaché, Cairo; dated 12 January 1962.
44 DM 00 to 48 DM 99	WV34	241-03730A to 24105958A	500	FFR RHD; dated 6 February 1962.
52 DM 74 to 61 DM 20	WV34	241-05959A to 241-07926A	847	FFR RHD; dated 6 February 1962.
08 EK 58 to 12 EK 93	WV496	241-05898A to 241-07225A	436	GS RHD; dated 11 May 1962.
16 EK 23 to 16 EK 25	KL/H/0803 R835	241-05557A to 241-05559A	3	Station Wagon RHD; Military Attaché, Bangkok, Military Attaché, Djakarta and Military Attaché, Kathmandu; dated 18 June 1962.
16 EK 41 to 16 EK 42	KL/H/0803 R836	n/a	2	Station Wagon LHD; Military Attaché, Sofia and Military Attaché, Damascus; dated 18 June 1962.
27 EK 41 to 30 EK 10	WV1328	244-07690B to 24409052B	270	GS LHD; dated 15 October 1962.
30 EK 11 to 31 EK 40	WV1328	241-08240B to 241-09164B	130	GS RHD; dated 15 October 1962.
31 EK 41 to 33 EK 40	WV1327	241-08241B to 241-09185B	200	FFR RHD; dated 15 October 1962.
33 EK 41 to 37 EK 40	WV1327	244-07688B to 24411244B	400	FFR LHD; dated 15 October 1962.
52 EK 69 to 67 EK 00	WV1327	241-09192B to 241-13302B	1432	FFR RHD; dated 15 October 1962.
67 EK 01 to 68 EK 60	WV1328	244-09506B to 244-11261B	160	GS LHD; dated 15 October 1962.
68 EK 61 to 74 EK 60	WV1328	241-09167B to 241-12508B	600	GS RHD; dated 15 October 1962.
61 EL 00 to 70 EL 91	WV2916	241-13853B to 241-15936B	992	GS RHD; dated 26 November 1963.
70 EL 92 to 75 EL 91	WV2916	244-13887B to 244-19592B	500	GS LHD; dated 26 November 1963.
83 EL 25 to 97 EL 19	WV2985	241-13851B to 241-19754B	1395	FFR RHD; dated 13 December 1963.
97 EL 20 to 99 EL 99	WV2985	244-13884B to 244-18801B	280	FFR LHD; dated 13 December 1963.
00 EM 01 to 00 EM 20	WV2985	244-18913B to 244-21398B	20	FFR LHD; dated 13 December 1963.
61 EN 91 to 63 EN 71	WV2916	241-18413B to 241-18690B	181	GS RHD; dated 26 November 1963.
63 EN 72 to 64 EN 51	WV2916	244-19594B to 244-20075B	80	GS LHD; dated 26 November 1963.
66 EN 33 to 75 EN 32	WV3691	241-18861B to 241-23047B	900	GS RHD; dated 10 September 1964.
75 EN 33 to 82 EN 82	WV3691	244-19946B to 244-26602B	750	GS LHD; dated 10 September 1964.

ARMY

(a) Mk 8 (88inch) (Continued)

Serials	Contract	Chassis Nos	Total	Remarks
82 EN 83 to 84 EN 32	WV3691	241-20414B to 241-21387B	150	GS RHD, Light Stone; dated 10 September 1964.
84 EN 33 to 89 EN 53	WV3692	241-19525B to 241-23735B	521	FFR RHD; dated 10 September 1964.
89 EN 54 to 92 EN 24	WV3692	244-21068B to 244-26599B	371	FFR LHD; dated 10 September 1964.
92 EN 25 to 92 EN 43	WV3692	241-21629B to 241-21627B	19	FFR RHD Light Stone; dated 10 September 1964.
35 EP 17	WV223 R1164	244-21090B	1	Station Wagon LHD; Military Attaché, Beirut; dated 8 October 1964.
38 EP 32 to 38 EP 36	WV2916	241-18847B to 241-18851B	5	GS RHD; dated 26 November 1963.
39 EP 32	WV223 R1178	271-04671B		GS Diesel RHD; dated 26 November 1964.
42 EP 03 to 43 EP 52	WV3691	241-23011B to 241-24128B	150	GS RHD; dated 10 September 1964.
10 ER 94 to 13 ER 43	WV3692	241-23622B to 241-24773B	250	FFR RHD; dated 10 September 1964.
14 ER 42 to 15 ER 15	WV3691	241-24164B to 241-24742B	70	GS RHD; dated 10 September 1964.
59 ER 15 to 61 ER 64	WV4629	241-23871C to 241-26761C	250	FFR RHD.
61 ER 65 to 64 ER 14	WV4629	244-27430C to 244-29493C	250	FFR LHD.
68 ER 23 to 80 ER 12	WV4631	241-23874C to 241-28838C	1190	GS RHD; 80 ER 13 to 86 ER 42 were cancelled.
86 ER 43 to 89 ER 72	WV4631	244-26102C to 244-28835C	330	GS LHD; 89 ER 73 to 94 ER 42 were cancelled.
03 ET 68	WV4052 R1377	315-00159C	1	Station Wagon RHD; to Military Attaché, Rawalpindi.
			Total 15,236	

RAF Note that chassis suffix letters are not shown in the RAF records.

(a) Mk 8 (88inch)

Serials	Contract	Chassis Nos	Total	Remarks
77 AA 27 to 79 AA 81	WV213	241-03731 to 241-05686	255	GS RHD.
79 AA 84 to 79 AA 87	WV213	241-05792 to 241-05815	4	GS Hard Top with windows, RHD.
79 AA 88 to 80 AA 25	WV213	241-05595 to 241-05787	38	GS RHD, Light Stone.
80 AA 26 to 80 AA 56	WV213	244-05301 to 244-05411	31	GS LHD.
80 AA 69 to 80 AA 78	WV625	271-01687 to 271-01709	10	GS RHD Diesel, 1962 delivery.
80 AA 79 to 81 AA 08	WV1698	241-08626 to 241-09176	30	GS RHD.
81 AA 09 to 81 AA 13	WV1698	241-09213 to 241-09268	5	GS RHD.
81 AA 26 to 81 AA 31	WV1698	244-08918 to 244-08971	6	GS LHD.
81 AA 32 to 81 AA 39	n/a	271-02222 to 271-02259	8	GS RHD Diesel.
81 AA 40 to 81 AA 57	WV2099	241-10564 to 241-10839	18	GS 24v RHD.
81 AA 58 to 81 AA 82	WV1698	241-11401 to 241-11771	25	GS RHD.
81 AA 83 to 81 AA 86	WV1698	271-02930 to 271-02937	4	GS RHD Diesel, 1963 delivery.
82 AA 19 to 82 AA 24	n/a	n/a	6	GS Diesel RHD; This batch was probably cancelled; it is blank on the register and there are no record cards at the RAF Museum.
82 AA 27 to 82 AA 32	WV1650	271-10033 to 271-10558	6	GS Diesel RHD, date recorded as 1963.
82 AA 36 to 82 AA 96	WV1698	241-10345 to 241-10633	61	GS RHD.
83 AA 17 to 84 AA 79	WV3314	241-17412 to 241-18813	163	GS RHD.
84 AA 80 to 85 AA 07	WV3299	241-16592 to 241-17675	28	24v RHD.
85 AA 54 to 85 AA 88	WV4010	241-20119 to 241-20186	35	GS RHD.
85 AA 89 to 86 AA 08	WV4010	241-20245 to 241-20173	20	GS RHD, Light Stone.
86 AA 09 to 86 AA 13	WV4010	271-04843 to 271-04940	5	GS Diesel RHD.
86 AA 29 to 86 AA 49	WV4180	241-21392 to 241-22122	21	GS RHD.
86 AA 60 to 86 AA 99	WV4254	241-23273 to 241-23334	20	GS RHD, date recorded as 12/65.
86 AA 80 to 86 AA 99	WV4254	241-23263 to 241-23262	20	GS RHD Light Stone.

RAF Note that chassis suffix letters are not shown in the RAF records.

(a) Mk 8 (88inch) (Continued)

Serials	Contract	Chassis Nos	Total	Remarks
87 AA 00 to 87 AA 14	WV4254	244-24837 to 244-25189	15	GS LHD.
87 AA 88 to 90 AA 11	WV4946	241-24543 to 241-25891	224	GS RHD, date recorded as 1/66.
90 AA 12 to 90 AA 27	WV4946	244-26918 to 244-26933	16	GS LHD, date recorded as 7/66.
90 AA 36 to 90 AA 53	WV5032	271-06673 to 271-06840	18	GS Diesel RHD.
90 AA 70 to 90 AA 78	WV4843	241-27090 to 241-27189	9	GS 24v RHD.
90 AA 85 to 91 AA 00	WV5223	241-28857 to 241-28897	16	GS RHD.
91 AA 01 to 91 AA 05	WV5223	244-29458 to 244-29474	5	GS LHD.
93 AA 21 to 93 AA 81	WV6836	241-29903 to 241-30683	61	GS RHD, date recorded as 7/69.
93 AA 82 to 93 AA 91	WV6836	244-31160 to 244-31180	10	GS LHD.
93 AA 92 to 94 AA 11	WV6836	271-07938 to 271-08307	20	GS Diesel RHD.
94 AA 12 to 94 AA 24	WV6836	274-04743 to 274-04763	13	GS Diesel LHD, date recorded as 7/67.
			Total 1240	

Note *According to the Land Rover despatch records held by BMIHT at the Heritage Motor Centre, Gaydon, 315-00435 (an 88-inch Station Wagon) was despatched to RAF Farnborough and was painted Royal Blue, the colour normally used on vehicles for the Royal Navy. Its RAF serial number, if it had one, is not known.*

ROYAL NAVY In the absence of official records, it is possible only to give some sample Navy registrations. The table below has been compiled from the Land Rover despatch records held by BMIHT at the Heritage Motor Centre, Gaydon.

(a) Mk 8 (88inch)

Serials	Contract	Chassis Nos	Total	Remarks
RN Serials	n/a	241-04153 to 24104158	6	Cargo; delivered June 1962.
RN Serials	n/a	241-04413 to 24104418	6	Cargo; delivered June 1962.
RN Serials	n/a	241-04468 to 241-04473	6	Cargo; delivered July 1962.
RN Serials	n/a	241-04494 to 24104498	6	Cargo; delivered July 1962.
08 RN 06 to 08 RN 09	n/a	241-07937 to 241-07940	4	Cargo; delivered February 1963.
RN Serials	n/a	241-10730 to 241-10762	6	Cargo; delivered October 1963.
RN Serials	n/a	241-11657 and 241-11658	2	Cargo; delivered November 1963.
RN Serials	n/a	241-14437 to 24114775	12	Cargo; delivered June 1964.
RN Serials	n/a	241-15075 to 241-15097	3	Cargo; delivered June 1964.
RN Serials	n/a	241-15242 to 24115324	5	Cargo; delivered July 1964.
RN Serials inc 46 RN 44	n/a	241-20943 to 241-21438	9	Cargo; delivered August 1965.
RN Serials	n/a	241-27636 to 241-27682	9	Cargo; delivered August 1966.
			Total 74	

ARMY

(b) Mark 9 (109-inch)

Serials	Contract	Chassis Nos	Total	Remarks
02 DM 06 to 03 DM 25	KL/H/01292	251-00102A to 251-00389A	120	GS RHD; dated 18 April 1961.
18 DM 01 to 20 DM 27	KL/H/01292	251-00394A to 251-00799A	227	GS RHD; dated 18 April 1961.
30 DM 79 to 32 DM 31	KL/H/01362	251-00456A to 251-01259A	153	FFR RHD; dated 1 August 1961.
40 DM 15	KL/H/0803 R767	264-00909A	1	Station Wagon LHD; Military Attaché vehicle, Kabul; dated 29 December 1961.
49 DM 00 to 50 DM 63	WV32	251-01269A to 251-02071A	164	GS RHD; dated 6 February 1962; 50 DM 64 to 50 DM 72 were cancelled and became part of WV33.
50 DM 64 to 50 DM 72	WV33	251-02016A to 25102068A	9	FFR RHD; dated 6 February 1962.
50 DM 73 to 51 DM 44	WV33	251-01270A to 25102015A	72	FFR RHD; dated 6 February 1962.
51 DM 83	KL/H/0803 R800	264-01299A	1	Station Wagon LHD; Military Attaché, Lagos; dated 26 February 1962.
52 DM 48 to 52 DM 67	WV329	n/a	20	GS RHD; for Somalia; dated 19 March 1962.
16 EK 01 to 16 EK 20	WV579	310-00002A to 310-00023A	20	APGP RHD; dated 7 June 1962.
16 EK 21 and 16 EK 22	KL/H/0803 R837	264-01709A and 264-01708A	2	Station Wagon LHD; to Military Attaché, Prague and Military Attaché, Warsaw; dated 18 June 1962.
20 EK 66 and 20 EK 67	KL/H/0803 R845	n/a	2	Station Wagon LHD; to BRIXMIS.
27 EK 30 to 27 EK 40	KL/H/0803 R720 It 13	261-00017A to n/a	11	Station Wagon RHD; Converted to "Truck, Sensitivity Test, No 2 Mk 1, SAGW, ¾ ton,4x4, Rover 9"; dated 4 August 1961.
52 EK 66 and 52 EK 67	WV1724	251-02698B and 251-02701B	2	Fire Tender RHD; dated 4 February 1963.
01 EL 01 to 01 EL 21	WV2086	251-02728B to 251-02771B	21	FFR RHD; 01 EL 22 to 01 EL 24 were cancelled.
18 EL 08 to 20 EL 16	WV2651	251-03450B to 251-03862B	209	GS RHD; dated 27 August 1963.
20 EL 17	WV2651	251-03863B	1	Station Wagon RHD; built to Rover 9 standard; dated 27 August 1963.
20 EL 18 to 24 EL 90	WV2651	251-03864B to 251-04665B	473	GS RHD; dated 27 August 1963.
24 EL 91 to 29 EL 97	WV2651	254-05108B to 251-08013B	507	FFR LHD; dated 27 August 1963.
29 EL 98 to 31 EL 47	WV2651	251-03868B to 251-04570B	150	FFR RHD; dated 27 August 1963.
31 EL 48 to 32 EL 61	WV2651	254-07274B to 254-08001B	124	FFR LHD; dated 27 August 1963.
78 EL 66 to 78 EL 70	WV2853	251-03875B to 251-04058B	5	FT/6 Forward Control Fire Tender RHD; dated 4 November 1963.
00 EM 21 to 01 EM 88	WV2926	251-04511B to 251-05020B	168	GS RHD; dated 13 December 1963.
01 EM 89 to 02 EM 88	WV2926	254-07877B to 254-09027B	100	GS LHD; dated 13 December 1963.
03 EM 73 to 03 EM 77	WV3025	251-04428B to 251-04431B	5	FT/6 Forward Control Fire Tender RHD; dated 9 January 1964.
03 EM 78	WV3025	254-07790B	1	FT/6 Forward Control Fire Tender LHD; dated 9 January 1964.
06 EM 41 to 11 EM 10	WV3268	251-05122B to 251-06216B	470	GS RHD; dated 31 March 1964.
11 EM 11 to 11 EM 40	WV3268	251-05292B to 251-05381B	30	GS RHD Light Stone; dated 31 March 1964.
11 EM 41 to 13 EM 40	WV3268	254-09069B to 254-10427B	200	GS LHD; dated 31 March 1964.
13 EM 41 to 14 EM 90	WV3269	251-06137B to 251-07457B	150	FFR RHD; dated 31 March 1964.
14 EM 91 to 15 EM 15	WV3269	251-06842B to 251-07035B	25	FFR RHD Light Stone; dated 31 March 1964.
15 EM 16 to 15 EM 40	WV3269	254-10324B to 254-11520B	25	FFR LHD; dated 31 March 1964.
23 EN 83 to 24 EN 70	WV3315	251-06126B to 251-08110B	88	Field Ambulance RHD; dated 28 May 1964.
24 EN 71 to 24 EN 82	WV3315	251-07155B to 251-07173B	12	Field Ambulance RHD, Light Stone; dated 28 May 1964.
24 EN 83 to 25 EN 82	WV3315	254-12188B to 251-00322B	100	Field Ambulance LHD; dated 28 May 1964.
48 EN 97 to 49 EN 00	WV223 R1085	251-05716B to 251-05758B	4	ACRT RHD; dated 13 May 1964.
49 EN 03 to 51 EN 50	WV3517	251-06271B to 251-06781B	248	GS RHD; dated 27 July 1964.
51 EN 51 to 53 EN 43	WV3517	254-10395B to 254-11079B	193	GS LHD; dated 27 July 1964.

ARMY
(b) Mark 9 (109-inch) (Continued)

Serials	Contract	Chassis Nos	Total	Remarks
53 EN 44 to 54 EN 10	WV3517	251-06646B to 251-06767B	67	GS RHD Light Stone; dated 27 July 1964.
54 EN 11 to 55 EN 21	WV3518	251-07549B to 251-07677B	111	FFR RHD; dated 27 July 1964.
55 EN 22 to 57 EN 25	WV3518	254-11525B to 254-12728B	204	FFR LHD; dated 27 July 1964.
57 EN 26 to 57 EN 46	WV3518	251-07075B to 251-07220B	21	FFR RHD Light Stone; dated 27 July 1964.
92 EN 44 to 96 EN 43	WV3693	254-11080B to 254-12231B	400	GS LHD; dated 10 September 1964.
96 EN 44 to 96 EN 63	WV3693	251-07251B to 251-07433B	20	GS RHD; dated 10 September 1964.
96 EN 64 to 96 EN 73	WV3693	251-07412B to 251-07431B	10	GS RHD Light Stone; dated 10 September 1964.
96 EN 74 to 98 EN 73	WV3694	251-07373B to 251-08957B	200	FFR RHD; dated 10 September 1964.
98 EN 74 to 99 EN 99	WV3694	254-12773B to 254-14269B	126	FFR LHD; dated 10 September 1964.
00 EP 01 to 01 EP 24	WV3694	254-14273B to 254-14351B	124	FFR LHD; dated 10 September 1964.
01 EP 25 to 01 EP 94	WV3694	254-14355B to 254-15318B	70	FFR RHD; dated 10 September 1964.
29 EP 29 to 29 EP 76	WV3517	251-06782B to 251-06841B	58	GS RHD Light Stone; dated 27 July 1964.
35 EP 18	WV223 R1161	264-05727B	1	Station Wagon, LHD; for Military Attaché, Rabat; dated 8 October 1964.
41 EP 50 to 41 EP 99	WV3693	251-08424B to 251-08623B	50	GS RHD; dated 10 September 1964.
15 ER 16 to 15 ER 22	WV3693	251-08969B to 251-09060B	7	GS RHD; dated 10 September 1964.
17 ER 97 to 20 ER 38	WV3694	251-08978B to 251-09494B	240	FFR RHD; dated 10 September 1964.
20 ER 39 to 20 ER 48	WV3694	251-09017B to 251-09043B	10	FFR RHD Light Stone; dated 10 September 1964.
20 ER 49 to 22 ER 08	WV3694	254-15437B to 254-16103B	160	FFR LHD; dated 10 September 1964.
43 ER 40 to 50 ER 73	WV4628	251-09168C to 251-12330C	734	GS RHD; dated 7 October 1965. (50 ER 74 to 57 ER 89 were cancelled.)
57 ER 90 to 58 ER 64	WV4628	254-15587C to 254-18171C	75	GS LHD; dated 7 October 1965. (58 ER 65 to 59 ER 14 were cancelled.)
64 ER 15 to 67 ER 64	WV4630	251-09166C to 251-11106C	350	FFR RHD; dated 7 October 1965.
67 ER 65 to 68 ER 22	WV4630	254-15585C to 254-17177C	68	FFR LHD; dated 7 October 1965.
96 ER 56 to 97 ER 32	WV4838	251-10834C to 251-10513C	77	Field Ambulance RHD; dated 23 December 1965.
97 ER 33 to 97 ER 41	WV5542	251-12902C to 251-12920D	9	Field Ambulance RHD; dated 19 September 1966.
97 ER 42 to 97 ER 44	WV4838	251-10943C to 251-10720C	3	Field Ambulance RHD; dated 23 December 1965.
97 ER 45 to 97 ER 70	WV4838	254-17687C to 254-17429C	26	Field Ambulance LHD; dated 23 December 1965.
28 ES 82 to 29 ES 96	WV4630	251-11843C to 251-12186C	15	FFR RHD.
29 ES 97 to 32 ES 56	WV4630	254-19244C to 254-20080C	260	FFR LHD.
03 ET 15 to 03 ET 23	WV4838	251-10727C to 251-10932C	9	Field Ambulance RHD; dated 23 December 1965.
03 ET 65 to 03 ET 67	WV4052 R1377	264-09445C to 264-09447C	3	Station Wagon LHD.
14 ET 21 to 14 ET 30	WV4052 R1375	261-02069C to 261-02078C	10	Station Wagon RHD.
14 ET 31	WV4052 R1376	251-12146C	1	Van RHD
14 ET 53	WV4052 R1394	315-00200C	1	Station Wagon RHD.
14 ET 92 to 15 ET 09	WV4052 R1410	264-09768C to 264-09893C	18	Station Wagon LHD.
15 ET 10 to 15 ET 15	WV4052 R1410	261-02101C to 261-02106C	6	Station Wagon RHD.
15 ET 16	WV4052 R1410	261-02107C	1	Station Wagon RHD.
		Total	7636	

RAF Note that chassis suffix letters are not normally shown in the RAF records. Vehicle batches are listed in serial number order, which does not necessarily correspond to delivery order.

(b) Mark 9 (109-inch)

Serials	Contract	Chassis Nos	Total	Remarks
13 AA 44 to 13 AA 64	WV3362	251-05863 to 251-06189	21	Airfield Crash Recue Truck, RHD; Body: KM/G/423 Foamite Ltd.
13 AA 65 to 13 AA 72	WV3491	251-06057 to 251-06226	8	Stretcher Carrier RHD; at least one was MDJR.
39 AA 74 to 39 AA 98	KM/G/0262	251-02087 to 251-02164	25	Airfield Crash Recue Truck RHD, recorded as 1962.
39 AA 99	n/a	264-03408	1	Station Wagon LHD; Air Attaché vehicle.
47 AA 25 to 47 AA 29	KL/J/0391	251-01878A to 251-01882A	5	Crash Rescue Ambulance RHD.
47 AA 31 and 47 AA 32	WV7421	254-22391 and 254-22401	2	GS LHD; 47 AA 32 to Air Attaché Teheran.
57 AA 00	n/a	261-00986	1	Station Wagon RHD.
79 AA 82	n/a	251-01911A	1	GS RHD.
79 AA 83	n/a	261-00187	1	Station Wagon Tropical RHD, to Air Attaché vehicle, Bangkok.
80 AA 57 to 80 AA 63	WV131	261-00091 to 261-00099	7	Station Wagon RHD, recorded as 1962.
80 AA 64 to 80 AA 68	WV585	251-01912A to 251-01916A	5	GS RHD, recorded as 1962.
81 AA 14 to 81 AA 24	WV1708	251-02704 to 251-02723B	11	GS RHD, recorded as 1963.
81 AA 25	n/a	26402923	1	Station Wagon LHD, Air Attaché vehicle, Ankara.
81 AA 87 to 82 AA 06	WV2098	251-03142 to 251-03183	20	Airfield Crash Recue Truck RHD, recorded as 12/63.
82 AA 25 and 82 AA 26	WV2098	251-02702 and 251-02703	2	Airfield Crash Recue Truck, RHD, recorded as 3/64.
82 AA 33 to 82 AA 35	WV2161	251-03138 to 251-03141	3	Ambulance Special, recorded as 1964; Body Contract was WV2568 with Mickleover.
82 AA 97 to 83 AA 03	WV3282	251-05222 to 251-05232	7	GS Window Hardtop RHD, recorded as 7/64.
83 AA 04 to 83 AA 07	WV3282	261-00996B to 261-01004B	4	Station Wagon RHD.
83 AA 08 to 83 AA 11	WV3282	254-09044 to 254-09047	4	GS LHD, recorded as 7/64.
83 AA 12 to 83 AA 16	WV3282	251-05254 to 251-05271	5	24v 90A RHD.
85 AA 08 to 85 AA 34	WV3470	251-06103 to 251-06373	27	Window Hardtop, RHD.
85 AA 35 to 85 AA 39	n/a	261-01091 to 261-01095	4	Station Wagon RHD.
85 AA 40 and 85 AA 41	n/a	n/a	2	Station Wagon RHD; for GCHQ. Chassis numbers not on register.
85 AA 42 to 85 AA 49	WV3534	251-06532 to 251-06686	8	Mountain Desert & Jungle Rescue RHD.
85 AA 50 to 85 AA 53	WV3417	251-07001 to 251-07038	4	Crash Rescue Ambulance RHD.
86 AA 50 and 86 AA 51	n/a	n/a	2	Station Wagon RHD; for GCHQ. Chassis numbers not on register.
86 AA 54 to 86 AA 59	WV4179	251-08246 to 251-08301	7	24v RHD, recorded as 7/65.
87 AA 15 to 87 AA 17	WV4121	251-07828 to 251-07932	3	Window Hardtop, RHD. Register says "Car, 10cwt, 4x4, 109 inch WB, Land Rover", but coding is for Station Wagon (16A/2710 and 1155-0764). Chassis prefix suggests Window Hardtop rather than Station Wagon.
87 AA 19 to 87 AA 33	WV4052 R1222	251-08403 to 251-08552	15	Window Hardtop, RHD.
87 AA 34 to 87 AA 43	WV4052	276-04454 to 276-04603	10	Window Hardtop, Diesel RHD.
87 AA 44	WV3653	251-08659	1	Crash Rescue Ambulance RHD; Body: Marshalls.
87 AA 45 to 87 AA 87	WV6652	251-11721 to 251-11805	43	Crash Rescue Ambulance RHD, recorded as 1/68.
90 AA 28 to 90 AA 35	WV4900	251-10100 to 251-10602	8	GS RHD.
90 AA 60 to 90 AA 69	WV4052	276-05753 to 276-05763	10	GS Hardtop Diesel RHD.
90 AA 79 to 90 AA 82	WV5096	251-11086 to 251-11089	4	GS Hardtop RHD.
90 AA 83 and 90 AA 84	WV5096	254-18119 and 254-18118	2	GS Hardtop LHD, recorded as 1/67.
91 AA 06 to 91 AA 17	WV5108	251-11820 to 251-11859	12	24v 90A RHD, recorded as 1/67.
91 AA 18 to 91 AA 26	WV5409	251-12052 to 251-12071	9	Airfield Crash Recue Truck RHD, recorded as 7/67.
91 AA 67 to 91 AA 75	KM/G/491	251-13024 to 251-13037	9	Airfield Crash Recue Truck RHD.

RAF

(b) Mark 9 (109-inch) (Continued)

Serials	Contract	Chassis Nos	Total	Remarks
91 AA 76 to 91 AA 99	WV6824	251-12332 to 251-12371	24	GS Hardtop RHD.
92 AA 00 and 92 AA 01	WV6824	254-20085 and 254-20084	2	GS Hardtop LHD.
92 AA 02	WV6824	251-12384	1	GS RHD; used to tow hearse trailer and based at RAF Uxbridge.
27 AG 37 to 27 AG 50	WV6723	251-12410C to 251-12422C	14	Truck Airfield Crash (Tactical) RHD.
30 AG 15	WV6723	251-12416C	1	Truck Airfield Crash (Tactical) RHD.
			Total 357	

ROYAL NAVY The lack of official records means it is possible only to give some sample RN serial numbers.

(b) Mark 9 (109-inch)

Serials	Contract	Chassis Nos	Total	Remarks
38 RN 04 to 38 RN 11	n/a	n/a	8	GS RHD.
36 RN 41 to 36 RN 52	n/a	n/a	12	GS RHD.
53 RN 88 to 53 RN 97	n/a	n/a	10	Ambulance RHD.
53 RN 20 to 53 RN 34	n/a	n/a	15	GS RHD.
52 RN 24 to 52 RN 31	n/a	n/a	8	Station Wagon RHD.
51 RN 47 to 52 RN 60	n/a	n/a	14	Station Wagon RHD.

Note: *Other Lomas-bodied ambulances included 00 RN 22 and possibly 00 RN 24 and 05 RN 03.*

Despatch records at BMIHT, Heritage Motor Centre, Gaydon reveal the following:

Serials	Contract	Chassis Nos	Total	Remarks
RN Serials	n/a	251-01412 to 251-01436	15	Cargo; delivered June 1962.
RN Serials	n/a	251-02205	1	Cargo; delivered December 1962.
RN Serials	n/a	251-02237 to 251-02339	21	Fire Tender or Rescue Van; delivered January 1963.
RN Serials	n/a	251-02466	1	Cargo; delivered March 1963.
RN Serials	n/a	251-02513	1	Cargo; delivered March 1963.
RN Serials	n/a	251-03037 to 251-03120	25	Cargo; delivered October 1963.
RN Serials	n/a	251-03202	1	Cargo; delivered December 1963.
RN Serials	n/a	251-05176 to 251-05328	20	Cargo; delivered August 1964.
RN Serials	n/a	251-05353 and 251-05380	2	Fire Tender or Rescue Van; delivered September 1964.
RN Serials	n/a	251-06024 to 251-06087	8	Cargo; delivered December 1964.
RN Serials	n/a	251-07952 to 251-08224	23	Cargo; delivered September 1965.
RN Serials	n/a	251-09164 and 251-09165	2	Cargo; delivered September 1965.
RN Serials	n/a	251-11007 to 251-11051	15	Cargo; delivered October 1966.
RN Serials	n/a	251-11988 to 251-12012	13	Cargo; delivered January 1967.
			Total 148	

ASSET CODES

Rover 8

1150-0759	Car, Utility, ¼ ton, 4x4, Rover 8
1620-0759	Truck, General Service, ¼ ton, 4x4, Rover 8
1620-5759	Truck, General Service, ¼ ton, 4x4, LHD, Rover 8
1621-0759	Truck, CL, ¼ ton, 4x4, Rover 8
1622-0759	Truck, General Service, mineplated, ¼ ton, 4x4, Rover 8
1625-0759	Truck, General Service, FFR, ¼ ton, 4x4, Rover 8 FV18021B
1625-5759	Truck, General Service, FFR, ¼ ton, 4x4, LHD, Rover 8
1627-0759	Truck, General Service, mineplated, ¼ ton, 4x4, FFR, Rover 8

Rover 8/1

No asset codes known.

Rover 8/2

1150-0761	Car, Utility, ¼ ton, 4x4, Rover 8/2
1150-3761	Car, Utility, ¼ ton, 4x4, tropical, Rover 8/2
1150-5761	Car, Utility, ¼ ton, 4x4, LHD, Rover 8/2
1620-0762	Truck, General Service, ¼ ton, 4x4, Rover 8/2
	Note: This is presumably a mis-coding for 1620-0761.
1625-0762	Truck, General Service, FFR, ¼ ton, 4x4, Rover 8/2 FV18021B

Rover 9

1040-0762	Ambulance, 2/4 stretcher, 4x4, Rover 9
1040-5762	Ambulance, 2/4 stretcher, 4x4, LHD, Rover 9
1041-0762	Ambulance, 2/1 stretcher, 4x4, Rover 9 FV18005
1146-0762	Car, Utility, Large, 4x4, Rover 9
1155-0762	Car, Utility, ¾ ton, 4x4, Rover 9
1155-1762	Car, Utility, ¾ ton, 4x4, w/winch, Rover 9
1155-3762	Car, Utility, ¾ ton, 4x4, Tropical, Rover 9
1155-5762	Car, Utility, ¾ ton, 4x4, LHD, Rover 9
1690-0762	Truck, Firefighting, ¾ ton, 4x4, Rover 9
1690-5762	Truck, Firefighting, ¾ ton, 4x4, LHD, Rover 9
1700-0762	Truck, Firefighting, Airfield Crash Rescue, ¾ ton, 4x4, Rover 9
1710-0762	Truck, General Service, ¾ ton, 4x4, Rover 9
1710-5762	Truck, General Service, ¾ ton, 4x4, LHD, Rover 9
1711-1762	Truck, Utility, CL, ¾ ton, 4x4, Plain Hard Top, Rover 9
1715-0762	Truck, GS, mineplated, ¾ ton, 4x4, Rover 9
1718-0762	Truck, General Service, Fitted For FACE, ¾ ton, 4x4, Rover 9
1720-0762	Truck, General Service, FFR, ¾ ton, 4x4, Rover 9
1720-5762	Truck, General Service, FFR, ¾ ton, 4x4, LHD, Rover 9
1722-0762	Truck, Utility, FFR, ¾ ton, 4x4, (Mineplated), Rover 9
2609-1762	Van, ¾ ton, 4x4, Rover 9
2614-0762	Van, DF Equipment, ¾ ton, 4x4, Rover 9
2616-0762	Van, GS, FFR, ¾ ton, 4x4, Rover 9
3620-5762	Printing Machine, Blueprint, Truck Mounted, ¾ ton, 4x4, LHD, Rover 9
3630-0762	Truck, Sensitivity Test, No 2 Mk 1, SAGW, ¾ ton, 4x4, Rover 9

Rover 9/1

1710-0763	Truck, General Service, ¾ ton, 4x4, Rover 9/1
1720-0763	Truck, General Service, FFR, ¾ ton, 4x4, Rover 9/1

Rover 9/2

1155-0764	Car, Utility, ¾ ton, 4x4, Rover 9/2
1155-5764	Car, Utility, ¾ ton, 4x4, LHD, Rover 9/2
1155-8764	Car, Utility, ¾ ton, 4x4, Tropical, LHD, Rover 9/2
1160-0764	Car, Utility, FFR, ¾ ton, 4x4, Rover 9/2

Rover 109 IIA (not including Forward Control)

1038-0769	Ambulance, 2 stretcher, FFR, 24v, Special Pilot Rescue, Rover 109 Series IIA (P)
1041-0769	Ambulance, 2/1 stretcher, 4x4, Rover 9 FV18005
1155-0769	Car, Utility, ¾ ton, 4x4, Rover 109 Series IIA (P)
1155-4769	Car, Utility, ¾ ton, 4x4, 12 seater, w trailer atts, Rover 109 S IIA
1155-9769	Car, Utility, ¾ ton, 4x4, 12 seater, w trailer atts, LHD, Rover 109 S IIA
1705-0769	Truck, GS, Plain Hard Top, 4x4, 24v 90A? Rover ??
1705-6769	Truck, Utility, ¾ ton, 4x4, LHD, Hard Top, Rover 11
1706-4769	Truck, Utility, ¾ ton, 4x4, 24v 90A rectified, Rover 11
1710-0769	Truck, Utility, ¾ ton, 4x4, Land Rover 109 Series IIA FV18061
1710-1769	Truck, Utility, ¾ ton, 4x4, Hard Top, Land Rover 109 Series IIA (Petrol)
1710-2769	Truck, Utility, ¾ ton, 4x4, 24v 40A rectified, Rover 109 Ser IIA
1710-3769	Truck, Utility, ¾ ton, 4x4, Stretcher Carrier, Land Rover 109 Series IIA
1710-4769	Truck, Utility, ¾ ton, 4x4, 24v 90A rectified, Rover 109 Ser IIA
1710-6769	Truck, Utility, ¾ ton, 4x4, Hard Top, LHD, Land Rover 109 Series IIA (Petrol)
1711-1769	Truck, CL, ¾ ton, 4x4, Hard Top, Rover 109 Series IIA
1711-2769	Truck, Utility, CL, ¾ ton, 4x4, Hard Top w/windows, Rover Series IIA
1711-4769	Truck, Utility, CL, ¾ ton, 4x4, Rover Series IIA
1720-0769	Truck, General Service, FFR, ¾ ton, 4x4, Hard Top, 24v AC rectified w radio eqt, Rover 109in
1745-0769	Truck, Pilot Rescue, ¾ ton, 4x4, Rover 109 Series IIA (P)

TECHNICAL SPECIFICATIONS, ROVER 8 AND ROVER 9 MODELS

ENGINE (PETROL):

2286cc (90.47mm x 88.9mm) four-cylinder with overhead valves and single Solex 40PA carburettor. 7.0:1 compression ratio. 77bhp at 4250rpm and 124 lb ft at 2500rpm.

ENGINE (DIESEL):

2286cc (90.47mm x 88.9mm) four-cylinder with overhead valves and indirect injection. 23:1 compression ratio. 56.2bhp at 4000rpm and 101 lb ft at 1800rpm.

TRANSMISSION:

Selectable four-wheel drive.
Four-speed main gearbox; ratios 3.60:1, 2.22:1, 1.50:1, 1.00:1, reverse 3.02:1. Synchromesh on third and fourth gears only.
Two-speed transfer gearbox; ratios 1.148:1 (High) and 2.888:1 (Low).
Axle ratio: 4.7:1

SUSPENSION, STEERING AND BRAKES:

Semi-elliptic leaf springs all round.
Recirculating-ball steering with 15:1 ratio; later 15.6:1 ratio.
Drum brakes on all four wheels; 10in x 1.5in on 88-inch Rover 8s and 11in x 2.25in on 109-inch Rover 9s; separate drum-type transmission parking brake.

ELECTRICAL SYSTEM:

12-volt with dynamo and positive earth; FFR models with 24-volt negative-earth system and 90-amp generator.

UNLADEN WEIGHT:

88in (minimum): 2900 lb (1315kg) with petrol engine (civilian model figures)
109in (minimum): 3294 lb (1494kg) with petrol engine (civilian model figures)

DIMENSIONS:

88-inch Rover 8:

Overall length:	142.4in (3617mm)
Wheelbase:	88in (2235mm)
Overall width:	64in (1626mm)
Unladen height:	77.5in (1968mm) maximum
Track:	51.5in (1308mm)

109-inch Rover 9

Overall length:	175in (4445mm)
Wheelbase:	109in (2769mm)
Overall width:	64in (1626mm)
Unladen height:	81in (2057mm) maximum
Track:	51.5in (1308mm)

PERFORMANCE

88in Rover 8 with 2.25-litre petrol engine:

0-50mph:	21secs
Maximum:	67mph approx (108km/h)
Fuel consumption:	26 mpg approx

88in Rover 8 with diesel engine:

0-50mph:	Figures not available
Maximum:	52mph approx (84km/h)
Fuel consumption:	30 mpg approx

109in Rover 9 with 2.25-litre petrol engine:

0-50mph:	29secs
Maximum:	58mph approx (93.3km/h)
Fuel consumption:	19 mpg approx

*This was the standard
installation of radios for both
Rover 8 and Rover 9 models*

LAND ROVER CHASSIS CODES

All Land Rovers in this period had a three-digit identifying prefix in the chassis code, which indicated the model type, steering position and other factors. Neither the model-year nor the calendar-year of manufacture was indicated. The ones relevant to the Rover 8 and Rover 9 models are shown below. The three-figure prefix was followed by a five-figure serial number that began at 00001 for each separate sequence, and this in turn was followed by a suffix letter. The suffix letter (between A and C on Rover 8 and Rover 9 models) indicated major changes in the vehicle's specification that affected servicing.

Note that the Land Rover model-year began in September and continued until the end of the following July, leaving August clear for the works' annual holiday and for preparing the assembly lines to take new models. A Land Rover built in the 1963 model-year could therefore have been built at any time between September 1962 and July 1963.

241	RHD 88in
244	LHD 88in
251	RHD 109in
254	LHD 109in
261	RHD 109in Station Wagon
264	LHD 109in Station Wagon
271	RHD 88in diesel
300	RHD 109in Forward Control, six-cylinder
310	RHD 109in APGP
315	RHD 88in Station Wagon

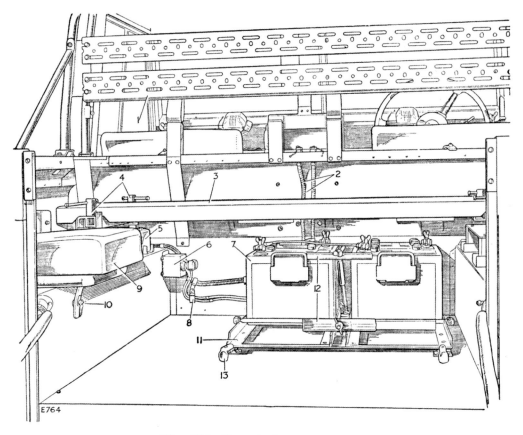

Fig. 106. Rear body compartment

1	Slotted angle framework.	8	Special cable clips.
2	Aerial co-axials.	9	Operator's seat.
3	Table top.	10	Seat locating stud.
4	Screw clamp for table top.	11	Radio battery carrier.
5	Runner mounting block	12	Clamp plates for batteries.
6	Insulated terminals.	13	Fastener for battery cover.
7	Radio batteries.		

ARMY SERIAL NUMBERS

The serial numbers allocated by the Army gave a clue to the date of the vehicle, although those issued by the RAF and Royal Navy did not. In this period, serial letters indicated the financial year in which the vehicle was purchased (which is not necessarily the same as the calendar year in which it was delivered). Those relevant to the Mark 8 and Mark 9 models are shown below.

As before, serial sequences began at 0001 (e.g. 00 DM 01) and ran to 9999 (e.g. 99 DM 99). There was not necessarily any correlation between chassis number order and military serial number within batches.

DM	1961-1962	EK	1962-1963	EL	1963-1964
EM	1963-1964	EN	1964-1965	EP	1964-1965
ER	1965-1966	ES	1965-1966	ET	1966-1967

CHAPTER 6:

THE ROVER 10 (SERIES IIA 88-INCH) AND ROVER 11 (SERIES IIA 109-INCH)

As the new Rover 1 or Lightweight took over the rôles previously assigned to the short-wheelbase Land Rovers in the later 1960s, fewer and fewer civilian-pattern 88-inch models were ordered. 35 ES 71 was one of these late Rover Mk 10 deliveries. (GF)

From the same batch was 35 ES 64, seen here towing a standard Sankey trailer. This time, the spare wheel is carried on the bonnet to give more cargo space in the body. Note the black panel on the wing, where information relevant to shipping weights would be chalked. The vehicle wears the markings of 5 (Airportable) Ordnance Field Park, RAOC and was seen at Aldershot in 1970. (RES)

Trends elsewhere in the motor industry persuaded Rover to build all its vehicles with a negative-earth electrical system from the mid-1960s, and on Land Rovers the change took place in May 1967. The revised models were still Series IIA types, and were initially identified by the chassis suffix D. These vehicles also had twin wipers operated by a single motor, a black instrument panel with a revised layout, and a key-operated starter. On the four-cylinder petrol engines that were used in MoD vehicles, a Zenith carburettor replaced the earlier Solex type. There were also some other and less significant changes.

From the military point of view, the most important of these changes was to the negative-earth electrical system (24-volt vehicles already had a negative earth) because few if any of the electrical ancillaries on the vehicle could be used on an earlier vehicle and vice versa. The revised vehicles were given new Asset Codes, and the short-wheelbase models were also reclassified as Rover 10 while the long-wheelbase types became Rover 11.

This was also the period when the new Lightweight (see Chapter 8) largely supplanted the older 88-inch models based on the civilian vehicle. The figures in the Appendix show that in the 1966-1967 Financial Year, no 88-inch vehicles were purchased for the Army as it awaited the arrival of the Lightweight. Although deliveries of conventional 88-inch Land Rovers did not cease altogether, many of those that entered military service had a more or less standard civilian specification (which made them cheaper to buy than the Lightweight) and were classified as CL types.

A further visible change in the specification of all Land Rovers occurred in April 1969. New traffic regulations in Europe – especially in Germany and the Low Countries where many of the British Army vehicles served – required headlamps to be a minimum distance from the sides of the vehicle. To meet this, the Land Rover's headlamps were relocated to a recessed position in each front wing; a larger, cross-shaped grille was fitted and the front number plate moved from the wing to the centre of the bumper on a support plate. The vehicles with this modification commenced with chassis suffix G.

More fundamental changes in the UK's defence posture affected military purchases of Land Rovers. Orders continued at reasonably high levels although much lower than at their peak as the UK's economic performance was

06 ET 55 is a Rover Mk 11, and is here towing a Sankey trailer. Earlier Mk 11 deliveries still had headlights in the grille panel, as here. (RES)

06 ET 65 was one of the rare Mk 11s equipped with a winch. The chalk plate is here behind the door rather than on the front wing. It was part of a REME trials unit attached to 3 Division which later became 10 Field Workshop, REME. (RES)

From 1969, the headlights were moved to the wing fronts, as seen on 32 FK 03, a later Rover Mk 11 109-inch GS vehicle. (Land Rover)

weak and defence cuts followed. The Labour government under Harold Wilson from 1964 had a fundamentally different perspective on the world and the UK from the previous Conservative administration, and a Defence Review followed under Minister of Defence Dennis Healey. The review reported to Parliament in 1966 but was followed with further policy documents in 1967 and 1968, largely as a result of the financial crisis that had forced a devaluation of Sterling (Wilson nevertheless famously insisted that "It does not mean that the pound . . .in your pocket . . . has been devalued." All this led to a requirement for the MoD to find further cost savings.

The review was to achieve substantial savings through the

Unusually, 08 ET 29 was delivered as a hardtop model. The jerrycan holder and associated relocation of the lights on the front bumper were a unit modification. It was photographed when serving with the Movement Control Detachment of 50 Movement Control Squadron, RCT in June 1971. (RES)

It is a common mistake to assume that every leaf-sprung Land Rover with headlights in the wing fronts is a Series 3; in fact, the revised headlights appeared on the later Mk 11s. This train-load was pictured on delivery to an Army vehicle depot when fresh from the manufacturer. (Unknown source)

Though it is hard to see on this black-and-white picture, the front wings of this Mk 11 attached to HQ Bomb Disposal Unit, RE and based at Rochester would have been painted bright red. (RE Smith Collection)

The extra-long tilt of this late Rover Mk 11 attached to the Royal Artillery indicates that is a Rapier Fire Unit Tractor vehicle. The extra long tilt covered the missile boxes which protruded from the rear of the vehicle.(GF)

There were Mk 11 Station Wagons, too, often seen with a rear tent extension as here. This one was in use with UK (SP) Postal and Courier Communications Unit, RE at Aldershot in June 1974.(GF)

cancellation of major equipment orders, including cancellation of further aircraft carrier construction, domestic aircraft programmes and the reorganisation and reduction by almost half of the Territorial Army. In order to reduce overseas expenditure and overstretch, decisions were also taken to reduce the UK's global presence and concentrate the deployment of the military in Europe. These changes led to reductions in British forces deployed in Germany, Cyprus and Malta, withdrawal from Aden, and accelerated withdrawal from Singapore and Malaysia and the Persian Gulf.

Army Rover 10 and Rover 11 deliveries

Army purchases had averaged just over 5000 Land Rovers per year between the 1961-1962 Financial Year and that for

Examples of the ACRT were still entering service in this period, 47 FG 09 being delivered for use on Army airfields. Some examples had the metal roof canopy pictured here, and it may be that the later vehicles (built by Merryweather) all did. (PH)

1965-1966. This fell quite dramatically to just over 1800 in the period between the 1966-1967 and 1971-1972 Financial Years. Nonetheless the usefulness of the Land Rover to UK forces and the number of special types purchased began to increase, as did the number of adaptations carried out in service by REME and unit workshops. The Army appear to have made no diesel purchases.

Commercial (CL) variants

No conventional 88-inch vehicles were purchased in 1966-1967 in anticipation of the Lightweight arriving late in 1968,

Marshall's ambulances continued to arrive in quantity on the Rover Mk 11 chassis. 57 FG 72 is fairly typical of the Army deliveries, although the bar on the front bumper is unusual. (GF))

The fuel filler behind the door gives away that 25 FJ 79 is a CL-specification vehicle; military-specification vehicles still had under-seat fillers for their twin tanks. This vehicle is in the markings of King's Troop, Royal Horse Artillery. (GF)

Some Rover Mk 11s were converted to light recovery vehicles by user units. This one was 36 ES 65. It was photographed during a 24 Airportable Brigade amphibious landing exercise on Westward Ho beach in 1970 and was with 15 Infantry Workshop (Airportable), REME. (RES)

but it soon became clear that there was still a rôle for the conventional 88-inch. There was a requirement that could be met by non-militarised Land Rovers and both the 88-inch and 109-inch were bought in CL form. These were more or less standard civilian-specification models, and their most obvious recognition feature was that they lacked the pusher bumpers front and rear and the drop-shackle suspension of the military-specification Land Rover. No oil cooler was fitted, and the standard four-blade engine fan was used.

Initially there were small purchases, with the first contract being for 15 LHD 88-inch CLs for the Joint Service Liaison Organisation (JSLO) in Hanover in BAOR. The JSLO acted as an intermediary between the UK Forces operating in BAOR and the civil powers, and so was responsible for customs clearance by British troops entering and leaving West Germany and Berlin. It also dealt with matters such as land for training, barracks and civilian labour matters and with the British Frontier Service (BFS) was responsible for border monitoring duties in West Germany between 1946 and 1991. This unit received the 15 88-inch CLs (53 FH 35 to 53 FH 49) in March 1970. A second batch of ten RHD 88-inch CLs (25 FJ 61 to 25 FJ 70) followed in 1970 and these mostly equipped experimental establishments of the Procurement Executive, the others initially going into storage.

A batch of eleven 109-inch vehicles (25 FJ 73 to 25 FJ 83) which was delivered in spring 1970 was issued to the Army School of Transport, King's Troop RHA , Royal School of Artillery, and to experimental establishments of the Procurement Executive. When the Series III arrived, these types went on to be purchased in much greater numbers and equipped many TA units based in the UK as well as units carrying out administrative transport supporting various garrisons in both the UK and BAOR.

Drone Recovery Vehicles

The UK adopted the Canadair CL-89 drone as an unmanned surveillance drone and it became "Midge" in UK service. This required a number of specialist vehicles including a Drone Recovery Vehicle based on the long-wheelbase Rover 11.

Although the Midge drone looked like a missile, it was in practice more like an aircraft and was launched from a zero-length launcher mounted on a truck. At its rear were four large surfaces for directing the drone, commanded by

The tall box body marks out 73 FG 02 as one of the rare drone recovery vehicles on Rover Mk 11 chassis. These were also used by Midge Drone Sections of Royal Artillery Observation Post Batteries. (GF)

for this purpose a Land Rover was kitted out for recovery of the drone. It had a pantechnicon body, and the rear opening was covered with canvas curtains rather than having a door. Inside on the left was a structure for supporting the inverted drone while the cameras and sensors were removed. This structure slid out and the rear end rested on the ground to allow the drone to be loaded. Once loaded, the drone stretched from the rear curtain to the front screen.

These vehicles were converted by Marshall's of Cambridge. Two RHD prototypes were built (27 ES 40 and 27 ES 41) and once testing was complete these were retained at Larkhill by 22 Locating Battery. A further 21 production examples were ordered (69 FG 34 to 69 FG 50 and 73 FG 01 to 73 FG 04) but some (around 7) were cancelled and remained as GS vehicles. Three were later created by conversion (49 FH 07, 49 FH 34 and 49 FH 53). At least one Drone Recovery was converted to a Drone Photographic Processing Interpretation Facility (PPIF) (see below). This means that the total number of vehicles produced was around 18.

Each Drone Troop had three Drone Recovery vehicles. From July 1969, each of the three locating batteries of 94 Locating Regiment, Royal Artillery had a Drone Troop, a Meteorological Troop and a Sound Ranging Troop. This meant that 94 Locating Battery needed 9 Drone Recovery Vehicles, while 22 Locating Battery in the UK had 4, giving a total of 13. The remainder were kept as War Reserve.

stabilisers mounted in the nose-cone. A booster rocket powered the drone off the launch rail and was quickly jettisoned in favour of a small turbojet used for the remainder of the flight. Landing was achieved with a parachute and two landing bags. There was a setting on the programmer which cut the engine, deployed the parachute and inflated the airbags. The parachute deployed from the bottom and the airbags from the top, which meant that the drone did a back-flip as it landed, in order to protect the cameras and sensors which were at the bottom.

Each drone was fitted with a small bleeper, which was powered by a battery which was triggered once the drone had landed. It was vital to recover the camera and sensors, and

Drone Photographic Processing Interpretation Facility (PPIF)

The Midge drone could carry three sensors, all of which produced conventional photographic film – two types of camera and an infra-red line scanner. There was an obvious requirement to process this film and to interpret it as quickly

The special bodywork and trailer of 25 FG 73 mark it out as a specialist Photographic Interpretation Facility (PPIF) unit. These were attached to the Midge Drone Sections of Royal Artillery Observation Post Batteries to process the film from the drones. (TMB)

as possible to pass on intelligence to senior commanders. The PPIF was designed to allow processing of photographic film and also provided space for analysis of the negatives. It was all housed inside a box body of fairly large proportions for the rear of a 109-inch vehicle! One vehicle based in the UK supported 22 Locating Battery Royal Artillery (RA) and supported the strategic reserve of 3 Division, while similar vehicles were used in BAOR by 94 Locating Regiment RA. Midge was replaced by Phoenix in the late 1980s and these PPIFs were no longer necessary as Phoenix captured digital imagery and transmitted it electronically to a ground-based receiving station.

Electronic Warfare Vehicles

Electronic Warfare (EW) was coming of age and the Army deployed a number of Direction Finding and Listening posts based on 109-inch chassis in BAOR as well as training and support units in the UK. These were the antecedents of the famous One-Tonne "Vampire" which is discussed in Chapter 12. The base 109s were purchased as 24-volt FFR versions but had a full hardtop and were variously designated as "Van, DF Equipment, ¾ ton, 4x4", "Van, GS, FFR, ¾ ton, 4x4" and "Van, GS, FFR, EW/Y, ¾ ton, 4x4". The exact meaning of that last designation is not clear; while EW clearly means Electronic Warfare, the Y may or may not refer to the Intercept Service.

This period of electronic warfare remains shrouded in mystery because aspects of it are still covered by the Official Secrets Act so that very little has been published. The first EW Land Rover conversion was of a standard Rover 9 FFR in 1966 which was used by 30 Signal Regiment – presumably for trials and training – from October 1966. An initial purchase was then made of three Station Wagons based on the Rover 9 chassis (03 ET 12 to 03 ET 14) fitted out as 24-volt FFR that were converted to their EW rôle by Park Royal Vehicles. They were then re-designated "Van, DF Equipment, ¾ ton, 4x4" and were issued to 224 Signal Squadron, Royal Corps of Signals at Garat's Hay in Leicestershire in early 1967. From photographs, it appears these vehicles were fitted with a rectangular aerial with round corners, about 3 feet across, mounted on a mast in the centre of the roof.

This first batch was followed by a much larger purchase of 30 FFR 109-inch vehicles fitted with hardtops that were again converted for their special rôle by Park Royal Vehicles. There were 25 LHD examples (48 FG 62 to 48 FG 86) and five with RHD (48 FG 87 to 48 FG 91). The LHD vehicles were then sent to 224 Signal Squadron for equipment to be fitted, and were issued to 225 Signal Squadron. This was based at Langenhangen near the Inner German Border (IGB), and had a detachment at Gatow inside West Berlin from around May 1970. The RHD vehicles also went to 224 Signal Squadron, but then were issued to 30 Signal Regiment at Blandford Forum which undertook Signals Intelligence

work in other parts of the world.

A further batch of 14 FFR hardtops, which the Army referred to as "Vans", was purchased the following year. Again the LHD types predominated, there being eight of them (48 FH 15 to 48 FH 22) as against six RHD types (48 FH 09 to 48 FH 14). The RHD examples were issued to 30 Signal Regiment but the LHD examples were surplus to requirements in BAOR in 1970 and three went to Hong Kong, possibly for EW duties with the Gurkha Signals. Two more went to the Royal School of Artillery (RSA). The following year, two more FFR Vans were purchased which also were issued to RSA.

SAS Pink Panthers

As described in Chapter 2, several Mk 5 88-inch Land Rovers were converted for SAS use. By the 1960s the SAS found the 109-inch offered the additional capacity it craved and began converting vehicles in its own workshops to replace the earlier short-wheelbase models. Although these vehicles could carry more than their predecessors, the engine was severely underpowered for the loads of weapons, ammuni-

The Special Air Service gradually developed their own specification for a long-range patrol vehicle on the basis of existing vehicles. This is one – although it is impossible to be certain whether this was a Rover Mk11 or a Rover Mk9. (A former soldier)

Not every "Pink Panther" was actually pink: the vehicles were delivered in the standard Bronze Green, and when that colour suited the theatre of operations, that was the colour they retained. 10 FG 89 was pictured when new. Note the sand tyres on 15-inch wheels. (PW)

The Swingfire missile system was installed on this vehicle, 05 ET 19. The installation is not known to have entered production for the UK armed forces. (RES)

tion, water, fuel and supplies that could be placed on the chassis.

There is some evidence to show that FVRDE trialled the APGP (see Chapter 5) in the SAS rôle in spring 1964 as photographs survive showing it fitted with 7.62mm General Purpose Machine Guns (GPMG) mounted front and rear. However, by 1965, one of the unit-converted 109-inch vehicles was in the hands of FVRDE showing many of the typical modifications – front-mounted spare wheel, GPMG mounted front and rear, jerry can stowage on the sides, behind the cargo bulkhead and on the front bumpers, ammunition stowage around the edges of cargo floor, and sand channels on the sides.

A prototype (18 DM 93) was produced by January 1967, with modifications selected from those that had been tried by the SAS and subsequently improved by FVRDE's engineers. By this stage, the vehicle had a front-mounted spare wheel, sand tyres, smoke dischargers front and rear, a 7.62mm GPMG on a revised mount on the scuttle and another on a pedestal in the rear load bed. It also had a revised and higher position for the front passenger, jerry cans on either side of the driver and passenger, a theodolite tripod on the passenger's side front wing, gun holsters on the front wings, sand channels either side of the cargo bay, a cargo bag on the rear supported by a drop down flap, large auxiliary fuel tanks either side of the rear-facing crew member in the load area, and much ammunition and weapons stowage alongside.

Marshall's of Cambridge were awarded the production contract (WV7293) for the modifications to 72 vehicles (10 FG 30 to 11 FG 01) ordered under Land Rover contract WV7318. The first example from the production batch was

receipted by 22 SAS on 14 February 1969 and the vehicles saw service in many parts of the world (including the Persian Gulf, BAOR and Northern Ireland) although all were sold by 1986. Many were used for desert work, where the SAS had found that dull pink paint was an effective camouflage, and as a result the vehicles generally were known by the nickname of Pink Panther, a name taken from the series of comedy films made in the 1960s and starring Peter Sellers as Inspector Jacques Clouseau. Several vehicles nevertheless remained green throughout their service lives.

Truck, Aircraft Crash Rescue (TACR)

The TACR was intended as the replacement for the ACRT in the late 1960s, although in practice the two types overlapped in service and often served alongside one another. It was introduced as the TACR type; subsequently a replacement based on the Range Rover was introduced as the TACR-2 and it was re-named the TACR-1. Although they were primarily RAF vehicles, in practice the TACRs saw service with the Army and Royal Navy as well as the RAF.

The TACR was intended as a light, fast fire tender which could get to a crashed aircraft quickly in order to evacuate the crew while heavier (and slower) fire appliances arrived on scene. It was also used for lesser incidents such as overheating brakes or aircraft landing with damaged undercarriage.

There were 22 vehicles registered as 28 AG 00 to 28 AG 16, 03 FK 04 to 03 FK 05, and 05 FK 86 to 05 FK 88. Their bodies were purpose-built by HCB-Angus Ltd on a Land Rover One Ton chassis, a high-payload development of the Rover 11's commercial equivalent. This was normally supplied with a six-cylinder petrol engine, but the TACRs were specially fitted with the 2¼-litre four-cylinder petrol engine to ensure maximum commonality with other Land Rovers then in British military service. They also had military-pattern fuel tanks under the seatbox.

Land Rover supplied them as truck cabs on a chassis fitted with military-pattern front bumper and rear cross-member, plus an RAF-pattern brush bar. HCB-Angus added a roof hatch to the cab and constructed a special back body. On a tray in the centre of the body was a 100-gallon water tank, which in later years was used to carry foam. There was a 150psi fire pump with side outlets, and the vehicle carried 100-foot hoses with a 1.25-inch bore.

Around the tray for the first-aid tank was a structure containing open side hoppers for the equipment, and rear-facing lockers with roller shutters. Between these lockers was a rearward-facing crew seat. There was a ladder-rack on the driver's side, and most TACR-1s carried a blue beacon on a stalk, a nine-inch Francis searchlight and a Plessey floodlight mounted on a telescopic mast which could raise it high above the scene of an incident. The vehicle was designed to accommodate a crew of three (two in the cab with the third crew member on the rearwards-facing seat), plus tools and loose equipment.

The first batch of 17 chassis for the RAF was ordered in the 1969-1970 Financial Year under contract WV8932; the bodies and firefighting equipment were supplied by HCB-Angus under contract K/69c/34. Orders for 38 more followed.

The Army version was slightly different and was used at the two UK AAC bases. The AAC were initially issued with five TACRs from late 1972, two at Netheravon (03 FK 04 and 03 FK 05) and three at Middle Wallop (05 FK 86 to 05 FK 88). These were painted the standard RAF red for fire appliances.

Further examples of the type were supplied on Series III chassis, including some for the Navy.

WOMBAT portees

WOMBAT L6 (Weapon of Magnesium Battalion Anti-tank) was a development of the BAT L1 (see Chapter 2). Both BAT L1 and MOBAT L4 were designed to be towed – MOBAT was often seen behind Champs – but in order to reduce weight further WOMBAT L6 was designed with only two small trolley wheels to aid manhandling. It was of 120mm calibre and was the largest recoilless rifle to be developed. To tackle tanks, it fired a High Explosive Squash Head (HESH) round and it was accurate to about one kilometre. This relatively short range, the huge back blast which kicked up dust and stones, and the loud report led soldiers to christen it "The VC Gun" for obvious reasons. Aiming the weapon was achieved via a spotting rifle ballistically matched to the L6 main armament and mounted co-axially.

WOMBAT L6 began to be replaced by the MILAN anti-

The early TACR crash rescue tenders were delivered on 109-inch One-Ton chassis, although they were classified as Rover Mk 11 types. This was the first one, which has now been beautifully preserved.
(Steve Shirley/RAF Fire Museum)

tank missile in the late 1970s although it remained in service with the Territorial Army for some time. Since it could not be towed, it was carried portee-style in both the 109-inch Land Rover and the FV432 armoured personnel carrier. Initially, Rover 9s were converted to the portee rôle from 1960 by adding ramps and a winch for pulling the weapon into the cargo compartment and the only known users were the Royal Marines. The ramps were stowed beneath the gun on the move. Stowage lockers were fitted either side of the cargo compartment and a total of six rounds were stored in tubes – three on each side. To enable the gun barrel to project over the bonnet, the windscreen was often folded and a rest for the gun barrel fitted above the scuttle with a clamp to secure it above the ammunition storage.

In 1971-1972 a contract was placed for 24 portees that were built as such. These were the last Rover 11s built and were never enough to equip all the infantry battalions equipped with WOMBAT.

Although more modern anti-tank weapons were entering service, the Wombat was still in use and some Rover Mk 11s, including this late example, were modified as portees. (GF)

SUMMARY OF ROVER 10 AND 11 DELIVERIES, 1967-1971

Lists cover vehicles ordered under contracts, and do not include vehicles transferred in from other services or elsewhere. RAF vehicles allocated to NATO are not included.

Note that there were special procurement arrangements for the Berlin Brigade. Vehicle purchases were treated as part of the offsetting agreements for the Berlin Garrison with the Senät (the executive body that governed the city) and were charged to that body. They are therefore not associated with any MoD contract numbers, and none of the official documents so far discovered show a contract number of any kind.

There were several "master" contracts (e.g. WV4052, WV8765) from which individual vehicles were ordered by "warrant". These contracts were in effect open documents and allowed individual or small-quantity vehicle purchases without the formalities associated with the larger contracts. Warrant Numbers covered the authority to purchase a vehicle or vehicles; Item Numbers were added to the contracts to record these purchases.

ARMY

(a) Rover 10 (88-inch)

Serials	Contract	Chassis Nos	Total	Remarks
32 ES 57 to 36 ES 22	WV5053	241-29317D to 241-31986D	366	GS RHD.
22 FG 78	WV4052 R1501	315-00389D	1	Station Wagon RHD.
68 FG 83	WV4052 R1585	318-03925D	1	Station Wagon LHD; to Military Attaché, Cairo.
30 FH 77 to 30 FH 78	WV4052 R1674	315-00489F and 315-00490F	2	Station Wagon RHD.
48 FH 28	WV4052 R1713	315-00502F	1	Station Wagon RHD; to Services Adviser, Malaw.i
53 FH 35 to 53 FH 49	WV4052 R1720	244-37962G to 244-37979G	15	CL LHD.
60 FH 46	WV4052 R1711	318-05968G	1	Station Wagon LHD; to Military Attaché, Budapest.
60 FH 47	WV4052 R1711	315-00533G	1	RHD Station Wagon; to Military Attaché, Kathmandu.
60 FH 48	WV4052 R1711	318-05969G	1	LHD Station Wagon; to Military Attaché, Sofia.
60 FH 49	WV4052 R1711	315-00534G	1	RHD Station Wagon; to Military Attaché, Tokyo.
25 FI 61 to 25 FI 70	WV8765 R1830	241-38056G to 241-38055G	10	RHD GS (CL).
25 FJ 72	WV8765 R1831	318-06461G	1	RHD Station Wagon; to Military Attaché, Bucharest; later to Army.
32 FJ 69 to 32 FJ 70	WV8765 R1862	318-06840G and 318-06839G	2	LHD Station Wagon; 32 FJ 69 to Military Attaché, Helsinki; 32 FJ 70 to Military Attaché, Tel Aviv.
46 FJ 77 to 46 FJ 81	WV8765 R1903	315-00645G to 315-00644G	5	RHD Station Wagon.
41 FK 84 to 41 FK 91	WV8765 R2031	318-09140H to 318-09139H	8	LHD Station Wagon.
41 FK 92 to 42 FK 00	WV8765 R2031	315-00745H to 315-00753H	9	RHD Station Wagon; 41 FK 93 to Military Attaché, Muscat.
48 FK 70 to 48 FK 75	WV8765 R2049	241-41531H to 241-41540H	6	RHD GS (CL).
48 FK 76	WV8765 R2049	244-44938H	1	LHD GS (CL).
30 XC 01 to 30 XC 31	(See note)	n/a to 244-33077D	31	LHD GS; Berlin Brigade.
			Total 463	

ROYAL NAVY
These figures have been calculated from Land Rover despatch records, in the absence of Royal Navy records.

(a) Rover 10 (88-inch)

Serials	Contract	Chassis Nos	Total	Remarks
RN Serials	n/a	241-32272 to 241-32320	17	Cargo; delivered March 1968.
RN Serials	n/a	241-36184 to 241-36223	10	Cargo; delivered July 1969.
RN Serials	n/a	241-39801 to 241-39830	12	Cargo; delivered September 1970.
RN Serials	n/a	241-40937 to 241-40939	3	Cargo; delivered March 1971.
includes 74 RN 40	n/a	241-42168 to 241-42187	20	Cargo; delivered July 1971.
			Total 62	

Although 92 AA 95 is an earlier RAF ambulance with the head-lights on the grille panel, it is here wearing the later RAF livery that included high-visibility yellow stripes. (GF)

39 AM 85 was an RAF crash rescue ambulance, delivered with the later chassis specification that included headlamps on the wing fronts. The anti-roll bar added to these ambulances is clearly visible between the grille and bumper. (GF)

This 109 with a hardtop and "tropical" roof mounts a "hydraulic filtration system" and was photographed at a display in the 1970s. The Royal Navy had many unusual pieces of equipment mounted inside Land Rovers. (GF)

By this stage, most RAF Regiment vehicles carried IRR paint and standard camouflage in service. The example on the left is a 24-volt hardtop; note the "24v" sign painted on the rear panel. (GF)

RAF

(a) Rover 10 (88-inch)

Serials	Contract	Chassis Nos	Total	Remarks
94 AA 25 to 95 AA 16	WV7129	241-30191 to 241-30783	92	24v GS RHD.
95 AA 17 to 95 AA 19	n/a	n/a	3	GS LHD. (No chassis numbers on register.)
95 AA 32 to 95 AA 43	WV7129	241-30793 to 241-30876	12	24v GS RHD.
95 AA 62 to 96 AA 71	WV7657	241-32382 to 241-32737	110	GS RHD.
96 AA 72 to 96 AA 87	WV7657	244-32382 to 244-32737	16	GS LHD.
97 AA 38 to 98 AA 63	n/a	24132400 to 241-32657	126	GS RHD.
99 AA 16	WV4053 R1653	318-05056F	1	Station Wagon LHD; to Air Attaché Belgrade (later 31 BT 53).
41 AM 95 to 42 AM 66	WV9138	n/a to 241-40339	72	GS RHD.
42 AM 67 to 43 AM 02	WV9138	244-40783 to 244-41764	36	GS LHD.
43 AM 61	WV8765 R1969	318-07520G	1	Station Wagon LHD; to Air Attaché Ankara (later 30 BT 26).
			Total 469	

ARMY
(b) Mark 11 (109-inch)

Serials	Contract	Chassis Nos	Total	Remarks
27 ES 40 to 27 ES 41	WV4837	n/a	2	Drone Recovery RHD.
36 ES 23 to 38 ES 30	WV5054	251-12458D to 251-13795D	208	GS RHD.
38 ES 31 to 39 ES 05	WV5054	254-20515D to 254-22058B	75	GS LHD.
03 ET 24 to 03 ET 33	WV5542	251-12942D to 251-12927D	10	Field Ambulance RHD.
03 ET 34 to 03 ET 64	WV5542	254-21167D to 254-21178D	31	Field Ambulance LHD.
04 ET 80 to 08 ET 73	WV5392	251-12547D to 251-14213D	394	FFR RHD.
08 ET 74 to 09 ET 73	WV5392	254-20747D to 254-22339D	100	FFR LHD.
00 FG 10	WV4052 R1457	251-13136D	1	Station Wagon RHD.
00 FG 18 to 00 FG 51	WV7217	251-13600D to 251-13733D	34	GS RHD.
02 FG 43	WV4052 R1362	261-002161D	1	Station Wagon RHD.
10 FG 28 to 10 FG 29	WV4052 R1484	261-02256D and 261-02257D	2	Station Wagon RHD; to 55 Signal Squadron, RCS (V).
10 FG 30 to 11 FG 01	WV7318	251-14139D to 251-14161D	72	SAS RHD.
11 FG 02	WV4052 R1483	261-02264D	1	Station Wagon RHD; to BDLS (who he?) New Delh.i
22 FG 76	WV4052 R1494	261-02273D	1	Station Wagon, Tropical RHD; to Military Attaché, Rangoon.
22 FG 79	WV4052 R1502	261-02279D	1	Station Wagon, Tropical RHD; converted from Tropical and issued to Welsh Depot.
23 FG 64 to 24 FG 13	WV7419	251-14356D to 251-15372D	50	FFR RHD.
24 FG 14 to 24 FG 78	WV7419	254-24238D to 254-25461D	65	FFR LHD.
24 FG 79 to 26 FG 58	WV7419	251-16195G to 251-17054G	80	GS RHD.
26 FG 59 to 28 FG 28	WV7419	254-28225G to 254-30069G	170	GS LHD.
28 FG 29 to 33 FG 33	WV7453	251-14359D to 252-23828D	505	GS RHD.
47 FG 09	WV7452	251-13833D	1	Airfield Crash Rescue RHD.
48 FG 62 to 48 FG 86	WV7499	254-23105D to 254-23377D	25	EW/Y Van RHD.
48 FG 87 to 48 FG 91	WV7499	251-14128D to 251-14145D	5	EW/Y Van LHD.
52 FG 34	WV4052 R1522	264-11432G	1	Station Wagon, Tropical LHD.
53 FG 97	WV4052 R1539	264-11475D	1	Station Wagon LHD; to Military Attaché, Warsaw.
57 FG 29 to 57 FG 78	WV7733	251-14264D to 251-14901D	50	Field Ambulance RHD.
64 FG 12	WV4052R1582	264-11840D	1	Station Wagon LHD; to Military Attaché, Prague then to Army 05/74.
69 FG 34 to 69 FG 50	WV8002	254-29206G and 254-29304	17	Drone Recovery LHD.
70 FG 96 to 71 FG 25	WV8058	251-14915D to 251-15177D	30	GS RHD.
71 FG 26 to 71 FG 55	WV8058	254-24663D to 254-24980D	30	GS LHD.
71 FG 56	WV4052 R1593	264-12190D	1	Station Wagon LHD; to Defence Attaché, Belgrade.
71 FG 94	WV4052 R1596	264-12098D	1	Station Wagon, Tropical LHD; to Military Attaché, Thailand.
71 FG 95	WV4052 R1599	264-12243D	1	Station Wagon LHD; to Military Attaché, Phnom Penh.
73 FG 01 to 73 FG 04	WV8002	254-29305G to 254-29308G	4	Drone Recovery LHD.
20 FH 01	WV4052 R1602	261-02244D	1	Station Wagon, Tropical LHD; to Military Attaché, Jeddah.
20 FH 02	WV4052 R1604	261-02420D	2	Station Wagon RHD.
20 FH 12	WV4052 R1614	264-12348D	1	Station Wagon LHD.
20 FH 29	WV4052 R1613	264-12464A	1	Station Wagon LHD, Tropical; to Services Attaché Vietnam.
30 FH 69 to 30 FH 76	WV4052 R1673	261-02513F to 261-02520F	8	Station Wagon RHD.
44 FH 04 to 44 FH 05	WV4052 R1699	261-02566F and 261-02567F	2	Station Wagon RHD
45 FH 88 to 47 FH 02	WV8626	254-29828G to 254-29796G	125	Field Ambulance LHD.
48 FH 09 to 48 FH 14	WV8627	251-16196G to 251-16478G	6	FFR Van RHD.
48 FH 15 to 48 FH 22	WV8627	254-28224G to 254-28762G	8	FFR Van LHD.

ARMY

(b) Mark 11 (109-inch) (Continued)

Serials	Contract	Chassis Nos	Total	Remarks
48 FH 24	WV4052 R1710	261-02563F	1	Station Wagon RHD, Tropical; to Military Attaché, Addis Ababa.
48 FH 29 to 51 FH 48	WV8678	251-17017G to 251-17563G	320	GS RHD.
51 FH 49 to 52 FH 88	WV8678	254-30106G to 254-30765G	140	GS LHD.
55 FH 50 to 55 FH 51	WV8627	251-16482G and 251-16486G	2	FFR Van RHD.
58 FH 52 to 58 FH 53	WV8815	251-17003G and 251-17005G	2	Field Ambulance RHD.
58 FH 68 to 59 FH 71	WV8876	251-16292G to 251-16450G	104	GS RHD.
59 FH 72 to 59 FH 86	WV8877	251-16916G to 251-16963G	15	FFR RHD.
59 FH 87 to 60 FH 42	WV8877	254-29582G to 254-29670G	56	FFR LHD.
60 FH 45	WV4052 R1741	261-02619G	1	Station Wagon RHD.
06 FJ 66	WV8765 R1779	264-15126G	1	Station Wagon LHD; to Military Attaché, Amman.
16 FJ 36 to 18 FJ 39	WV9257	251-18460G to 251-19895G	204	GS RHD.
18 FJ 40 to 20 FJ 39	WV9257	254-32128G to 254-34478G	200	GS LHD.
20 FJ 40 to 22 FJ 61	WV9226	251-17597G to 251-17964G	222	GS RHD.
22 FJ 62 to 24 FJ 12	WV9227	251-17526G to 251-18032G	151	FFR RHD.
25 FJ 38 to 25 FJ 60	WV8765 R1828	261-02821G to 261-02843G	23	Station Wagon RHD.
25 FJ 73 to 25 FJ 83	WV8765 R1829	251-18045G to 251-18055G	11	CL RHD.
29 FJ 82 to 30 FJ 56	WV9319	251-18754G to 251-18965G	75	Field Ambulance RHD.
31 FJ 77 to 32 FJ 54	WV8765 R1856	261-02881G to 261-02982G	78	Station Wagon RHD.
32 FJ 71	WV7865 R1861	264-16231G	1	Station Wagon, Tropical LHD; to Military Attaché, Baghdad; to Military Attaché, Beirut, 09/72.
32 FJ 72	WV7865 R1861	261-03002G	1	Station Wagon RHD; to Services Adviser, Cyprus; to Army, 12/77.
32 FJ 73	WV7865 R1861	264-16230G	1	Station Wagon, LHD Tropical; to Military Attaché, Teheran.
32 FJ 74 to 35 FJ 69	WV9398	251-18732G to 251-19825G	296	FFR RHD..
35 FJ 70 to 38 FJ 64	WV9398	254-32249G to 254-34111G	295	FFR LHD
44 FJ 46 to 44 FJ 69	WV9565	251-18199G to 251-18198G	24	FFR RHD.
49 FJ 61 to 49 FJ 65	WV8765 R1912	261-03058G to 261-03062G	5	Station Wagon RHD.
49 FJ 66	WV8765 R1911	264-16443G	1	Station Wagon LHD.
53 FJ 51 to 54 FJ 50	WV9729	254-34115G to 254-34421G	100	FFR LHD.
00 FK 01 to 01 FK 00	WV9728	254-33226G to 254-34740G	100	GS LHD.
03 FK 01	WV9872	251-19590G	1	Field Ambulance RHD.
03 FK 06	WV8765 R1954	264-117173G	1	Station Wagon LHD;to Military Attaché, Saigon.
04 FK 86 to 04 FK 88	WV10176	254-35374H to 254-35387H	3	GS LHD.
05 FK 89 to 07 FK 63	WV10000	254-35844H to n/a	175	Field Ambulance LHD.
07 FK 64 to 07 FK 83	WV10000	251-21203H to 251-21228H	20	Field Ambulance RHD.
07 FK 84 to 08 FK 22	WV10634	254-37409H to 254-38945H	39	Field Ambulance LHD.
32 FK 00 to 34 FK 19	WV10275	251-20252H to 251-21430H	220	GS RHD.
34 FK 20 to 38 FK 19	WV10275	254-36541H to 254-38749H	400	GS LHD.
39 FK 30	WV8765 R2023	261-03348H	1	Station Wagon, Tropical RHD; to Military Attaché, Khartoum.
39 FK 31 to 39 FK 32	WV8765 R2023	264-17921H to 264-17941H	2	Station Wagon, Tropical LHD; 39 FK 31 to Military Attaché, Kinshasa; 39 FK 32 to Military Attaché, Rabat.
39 FK 33 to 39 FK 35	WV8765 R2023	261-03350H to 261-03349H	3	Station Wagon, Tropical LHD; 39 FK 33 to Military Attaché, Lagos; 39 FK 34 to Military Defence Adviser, Zambia; 39 FK 35 to British High Commission, Colombo.

ARMY

(b) Mark 11 (109-inch) (Continued)

Serials	Contract	Chassis Nos	Total	Remarks
48 FK 77 to 51 FK 30	WV10368	254-37169H to 254-39038H	254	FFR LHD.
51 FK 31 to 57 FK 10	WV10368	251-20537H to 251-21878H	580	FFR RHD.
62 FK 29 to 63 FK 78	WV10367	251-21653H to 251-21676H	150	GS RHD.
63 FK 79 to 64 FK 78	WV10367	254-38779H to 254-38959H	100	GS LHD.
02 FL 23 to 02 FL 28	WV10561	251-21737H to 251-21750H	6	Field Ambulance RHD.
06 FL 45 to 06 FL 47	WV10635	251-21880H to 251-21884H	3	24v GS RHD.
08 FL 07 to 08 FL 36	WV10634	254-38932H to 254-37120H	30	Field Ambulance LHD.
08 FL 37 to 08 FL 52	WV10000	254-37708H to 254-36510H	16	Field Ambulance LHD.
08 FL 53 to 08 FL 91	WV10000	251-20793H to 251-21244H	39	Field Ambulance RHD.
08 FL 92 to 08 FL 94	WV10634	254-38983H to 254-38979H	3	Field Ambulance LHD.
59 FL 74 to 59 FL 97	WV10829	251-21996H to 251-22019H	24	WOMBAT portee RHD.
04 XC 31	(See note)	254-39054H	1	FFR LHD; Berlin Brigade.
27 XC 93 to 27 XC 96	(See note)	n/a	4	FFR LHD; Berlin Brigade.
			Total 6630	

Note: Berlin vehicles were not purchased under contract but were ordered on a "warrant" system via the Berlin Senät who then ordered the vehicles from Brüggeman, a major Land Rover dealer in West Germany.

RAF

(b) Mark 11 (109-inch)

Serials	Contract	Chassis Nos	Total	Remarks
92 AA 86 to 93 AA 15	WV6872	251-13038 to 251-13164	30	Crash Rescue Ambulance RHD.
95 AA 29 to 95 AA 31	WV6652	251-13063 to 251-13169	3	Crash Rescue RHD Ambulance.
95 AA 47	n/a	261-02270	1	RHD Station Wagon, Tropical; to Air Attaché (later 29 BT 54).
96 AA 88 to 97 AA 36	WV7725	251-14853 to 251-14708	49	RHD Crash Rescue Ambulance.
98 AA 77 to 98 AA 78	WV7726	251-14309 and 251-14310	2	RHD Station Wagon, Tropical.
99 AA 04 to 99 AA 09	WV8009	251-15484 to 251-15507	2	24v Rectified GS RHD.
99 AA 10 to 99 AA 11	n/a	251-15510 and 251-15514	2	24v RHD.
82 AA 08 to 82 AA 17	WV8765	251-17035G to n/a	10	24v GS RHD.
28 AG 00 to 28 AG 16	WV8932	231-00001G to 231-00019H	17	TACR RHD.
39 AM 75 to 40 AM 00	WV8628	251-19541 to 251-19519	26	RHD Crash Rescue Ambulance.
28 AA 34	WV8765	264-15492G	1	Station Wagon LHD; to Air Attaché, Ankara (later 30 BT 25).
40 AM 43	WV8765 R1858	264-16195G	1	LHD Station Wagon; to Air Attaché, Jeddah (later 30 BT 40).
40 AM 44 to 40 AM 45	WV8765 R1858	261-02993 to n/a	2	RHD Station Wagon.
41 AM 26 to 41 AM 27	WV9384	254-32189 to 254-32190	2	LHD 24v/90a Van (Hardtop).
43 AM 04	WV8765 R1922	251-18723	1	RHD Van (Hardtop).
43 AM 05	WV8765 R1922	251-18722	1	RHD Van (Hardtop) (CL).
43 AM 62	WV8765 R1969	264-17181	1	LHD Station Wagon; to UKPMD, Ankara (later 30 BT 24).
43 AM 66 to 43 AM 68	WV8765 R1997	261-03124 to 261-03126	3	RHD Station Wagon.
48 AM 33	WV8765 R2084	351-01064	1	RHD Station Wagon; for NATO rôle.
			Total 155	

ROYAL NAVY These figures have been calculated from Land Rover despatch records, in the absence of Royal Navy records.

(b) Mark 11 (109-inch)

Serials including	Contract	Chassis Nos	Total	Remarks
05 RN 22 and 05 RN 23	n/a	251-14193 to 251-14251	14	Cargo; delivered March 1968.
RN Serials	n/a	276-08756 to 276-08758	3	diesel; delivered November 1968.
RN Serials	n/a	251-16451 to 251-16470	15	Cargo; delivered August 1969.
RN Serials	n/a	251-17528 to 251-17555	8	Cargo; delivered March 1970.
RN Serials	n/a	251-18745 to 251-18770	6	Cargo; delivered November 1970.
			Total 46	

ARMY SERIAL NUMBERS

The serial numbers allocated by the Army gave a clue to the date of the vehicle, although those issued by the RAF and Royal Navy did not. In this period, serial letters indicated the financial year in which the vehicle was purchased (which is not necessarily the same as the calendar year in which it was delivered). Those relevant to the Rover 10 and Rover 11 models are shown below.

As before, serial sequences began at 0001 (eg 00 FG 01) and ran to 9999 (eg 99 FG 99). There was not necessarily any correlation between chassis number order and military serial number within batches.

Serials were normally allocated at the time the contract was placed, or when an amendment to a previous contract was made, or when a warrant was issued as part of a "rolling" contract.

ES	1965-1966
FG	1967-1968
FH	1968-1969
FJ	1969-1970
FK	1970-1971
FL	1971-1972

LAND ROVER CHASSIS CODES

All Land Rovers in this period had a three-digit identifying prefix in the chassis code, which indicated the model type, steering position and other factors. Neither the model-year nor the calendar-year of manufacture was indicated. The ones relevant to the Rover 10 and Rover 11 models are shown below. The three-figure prefix was followed by a five-figure serial number that began at 00001 for each separate sequence, and this in turn was followed by a suffix letter. The suffix letter (between D and H on Rover 10 and Rover 11 models) indicated major changes in the vehicle's specification that affected servicing.

Note that the Land Rover model-year began in September and continued until the end of the following July, leaving August clear for the works' annual holiday and for preparing the assembly lines to take new models. A Land Rover built in the 1968 model-year could therefore have been built at any time between September 1967 and July 1968.

231	RHD 109in One Ton
241	RHD 88in
244	LHD 88in
251	RHD 109in
254	LHD 109in
261	RHD 109in Station Wagon
264	LHD 109in Station Wagon
315	RHD 88in Station Wagon
318	LHD 109in Station Wagon

The Berlin Brigade escort vehicles were particularly smartly presented in gloss black with chromed features and white upholstery. This vehicle is now preserved in the REME Museum at Bordon. (JT)

There were similar features on 30 XC 16, the Berlin Brigade's review vehicle. The special hubcaps are said to be VW Beetle items! This one is also preserved at the REME Museum in Bordon. (JT)

TECHNICAL SPECIFICATIONS, ROVER 10 AND 11 MODELS

05 ET 64 was one of a large batch of FFR models with right-hand drive. The layout of the back body, with two inward-facing seats for the radio operators and Dexion racking at the front, is clear in this picture. (RES)

ENGINE (PETROL):

2286cc (90.47mm x 88.9mm) four-cylinder with overhead valves and single Zenith 36 IV carburettor. 7.0:1 compression ratio. 77bhp at 4250rpm and 124 lb ft at 2500rpm.

ENGINE (DIESEL):

2286cc (90.47mm x 88.9mm) four-cylinder with overhead valves and indirect injection. 23:1 compression ratio. 56.2bhp at 4000rpm and 101 lb ft at 1800rpm.

TRANSMISSION:

Selectable four-wheel drive.
Four-speed main gearbox; ratios 3.60:1, 2.22:1, 1.50:1, 1.00:1, reverse 3.02:1. Synchromesh on third and fourth gears only.
Two-speed transfer gearbox; ratios 1.148:1 (High) and 2.888:1 (Low); later 2.350:1 (Low)
Axle ratio: 4.7:1

SUSPENSION, STEERING AND BRAKES:

Semi-elliptic leaf springs all round.
Recirculating-ball steering with 15:1 ratio.
Drum brakes on all four wheels; 10in x 1.5in on 88-inch Rover 10s and 11in x 2.25in on 109-inch Rover 11s; separate drum-type transmission parking brake.

ELECTRICAL SYSTEM:

12-volt with dynamo and negative earth; FFR models with 24-volt negative-earth system and 90-amp generator.

UNLADEN WEIGHT:

88in (minimum): 2900 lb (1315kg) with petrol engine (civilian models)
109in (minimum): 3294 lb (1494kg) with petrol engine (civilian models)

PERFORMANCE

88in Rover 10 with 2.25-litre petrol engine:
0-50mph: 21secs
Maximum: 67mph approx (108km/h)
Fuel consumption: 26 mpg approx

109in Rover 11 with 2.25-litre petrol engine:
0-50mph: 29secs
Maximum: 58mph approx (93.3km/h)
Fuel consumption: 19 mpg approx

DIMENSIONS:

88-inch Rover 10:
Overall length: 142.4in (3617mm)
Wheelbase: 88in (2235mm)
Overall width: 64in (1626mm)
Unladen height: 77.5in (1968mm) maximum
Track: 51.5in (1308mm)

109-inch Rover 11
Overall length: 175in (4445mm)
Wheelbase: 109in (2769mm)
Overall width: 64in (1626mm)
Unladen height: 81in (2057mm) maximum
Track: 51.5in (1308mm)

ASSET CODES

Rover 10

1150-0765	Car, Utility, ¼ ton, 4x4, Rover 10
1150-5765	Car, Utility, ¼ ton, 4x4, LHD, Rover 10
1151-0765	Car, Utility, SAAS, ¼ Tonne, 4x4, Rover
1151-5765	Car, Utility, SAAS, ¼ ton, 4x4, Rover 10
1618-1765	Truck, General Service, 24v 90A, ¼ ton, 4x4, Rover 10
1620-0765	Truck, Utility, GS, ¼ ton, 4x4, Rover 10
1620-1765	Truck, General Service, ¼ ton, 4x4, 24v, Rover 10
1620-5765	Truck, Cargo, GS, ¼ ton, 4x4, LHD, Rover 10
1621-0765	Truck, Utility, CL, ¼ ton, 4x4, Rover 10
1621-5765	Truck, Utility, CL, ¼ ton, 4x4, LHD, Rover 10

Rover 11

1040-0766	Ambulance, 2/4 stretcher, 4x4, Rover 11
1040-5766	Ambulance, 2/4 stretcher, 4x4, LHD, Rover 11
1043-0766	Ambulance, Crash Rescue, 2/4 stretcher, 4x4, Rover 11 FV18068
1155-0766	Car, Utility, ¾ ton, 4x4, Rover 11
1155-3766	Car, Utility, ¾ ton, 4X4, Tropical, Rover 11
1155-5766	Car, Utility, ¾ ton, 4x4, LHD, Rover 11
1155-8766	Car, Utility, ¾ ton, 4x4, Tropical, LHD, Rover 11
1159-0766	Car, Utility, E1410, ¾ ton, 4x4, Rover 11
1161-5766	Car, Utility, SAAS, Medium, 4x4, Rover 109
1700-0766	Truck, Firefighting, airfield crash rescue, ¾ ton, 4x4, Rover 11
1702-0766	Truck, Firefighting, Crash (Tactical), ¾ ton, 4x4, Rover 11
1709-1766	Truck, Utility, ¾ ton, 4x4, 24v, Rover 11
1710-0766	Truck, Utility, ¾ ton, 4x4, Rover 11
1710-1766	Truck, Utility, ¾ ton, 4x4, 24 volt, Rover 11
1710-2766	Truck, Utility, w/winch, ¾ ton, 4x4, Rover 11
1710-5766	Truck, Utility, ¾ ton, 4x4, LHD, Rover 11
1710-8766	Truck, Utility, CL, ¾ ton, 4x4, Plain Hard Top, Land Rover [LHD]
1710-9766	Truck, Utility, ¾ ton, 4x4, LHD, Hard Top, 24v 90A rectified, Rover 11
1711-0766	Truck, Utility, CL, ¾ ton, Rover 11
1711-1766	Truck, CL, ¾ ton, 4x4, Plain Hard Top , Rover 11
1718-0766	Truck, General Service, Fitted For FACE, ¾ ton, 4x4, Rover 11
1720-0766	Truck, General Service, FFR, ¾ ton, 4x4, Rover 11
1720-2766	Truck, General Service, FFR, Survey Computing RA, ¾ ton, 4x4, Rover 11
1720-5766	Truck, General Service, FFR, ¾ ton, 4x4, LHD, Rover 11
1720-6766	Truck, General Service, FFR, ¾ ton, 4x4, LHD, Hard Top, Rover 11
1725-0766	Truck, Utility, SAS, ¾ ton, 4x4, Rover 11
1730-0766	Truck, Utility, Wombat, ¾ ton, 4x4, Rover 11
2616-0766	Van, GS, FFR, ¾ ton, 4x4, no 32, Rover
2616-5766	Van, GS, FFR, EW/Y, ¾ ton, 4x4, LHD, Rover 11
2617-0766	Van, GS, FFR, EW/Y, ¾ ton, 4x4, Rover 11
2617-5766	Van, GS, FFR, EW/Y, ¾ ton, 4x4, LHD, Rover 11
3600-0766	Automatic Test Equipment, Truck Mounted, ¾ ton, 4x4, Rapier, Rover 11
3611-0766	Drone, Recovery Eqt, Truck Mounted, ¾ ton, 4x4, Rover 11
3611-5766	Drone, Recovery Eqt, Truck Mounted, ¾ ton, 4x4, LHD, Rover 11
3612-0766	Electronic Velocity Analysing Set, Truck-Mounted, ¾-ton, 4x4, Rover 11
3621-0766	Radar Set, Truck Mounted, Radar, GS, No 17 Mk 1, ¾ ton, 4x4, Rover 11

This publicity picture from BAC, makers of the Rapier missile system, shows 58 FH 77 with a civilian operator at the controls of the Automatic Test Equipment and the sides of the tall tilt rolled up to expose the equipment underneath.

109 Series IIA

Whilst the Army designated its negative-earth 109 inch vehicles as Mark 11 the RAF used the designation "109 inch IIA".

1038-0769	Ambulance, 2 stretcher, FFR, 24v, Special Pilot Rescue, Rover 109 Series IIA (P)
1041-0769	Ambulance, 2/1 stretcher, 4x4, Rover 9 FV18005
1155-0769	Car, Utility, ¾¾ ton, 4x4, Rover 109 Series IIa (P)
1155-4769	Car, Utility, ¾ ton, 4x4, 12 seater, w trailer atts, Rover 109 S IIA
1155-9769	Car, Utility, ¾ ton, 4x4, 12 seater, w trailer atts, LHD, Rover 109 S IIA
1690-0769	Truck, Firefighting, ¾ ton, 4x4, Domestic, Rover 109in
1690-1769	Truck, Firefighting, ¾ ton, 4x4, Domestic, Mk 2, Rover 109in
1705-0769	Truck, GS, Plain Hard Top, ¾ ton, 4x4, 24v 90A Rover 109in
1705-6769	Truck, Utility, ¾ ton, 4x4, LHD, Hard Top, Rover 11
1706-4769	Truck, Utility, ¾ ton, 4x4, 24v 90A rectified, Rover 11
1710-0769	Truck, Utility, ¾ ton, 4x4, Land Rover 109" Series IIa FV18061
1710-1769	Truck, Utility, ¾ ton, 4x4, Hard Top, Land Rover 109" Series IIA (Petrol)"
1710-2769	Truck, Utility, ¾ ton, 4x4, 24v 40A rectified, Rover 109 Ser IIA
1710-3769	Truck, Utility, ¾ ton, 4x4, Stretcher Carrier, Land Rover 109" Series IIA
1710-4769	Truck, Utility, ¾ ton, 4x4, 24v 90A rectified, Rover 109 Ser IIA
1710-6769	Truck, Utility, ¾ ton, 4x4, Hard Top, LHD, Land Rover 109" Ser IIA (Petrol)
1711-1769	Truck, CL, ¾ ton, 4x4, Hard Top, Rover 109 Series IIA
1711-2769	Truck, Utility, CL, ¾ ton, 4x4, Hard Top w/windows, Rover Series IIA
1711-4769	Truck, Utility, CL, ¾ ton, 4x4, Rover Series IIa
1720-0769	Truck, General Service, FFR, ¾ ton, 4x4, Hard Top, 24v AC rectified w radio eqt, Rover 109in
1723-6769	Armoured Patrol, ¾ tonne, 4x4, Shorland Mk 3 [RHD]
1723-7769	Truck, Armoured Personnel Carrier, ¾ Tonne, 4x4, LHD, Shorland Mk 5
1745-0769	Truck, Pilot Rescue, ¾ ton, 4x4, Rover 109 Series IIa (P)

CHAPTER 7:

THE FORWARD CONTROL MODELS

This was the Series IIA Forward Control. The rear view demonstrates one of the big disadvantages of the standard Forward Control models. They were tall and somewhat ungainly vehicles, high off the ground for loading and less able on side-slopes than traditional Land Rovers. (TMB)

Land Rover introduced a Forward Control version of its 109-inch chassis in 1962, initially only with the 2¼-litre four-cylinder petrol engine but from 1963 also with the 2.6-litre six-cylinder as an option. Mechanically similar to the contemporary Rover 9 models, the Forward Controls had a 30cwt payload within a footprint that was little larger than that of the normal-control vehicle. The cab was pushed up and forwards so that the driver sat roughly above the front axle, making room for a larger load space behind.

These early Forward Controls, known as Series IIA models like the contemporary normal-control types, were somewhat troublesome and did not earn a good reputation. So it was no surprise that the British military did not show any great interest in them. Nevertheless, a single vehicle was purchased in late 1965 or early 1966 for experiments at FVRDE with a screw propulsion system. The RAF also bought a small number fitted with special bodywork as domestic fire tenders.

In the meantime, Rover had attempted to interest the British military authorities in a special forward-control model, this one considerably larger and more robust than the production type, but still intended to take a 30cwt payload. Although FVRDE examined two prototypes between 1963 and 1967, neither attracted much enthusiasm from the military and the design was eventually abandoned.

However, the principle of a forward-control design did have some appeal, and by 1967 FVRDE had come up with its own design, which it then passed to Rover for further development. This subsequently evolved into the 1-Tonne model, which is the subject of Chapter 12. As part of its evaluation of forward-control designs at the time, FVRDE also took two examples of the civilian Series IIB model, an improved design with 110-inch wheelbase and wider-track axles for better stability, during the first half of 1967. A third example, specially equipped with a more powerful engine, passed through FVRDE hands in summer that year en-route for trials with the Trucial Oman Scouts.

The only Forward Control models purchased in quantity were configured as fire tenders. (Note that there were also some forward-control conversions of the Rover 9, which are discussed in Chapter 5.) After the domestic RAF fire tenders on Series IIA chassis, both the RAF and the Army Fire Service took a number of vehicles on the Series IIB 110-inch chassis with commercial-pattern bodywork by HCB-Angus. The last of these entered service in 1972, the year when Land Rover ceased to manufacture its Forward-Control models, which had always been slow sellers.

The experimental Forward Controls

Although the Land Rover was capable of taking over most of the rôles formerly allocated to 1 ton vehicles in the British Army, there were some which it could not handle. So a requirement was drawn up for a 30cwt load-carrier, and Rover was asked to submit a vehicle for assessment. A 30cwt normal-control model on a 129-inch wheelbase was under development and the fifth prototype, number 129/5 with 2.5-litre turbocharged diesel engine, went to FVRDE for examination in mid-1963, but did not meet with approval.

For the formal trials, Land Rover decided to develop a special Forward-Control model, the standard production type presumably being ruled out after FVRDE ran some informal comparison trials with a civilian-specification model in August 1963 (see below). The new design was much larger than the existing production models, with a 120-inch wheelbase and an 8.5-inch increase in track width. The first prototype was built as a dropside truck with a 24-volt FFR specification and a 110bhp Rover 3-litre petrol engine. However, the MoD was interested in multi-fuel engines at the time, so the vehicle was re-fitted with the 105bhp multi-fuel version of the Perkins 6.354 six-cylinder diesel engine that was also to be used in the Commer entry for the 30cwt truck trials.

The 120-inch Forward Control showed promise, but the Army found it was too big. So a second prototype was built on a shorter wheelbase of 112 inches, again with the multi-fuel Perkins engine. Its dropside body was designed to take the standard Army 1 ton container of the time. This second prototype went to FVRDE in 1965, when it is said to have been by far the best vehicle in the trials. It was shown as a "project in progress" at the 1966 SMMT-FVRDE exhibition alongside its rivals from Austin, Bedford and Commer, and at a Rover and Alvis military display at Chadwick Manor in May that year.

However, the MoD expressed no further interest. Military thinking had already moved on from the idea of a 30cwt vehicle to focus on a 1 ton type, and a standard Forward Control model, in its latest Series IIB guise, was already at FVRDE for consideration by mid-1966. In the absence of a military fleet order, the Rover Company was not interested in looking at commercial applications, and the big Forward Control project was abandoned.

The Series IIA trials vehicles

As already noted, FVRDE borrowed a Series IIA 109-inch Forward Control model for a test of civilian 4x4s carried out in August 1963. It was tested against a standard civilian-specification Land Rover 109-inch pick-up, an Austin Gipsy, a Toyota Land Cruiser, a Nissan Patrol and an International Harvester Scout. Nothing seems to have come directly of this, but in late 1965 or early 1966 FVRDE did take a further Series IIA 109-inch Forward Control which was transferred to its Research Division for trials of an experimental propulsion system. This was on chassis number 286-00302B; it attracted FVRDE wing number 6939 and became 02 SP 36.

The experimental propulsion system depended on a pair of Archimedes screws mounted between the axles, one on each side of the vehicle. The screws could be raised for travelling

This was Rover's first attempt at a military-special Forward Control. Bearing FVRDE trials number 7017 in these pictures, it had a 120-inch wheelbase and a Perkins six-cylinder diesel engine. (TMB)

When the 120-inch Forward Control proved too big, Rover built a second prototype with a 112-inch wheelbase. Note the differences in the body sides and below the tailgate at the rear. This one later became Rover's works breakdown truck, and still exists.
(Left – TMB, above – BMIHT)

FVRDE used this Series IIA Forward Control for research into an experimental screw propulsion system. The screws could be raised out of the way on channels when not needed, but the supporting hardware would have severely compromised the vehicle's rough-terrain ability. (TMB)

21 BT 29 was FVRDE's 7146P, and was a Series IIB 110-inch model. The lower headlights were an easy recognition feature on these later Forward Controls. (TMB)

This was the six-cylinder Forward Control, 22 BT 25. It was pictured here during Exercise Wagon Train at Lee-on-Solent. Behind it on the landing craft is the experimental 112-inch Forward Control.(Land Rover)

(and the Forward Control provided the necessary extra ground clearance for this to be feasible) and lowered to give propulsion across marshy ground. It appears not to have met military requirements, as no further vehicles were built with it. Nevertheless, the host vehicle remained in FVRDE ownership until February 1979.

The Series IIB trials vehicles

In the mean time, Rover had been developing its Forward Control model further, notably fitting different gearing and wider-track axles for better stability. To avoid a foul condition with the wider tracks, the wheelbase was also increased to 110 inches. This revised version was known as the Series IIB model, and became commercially available in early 1967.

FVRDE obtained one of the very first examples with the 2¼-litre four-cylinder petrol engine, and displayed it at the SMMT-FVRDE military vehicles exhibition that opened in late September 1966. The catalogue for that exhibition noted that the vehicle was undergoing assessment as a 1-ton load carrier, and that it had a possible alternative rôle as an ambulance. Wearing serial number 21 BT 29 and carrying FVRDE wing number 7146P, this vehicle did not lead directly to further orders but may have helped to firm up FVRDE thinking about the 1 ton Forward Control that it did want – which later materialised as the 101 1-Tonne and did have an ambulance variant.

FVRDE obtained two further examples of the Series IIB model in February 1967, this time with the more powerful 2.6-litre six-cylinder engine. These were on chassis numbers 330-00016A and 330-00019A and were given serial numbers 22 BT 26 and 22 BT 25 respectively. 22 BT 25 was trialled alongside the 112-inch Forward Control prototype during Operation Wagon Train, an exercise at Lee-on-Solent which included amphibious landings. Almost certainly, the objective

was once again to assess what really would be needed in a new Forward Control design.

There was a fourth Series IIB Forward Control in the trials series. This one had been specially fitted by Rover with its most powerful 3-litre six-cylinder engine, that delivered 110bhp. It had chassis number 335-00011A and gained the military serial 00 SP 47 – making it one of the first vehicles to

Yet another experimental vehicle was the 3-litre-engined Forward Control, 00 SP47. It is seen here being unloaded from the vessel which took it to Oman for desert trials. Note the large sand tyres and the exterior sun visor on the cab. (TMB)

ASSET CODES	
1690-0769	Truck, Firefighting, ¾ ton, 4x4, Domestic, Rover 109in
1690-1769	Truck, Firefighting, ¾ ton, 4x4, Domestic, Mk 2, Rover 109in
1820-0775	Truck, Cargo, GS, 1 ton, 4x4, Land Rover 110 Forward Control
1896-0750	Truck, Firefighting, 1¼ ton, 4x4, Rover
1896-5750	Truck, Firefighting, 1¼ ton, 4x4, LHD, Rover

be numbered in the new SP series for Special Projects vehicles. Fitted with oversize 11.00 x 16 sand tyres (the standard bar-tread size was 9.00 x 16), this one was shipped out to Sharja in the Persian Gulf for trials with the Trucial Oman Scouts in October or November 1967. The results of those trials fed directly into the programme to produce the new 1-Tonne Forward Control model. 00 SP 47 was later re-serialled in the EP series (see Chapter 13 for details).

Military records show that a fifth vehicle was purchased and became 02 SP 72. At present, no information about this vehicle or its use has come to light.

The RAF domestic fire tenders

Although the Army's interest in the Forward Control Land Rover was initially as a load carrier and later as a means of refining its ideas about a purpose-built model, the RAF recognised its potential as a domestic fire tender. The 109 Forward Control was commonly turned into a fire tender for volunteer fire brigades in the Alpine regions of Europe,

although less commonly in the UK.

The first known contract for a domestic fire tender was KM/G/416, which in 1965 was met by a four-cylinder Series IIA 109 Forward Control on chassis number 286-00351 which received the serial number 01 AG 32. The vehicle was bodied by fire tender specialist HCB-Angus to an apparently new design with folding entrance doors behind the rear section of the cab. It was sent in January 1965 to provide fire cover at RAF Fylingdales, the signals intercept station in Yorkshire. The RAF knew it as a 'Truck, Firefighting, ¾ ton, 4x4, Domestic, Rover 109in', and it appears to have been the only one of its kind. Its asset code was 1690-0769.

The four-cylinder engine in this vehicle probably proved unsatisfactory, because the next known contract called for a six-cylinder chassis with the same bodywork. Once again, the vehicle was a Series IIA 109-inch model, which was in theory not available in the UK with the six-cylinder engine (although that engine could be supplied for export). The RAF must therefore have done some special pleading. Contract KM/G/515 was met by 27 AG 24, with chassis number 300-00002A and one of only two six-cylinder Home Market chassis built. It had asset code 1690-1769, was a 'Truck, Firefighting, ¾ ton, 4x4, Domestic, Mk 2, Rover 109in', and was based at No 1 ACC (Air Control Centre) at Wattisham in Suffolk from December 1966.

These appear to be the only two vehicles of their kind supplied to the RAF before it moved on to a second design of Forward Control fire tender, this time on the Series IIB 110-inch chassis. There was, however, a third vehicle for the RAF. Bearing serial number 88 AA 52, this was acquired on behalf of GCHQ and was presumably used for signals intercept work. No further details of it are known.

01 AG 32 was the only four-cylinder Forward Control taken into RAF service. It did duty as a domestic fire tender. (RAF Fylingdales via Gordon Smith)

27 AG 24 was the second vehicle for the RAF domestic fire service. It had bodywork similar to that on 01 AG 32 but was powered by a six-cylinder engine. It, too, remained unique. (Unknown source)

The RAF also took a number of the standardised Forward Control fire tenders. This was 05 AG 47, pictured at RAF Rudloe Manor. (GF Collection)

The standardised fire tender was available commercially under the HCB-Angus brand name of Firefly. This one, 24 FK 41, was pictured providing fire cover at a military display. (GF)

The standardised fire tender body by HCB-Angus is seen here on 24 FK 45, a Series IIB six-cylinder Forward Control belonging to the Army Fire Service. (GF)

The standardised fire tenders

The more ready availability of the six-cylinder engine made the Forward Control models a much more attractive proposition for the fire engine specialists, and several designs now became available. The one that appealed to the MoD was by HCB-Angus, who had also built the bodies for the earlier RAF domestic fire tenders. This body was a further development of that design, now with conventional side doors for the rear cab.

Four warrants drawn on rolling contract WV4052 called for a total of 21 such vehicles, of which six went to the RAF, eight were intended for the Royal Navy and seven for the Army. However six went to the RAF and the other 15 went to the Army Fire Service to provide cover at establishments such as MVEE in Chobham. These were delivered between February 1969 and May 1970, and all except two had right-hand drive. HCB-Angus build records then show five more vehicles delivered in 1970, two with Army serial numbers but the other three with civilian registrations.

A final quantity of 43 was ordered by warrant (R2039) under rolling contract WV8765, this time all for the Army Fire Service; these were delivered in 1970 and 1971, and the final batch of 19 had left-hand drive. A grand total of 75 Series IIB Forward Controls of the standardised pattern was acquired, including the six for the RAF, between 1968 and 1971. Most survived in service until the mid-1980s; 05 AG 49 was transferred to the Army as 37 BT 02, and 24 FK 38 was transferred to the RAF as 01 AY 66.

ARMY SERIAL NUMBERS

The serial numbers allocated by the Army gave a clue to the date of the vehicle, although those issued by the RAF and Royal Navy did not. In this period, serial letters indicated the financial year in which the vehicle was purchased (which is not necessarily the same as the calendar year in which it was delivered). Those relevant to the Forward Control models are shown below.

As before, serial sequences began at 0001 (eg 00 DM 01) and ran to 9999 (eg 99 DM 99). There was not necessarily any correlation between chassis number order and military serial number within batches.

BT	No date association; the BT series included vehicles purchased individually, second-hand or transferred ex-RN or ex-RAF; see also Chapter 13
FG	1967-1968
FH	1968-1969
FJ	1969-1970
FK	1970-1971
SP	No date association; the SP series was for Special Projects vehicles used for research and development. See also Chapter 13.

SUMMARY OF FORWARD CONTROL MODEL DELIVERIES, 1963-1972

ARMY

(a) Experimental 120-inch and 112-inch Forward Controls

Serials	Contract	Chassis Nos	Total	Remarks
None allocated	n/a	Probably 120/1	1	RHD, 120-inch wheelbase, dropside truck. FVRDE wing number 7017.
None allocated	n/a	Probably 112/1	1	RHD, 112-inch wheelbase, dropside truck. FVRDE wing number 7044.
			Total 2	

(b) Series IIA (109-inch)

Serials	Contract	Chassis Nos	Total	Remarks
02 SP 36	n/a	286-00302B	1	RHD, 2.25-litre four-cylinder. FVRDE wing number 6939. Fitted with Archimedes screw propulsion.
			Total 1	

(c) Series IIB (110-inch)

Serials	Contract	Chassis Nos	Total	Remarks
21 BT 29	n/a	n/a	1	GS truck. FVRDE wing number 7146P.
22 BT 25 and 22 BT 26	n/a	330-00019A and 330-00016A	2	GS truck. 2.6-litre six-cylinder, RHD.
00 SP 47	n/a	335-00011A	1	GS truck. 3.0-litre six-cylinder, RHD.
02 SP 72	n/a	n/a	1	No details known.
22 FG 67 to 22 FG 73	WV4052 R1504	330-00094D to 330-00095A	7	Fire tenders by HCB-Angus, all RHD.
22 FG 74 and 22 FG 75	WV4052 R1504	333-00127A and 333-00128A	2	Fire tenders by HCB-Angus, LHD models.
59 FG 31	WV4052 R1533	330-00078A	1	RHD Fire tenders by HCB-Angus.
28 FH 78	WV4052 R1646	330-00129C	1	RHD Fire tenders by HCB-Angus.
31 FH 30 to 31 FH 33	WV4052 R1675	330-00159D to 330-00162D	4	RHD Fire tenders by HCB-Angus. [Details from HCB-Angus records].
ARE 976J	n/a			
ELA 824J	824 was 330-00240D; others not known			
ELA 825J			3	Fire tenders by HCB-Angus, 1970 deliveries. ARE 976J to ROSM Featherstone; ELA 824J to RAF Westcott, ELA 825J to RAF Pystock.
06 FJ 67 and 06 FJ 68	WV8765 R1784	330-00210D and 330-00207D	2	Fire tenders by HCB-Angus, RHD models.
24 FK 36 to 24 FK 57	WV8765 R2039	330-00289E to 330-00311E	22	Fire tenders by HCB-Angus, RHD Models.
24 FK 58 to 24 FK 76	WV8765 R2039	333-00351E to 333-00366E	19	Fire tenders by HCB-Angus, LHD models..
			Total 74	

RAF

(c) Series IIB (110-inch)

Serials	Contract	Chassis Nos	Total	Remarks
05 AG 45 to 05 AG 50	WV4052 R1709	330-00169D to 330-00179D (range)	6	All RHD.
			Total 6	

No deliveries of Forward Control models to the Royal Navy are known.

TECHNICAL SPECIFICATIONS, FORWARD CONTROL MODELS

ENGINES:

2286cc (90.47mm x 88.9mm) four-cylinder with overhead valves and single Solex carburettor. 7.0:1 compression ratio. 77bhp at 4250rpm and 124 lb ft at 2500rpm.

2625cc (77.8mm x 92.1mm) six-cylinder with overhead inlet and side exhaust valves; single Zenith 175 CD-2S carburettor. 7.8:1 compression ratio. 85bhp at 4500rpm and 132 lb ft at 1500rpm.

2995cc (77.8mm x 105mm) six-cylinder with overhead inlet and side exhaust valves; single Zenith 175 CD-2S carburettor. Compression ratio not known. 110bhp at 4500rpm and 152 lb ft at 1500rpm.

TRANSMISSION:

Selectable four-wheel drive.
Four-speed main gearbox; ratios 3.60:1, 2.22:1, 1.50:1, 1.00:1, reverse 3.02:1. Synchromesh on third and fourth gears only.
Two-speed transfer gearbox; ratios 1.53:1 (High) and 2.92:1 (Low) on 109-inch Series IIA; 3.27:1 (Low) on 110-inch Series IIB.
Axle ratio: 4.7:1

SUSPENSION, STEERING AND BRAKES:

Semi-elliptic leaf springs all round. Recirculating-ball steering with 19.6:1 ratio. Drum brakes on all four wheels, with servo assistance; 11in x 3in at the front, 11in x 2.25in at the rear; separate drum-type transmission parking brake.

ELECTRICAL SYSTEM:

12-volt with dynamo.

UNLADEN WEIGHT:

109in (minimum): 4200lb (1904kg) with four-cylinder petrol engine
110in (minimum): 4341lb (1969kg) with four- or six-cylinder petrol engine

PERFORMANCE

With 2.25-litre petrol engine:

0-50mph:	29.5secs
Maximum:	57mph approx (92km/h)
Fuel consumption:	12-14 mpg

With 2.6-litre petrol engine:

0-50mph:	23.2secs
Maximum:	62mph approx (100km/h)
Fuel consumption:	12-14 mpg

DIMENSIONS:

109-inch models:

Overall length:	193in (4902mm)
Wheelbase:	109in (2769mm)
Overall width:	75.5in (1918mm) across mirrors
Unladen height:	102in (2591mm) with tilt
Track:	53.5in (1359mm)

110-inch models:

Overall length:	193in (4902mm)
Wheelbase:	109.75in (2788mm)
Overall width:	75.5in (1918mm) across mirrors
Unladen height:	102in (2591mm) with tilt
Track:	57.5in (1460mm)

LAND ROVER CHASSIS CODES

All Land Rovers in this period had a three-digit identifying prefix in the chassis code, which indicated the model type, steering position and other factors. Neither the model-year nor the calendar-year of manufacture was indicated. The ones relevant to the production Forward Control models are shown below. The three-figure prefix was followed by a five-figure serial number that began at 00001 for each separate sequence, and this in turn was followed by a suffix letter. The suffix letter (A, B or D on Series IIA models and A to E on Series IIB types) indicated major changes in the vehicle's specification that affected servicing.

Note that the Land Rover model-year began in September and continued until the end of the following July, leaving August clear for the works' annual holiday and for preparing the assembly lines to take new models. A Land Rover built in the 1963 model-year could therefore have been built at any time between September 1962 and July 1963.

Prototype vehicles had special numbers (eg 129/5, 120/1) and are not included in these lists.

286	RHD 109in Series IIA Forward Control, four-cylinder petrol
300	RHD 109in Series IIA Forward Control, six-cylinder petrol
330	RHD 110in Series IIB Forward Control, six-cylinder petrol
333	LHD 110in Series IIB Forward Control, six-cylinder petrol

CHAPTER 8:
THE HALF-TON ROVER 1 (SERIES IIA)

The weight reduction was necessary so that the vehicle could be air-lifted by the Wessex helicopters then in service.
(Land Rover)

In the early 1960s, the United Kingdom still had responsibilities across the globe from Singapore and Hong Kong in the Far East, to Cyprus, Aden in the Near East and Gibraltar and Malta nearer to home. There still remained a few colonies in Africa and the Caribbean, although most were heading for independence. As already noted in Chapter 5, a decision had been taken to reduce the cost of overseas garrisons by creating an Army Strategic Reserve whose Brigades could be deployed swiftly by air to trouble spots. These Brigades needed airportable vehicles, and experiments were conducted in the early 1960s with a variety of contenders, including the British-built Mini Moke. However, none of these vehicles proved satisfactory.

The Royal Marines also needed a light vehicle which could be lifted from ship to shore as they had a responsibility for establishing a beachhead which could be exploited by other forces. In 1965, 40 and 42 Commando were in Singapore, while 45 Commando was in Aden covering the insurgency there. All three of these units needed a light deployable vehicle. As an interim measure, the Royal Marines on the commando carrier HMS Bulwark had been using Citroën 2CV pickups since 1958, and also the Steyr-Daimler-Puch Haflinger. A key reason for their choice was that each vehicle had to be light enough to be carried under

This stripped-down unit conversion was not part of the Lightweight programme, but it does illustrate that the demand for such a vehicle existed. It was converted from 07 DM 79, a Rover Mk 8, in 1963-1964 at RNAS Sembawang in Singapore, on the initiative of Captain Paterson-Knight of 42 Commando, Royal Marines. The vehicle was used to carry an anti-tank gun.("Marine"/EMLRA)

a helicopter from Aden for deployment in the mountainous territory to the North.

In 1964 the Wessex HU5 helicopter had entered service with the Fleet Air Arm and the similar Wessex HC Mark 2 with the Royal Air Force. Under the conditions described above in Aden, these helicopters could lift 2500lb, and this determined the stripped weight of the vehicle that the Marines needed. For long-distance deployment, RAF transport aircraft would be used, and their capabilities also came into the picture. In service at that time were the Britannia, Argosy, Andover and Beverley. The Beverley was due to be replaced by the Hercules from 1967. The Britannia could only carry cargo loaded through a side door and the Andover was rather limited in payload, so the focus was on the Argosy in the short term. In order to load two vehicles side by side in an Argosy, those vehicles had to have a maximum width of 60 inches each. A standard Land Rover of the time was too wide.

When word of the Royal Marines' requirement reached Rover at Solihull, the company immediately set about developing a vehicle to meet it. Even though there was no major contract in the offing at this stage (the Royal Marines needed fewer than 100 vehicles to replace their Citroëns and Haflingers), Rover saw military sales as so important that it was prepared to create whatever the MoD wanted. Clearly, though, there was a chance that the new Land Rover might meet at least some of the MoD's other requirements for an airportable vehicle, and Rover were prepared to gamble on that.

After a feasibility prototype had been created from a standard 88-inch Series IIA, the MoD issued a General Statement of Requirements. This called for a "lightweight version of the short-wheelbase Land Rover". It had to be no wider than 60 inches to meet the size limitations of the Argosy transport aircraft. Its unladen weight in 12-volt form had to be no more than 2500lb so that it could be carried under a Wessex helicopter (although a weight of 3100lb would be permissible for 24-volt FFR versions). It had to carry a payload of 1000lb including the driver, be capable of towing a 10cwt (1120lb) trailer, and have a range of 300 miles. To avoid complicating the MoD's spares and servicing arrangements, it also had to retain the standard engine, gearbox, axles, steering and suspension of the existing production Land Rover 88-inch.

All this meant that the new "lightweight" Land Rover had to be about 500lb lighter than its standard military equivalent, and four inches narrower. If the main mechanical elements had to remain unchanged, the weight would therefore all have to be shed from the bodywork. Although the development was done at Rover, the project team kept in close contact with FVRDE throughout.

The width was reduced by designing a new and narrower bulkhead, and by using flat side panels instead of the barrelsides of the standard Land Rover. The axles then had to be

narrowed to suit, and despite the MoD's original request that all mechanical elements should remain standard, the engineers obtained agreement to use narrow-track types with shorter half-shafts and redesigned drive flanges.

Weight was shed in several ways. Standard civilian road springs were used instead of the heavy-duty military type, the military-standard oil cooler was left off, and 6.00 x 16 tyres on standard single-piece disc wheels were fitted in place of 6.50 x 16s on military split-rim wheels. The front wings were replaced by simple splash-guards, and a new angular bonnet was designed to suit.

But the crucial weight-saving ploy lay in the use of demountable elements. FVRDE agreed that the front bumper, windscreen, doors, soft top and frame, rear side panels and rear seat were not essential, as long as the basic driveable platform had been delivered to the battle front. These elements could follow on and be reunited with the vehicle as time allowed. Without the demountable elements, the new "lightweight" Land Rover just scraped in under the 2500lb weight ceiling, and a first prototype to these specifications was ready for test over the summer of 1965. Two further vehicles were delivered to FVRDE at the end of 1965 or in early 1966. Both had chassis numbers in the Rover prototype sequence, and they were allocated serials 20 BT 90 and 20 BT 91.

In service, it became quite common for the Rover 1 to be mounted in an MSP, carried in a transport aircraft and then dropped by parachute.
(Land Rover)

This is probably the first Rover 1 delivered to FVRDE in early 1966, and the headlamp and grille arrangement marks it out as one of the early prototypes, probably LW2 or LW3. These early vehicles were later given the production front end design. (TMB)

The same prototype is seen in stripped-down condition at FVRDE, and the top photograph shows the items that could be demounted to reduce weight for air-lifting by helicopter. (Left – TMB; above – Land Rover)

THE FVRDE PROTOTYPE AND TRIALS VEHICLES

The first Lightweights delivered to FVRDE were Engineering Prototypes, and did not have chassis numbers in the production sequences. The first two were numbered as prototypes (LW2 and LW3) and the next six were numbered in the standard Series IIA 88-inch sequences with 241 (RHD) or 244 (LHD) prefixes.

These eight vehicles had various changes of serial number, being re-serialled in the SP series during June 1967; four were re-numbered in the EP series in March 1970.

LW2	20 BT 90		
LW3	20 BT 91		
241-25521C	21 BT 92	00 SP 13	60 EP 78
241-25945C	21 BT 85	00 SP 15	
241-26991C	21 BT 94	00 SP 17	
241-27158C	21 BT 95	00 SP 18	60 EP 80
244-26934C	21 BT 84	00 SP 14	60 EP 79
244-27323C	21 BT 93	00 SP 16	60 EP 81

That early prototype shows the simplified bonnet and wing arrangement, and the 2¼-litre petrol engine as well. The peak over the front lamps was found only on the early trials vehicles. (TMB)

Around a year later, in July 1966 contract number WV5101 called for six more prototypes for evaluation trials. All were built on modified standard 88-inch chassis, four with right-hand drive and two with left-hand drive. They were initially given serial numbers 21 BT 84 and 21 BT 85, and 21 BT 92 to 21 BT 95, although some were later renumbered as "Special Project" vehicles (SP), and some were renumbered yet again in the EP series around three years later.

Two prototype vehicles, one a 12-volt and the other a 24-volt FFR type, were displayed at the SMMT-FVRDE exhibition in October 1966. By this stage, the military designation Rover Mk 1 had been chosen, although it would later be changed to Rover 1 to avoid confusion with the original 80-inch Rover Mk 1. At the Chertsey exhibition, the vehicles were classified as ¼ ton capacity, but they became ½ ton types in service. This reflected a change in the Army's method of classifying vehicles: the new figure reflected the overall payload rather than only the load that could be carried in the load bed.

Trials were meanwhile under way at FVRDE, and in August 1967 the first contracts for production vehicles were issued. The anticipated Marines contract was numbered WV7477 and called for 92 vehicles, but the bonus was an order for 1000 more for the Army under contract WV7478. The first deliveries of these production contracts were made to Vehicle Depot Hilton in December 1968 and priority for issue was given to the Royal Marine Commandos whose need for the vehicle was seen as the greatest. Almost all of WV7477 went to Singapore for 3 Commando Brigade and the first hundred of WV7478 went to 41 Commando and 45 Commando and other supporting units based in Plymouth. Once the Royal Marines were equipped, the next vehicles produced went to the Army's Strategic Reserve – 5 Airportable Brigade in Tidworth, 19 Airportable Brigade in Colchester and 24 Airportable Brigade in Plymouth (later Catterick). All these Brigades formed part of 3 Division.

The new basic vehicle was designated "Truck, General Service, ½ ton, 4x4, Rover 1" (although "General Service" would be deleted in favour of "Utility" in late 1972). It was given the military type code FV18101 in 12-volt GS form, and was initially given an asset code 1670-0772 to distinguish it from the Land Rover 88-inch GS (coded 1620-...). However, once the MoD had decided to replace the previous generation of Land Rover 88-inch models completely by the Lightweight, this different Asset Code caused administrative problems: units which had an establishment for Asset Code 1620 could not take vehicles with a 1670 Asset Code. So the Lightweights were recoded 1620-0772 before the first issue was made, in order to avoid this bureaucratic difficulty.

In practice, however, the Lightweight did not become the universal short-wheelbase Land Rover in British military service. It was more expensive than the standard 88-inch

38 FG 25 was from the second production contract for Rover 1s. It was seen here as delivered to FVRDE, and then in later use as the transport of a four-star officer. Note the absence of a spare wheel in the later picture. (RES/TMB)

Series IIA model, and so more contracts for these were also placed for rôles where airportability was not necessary. These rôles included driver training, depots and schools and the type was designated 'Truck, Utility, CL, ...' with CL standing for 'commercial'.

All the Series IIA Lightweights, built between December 1967 and March 1972, had an instrument panel in the centre of the dash. Up to late 1970, they also had their headlamps mounted in the grille panel, but the lamps were subsequently relocated on new vertical panels hanging down from the front wings, in order to meet new regulations in Europe –

The later Rover 1s had their headlights repositioned on the front wings. Despite the regimental markings, NXC 25H was actually a Rover demonstrator – and when new, it had the earlier headlight configuration. (Land Rover)

35 FG 68 shows clearly the early Rover 1 configuration with headlights in the grille panel. Note also the plate over the gap between the double bumpers on one side; this was a unit marking painted over when the newer "SW/350" stencilled marking was added. (GF)

This was another early Rover 1 delivery, seen here in service with the Royal Regiment of Fusiliers. (Land Rover)

notably in Germany and the Low Countries where many of the British Army vehicles served. The exact changeover point remains unknown, but the best research so far suggests that there were 1500 vehicles with the original headlamp configuration. To meet the MoD contracts, the Series IIA Lightweight remained in production until March 1972, several months after civilian Land Rover production had switched completely to Series III models in autumn 1971. It was followed by a Series III version, which is the subject of Chapter 10.

All of the 2989 production Series IIA Lightweights were delivered to the British armed forces, with the exception of a few retained at Rover for engineering development and as demonstrators. All of them had the 2¼-litre four-cylinder petrol engine and were delivered as soft tops. They had 6.50 x 16 tyres and oil coolers, as the weight-saving requirement which had brought about the oil cooler's deletion and the use of 6.00 x 16 tyres on the prototypes had been relaxed before production began. There were 1893 with right-hand drive and a further 1096 with left-hand drive. The Army received 1710 and the RAF 128, while the Royal Navy received at least 17 and possibly as many as 30 (see tables below). In addition Rover retained a small number as prototypes.

Ironically, many of the factors which had shaped the design of the Lightweight had changed by the time the vehicles entered service. The arrival of the C-130 Hercules transport aircraft from 1967 meant that the reduced width was no longer critical for air transport, and the gradual arrival of more powerful helicopters meant that the weight

A change made on the production Rover 1 added this stowage box in the left-hand rear wheel arch for the wheel-changing jack. It was usually secured by something stronger than the wire seen here! (JT)

Stripped down for air-lifting, this Rover 1 carries the chains needed for the operation. It is 33 FG 89 and was serving with 95 Commando Light Regiment, Royal Artillery at Larkhill Artillery Day in July 1969. (RES)

ROVER 1 VARIANTS

The majority of the Series IIA Lightweights were 12-volt models with soft tops, but there were several variations on the theme.

Another early Rover 1 shows the bridge plate often attached to the double-bumpers. This one has been through the wading trough at FVRDE. (TMB)

Amphibious Lightweight

FVRDE experimented early on with an appliqué kit which was intended to make the Lightweight fully amphibious. The vehicle chosen for the experiments was a right-hand drive prototype, registered as 20 BT 91 while with FVRDE but probably owned by Rover. It was given pontoon-like floats and a water propulsion system.

No report of the trials has been found, although several photographs exist, and no other Lightweights are known to have been modified in this way.

FFR models

The General Service version was quickly followed by a 24-volt Fitted For Radio (FFR) version, to be used in command and liaison roles where radio operation was a pre-requisite. The FFRs were delivered from February 1969 and the radio station came as a completely demountable unit to reduce weight for helicopter lifting. The radio station itself was fitted with eyes so it could be lifted by helicopter as a separate load. Where the 12-volt models had three-abreast seating in the front, the 24-volt FFR models had a large battery box in place of the central seat in the driving compartment. The FFR models had military code FV18102.

constraint was no longer as important. One result was that Lightweights were only rarely seen completely stripped down in the way originally planned. Nevertheless, the demountable body elements were much appreciated as a way of lowering the profile of the vehicles for certain types of operation.

The Series IIA Lightweight saw service all over the world and was used in BAOR, Gibraltar, Cyprus, Hong Kong, Singapore, Malta and also Northern Ireland. There is no photographic record for the Series IIA Lightweight serving in the Falklands in 1982 as most had been sold off by then. Similarly there is no evidence for it serving with the resident Royal Marine detachment there (Naval Party 8901 – NP8901).

20 BT 91 was one of the prototype vehicles, and was used for flotation trials with this appliqué kit. Power came from a Dowty water jet at the rear. It is shown during trials at Horsey Island, Portsmouth. (TMB)

The demountable radio station is seen here both in and out of a vehicle. (TMB)

Hard Tops

The decision to replace most of the existing 88-inch Land Rovers with Lightweights meant that some examples were fitted with hard tops in order to replace earlier hard top vehicles. This seemed an anomaly as it was totally at odds with the original concept of a vehicle that could be stripped for airportability. However once the vehicle replaced the older 88-inch vehicles in rôles that required hard tops – such as with AMF – it became vital.

Linelayers

The Linelaying Kit which had traditionally been fitted to the Series IIA 88-inch was modified so that it would fit the Lightweight.

Vehicle Protection Kit (VPK)

A number of Rover 1 models served in Northern Ireland with a VPK or Vehicle Protection Kit. VPK-equipped Lightweights were usually fitted with Aeon hollow rubber spring assisters to deal with the additional weight of the GRP armour. There is more detail about the VPK in Chapter 5.

WOMBAT portees

The WOMBAT portee was a variant developed for the Royal Marines. It allowed the 120mm anti-tank weapon to be carried in the rear cargo area with its barrel projecting over the bonnet and clamped to a frame that replaced the windscreen. Although the Royal Marines were committed to this version, the Army continued to use the Land Rover 109-inch as a WOMBAT portee. The vehicles converted as WOMBAT portees were given new asset codes beginning with 1645, but this was found on paperwork only and the vehicles retained their original data plates. Each Commando seems to have been issued with six such vehicles between 1969 and 1971.

RAF Rover 1 deliveries

The RAF used Lightweights to equip their tactical units, including RAF Regiment, Mobile Air Movements Teams and Signals Units.

Glider recovery

Many RAF Lightweights were converted for use as glider recovery vehicles. The conversion seems to have involved little more than transparent panels in the roof of the tilt, an overall yellow paint scheme and occasionally an orange flashing beacon. The latter two were to make the vehicles more visible when moving around an airfield in a non-tactical rôle; the transparent panels gave the crew a better view of what was happening in the air. These vehicles were given an Asset Code prefix of 1614, although the original data plates were retained unchanged.

One of the early trials vehicles was pictured here at FVRDE during evaluation as a WOMBAT portee. By this time, it had been fitted with a production-style tool box in the rear wheelarch. The WOMBAT portee version was used exclusively by the Royal Marines. (TMB)

ASSET CODES

1620-0772	Truck, General Service, ½ Ton, 4x4, Rover 1 (RHD)
1620-5772	Truck, General Service, ½ Ton, 4x4, Rover 1 (LHD)
1625-0772	Truck, General Service, FFR, ½ Ton, 4x4, Rover 1 (RHD)
1625-5772	Truck, General Service, FFR, ½ Ton, 4x4, Rover 1 (LHD)
1645-0772	Truck, Utility, Wombat, ½ ton, 4x4, Rover 1
1670-0772	Truck, General Service, ½ Ton, 4x4, Rover 1 (RHD, RAF and RN); recoded to 1620-0772
1670-5772	Truck, General Service, ½ Ton, 4x4, Rover 1 (LHD, RAF and RN); recoded to 1620-5772
1674-0772	Truck, General Service, FFR, ½ Ton, 4x4, Rover 1 (RHD, RAF and RN); recoded to 1625-0772
1678-0772	Truck, Utility, Wombat, ½ ton, 4x4, Rover 1

ARMY SERIAL NUMBERS

The serial numbers allocated by the Army gave a clue to the date of the vehicle, although those issued by the RAF and Royal Navy did not. In this period, serial letters indicated the financial year in which the vehicle was purchased (which is not necessarily the same as the calendar year in which it was delivered). Those relevant to the Rover 1 models are shown below.

As before, serial sequences began at 0001 (e.g. 00 FL 01) and ran to 9999 (e.g. 99 FL 99). There was not necessarily any correlation between chassis number order and military serial number within batches.

BT	No date association; the BT series included vehicles purchased individually and second-hand; see also Chapter 13.
EP	1964-1965
FG	1967-1968
FH	1968-1969
FJ	1969-1970
FK	1970-1971
FL	1971-1972
SP	No date association; the SP series was for Special Projects vehicles used for research and development and was allocated from mid-1967 until around 2002. See also Chapter 13.

SUMMARY OF ROVER 1 MODEL DELIVERIES, 1966-1972

Lists cover vehicles ordered under contracts, and do not include vehicles transferred in from other services or elsewhere.

ARMY

Serials	Contract	Chassis Nos	Total	Remarks
20 BT 90, 20 BT 91		LW2, LW3	2	
21 BT 84, 21 BT 85	WV5101	244-26934C, 241-25945C	2	Later re-serialled; see above.
21 BT 92, 21 BT 93	WV5101	241-25521C, 244-27323C	4	Later re-serialled; see above.
21 BT 94, 21 BT 95		241-26991C, 241-27158C		
71 FG 97 to 72 FG 88	WV7477	236-00002A to 236-00118A	92	GS RHD, 1969 deliveries. Nominally a Royal Navy (i.e. Marines) contract.
33 FG 35 to 43 FG 34	WV7478	236-00004A to 236-01163A	100	GS RHD, 1969 deliveries.
59 FG 61 to 60 FG 16	WV7850	236-00761A to 236-00757A	56	FFR RHD, 1969 deliveries.
30 FH 49 to 30 FH 52	WV8459	236-00758A to 236-00627A	4	FFR RHD, 1969 deliveries.
53 FH 54 to 55 FH 40	WV8679	239-00006A to 239-00192A	87	GS LHD, 1969-1970 deliveries.
53 FJ 12 to 53 FJ 49	WV9753	236-01326A to 236-01363A	38	FFR RHD, 1971 deliveries. Nominally a Royal Navy (i.e. Marines) contract; most vehicles were issued to RM units.
26 FK 88 to 28 FK 39	WV10193	236-01371B to 236-01522B	152	GS RHD, 1971 deliveries.
28 FK 40 to 31 FK 99	WV10193	239-00193B to 239-00706B	360	GS LHD, 1971 deliveries.
57 FK 11 to 60 FK 28	WV10318	239-00284B to 239-01058B	318	FFR LHD, 1971-1972 deliveries.
60 FK 29 to 62 FK 28	WV10318	236-01523B to 236-01852B	200	FFR RHD, 1971-1972 deliveries.
64 FK 79 to 65 FK 78	WV10366	236-01630B to 236-01789B	100	GS RHD, 1972 deliveries.
65 FK 79 to 67 FK 28	WV10366	239-00707B to 239-00856B	150	GS LHD, 1972 deliveries.
00 FL 62 to 00 FL 86	WV10552	236-01883B to 236-01837B	25	GS RHD, 1972 deliveries. Nominally a Royal Navy (i.e. Marines) contract, but most vehicles went to Army units.
00 FL 87 to 01 FL 14	WV10551	236-01853B to 236-01881B	28	FFR RHD, 1972 deliveries. Nominally a Royal Navy (i.e. Marines) contract, but most vehicles went to Army units.

Total 1718

RAF

Serials	Contract	Chassis Nos	Total	Remarks
13 AA 73 to 14 AA 12	WV8551	23601164 to 23601203	40	GS RHD, 1969 deliveries.
99 AA 42 to 99 AA 75	WV8391	23601204A to 23601237A	34	GS RHD, 1969 deliveries.
71 AA 17 to 71 AA 48	WV8391	23601238 to 23601269	32	FFR RHD, 1969 deliveries.
99 AA 76 to 99 AA 97	WV8391	23601270A to 23601291A	22	FFR RHD, 1969 deliveries.

Total 128

ROYAL NAVY ROVER 1 DELIVERIES

The absence of contract records means that no definitive list of Rover 1s delivered to the Royal Navy can be established at present. However, it is clear that there were four contracts, numbered WV7835, WV9322, WV9383 and WV10274. The contract numbers suggest (but do not prove) that the contracts were issued in 1968 (WV7835), 1969 (WV9322 and WV9383) and 1971 (WV10274).

By a process of elimination it appears probable that the Royal Navy had a total of 30 Rover 1s. These were all RHD models in the 236- chassis series and had chassis numbers 00008A, 0388A, 0648A to 652A, 1293A to 1296A, 1316A to 1325A, 1370A, 1624B to 1629B, 1854B and 1882B. It has not yet been possible to tie these numbers to either serial numbers or contracts.

Known Examples

Serials	Contract	Chassis Nos	Total	Remarks
64 RN 00 to 64 RN 05	n/a	n/a	6	GS RHD. Note that 64 RN 00 was struck off and the serial re-allocated to a Series 3 Lightweight in 1979.
26 RN 85 to 26 RN 93	n/a	n/a	9	GS RHD
16 RN 84 to 16 RN 85	n/a	n/a	2	GS RHD; 16 RN 85 was converted to a WOMBAT Portee

TECHNICAL SPECIFICATIONS, SERIES IIA LIGHTWEIGHT MODELS

ENGINE:
2286cc (90.47mm x 88.9mm) four-cylinder with pushrod OHV and Solex carburettor. 8:1 compression ratio. 77bhp at 4250rpm and 124 lb ft at 2500rpm.

TRANSMISSION:
Selectable four-wheel drive. Four-speed main gearbox; ratios 3.6:1, 2.22:1, 1.512:1, 1.0:1, reverse 3.0:1. Synchromesh on third and fourth gears only. Two-speed transfer gearbox; ratios 1.148:1 (High) and 2.4:1 (Low) Axle ratio: 4.7:1

SUSPENSION, STEERING AND BRAKES:
Semi-elliptic leaf springs all round. Recirculating-ball steering with 15.6:1 ratio. Drum brakes all round and separate drum-type transmission parking brake.

ELECTRICAL SYSTEM:
12-volt with dynamo, or 24-volt with 90-amp alternator.

UNLADEN WEIGHT:
12-volt GS soft top   3210 lb (1456kg); 2660 lb (1206.5kg) when stripped

PERFORMANCE
0-50mph:	21 secs approximately
Maximum:	65mph (105km/h)
Fuel consumption:	15-18 mpg

DIMENSIONS:
Overall length:	144in (3650mm)
Wheelbase:	88in (2235mm)
Overall width:	60in (1520mm)
Unladen height:	77in (1950mm) – GS soft top
Track:	51.5in (1310mm)
Ground clearance:	8.5in (210mm)

The later front end design is pictured here on 28 FK 32. This vehicle is fleet number "76" of the Royal School of Artillery and was photographed at RAF St Mawgan in August 1973. (GF)

This was the military identification plate of an early LHD Rover 1, 54 FH 42 with chassis number 239-00064A. Note that the early Asset Code 1670-0772 has had the first "7" scratched out when the code was changed to 1620-0772. (GF)

LAND ROVER CHASSIS CODES
All Land Rovers in this period had a three-digit identifying prefix in the chassis code, which indicated the model type, steering position and other factors. Neither the model-year nor the calendar-year of manufacture was indicated. The ones relevant to the Rover 1 models are shown below. The three-figure prefix was followed by a five-figure serial number that began at 00001 for each separate sequence, and this in turn was followed by a suffix letter. The suffix letter indicated major changes in the vehicle's specification that affected servicing.

Note that the Land Rover model-year began in September and continued until the end of the following July, leaving August clear for the works' annual holiday and for preparing the assembly lines to take new models. A Land Rover built in the 1969 model-year could therefore have been built at any time between September 1968 and July 1969.

236   RHD 12-volt and 24-volt
239   LHD 12-volt and 24-volt
241   RHD standard 88in (prototypes only)
244   LHD standard 88in (prototypes only)

CHAPTER 9:
SERIES III 109

This group of Series 3 models shows three different configurations. From the left are a GS soft top, a GS hardtop and an FFR hardtop. The vehicles are from 5 Battalion Royal Regiment of Fusiliers (V) in the early 1990s. (Land Rover)

In September 1971 Rover-British Leyland (as it had become known) launched a face-lifted and uprated version of its traditional Land Rover range. This was known on the civilian market as a Series III, and it was intended to address some of the shortcomings of the Series

IIA in order to combat the increasing tide of competition from Japan in the civilian market place, particularly outside the UK. The most important change was an all-new synchromesh gearbox but alongside this the 9½-inch diameter heavy-duty clutch formerly fitted to only the diesel and six-cylinder models became standard across the range. New, stronger, half-shafts were also introduced on the long wheelbase model along with a tougher rear axle made by Salisbury. A new brake system was fitted with revised brake drums, re-routed brake pipes and a translucent brake fluid reservoir to ease inspection and so meet regulations in some export territories.

Externally the recognition point for the new model was the silver-grey injection-moulded ABS radiator grille replacing the galvanised wire mesh of earlier models. The door hinges were also tidied up to reduce protrusion and a circular heater inlet appeared on the nearside wing just ahead of the front door. Internally the facia was revised and offered a full width parcel shelf, and there was relocation of controls and

Rather too smart to be air-dropped, this Series 3 109 was pictured at the British Army Equipment Exhibition on an MSP. This vehicle was one used by the Joint Air Transport Establishment for displays. (Dave Shephard)

switches so that they could all be reached whilst wearing a seat belt. In general, attempts were made to improve interior comfort from the previous rather spartan levels.

The Ministry of Defence (MoD) appeared to take the change in its stride and when the new models came down the production line they slipped into service seamlessly. The Army began to receive examples in December 1971, and baptised them as Series 3 types, following its traditional resistance to Roman numerals. The first military specification Series 3s were a mixed batch of General Service Utility 109 vehicles, Fitted For Radio (FFR) 109-inch vehicles and some Lightweights (see Chapter 10). Most of these models were also acquired in Left Hand Drive (LHD) form so that they could be deployed to BAOR and other places where that was the norm. Meanwhile, the rolling contract for "administrative" Land Rovers and Rover cars – WV8765 – started delivering civilian specification 109-inch vehicles and Station Wagons on both the 88-inch and 109-inch chassis from early 1972, following on from deliveries of Series IIA models.

For the first time, some 109-inch Land Rovers were acquired with the six-cylinder petrol engine; some were Station Wagons and others were special-purpose conversions, notably the Shorland armoured car and some three-axle types. On the production lines at Rover, this engine was phased out during 1978-1979 and was replaced by a V8 petrol engine. Models with the V8 engine differed visually by having a black-painted grille in a panel set level with the wing fronts (rather than recessed). They were known to the manufacturer as Stage 1 V8 types. The only MoD purchases of V8-engined Land Rovers in this period were special-purpose conversions, notably the Laird Centaur (see Chapter 13).

Note that the four-cylinder engines delivered from late 1980 were known to Land Rover as 2.3-litre types; earlier ones had been 2¼-litre types. In practice, there was no difference in the bore and stroke sizes, but the later engines had five main bearings instead of the original three. Metricated fittings were also introduced progressively, beginning in 1982.

Army deliveries

The 12-volt "utility" versions of the 109-inch chassis– cargo with soft top – and the FFR models with their 24-volt electrical systems were capable of carrying out a number of rôles with little or no modification. Most army units had the "utility" for cargo carrying, and until the arrival of the Land Rover 101 gun tractor, the Series 3 109-inch also towed the 105mm Pack Howitzer in light artillery regiments. The FFR was also used for command rôles in almost all tactical units such as infantry battalions, Royal Armoured Corps regiments and artillery regiments.

The last Series 3 vehicles were delivered to the Army in early 1985, just before the diesel-engined Land Rover One Tens began to enter service. They soldiered on until about

65 HG 54 was delivered as a Cargo vehicle but is carrying radios and has twin aerial tuners on the wings. (GF)

1998 when the pressure to move to an all-diesel fleet led to their withdrawal. It is worth noting that some of the Land Rovers (by then known as Defenders) that replaced those Series 3 vehicles were still in service some 20 years later. Many of them went through a rebuild programme under Project Tithonus.

18 GN 39 was serving with the Military Police when photographed. Note the additional bracket on which the blue beacon is mounted. (GF)

When needs must.... 28 HF 16 was smartened up to represent its unit as a recruitment vehicle. Note also the badge bar and additional lights at the front.(GF)

02 GN 24 represents the Series 3 109 FFR. Clearly visible are the side aerial mount and the Dexion racking in the rear. This vehicle had not entered service when pictured: it was still in glossy Bronze Green paint, and the galvanised capping on the door was as it had left the factory. It was issued to one of the Guards Battalions in London. (Land Rover)

26 HF 99 and 98 KA 16 were both long-wheelbase Cargo models, but their specifications differ. 26 HF 99 still has "pusher" front bumpers and the older pattern of FV sidelights and turn signals with "eared" lenses. 98 KA 16, dating from the early 1980s, has a single front bumper and the later screw-on lenses for sidelights and turn signals. (GF)

16 GN 07 was new enough when these pictures were taken not to have had any camouflage applied. The Tactical Command Post vehicles had a window on one side of the hardtop but not on the other. (HQ BAOR)

ROVER SERIES 3 VARIANTS

Berlin Brigade

Series 3 versions of the 109-inch vehicle were purchased by the Senät for the Berlin Garrison. Although these vehicles were identical to the ones purchased by the MoD, they were not on normal contracts. Some were retained after the Berlin Garrison closed in September 1994 and then given new serials in the current registrations of the later period.

Carawagon Tactical Command Post (TCP)

In order to provide sleeping accommodation in the field for very senior officers – Brigadiers and Generals – the British Army had used converted trailers which were deployed with the appropriate formation Headquarters including HQ I (BR) Corps. By the mid-1970s a mobile caravan based on the Land Rover 109-inch pick-up became a possibility.

Searle Ltd of Sunbury on Thames was both a Land Rover dealer and a conversion specialist. It offered a range of conversions of basic Land Rovers including a caravan based on the Land Rover 109 pick-up and known as the Carawagon De Luxe. This had an elevating roof to increase headroom, a roof rack over the cab and up to four beds as well as a refrigerator, a cooker and a toilet.

By 1977 a prototype had been built on a military-specification Land Rover 109-inch LHD vehicle (62 GF 86), using the same external bodywork including the roof rack. The

The roof of the TCP folded down to give a lower profile for travelling. It was seen at the RLC Corps Day in June 1996. (GF)

The TCP roof sometimes gave trouble with leaks. Two remedies are seen here: 16 GN 53 has a (presumably) waterproof cover and 16 GN 06 had been fitted with a fixed roof by the time it was sold into preservation. (Left – FMW; right – JT)

The TCP provided a working table and basic living facilities. The seat on the left doubled as a bed. This was 16 GN 07. (HQ BAOR)

elevating roof provided standing headroom of about 1.9m over the full length of the cargo area. The roof rack over the cab provided space for stowage of camouflage nets and an additional tent (2.75m wide x 2.13m long) that could be fitted over the rear door.

The internal arrangement was rather different from the civilian version. Along the right-hand side, a fitted cabinet provided a working area for up to three people and had cupboards and drawers below. A vertical map board above the work area was provided together with a drop-down table. Searles were rather proud of the plastic-faced working surfaces that were covered with Formica – the latest thing in those days! One of the cupboards by the rear door concealed a stainless steel sink, and a foot-operated pump supplied the tap. On the left-hand side there was a cushioned bench seat and back rest which was convertible to a single bed. A wardrobe was provided for hanging clothes opposite the basin, and lockers provided space for water jerrycans, bedding and other supplies.

Production began in late 1978 with Land Rover 109-inch vehicles from the current GS batch in both LHD and RHD forms being sent to Sunbury for conversion. In all, three RHD (15 GN 59, 15 GN 69 and 15 GN 76) and 32 LHD (the prototype 62 GF 86, and the others drawn from 15 GN 90 to 16 GN 53, apparently at random) were converted to make a total of 35 in all. The converted vehicle was known as "Truck, Caravan, Commanders, 1 berth, ¾ Tonne, 4x4," although it was also called a Tactical Command Post (TCP). One other was known to have carried 04 BT 03 but is believed to have been Carawagon's demonstrator (see Chapter 13).

Initially the RHD examples were issued to the Commanders of the UK-based Field Forces. These had been formed from the Airportable Brigades of the Strategic Reserve and 16 Parachute Brigade during 1977 and 1978. As one of the consequences of the 1975 Defence Review, 3 Division moved to BAOR on 1 January 1978 to join 1, 2, and 4 Divisions and each division would consist of two task forces rather than brigades. During 1979 and early 1980 these four divisions were each equipped with three LHD TCPs – presumably one for the Divisional Commander and one for each of the subordinate Task Force Commanders. A further

Some Station Wagons were taken onto the strength of the CL fleet. 27 GB 86, seen at Ashchurch Vehicle Depot, still had the civilian-standard Limestone-coloured roof when pictured. The later vehicle (above) has door-mounted mirrors, which replaced wing mirrors in the early 1980s and is shown when serving with Post and Courier Depot, Royal Engineers. (GF)

The CL vehicles came as both hardtops and soft tops. 19 FM 08 was used by "recruitment and Liaison Staff" and was in an orange and brown "camouflage" scheme. It was used to tow a recruitment caravan – not the fron civilian towing hook. 14 KA 50 (above) is typical of the type of vehicle used by TA units including University Officer Training Corps. (Above – JT; right – GF))

12 GN 61 and 12 GN 65 were CL specification soft tops, with standard civilian-pattern head-lamps and standard production front bumpers. Note the non-matching wing mirrors on 12 GN 65; workshops used what they had to hand when a replacement was needed. These vehicles were in service with 37 Signal Regiment, Royal Corps of Signals in June 1981. (GF)

12 or 13 of the LHD examples were issued to HQ I (BR) Corps during 1980 and early 1981 to provide accommodation for the most senior officer of the Corps, including the Corps Commandant and the commanders of each arm of service. After brigades were re-instated from 1 January 1981 there were some further issues and re-allocations.

In late 1983 and 1984 deliveries of some new TCPs (71 KB 43 to 71 KB 52) were made – five with RHD and five with LHD. These had been built from scratch by Carawagon Ltd (under which name Searles now traded) rather than as conversions of existing GS vehicles. One further vehicle (64 KC 84) was delivered in 1985 and another (95 KA 67) is alleged to have been re-built from the bodywork of one of the 1978 batch. All the Carawagons were withdrawn by 2002. In all a total of 46 new vehicles and one rebuild are known.

Commercial (CL) versions

The Army and RAF at this time used a standard commercial version of both the 88-inch and the 109-inch vehicles. These versions had the designation "Truck, Utility, CL,..." where CL indicated "commercial" rather than the military version. These CL versions were cheaper to procure and were allocated to units who did not need the full military specification. They were often used by Garrison Transport Units and Driver Training Units, and many ended up at Leconfield with the Army School of Mechanical Transport. The 88-inch in CL form was quite a contrast to the military specification Lightweight but the 109-inch CL is remarkably similar to its military counterpart. The 109-inch CL can be distinguished, however, by noting that the push-start bumperettes at the front and rear of the vehicle are missing. The 109-inch CL was also used in Hard Top and Window Hard Top forms. Notable users of the Hard Top version were Explosive Ordnance Disposal units of the Royal Engineers.

Field Ambulance

The Field Ambulance on the Series 3 chassis was a continuation of the design introduced to service in 1960 on Series II (Rover Mk 7) chassis and continued through the Series IIA (Rover 9 and Rover 11) deliveries. Once again the body was built by Marshall's of Cambridge.

Midge drone vehicles

More major modifications to the Series 3 enabled it to carry out several other rôles. One of the more interesting and rarest modifications carried out was to provide vehicles for 94 Locating Regiment, Royal Artillery. The regiment was organised as three batteries each equipped with the Midge drone (see Chapter 6). The Command section of each Battery consisted of a Command Post (CP), the Photographic Interpretation Facility (PPIF) and the Photographic Interpretation Vehicle (PPIV). The PPIF was a Land Rover 109 with a special body, and the PPIV a 4 ton flat platform with specialist container. In addition, there was another specialist vehicle with a van body based on a Land Rover 109-inch which was used for drone recovery, and its specification was essentially the same as it had been on Rover 11 chassis.

MOULD and MOULD repair

In the early 1980s a new VHF radio system (MOULD) was introduced to provide emergency links between the Regular Army, TA Home Defence Battalions, Army District Headquarters and Regional Government Headquarters. Its purpose was to provide communications links to enable the government to control the country after a nuclear strike.

To provide national coverage, a network of 150 hilltop sites was established that provided the necessary links across the regions. Since there was always the possibility that a hilltop site could be out of action as a result of a strike or simply a fault, "Insertion Vehicles" were operated by TA Royal Corps of Signals units which would provide mobile MOULD radios to replace the hilltop site whilst it was out of action. Each "Insertion Vehicle" was based on a Series 3 CL Cargo fitted with a Hard Top and with Pye Pegasus radios mounted in the rear.

It was equipped with a substantial roofrack for carrying the 12-metre Clark mast, and a pair of jerrycans could be clamped to the front bumper. There was a canvas flap on each side of the hard top behind the driver and passenger doors to allow connections to be made to the antenna. At the rear were a power inlet from the generator and earthing points. On the rear door was mounted a reel to carry the cables for connecting the radios to the aerial. The "Insertion

The Series 3 version of the Marshall's field ambulance was essentially the same as earlier versions. 01 GN 17 was seen wearing the pattern of camouflage used in both Cyprus and Canada. (GF)

03 HJ 78 was one of a small batch of hardtops dedicated to MOULD insertion duties. The front end indicates that these were essentially civilian-specification vehicles. This vehicle was serving with 94 (Berkshire Yeomanry) Signal Squadron of 71 Signal Regiment (V). (GF)

Few details of the MOULD vehicles became available when they were in service, but this example was displayed at a military exhibition. It was not normally distinctive, being based on a RHD GS hardtop. (GF)

Vehicle" was accompanied by a standard 109-inch GS "stores vehicle" which also towed a generator to provide a power supply if necessary.

In addition, there were "Technician Repair Vehicles" to provide technical support of the system, and each carried spares and test equipment. In all, 22 "Insertion Vehicles" were purchased along with 11 "Technician Repair Vehicles", and these were issued to TA Signal Regiments in late 1982 or early 1983. This number of vehicles meant that each region had two "Insertion Vehicles" and one "Technician Repair Vehicle" (except for Scotland which had two).

The vehicle conversions were carried out by Hunting

Hivolt Ltd during 1982. The MOULD vehicles were withdrawn around 2003.

Shorland

The Shorland was an armoured car based on an uprated Land Rover 109-inch chassis. It had been developed in the early 1960s by Short Brothers & Harland to meet a requirement of the Royal Ulster Constabulary, and the RUC had purchased 16 Shorlands by the time it was restructured in the wake of the Hunt Report.

As a result, 15 of the 16 RUC Shorland Mk 1 vehicles were taken on Army Census as "transfers" and were given serials 27 BT 50, 27 BT 51, and 27 BT 62 to 27 BT 74; the other Shorland had been destroyed by fire while in storage after their withdrawal following the Hunt Report. The vehicles were refurbished and divided among the newly formed Ulster Defence Regiment (UDR) battalions in July 1971, although 1 UDR and 7 UDR did not receive any while each of the others received between two and four.

By this time, the latest version of Shorland was based on the Series 3 Land Rover chassis and was known as Shorland Mk 3. The Mk 3 had the six-cylinder engine in the One Ton chassis (invariably bearing export numbering), and had been introduced during 1969, so some were built on Series IIA chassis before the Series 3 entered production. In July 1971, MVEE conducted ballistic tests which made clear that the armour on Mk 3 models offered superior performance.

The Army subsequently placed a contract (FV15765) for 39 further Mk 3 vehicles, to be delivered in three batches, which gained serials 11 FL 92 to 12 FL 17, 60 FL 30 and 60 FL 31, and 77 FL 07 to 77 FL 27. Most of the deliveries were

FL 20 to 77 FL 27) were not issued but were retained as a reserve in Vehicle Sub-Depot, Northern Ireland. By late 1973, 6 UDR had the most with nine, while 8 UDR had only four so the distribution amongst the battalions was certainly not even.

Station Wagon

In addition, the Station Wagon version of the Series 3 also was used in various rôles, being known in army parlance as the "Car, Utility, ¼ Tonne" or "Car, Utility, ¾ Tonne" depending on wheelbase. The ¼ Tonne was used by various field commanders, by research and development establishments and also by Military Attachés. The ¾ Tonne was used by Postal & Courier detachments of the Royal Engineers and by Army Youth Teams. The rôle of Army Youth Teams was to take groups of young potential recruits on adventure training. These 'Car, Utilities' had only a few military modifications to the civilian specification, which included the colour scheme and a fire extinguisher.

TACR

As Chapter 6 explains, the TACR crash-rescue tender was originally developed on Series IIA (Rover 11) chassis and primarily for RAF use. However, the type proved sufficiently useful for all three services to take similar vehicles based on the Series 3 chassis. The Army Air Corps took just six examples, with serials 46 GF 35 to 46 GF 40.

Where the Rover 11 variants had used a 109 One Ton chassis specially fitted with a four-cylinder engine, the Series 3 types used standard military 109-inch chassis uprated to One Ton specification. The end result was more or less the same! When the Range Rover-based six-wheel TACR-2 crash rescue tender was introduced, these vehicles became known

60 FL 31 was one of a 39-strong order for Shorland armoured patrol vehicles that were destined for use by the UDR in Northern Ireland. (TMB)

made direct to the Army's Vehicle Sub-Depot at Long Kesh during the latter part of 1972 although the contract was not finally complete until 1974.

This contract gave the Army enough to equip three of the four newly raised battalions with Shorlands (although 10 UDR received none, probably because the vehicle was not considered useful in the streets of Belfast), to equip 1 UDR and to strengthen the existing six battalions using the Shorland Mk 1. In addition nine Shorlands (77 FL 16 and 77

A third crew member was carried on the rearward-facing seat at the back, and a simple speaking-tube allowed communication between him and the cab. (GF)

retrospectively as TACR-1 types.

Details of the RAF and RN TACR vehicles are given below.

Three-axle vehicles

From the late 1970s, Land Rover worked with a small number of specialist companies to develop three-axle, high-payload conversions of its utility models, supposedly with military contracts in mind. The Army purchased three such vehicles in the early 1980s, but took the idea no further.

Two of these, purchased at the end of October 1983, were Hotspur "Sandringham 6" conversions, and both were allocated to the Royal Artillery ranges in the Hebrides. 99 KB 84 and 99 KB 85 were on the 139-inch wheelbase version of this commercially-available chassis, which was designed by SMC in Bristol and commercialised through Hotspur Armoured Products of Neath, Glamorgan. Both had dropside bodies with a crane mounted behind the cab and were described as "Carrier, Wheeled, Utility, with crane, 6x6, Land Rover Sandringham". Few details of these vehicles are available but it is likely that they had the 2.6-litre six-cylinder engine rather than the military's preferred four-cylinder, which would have made them distinctly under-powered. They remained in service until 1996 (99 KB 84) and 2000 (99 KB 85).

RAF DELIVERIES

The RAF again took large quantities of the long-wheelbase Land Rover in its Series 3 form. There were types with both right-hand and left-hand drive, many for Cargo duties but also some Station Wagons and some FFR and other 24-volt vehicles. Most of the Cargo vehicles were to military specification with soft tops, but there were some with plain hard tops as well, and a number of vehicles were delivered with the close-to-civilian CL specification. As with its deliveries of Rover 11 models, the RAF tended to favour the window hard top body that was not available on the UK civilian market for tax reasons, and some of these were used by the RAF Police.

RAF vehicles delivered after the introduction of the tri-service serials in 1982 were obviously less easy to distinguish from those supplied to the other services, but they typically performed the same rôles. Some units also took pride in displaying an RAF roundel on the front and rear of the vehicle, although this was certainly not standard. Vehicles delivered in green (usually IRR Green) but used on airfields were given yellow side stripes to make them more visible.

Crash-rescue ambulance

The RAF continued to buy the Marshall-bodied ambulance for airfield crash-rescue duties. As with its Rover 11 deliveries, these had equipment differences from the similar vehicles supplied to the Army to suit their special rôle.

99 KB 85 was one of just two six-wheel conversions by Hotspur that were used on the artillery ranges in the Hebrides. It was pictured on Benbecula. (Roger Conway)

The RAF ordnance disposal teams used Series 3 Station Wagons like this one. 47 AM 33 has red-painted wings front and rear to mark out its special rôle. Note the Lucas fog lamps with their plastic covers above the front bumper. (GF)

Helicopter Support

As Chapter 10 explains, special versions of the Lightweight were developed to provide Ground Handling Support for helicopters. These were followed after around 18 months by similar conversions of the Series 3 109-inch vehicle, and from early 1978 the long-wheelbase conversions began to equip helicopter units of the RAF, principally 33 Squadron at Odiham and 230 Squadron at Gütersloh.

The vehicles chosen for conversion were hard tops, some fitted with windows, and all had the 24-volt, 90-amp electrical system that enabled them to act in the Helicopter Start rôle. The conversion work involved fitting a working platform above the hard top with a fold-down safety rail, and also providing an external socket for the "heli-start" connection in the hard top to the rear of the driver's door. The platform enabled technicians to work on the engines of helicopters and the tail rotor without needing specialist

Wearing one of the later tri-service serials, this RAF window hardtop was equipped with a public address system. The amber beacon on the roof and the yellow stripes on the bodywork and bumpers were to make the vehicle more visible when operating on an airfield.(GF)

The window hardtop was a model not sold on the civilian market in the UK for tax reasons. This example is typical of a great many that belonged to the RAF. (GF)

platforms.

These conversions were followed by some similar vehicles built with the Helicopter Support specification from new, and in 1981 these began to enter service and replace the earlier conversions. They were known as "Truck, Helicopter Ground Handling, ¾ ton, 4x4, 24v, Rover Series 3" types. Eventually these vehicles were transferred to the 'Support

Helicopter Force' and with that unit some saw service in Operation Granby – the first Gulf War in 1990.

MDJR

Also unique to the RAF were the Mountain, Desert and Jungle Rescue (MDJR) versions of the Series 3 109-inch vehicle which equipped the various rescue teams around the

The Series 3 109 also appeared as a helicopter starting and servicing vehicle, when it used a modified hardtop body. The RAF's 73 AM 29 is seen here while under evaluation at FVRDE in Chertsey, both with and without the roof-mounted platform deployed. (TMB)

The RAF favoured window hardtop models for many rôles, including that of the Mountain, Desert and Jungle Rescue ambulance. (Far left – TMB; left – GF)

world including the UK-based Mountain Rescue Teams. At least two such versions are known, one a command and control vehicle and the other a two-stretcher ambulance.

TACR

The RAF took the lion's share of the TACR crash-rescue vehicles, with a total of 29 that were serialled as 30 AG 42 to 30 AG 70.

The TACR was used by all three branches of the armed forces. 91 RN 48 was pictured by the body manufacturer before delivery to the Royal Navy. (HCB-Angus)

The Royal Navy also continued to buy Station Wagons. The two vehicles have different roof racks and carry their spare wheels there instead of in the standard positions on the tail door or the bonnet. There is a rack on the tail door to carry a jerrycan, and the styles of rear number-plate also differ. (HMS Heron)

ROYAL NAVY DELIVERIES

The Royal Navy took its usual selection of Station Wagons and soft top Land Rovers, but also bought a number of window hard top models and fell into line with the Army and RAF by purchasing some Marshall-bodied ambulances to the standard pattern. As was the case with RAF vehicles, the Land Rovers delivered for Royal Navy use after the introduction of the tri-service serials in 1982 were less easy to distinguish from those supplied to the other services, but typically performed the same rôles as before.

TACR

The Royal Navy took 23 of the 67 TACR vehicles built on Series 3 chassis, and gave them serials 06 RN 24, 71 RN 50 to 71 RN 54, 90 RN 63 to 90 RN 69, 91 RN 48 and 91 RN 49, 93 RN 02, 96 RN 01 to 96 RN 02 and 96 RN 57, 96 RN 59, 96 RN 63, 96 RN 66 and 96 RN 67.

The TACRs had Series IIA door hinges so that their cab doors could be opened flat against the body sides for ease of access. 46 GF 36 was pictured on service at Dehekelia in Cyprus in a "dayglo" reflective colour scheme. (GF)

Pictured when new, 38 FL 83 was one of a large batch of RHD Cargo vehicles. Note that the vehicles were delivered in Bronze Green with many galvanised parts bare but they quickly were re-sprayed in black over green camouflage in most cases. (Land Rover)

16 GX 78 was a RHD FFR soft-top, seen here being driven with some enthusiasm by a representative of the manufacturer. Despite this vehicle being RHD it was initially issued to Ordnance Depot Antwerp before returning to the UK without issue. (Land Rover)

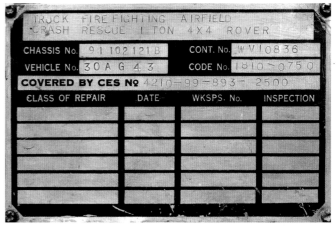

As the plate from 30 AG 43 shows, this was a 'Truck, Firefighting, Airfield Crash Rescue, 1 Ton, 4x4, Rover'. (GF)

27 HF 03 was delivered as a GS vehicle, but was modified to mine-protected status. It was seen here after withdrawal and purchase by a civilian collector. A number of vehicles from this contract were converted for use during Operation Agila. This was the operation to monitor the ceasefire and handover of weapons in Northern Rhodesia and the country's transition into Zimbabwe. (John Craddock)

SUMMARY OF ROVER SERIES 3 DELIVERIES, 1971-1985

The earliest contracts for Series 3 109 models were numbered in the old WV series. However, the file code for these contracts changed in 1976 (approximately), and the later contracts had an FVE prefix.

Lists cover vehicles ordered under contracts, and do not include vehicles transferred in from other services or elsewhere. RAF vehicles allocated to NATO are not included. Chassis suffix letter codes are given where available. For brevity, the tables show only the serial numbers (and not the prefix code) of vehicles built with VIN numbers.

Note that there were special procurement arrangements for the Berlin Brigade. Vehicle purchases were treated as part of the offsetting agreements for the Berlin Garrison with the Senät (the executive body that governed the city) and were charged to that body. They are therefore not associated with any MoD contract numbers, and none of the official documents so far discovered show a contract number of any kind.

There were several "master" contracts (e.g. WV8765, FVE 22A/44 and FVE 22A/140) from which individual vehicles were ordered by "warrant". These contracts were in effect open documents and allowed individual or small-quantity vehicle purchases without the formalities associated with the larger contracts. Warrant Numbers covered the authority to purchase a vehicle or vehicles; Item Numbers were added to the contracts to record these purchases.

When chassis numbers reached 911-99999C, the next number allocated was 911-00001D! Although this resulted in some duplication of the serial numbers, the different suffix codes ensured that there was no confusion. For numbers allocated under the ISO VIN system see the panel on page 141.

ARMY & TRI-SERVICE DELIVERIES

Serials	Contract	Chassis Nos	Total	Remarks
00 FL 10 to 00 FL 31	WV8765 R2079	911-00423A to 911-00444A	22	CL Cargo RHD.
05 FL 49 to 05 FL 66	WV8765 R2099	934-01346A to 934-01363A	18	Station Wagon LHD.
06 FL 33	WV8765 R2102	934-00808A	1	Station Wagon LHD; to Military Attaché, Warsaw.
06 FL 34	WV8765 R2129	934-01057A	1	LHD Station Wagon; to Military Attaché, Buenos Aires.
11 FL 92 to 12 FL 17	FV15765	942-00047A to 942-00074A	26	RHD? Shorland APV.
12 FL 18 to 12 FL 23	WV8765 R2154	911-00482A to 911-00487A	6	CL Cargo RHD Hard Top.
14 FL 99	WV8765 R2163	911-01082A	1	CL Cargo RHD.
22 FL 68 to 22 FL 75	WV8765 R2164	931-00388A to 931-00395A	8	Station Wagon RHD.
22 FL 76 to 22 FL 86	WV8765 R2164	934-02201A to 934-02193A	11	Station Wagon LHD.
22 FL 87 and 22 FL 88	WV8765 R2177	914-01249A and 914-01250A	2	CL Cargo LHD.
35 FL 68 to 35 FL 71	WV10817	911-01937B to 911-01934B	4	Field Ambulance RHD.
35 FL 74	WV8765 R2204	931-00086A	1	Station Wagon RHD; to Services Adviser Pakistan.
38 FL 76 to 41 FL 26	WV10786	911-00924A to 911-02575B	251	Cargo RHD.
41 FL 27 to 43 FL 82	WV10786	914-01554A to 914-06158B	266	Cargo LHD.
43 FL 84 to 44 FL 51	WV10776	911-01148A to 911-02364B	68	FFR RHD.
44 FL 52 to 45 FL 35	WV10776	914-02604A to 914-05857B	84	FFR LHD.
59 FL 98	WV8765 R2224	931-00481A	1	Station Wagon RHD; to Military Attaché, Pretoria.
59 FL 99	WV8765 R2225	934-02375A	1	Station Wagon LHD; to Military Attaché, Addis Ababa.
60 FL 00	WV8765 R2226	934-02736A	1	Station Wagon LHD; to Military Attaché, Seoul.
60 FL 01	WV8765 R2227	934-02737A	1	Station Wagon LHD.
60 FL 02	WV8765 R2228	934-02830A	1	Station Wagon LHD; to Military Attaché, Warsaw.
60 FL 30 to 60 FL 31	FV15765	942-00073A and 942-00072A	2	Shorland APV, RHD.
77 FL 07 to 77 FL 27	FV15765	942-00132A to 942-00274B	21	Shorland APV RHD; Note that although these vehicles have LHD chassis numbers they were in fact RHD!
00 FM 78 to 00 FM 82	WV8765	931-00540A to 931-00544A	5	Station Wagon RHD.
03 FM 12	WV8765	934-03748B	1	Station Wagon LHD; to Military Attaché, Manila.
03 FM 80	WV8765	934-03855B	1	Station Wagon LHD; to Military Attaché, Belgrade; to Army 05/77.
04 FM 64	WV8765	931-01196B	1	Station Wagon RHD; to Military Defence Adviser Uganda, to Kenya 04/75.
04 FM 65 and 04 FM 66	n/a	934-03506B and 934-03507B	2	Station Wagon LHD; to NATO rôle.
18 FM 78 to 19 FM 16	WV8765	911-03915B to 911-04719B	39	CL Cargo RHD.

ARMY & TRI-SERVICE DELIVERIES

Serials	Contract	Chassis Nos	Total	Remarks
34 FM 79 and 34 FM 80	WV8765	934-05133B and 934-05134B	2	Station Wagon LHD; 34 FM 79 to Military Attaché, Bangkok and then Vientiane, 34 FM 80 to Military Attaché, Rangoon.
34 FM 81	WV8765	931-01180B	1	Station Wagon RHD; to Military Attaché, Djakarta.
34 FM 82	WV8765	934-05135B	1	Station Wagon LHD; to Military Attaché, Teheran.
34 FM 83 to 42 FM 93	WV11138	911-02677B to 911-05443B	811	Cargo RHD.
42 FM 94 to 45 FM 07	WV11138	914-07933B to 914-10431B	214	Cargo LHD.
49 FM 27 to 51 FM 81	WV11180	914-08729B to 914-11538C	255	FFR LHD.
51 FM 82 to 56 FM 26	WV11180	911-03360B to 911-05095B	445	FFR RHD.
57 FM 18	WV8765	911-03110B	1	CL Cargo RHD.
61 FM 60 to 61 FM 72	WV8765	931-01354B to 931-01366B	13	Station Wagon RHD.
61 FM 73 to 62 FM 00	WV8765	934-05764B to 934-05789B	28	Station Wagon LHD.
65 FM 25 to 67 FM 14	WV11138	911-05014B to 911-05431B	190	Cargo RHD.
75 FM 40 to 77 FM 33	WV11180	914-11524C to 914-10674C	194	FFR LHD.
77 FM 34 to 79 FM 53	WV11180	911-05098B to 911-05666C	220	FFR RHD.
01 GB 08 to 01 GB 63	WV8765	911-04351B to 911-04708B	56	CL Cargo RHD.
05 GB 41 to 05 GB 48	WV8765	911-03900B to 911-03911B	8	CL Cargo RHD.
06 GB 04	WV8765	949-01130B	1	Station Wagon 6 cyl, LHD; to UK National Support Element, Turkey.
22 GB 93	WV8765	931-01423B	1	RHD Station Wagon Tropical; to Service Attaché, Bangkok.
27 GB 22 to 27 GB 26	WV11406	911-06699C to 911-06712C	5	FFR RHD.
27 GB 68 to 27 GB 88	WV8765	931-01437B to 931-01457B	21	Station RHD Wagon.
27 GB 89 to 28 GB 03	WV8765	934-06363B to 934-06376B	15	Station Wagon LHD.
28 GB 05 to 28 GB 39	WV8765	911-07155C to 911-07350C	35	CL Cargo RHD.
29 GB 07 to 30 GB 51	WV11403	911-06288C to 911-07042C	145	Cargo RHD.
30 GB 52 to 30 GB 96	WV11403	914-15078C to 914-15286C	45	Cargo LHD.
38 GB 83	WV8765	931-01760C	1	Station Wagon Tropical RHD; to Services Advisor, Cyprus.
38 GB 84	WV8765	934-08121C	1	Station Wagon LHD; to Service Attaché, Brazil.
38 GB 93	WV8765	934-08131C	1	Station Wagon LHD; to Defence Attaché, Seoul.
38 GB 94	WV8765	934-08132C	1	Station Wagon LHD; to Defence Attaché, Muscat/Oman.
42 GB 13	WV8765	931-01765C	1	Station Wagon RHD; to Service Advisor, Colombo, later BDLS India.
43 GB 04 to 43 GB 21	WV8765	911-07209C to 911-16941C	18	CL Cargo RHD.
43 GB 22 to 44 GB 24	WV11402	911-06183C to 911-06939C	103	FFR RHD.
44 GB 25 to 45 GB 24	WV11402	914-14724C to 914-16036C	100	FFR LHD.
46 GB 72	WV8765	931-01766C	1	Station Wagon RHD.
00 GF 04	WV8765	934-18439C	1	Station Wagon LHD; to Services Advisor, Nigeria.
01 GF 39 to 02 GF 38	WV11587	911-06989C to 911-07205C	100	FFR RHD.
04 GF 54 to 04 GF 74	WV11402	911-06942C to 911-06988C	21	FFR RHD.
06 GF 99 to 07 GF 25	WV8765	911-06635C to 911-07154C	27	CL Cargo Hard Top with Windows RHD; all for 1 Ammo IDU.
07 GF 65	WV8765	934-08380C	1	Station Wagon Tropical RHD; to Service Attaché, Baghdad.
19 GF 22 to 20 GF 74	WV8765	911-07059C to 911-17802C	153	CL Cargo RHD.
46 GF 35 to 46 GF 38	WV11629	911-25894C to 911-25899C	4	TACR RHD.
46 GF 39 to 46 GF 40	WV11629	914-25913C to 914-5932C	2	TACR LHD.
46 GF 42	WV8765	934-24967C	1	Station Wagon LHD; to Services Attaché, Amman.
46 GF 43	WV8765	934-21951C	1	Station Wagon LHD; to Services Attaché, Ankara.

ARMY & TRI-SERVICE DELIVERIES

Serials	Contract	Chassis Nos	Total	Remarks
46 GF 44 to 46 GF 45	WV8765	949-15403C to 949-15082C	2	Station Wagon 6 cyl LHD; to UK Support Element, Turkey.
46 GF 46	WV8765	949-15083C	1	Station Wagon 6 cyl LHD; to Services Attaché, Caracas, later to Army.
46 GF 47	WV8765	934-23321C	1	Station Wagon LHD; to Defence Attaché, Kinshasa.
46 GF 48	WV8765	934-23320C	1	Station Wagon LHD; to Services Attaché, Budapest.
46 GF 49	WV8765	934-21951C	1	Station Wagon LHD; to Services Attaché, Ankara.
46 GF 51 to 46 GF 90	WV8765	931-22091C to 931-23975C	40	Station Wagon RHD.
46 GF 91 to 46 GF 96	WV8765	934-23989C to 934-23996C	6	Station Wagon LHD.
47 GF 49 to 47 GF 60	WV11761	942-00425C to 942-00463C	12	Shorland Mark 3 RHD; although built on LHD chassis these vehicles were RHD.
47 GF 62	WV11704	914-24707C	1	Cargo LHD.
47 GF 63	WV11702	914-24812C	1	FFR LHD.
47 GF 64 to 51 GF 69	WV11702	911-25358C to 911-28749C	410	Cargo RHD.
51 GF 70 to 52 GF 10	WV11702	914-24039C to 914-22855C	41	Cargo LHD.
56 GF 58 to 59 GF 02	WV11713	911-24862C to 911-27343C	245	Cargo RHD.
59 GF 03 to 59 GF 62	WV11713	914-24712C to 914-24702C	60	Cargo LHD.
62 GF 73 to 63 GF 57	WV11713	914-33302C to 914-34485C	185	Cargo LHD.
63 GF 58 to 64 GF 57	WV11703	911-27450C to 911-28461C	100	Cargo RHD.
64 GF 58 to 65 GF 07	WV11703	914-28663C to 914-29470C	50	Cargo LHD.
20 GJ 40 to 21 GJ 53	WV8765	911-48491C to 911-49982C	114	CL Cargo RHD.
21 GJ 54 to 23 GJ 45	WV8765	914-49372C to 914-50672C	192	CL Cargo LHD.
52 GJ 05 to 55 GJ 31	WV11990	911-49442C to 911-60898C	327	FFR RHD.
55 GJ 32 to 58 GJ 51	WV11990	914-53853C to 914-61229C	320	FFR LHD.
58 GJ 91 to 58 GJ 96	WV8765	931-51379C to 931-51386C	6	Station Wagon RHD.
58 GJ 97 to 59 GJ 11	WV8765	934-51827C to 934-52170C	15	Station Wagon LHD.
67 GJ 15 to 67 GJ 24	WV8765	931-51388C to 931-51834C	10	Station Wagon RHD.
67 GJ 25 to 67 GJ 44	WV8765	934-52178C to 934-53040C	20	Station Wagon LHD.
00 GN 17 to 00 GN 21	WV8765	934-54528C to 934-54533C	4	Station Wagon Tropical LHD; 17 to Services Attaché, Teheran; 18 to Services Attaché, Jeddah; 19 to Defence Attaché, Rabat; 20 Cancelled; 21 to Services Attaché, Khartoum; 22 to Services Attaché, Oslo.
00 GN 88 to 01 GN 52	WV12088	911-95673C to 911-60475C	65	Field Ambulance RHD.
02 GN 12 to 02 GN 61	WV12087	911-62339C to 911-72907C	50	FFR RHD.
02 GN 62 to 03 GN 11	WV12087	914-61382C to 914-62260C	50	FFR LHD.
03 GN 53 to 05 GN 32	WV8765	911-66818C to 911-68117C	180	CL Cargo RHD.
05 GN 33 to 05 GN 72	WV8765	914-65181C to 914-70536C	40	CL Cargo LHD.
06 GN 25 to 06 GN 30	WV12145	914-61288C to 914-61368C	6	FFR LHD.
12 GN 11 to 13 GN 10	WV8765	911-70241C to 911-78357C	100	CL Cargo RHD.
15 GN 57 to 15 GN 86	FVE 22A/12	911-66325C to 911-66623C	30	Cargo RHD; several to Carawagon TCP.
15 GN 87 to 16 GN 56	FVE 22A/12	914-66623C to 914-67240C	70	Cargo LHD; several to Carawagon TCP.
16 GN 57 to 19 GN 56	FVE 22A/11	911-67204C to 911-71807C	300	FFR RHD.
19 GN 57 to 22 GN 56	FVE 22A/11	914-72422C to 914-78794C	300	FFR LHD.
23 GN 55	WV8765	934-62541C	1	Station Wagon LHD; to Services Attaché, Warsaw.
25 GN 76	WV8765	934-83585C	1	Station Wagon Tropical LHD; to Services Attaché, Jeddah.
03 GT 18 to 04 GT 00	WV8765	911-82963C to 911-84929C	83	CL Cargo RHD.
04 GT 01 to 04 GT 17	WV8765	914-83152C to 914-83918C	17	CL Cargo LHD.
28 GT 44 to 31 GT 02	FVE 22A/47	911-92772C to 911-97028C	259	FFR RHD.
31 GT 03 to 34 GT 43	FVE 22A/47	914-97084C to 914-00275D	341	FFR LHD.

ARMY & TRI-SERVICE DELIVERIES

Serials	Contract	Chassis Nos	Total	Remarks
34 GT 50 to 35 GT 22	FVE 22A/49	911-98641C to 911-00444D	73	Cargo RHD.
35 GT 23 to 39 GT 04	FVE 22A/49	914-89262C to 914-92277C	382	Cargo LHD.
42 GT 58 to 46 GT 21	FVE 22A/44	911-84930C to 911-99825C	364	CL Cargo RHD.
46 GT 22 to 46 GT 68	FVE 22A/44	914-04866D to 914-09254D	47	CL Cargo LHD.
46 GT 69 to 46 GT 80	FVE 22A/61	911-01103D to 911-01100D	12	FFR RHD.
92 GT 73 to 92 GT 77	FVE 22A/44 R3200	931-87983C to 931-87998C	5	Station Wagon RHD.
92 GT 78 to 93 GT 18	FVE 22A/44 R3200	931-88001C to 931-97035C	41	Station Wagon RHD.
93 GT 19 to 93 GT 28	FVE 22A/44 R3200	934-91521C to 934-95156C	10	Station Wagon LHD.
00 GX 01 to 00 GX 78	FVE 22A/49	911-96726C to 911-98637C	78	Cargo RHD.
00 GX 79 to 02 GX 04	FVE 22A/49	914-86116C to 914-89551C	126	Cargo LHD.
10 GX 17 to 10 GX 58	FVE 22A/71	911-96664C to 911-97820C	42	Cargo RHD.
16 GX 48 to 21 GX 01	FVE 22A/69	911-10384D to 911-13997D	454	FFR RHD.
21 GX 02 to 22 GX 50	FVE 22A/69	914-16030D to 914-16061D and 100090 to 101808	149	FFR LHD.
16 GX 14	FVE 22A/44 R3261	931-97309C	1	Station Wagon Tropical RHD; to Services Attaché, Djakarta.
05 HF 28	FVE 22A/44 R3276	931-97746C	1	Station Wagon Tropical RHD; to Services Adviser, Pakistan.
26 HF 64 to 31 HF 53	FVE 22A/87	911-11094D to 911-16058 and 100068 to 104443	490	Cargo RHD.
31 HF 54 to 33 HF 04	FVE 22A/87	104619 to 107728	151	Cargo LHD.
45 HF 23	FVE 22A/44 R3329	931-09778D	1	Station Wagon RHD; to Service Adviser, Kenya.
60 HF 78 to 61 HF 13	FVE 22A/44 R3353	911-12367D to 911-15989D	36	CL Cargo RHD.
17 HG 17 to 19 HG 56	FVE 22A/95	108995 to 113792	240	Cargo RHD.
19 HG 57 to 20 HG 46	FVE 22A/95	113962 to 115604	90	Cargo LHD.
20 HG 47 to 21 HG 40	FVE 22A/95	911-14052D to 911-14790D and 103119 to 103419	94	FFR RHD.
21 HG 41 to 22 HG 07	FVE 22A/95	104856 to 106033	67	FFR LHD.
23 HG 01	FVE 22A/44 R3376	112305	1	Station Wagon LHD; to Services Attaché, Buenos Aires; later Defence Attaché, Montevideo.
37 HG 72 to 38 HG 29	FVE 22A/44 R3397	107853 to 116343	58	CL Cargo RHD.
45 HG 37 to 45 HG 39	FVE 22A/115	108439 to 118191	3	Cargo LHD.
45 HG 40 to 45 HG 56	FVE 22A/115	118197 to 118293	17	Cargo RHD.
57 HG 40 to 60 HG 68	FVE 22A/115	118805 to 123081	329	Cargo LHD.
60 HG 69 to 65 HG 63	FVE 22A/115	123983 to 131140	495	Cargo RHD.
65 HG 64 to 67 HG 23	FVE 22A/115	110930 to 113790	160	FFR LHD.
67 HG 24 to 70 HG 58	FVE 22A/115	114162 to 119384	335	FFR RHD.
70 HG 93	FVE 22A/44 R3407	125943	1	Station Wagon LHD; to SAAS.
70 HG 94	FVE 22A/44 R3413	125947	1	Station Wagon LHD; to Services Adviser, Nigeria.
70 HG 99	FVE 22A/44 R3415	128870	1	LHD Station Wagon; to Services Attaché, Prague.
72 HG 53	FVE 22A/44 R3439	128161	1	Station Wagon LHD; to Services Attaché, Baghdad.
00 HH 01 to 00 HH 06	FVE 22A/44 R3441	125648 to 126569	6	Station Wagon RHD.
00 HH 07 to 00 HH 10	FVE 22A/44 R3441	126590 to 128163	4	Station Wagon LHD.
04 HH 28 to 05 HH 37	FVE 22A/115	131627 to 132089	110	Cargo RHD.
05 HH 77 to 06 HH 67	FVE 22A/115	130766 to 132436	91	FFR RHD.
09 HH 78	FVE 22A/44 R3507	144189	1	Station Wagon RHD; to Services Attaché, Nepal.
09 HH 79	FVE 22A/44 R3506	146180	1	Station Wagon RHD; to Service Attaché, Budapest.
03 HJ 45	FVE 22A/140	157488	1	Station Wagon LHD; to Defence Attaché, Khartoum.
03 HJ 71 to 03 HJ 92	FVE 22A/140	154829 to 155722	22	CL Cargo Hard Top RHD; for MOULD Insertion Vehicle.
03 HJ 93 to 04 HJ 03	FVE 22A/140	153842 to 153834	11	CL Cargo Hard Top RHD; for MOULD Repair.

ARMY & TRI-SERVICE DELIVERIES

Serials	Contract	Chassis Nos	Total	Remarks
08 KA 01 to 10 KA 53	FVE 22A/140 R3527	158851 to 159280	253	CL Cargo RHD.
14 KA 25	FVE 22A/140 R3536	168351	1	Station Wagon LHD; to Services Adviser, Ghana.
14 KA 26 to 15 KA 61	FVE 22A/140 R3527	160520 to 160750	136	CL Cargo RHD.
15 KA 62 to 16 KA 61	FVE 22A/140 R3527	160419 to 160519	100	CL Cargo LHD.
16 KA 90 to 16 KA 91	FVE 22A/140 R3557	174557 and 174608	2	CL Cargo Hard Top RHD w/Windows (Diesel).
17 KA 50 to 17 KA 80	FVE 21B/229	169903 to 171013	31	FFR RHD.
17 KA 81 to 18 KA 25	FVE 21B/229	170013 to 191527	45	FFR RHD; possibly USAF funded for RAF Regiment.
18 KA 26 to 18 KA 60	FVE 21B/229	170011 to 191128	35	Cargo RHD; possibly USAF funded for RAF Regiment.
18 KA 61 to 18 KA 65	FVE 21B/229	170168 to 170322	5	Cargo RHD.
18 KA 66 to 18 KA 72	FVE 21B/229	169901 to 170303	7	Cargo LHD.
18 KA 73 to 18 KA 83	FVE 21B/229	173635 to 173682	10	Cargo Hard Top RHD w/windows; for RAF.
20 KA 25	FVE 22A/140 LR3563	177843	1	Station Wagon LHD; for Services Attaché, Ankara.
36 KA 64 to 36 KA 74	FVE 22A/140 LR3584	175095 to 175733	11	Station Wagon RHD.
36 KA 75 to 37 KA 27	FVE 22A/140 LR3584	177981 to 180024	53	Station Wagon LHD.
37 KA 28 to 37 KA 31	FVE 22A/140 LR3584	180024 to 180082	4	Station Wagon Tropical LHD.
37 KA 40 to 38 KA 11	FVE 22A/140 LR3586	175146 to 175762	72	CL Cargo RHD.
38 KA 12 to 38 KA 53	FVE 22A/140 LR3586	178674 to 179299	42	CL Cargo LHD.
82 KA 22 to 83 KA 51	FVE 21B/244	175436 to 180180	130	FFR LHD.
85 KA 52 to 86 KA 80	FVE 21B/244	174556 to 176373	129	Cargo RHD.
86 KA 81 to 88 KA 51	FVE 21B/244	174552 to 177345	171	Cargo LHD.
88 KA 52 to 91 KA 95	FVE 21B/244	180192 to 184155	344	FFR LHD.
93 KA 89 to 96 KA 66	FVE 21B/244	176375 to 180189	278	Cargo LHD.
96 KA 67 to 98 KA 74	FVE 21B/244	180194 to 182357	208	Cargo RHD.
98 KA 75 to 98 KA 87	FVE 21B/244	182403 to 182495	13	Cargo RHD.
98 KA 88 to 99 KA 57	FVE 22A/140 LR3600	182515 to 183268	70	CL Cargo RHD.
99 KA 58 to 99 KA 97	FVE 22A/140 LR3600	183744 to 184281	70	CL Cargo LHD.
18 KB 19 to 19 KB 19	FVE 22A/140 LR3600	180447 to 183686	101	CL Cargo RHD.
21 KB 49 to 21 KB 52	FVE 22A/140 LR3604	183766 to 183793	4	Cargo Hard Top RHD w/windows Anti-Spark (Diesel); to RAF.
21 KB 53 to 21 KB 55	FVE 22A/140 LR3604	185371 to 184802	3	Cargo Hard Top LHD w/windows Anti-Spark (Diesel); to RAF.
22 KB 80 to 23 KB 04	FVE 21B/244	185344 to 185465	25	Cargo RHD.
23 KB 05	FVE 21B/244	185543	1	Cargo Hard Top RHD with windows, 24v 90A; to RAF.
23 KB 06	FVE 21B/244	185543	1	Cargo Hard Top RHD, w/side windows; to RAF.
23 KB 16 to 23 KB 21	FVE 21B/244	185550 to 185665	6	Cargo Hard Top RHD with windows, 24v 90A; to RAF.
23 KB 42	FVE 21B/244	185431	1	Cargo RHD.
23 KB 43 to 23 KB 61	FVE 21B/244	185672 to 186026	19	Cargo RHD.
29 KB 71	-	158849	1	For Defence Sales Tour – details n/a.
30 KB 40	FVE 21B/244	192169	1	FFR RHD.
41 KB 11	FVE 22A/140 LR3649	195338	1	Station Wagon LHD; to Defence Attaché, Seoul.
41 KB 15 to 41 KB 16	FVE 21B/229	194637 and 194639	2	FFR RHD.
45 KB 48	FVE 22A/140 LR3664	195369	1	Station Wagon Tropical RHD; to Services Adviser, Bangladesh.
48 KB 49	FVE 22A/140 LR3663	202498	1	Station Wagon LHD; to Services Attaché, Amman.
51 KB 01	FVE 22A/140 LR3682	188916	1	Station Wagon LHD; to Services Attaché, Tel Aviv.
58 KB 36 to 61 KB 35	FVE 22A/225	197261 to 200236	300	Cargo RHD.
61 KB 36 to 64 KB 85	FVE 22A/225	196908 to 203827	350	FFR RHD.
65 KB 80	Local Purchase	175011	1	Station Wagon Tropical RHD; for Defence Attaché, Jedda.
71 KB 42	FVE 22A/227	199762	1	RHD FFR.

ARMY & TRI-SERVICE DELIVERIES

Serials	Contract	Chassis Nos	Total	Remarks
71 KB 43 to 71 KB 47	FVE 22A/227	200301 to 200583	5	Carawagon TCP LHD; batch contains one vehicle with an RHD VIN prefix – 71 KB 46.
71 KB 48 to 71 KB 52	FVE 22A/227	200240 to 200294	5	Carawagon TCP RHD; batch contains one vehicle with an LHD VIN prefix – 71 KB 52.
71 KB 55 to 71 KB 59	FVE 22A/227	201528 to 201549	5	Cargo LHD.
72 KB 29 to 72 KB 53	FVE 22A/227	201554 to 201719	25	Cargo LHD; purchased for Air Bottle Charging Equipment (ABCE).
73 KB 67	Local Purchase	537198	1	Station Wagon RHD; for Defence Attaché, Pretoria; assembled in South Africa from CKD kit and given South African Chassis number.
73 KB 68 to 73 KB 72	FVE 22A/227	205892 to 206192	5	RHD Cargo.
82 KB 64 to 84 KB 25	FVE 22A/240	206644 to 210405	162	FFR RHD.
85 KB 32 to 86 KB 00	FVE 22A/240	205493 to 209695	69	Cargo RHD.
86 KB 01 to 86 KB 41	FVE 22A/240	206961 to 208009	41	Cargo LHD.
86 KB 42 to 87 KB 10	FVE 22A/240	206891 to 207411	69	FFR RHD.
88 KB 25 to 88 KB 27	FVE 22A/140 LR3762	209533 to 209540	3	Cargo Hard Top RHD w/windows; to RAF.
88 KB 28 to 88 KB 33	FVE 22A/140 LR3762	209649 to 209748	6	Cargo Hard Top LHD w/windows; to RAF.
88 KB 34 to 88 KB 35	FVE 22A/140 LR3759	209650 and 209653	2	Station Wagon RHD.
90 KB 68 to 90 KB 90	FVE 22A/240	209705 to 210400	23	Cargo RHD.
90 KB 91 to 91 KB 14	FVE 22A/240	209828 to 210016	24	FFR RHD.
99 KB 84 and 99 KB 85	ML22A/433	193627 and 193629	2	Hotspur three-axle conversion, RHD.
07 KC 36	Local Purchase	180242	1	Cargo Hard Top RHD w/side windows, Diesel.
21 KC 52	FVE 22A/140 LR3772	210351	1	Station Wagon RHD; to Services Adviser, Cyprus.
44 KC 95 to 45 KC 14	FVE 22A/251	219525 to 226446	20	Cargo LHD.
45 KC 15 to 46 KC 63	FVE 22A/251	219528 to 225610	149	Cargo RHD.
61 KC 79 to 62 KC 31	FVE 22A/251	220697 to 225878	53	Cargo RHD.
62 KC 32 to 62 KC 43	FVE 22A/251	220186 to 226895	12	Cargo LHD.
62 KC 44 to 62 KC 53	FVE 22A/251	221126 to 226032	10	Cargo RHD.
62 KC 54 to 63 KC 16	FVE 22A/251	228574 to 228563	63	Cargo LHD.
63 KC 17 to 64 KC 83	FVE 22A/251	221145 to 228043	167	Cargo RHD.
64 KC 84	FVE 22A/251	223111	1	Carawagon TCP RHD.
64 KC 85 to 64 KC 97	FVE 22A/251	221954 to 222264	13	FFR LHD.
64 KC 98 to 65 KC 16	FVE 22A/251	224987 to 227695	19	FFR RHD.
65 KC 17 to 65 KC 23	FVE 22A/251	222268 to 222453	7	FFR LHD.
65 KC 24 to 65 KC 33	FVE 22A/251	224970 to 228040	10	FFR RHD.
65 KC 34 to 65 KC 43	FVE 22A/251	222458 to 224191	10	FFR LHD.
65 KC 44 to 65 KC 49	FVE 22A/251	228046 to 228210	6	FFR RHD.
67 KC 10	Local Purchase	540649	1	Station Wagon Tropical RHD; to Defence Attaché, Djakarta; built from CKD kit, possibly in South Africa.
72 KC 52 to 73 KC 51	FVE 22A/251	219553 to 228991	100	FFR LHD.
73 KC 52 to 76 KC 51	FVE 22A/251	219542 to 227840	300	FFR RHD.
76 KC 52 to 76 KC 57	FVE 22A/251	221945 to 222255	6	CL Cargo RHD.
76 KC 58 to 78 KC 57	FVE 22A/251	219548 to 228373	200	CL Cargo LHD.
78 KC 58 to 80 KC 57	FVE 22A/251	220667 to 228564	200	CL Cargo RHD.
80 KC 58	FVE 22A/251	223937	1	Station Wagon LHD.
80 KC 59 to 81 KC 03	FVE 22A/251	222060 to 223929	45	Station Wagon RHD.
81 KC 04	FVE 22A/251	223729	1	Station wagon V8 LHD; to Defence Attaché, Bucharest.
81 KC 05 to 81 KC 07	FVE 22A/251	229332 to 229515	3	Cargo Hard Top LHD.
81 KC 08 to 81 KC 34	FVE 22A/251	228346 to 229509	27	Cargo Hard Top RHD

ARMY & TRI-SERVICE DELIVERIES

Serials	Contract	Chassis Nos	Total	Remarks
81 KC 97	FVE 22A/251	224363	1	Station Wagon LHD; to Services Adviser, Nigeria.
81 KC 98 to 82 KC 01	FVE 22A/274	228839 to 228587	4	FFR RHD.
82 KC 02 to 82 KC 04	FVE 22A/152	221950 to 222711	3	Station Wagon RHD; for RN.
82 KC 05	FVE 22A/152	223289	1	Station Wagon Diesel RHD; for RN.
04 KD 12 and 04 KD 13	FVE 22A/251	227436 and 227441	2	Helicopter Ground Handling LHD; to RAF.
04 KD 14 and 04 KD 15	FVE 22A/251	228204 and 235938	2	Helicopter Ground Handling RHD; to RAF.
04 KD 16 to 04 KD 22	FVE 22A/251	226657 to 227328	7	CL Cargo Diesel RHD; to RAF.
04 KD 23 to 04 KD 30	FVE 22A/251	227411 to 228041	8	CL Cargo Diesel RHD; to RAF.
04 KD 31 to 04 KD 41	FVE 22A/251	228783 to 229640	11	Anti-Spark, Hard Top LHD w/windows Diesel; to RAF.
04 KD 42 to 04 KD 44	FVE 22A/251	226400 to 226456	3	Anti-Spark, Hard Top RHD w/windows Diesel; to RAF.
04 KD 45 to 04 KD 50	FVE 22A/251	228597 to 228914	6	FFR RHD Van.
09 KD 26 to 09 KD 31	FVE 22A/251	n/a	6	CL Cargo Hard Top RHD w/windows.

Total 17,692

RAF DELIVERIES

Serials	Contract	Chassis Nos	Total	Remarks
27 AJ 48 to 27 AJ 77	WV10104	911-01726B to 911-01903B	30	RHD Cargo.
30 AG 42 to 30 AG 44	WV10836	911-02117B to 911-02119B	3	RHD TACR Mk 1.
47 AM 27 to 47 AM 34	n/a	n/a	8	LHD Station Wagon.
48 AM 32	WV8765	n/a	1	LHD Station Wagon; to Air Attaché, Teheran; later to 30 BT 73.
58 AM 19 and 58 AM 20	WV10867	911-02467B and 911-02469B	2	RHD MDJR Control.
58 AM 21 to 58 AM 23	WV10879	911-02472B to 911-02475B	3	RHD MDJR Control.
60 AM 29 to 60 AM 34	WV11099	911-04064B to 911-04071B	6	RHD MDJR Cargo/2 Stretcher Ambulance.
60 AM 35 to 60 AM 49	WV11099	911-03305B to 911-04062B	15	RHD Cargo.
60 AM 50 to 60 AM 59	WV11099	914-08344 to 914-08343	10	LHD Cargo.
60 AM 60 to 60 AM 74	WV11099	911-03392B to 911-03113B	15	RHD Cargo Plain Hard Top.
60 AM 75 to 60 AM 84	WV11099	911-03322B to 911-03326B	10	RHD Cargo.
30 AG 45 to 30 AG 79	WV11110	911-03299B to 911-06447C	35	RHD TACR Mk 1.
28 AJ 63 to 28 AJ 83	WV11285	914-10763B to 914-10719B	21	LHD Cargo.
28 AJ 84 to 28 AJ 86	WV11285	914-10721B to 914-10725B	3	LHD Cargo.
28 AJ 87 to 28 AJ 88	WV8765	916-03600 to 916-03467	2	RHD Cargo Hard Top w/windows Diesel.
66 AM 24 to 66 AM 29	WV11286	914-15552 to 914-15572	6	LHD FFR.
29 AJ 51 to 29 AJ 54	WV8765	916-06933C to 916-06936C	4	RHD CL Cargo Hard Top w/windows.
71 AM 19	WV8765	931-01767	1	RHD Station Wagon.
71 AM 28	WV11431	911-06676C	1	RHD MDJR Control.
72 AM 81 to 72 AM 96	WV11437	911-07159 to 911-07095	16	RHD Cargo.
72 AM 97 to 73 AM 06	WV11437	911-07101 to 911-07232	10	RHD Cargo Plain Hard Top.
73 AM 08 to 73 AM 21	WV11432	914-14736C to 914-14756C	14	RHD Cargo 24v 90A.
73 AM 22 to 73 AM 24	WV11432	911-06208C to 911-06439C	3	RHD FFR.
73 AM 25 to 73 AM 32	WV11432	911-07225 to 911-07276	8	RHD Cargo 24v 90A.
76 AM 49	WV8765	931-22802	1	RHD Station Wagon w/Winch.
76 AM 88 to 77 AM 02	WV11714	911-28465C to 911-28614C	15	RHD Cargo.
77 AM 03 and 77 AM 04	WV117376	911-37581C and 911-37587C	2	RHD Cargo 24v 90A.
29 AJ 73 to 29 AJ 82	WV11869	911-43074C to 911-43216C	10	RHD Cargo.
29 AJ 97	WV11870	911-39057C	1	RHD MDJR Control.
77 AM 79 to 77 AM 83	WV11871	911-42957C to 911-42992C	5	RHD Cargo 24v 90A.
30 AJ 06 to 30 AJ 13	WV8765	916-17525C to 916-18115C	8	RHD CL Cargo Hard Top w/windows Diesel.
30 AJ 86	WV8765	916-22081C	1	RHD CL Cargo Hard Top w/windows Diesel.

RAF DELIVERIES

Serials	Contract	Chassis Nos	Total	Remarks
80 AM 88 to 80 AM 97	WV11990	911-59648C to 911-59670C	10	RHD FFR.
86 AM 22 to 86 AM 24	WV8765	93163124C to 93163129C	3	RHD Station Wagon.
84 AM 69 to 84 AM 84	FVE 22A/10	n/a	16	RHD FFR.
86 AM 50 to 86 AM 55	FVE 22A/10	91171479 to 91172139	6	RHD FFR.
86 AM 77 to 86 AM 79	WV8765	93187328C to 93187330C	3	RHD Station Wagon.
88 AM 87 to 89 AM 13	FVE 22A/23	91172663C to 91174059C	27	RHD Cargo.
89 AM 14 to 89 AM 30	FVE 22A/23	91174064 to 91175145C	17	RHD Cargo Hard Top.
89 AM 31 to 89 AM 54	FVE 22A/23	91472679 to 91474829C	24	LHD Cargo.
31 AJ 12 to 31 AJ 37	FVE 22A/33	91188728C to 91188644C	26	RHD Cargo.
31 AJ 38 to 31 AJ 47	FVE 22A/33	91188855C to 91188724C	10	RHD Cargo Plain Hard Top.
31 AJ 48 to 31 AJ 53	FVE 22A/33	91486084 to 91486109	6	LHD Cargo.
31 AJ 63	WV8765	91622082C	1	RHD CL Cargo Hard Top w/windows Diesel.
34 AJ 52 and 34 AJ 53	FVE 22A/69	91110376 and 91110380	2	RHD FFR.
34 AJ 54 to 34 AJ 66	FVE 22A/69	91415105 to 91415141	13	LHD FFR.
34 AJ 67 to 34 AJ 75	FVE 22A/74	91101122D to 91101311D	9	RHD Cargo 24v 90A.
34 AJ 76 to 35 AJ 02	FVE 22A/34	91100785D to 91100565D	27	RHD Cargo 24v 90A.
35 AJ 03	WV8765	91629106	1	RHD CL Cargo Hard Top w/windows Diesel.
35 AJ 05 to 35 AJ 22	FVE 22A/33	91188860 to 911-89252	18	RHD Cargo.
35 AJ 23 to 35 AJ 27	FVE 22A/33	911-89257C to 911-89198C	5	RHD Cargo Hard Top.
35 AJ 28 to 35 AJ 30	FVE 22A/33	914-88233C to 914-88242C	3	LHD Cargo.
89 AM 81 to 90 AM 00	FVE 22A/34	911-91074C to 911-92275C	20	RHD FFR.
90 AM 01 to 90 AM 20	FVE 22A/34	914-90985C to 914-92659C	20	LHD FFR.
36 AJ 01 to 36 AJ 32	FVE 22A/74	911-09948D to 911-10373D	32	RHD Cargo 24v 90A.
92 AM 11 to 92 AM 18	FVE 22A/34	914-92665C to 914-92743C	8	LHD FFR.
40 AJ 75 to 40 AJ 78	FVE 22A/44	916-33512C to n/a	4	RHD CL Cargo Hard Top w/windows Diesel.
40 AJ 79 to 40 AJ 84	FVE 22A/44	n/a to 916-34588C	6	RHD CL Cargo Hard Top w/windows Diesel.
40 AJ 85 and 40 AJ 86	FVE 22A/44	931-16087 and 931-16109D	2	RHD Station Wagon.
40 AJ 87	FVE 22A/44	934-09548D	1	LHD Station Wagon.
41 AJ 91 to 42 AJ 52	FVE 22A/95	107946 to 108989	62	RHD Cargo.
42 AJ 53 to 42 AJ 95	FVE 22A/95	n/a to 107936	43	LHD Cargo.
43 AJ 17 to 43 AJ 24	FVE 22A/115	113187 to 113209	8	LHD Cargo Hard Top w/windows.
99 AM 87 to 99 AM 95	FVE 22A/44	123906 to 125630	1	RHD Station Wagon; 99 AM 88 stolen before delivery – 11 AF 09 replaced it.
43 AJ 28 to 43 AJ 45	FVE 22A/115	133216 to 133355	18	LHD Cargo.
43 AJ 46 to 43 AJ 65	FVE 22A/115	132816 to 133182	20	RHD Cargo.
43 AJ 66 to 43 AJ 68	FVE 22A/115	131142 to 131149	3	RHD Cargo.
45 AJ 09 to 45 AJ 12	FVE 22A/115	119560 to 119702	4	LHD FFR.
45 AJ 13 to 45 AJ 24	FVE 22A/115	119975 to 120641	12	RHD FFR.
45 AJ 50 to 45 AJ 64	FVE 22A/115	119904 to 120953	15	LHD FFR.
45 AJ 65 to 46 AJ 06	FVE 22A/115	120649 to 121210	42	RHD FFR.
46 AJ 07	FVE 22A/115	123890	1	RHD MDJR Control.
47 AJ 71	FVE 22A/115	133211	1	LHD Cargo Hard Top w/windows.
47 AJ 72 to 48 AJ 08	FVE 22A/115	n/a to 131625	37	RHD Cargo.
48 AJ 17 to 48 AJ 25	FVE 22A/115	120625 to 119768	9	LHD FFR.
48 AJ 26 to 48 AJ 43	FVE 22A/115	120005 to 120466	18	RHD FFR.
48 AJ 44 to 48 AJ 51	FVE 22A/115	131151 to 131260	8	RHD Cargo Hard Top w/windows.
49 AJ 31 to 49 AJ 37	FVE 22A/140	145861 to 147760	7	RHD CL Cargo Hard Top w/windows Diesel.
11 AF 09	FVE 22A/44	147187	1	RHD Station Wagon.
51 AJ 54 to 51 AJ 87	FVE 21B/173	146788 to 148712	34	RHD Cargo Hard Top w/windows.

RAF DELIVERIES

Serials	Contract	Chassis Nos	Total	Remarks
51 AJ 88 to 52 AJ 01	FVE 21B/173	148480 to 148499	14	LHD Cargo Hard Top w/windows.
52 AJ 02 to 52 AJ 39	FVE 21B/173	148989 to 149184	38	RHD FFR.
52 AJ 40 to 52 AJ 43	FVE 21B/173	148982 to 148986	4	RHD Cargo.
52 AJ 68 to 52 AJ 92	FVE 21B/173	148111 to 148147	25	RHD Helicopter Ground Handling.
52 AJ 93 to 52 AJ 97	FVE 21B/173	148104 to n/a	5	LHD Helicopter Ground Handling.
00 AY 08 to 00 AY 12	FVE 21B/229	n/a	5	RHD MDJR Cargo/2 Stretcher Ambulance.
00 AY 13 to 00 AY 17	FVE 21B/229	n/a	5	RHD MDJR Control.

Total 1030

BERLIN SENÄT PURCHASES

Serials	Contract	Chassis Nos	Total	Remarks
28 XC 11 to 28 XC 22	-	n/a to 914-05883B	12	LHD FFR
28 XC 41 to 28 XC 51	-	n/a to 914-15499B	11	LHD FFR
05 XC 74 to 05 XC 80	-	914-15776C to n/a	7	LHD Cargo
57 XB 66 to 57 XB 82	-	914-47207 to 914-47184C	17	LHD Cargo
27 XH 45 to 27 XH 48	-	914-82125C to 914-82159C	4	LHD FFR
43 XB 96 to 44 XB 11	-	914-93482C to 914-93722C	16	LHD Cargo
44 XB 13 to 44 XB 20	-	914-91983C to 914-91973C	8	LHD FFR
56 XB 68 to 56 XB 87	-	n/a	20	LHD Cargo
61 XB 02 to 61 XB 04	-	108662 to 108680	3	LHD FFR
59 XB 84 to 59 XB 99	-	108726 to 108744	16	LHD FFR
61 XB 50 to 61 XB 61	-	108884 to 108646	12	LHD FFR
59 XB 57 to 59 XB 76	-	115638 to 115937	20	LHD Cargo
61 XB 84 to 61 XB 88	-	115817 to 115634	5	LHD Cargo
04 XC 37	-	n/a	1	LHD FFR
04 XC 38	-	n/a	1	LHD FFR
28 XC 58 to 28 XC 77	-	134230 to 134257	20	LHD Cargo
29 XC 64 to 29 XC 77	-	143273 to 143782	14	LHD Cargo
30 XC 68	-	164534	1	LHD FFR
46 XB 20 to 46 XB 30	-	164700 to 164716	11	LHD FFR
00 XK 25 to 00 XK 65	-	181537 to 183251	41	LHD Cargo Hard Top; although believed to have been Cargo Hard Top, possibly with side windows, these vehicles were given Asset Codes suggesting they were Station Wagons.
01 XK 22 to 01 XK 34	-	183255 to 181651	13	LHD Cargo Hard Top; although believed to have been Cargo Hard Top, possibly with side windows, these vehicles were given Asset Codes suggesting they were Station Wagons.
01 XK 50 to 01 XK 52	-	196209 to 196199	3	LHD FFR
03 XK 30 to 03 XK 32	-	219526 to 219537	3	LHD FFR

Total 259

Hardtop 02 GF 04 displays an unusual camouflage scheme, and is seen here with blackout canvas over the cab windows and wind-screen. Just visible on the upper part of the hardtop are what appear to be two small hatches.(GF)

ROYAL NAVY PURCHASES

The following list is incomplete but gives some idea of Royal Navy purchases. The authors are aware of other examples but have included those vehicles where there is detailed information from reliable sources.

Royal Navy vehicles were ordered under a Navy "warrant" of the form 123-79-1 where 79 was the Financial Year and 123 was a serial number. These later were given WV contract numbers.

Serials	Contract	Chassis Nos	Total	Remarks
06 RN 24	n/a	n/a	1	TACR RHD.
90 RN 63 to 90 RN 69	099-90-1	911-04497B to n/a	7	TACR RHD; it is not known why the warrant on this vehicle refers to FY 90.
96 RN 66	n/a	911-82107C	1	TACR RHD.
96 RN 01 to 96 RN 02	n/a	911-82116C to 911-82113C	2	TACR RHD.
24 RN 84 to 24 RN 98	063-72-1	911-02394B to n/a	15	CL Recovery RHD.
15 RN 92 to 16 RN 06	033-76-1	931-51275C to 931-51282C	15	Station Wagon RHD.
19 RN 94 to 20 RN 03	049-76-1 = WV8765 R2942	911-59627C to n/a	10	Cargo CL RHD.
15 RN 85 to 15 RN 89	049-76-1	911-59657C to 911-59663C	5	Cargo CL RHD.
10 RN 31 to 10 RN 32	066-76-1	911-59013C to 911-59014C	2	Cargo CL RHD.
10 RN 40 to 10 RN 43	066-76-1	911-59015C to 911-59018C	4	Cargo CL RHD.
10 RN 47 to 10 RN 48	066-76-1	911-59019C to 911-59020C	2	Cargo Hard Top w/Winch EOD RHD.
10 RN 89 to 10 RN 99	066-76-1	911-59023C to 911-59034C	11	Cargo CL RHD.
26 RN 35	033-78-1	911-01119D	1	FFR RHD.
67 RN 04	WV8765 R2717	n/a		Cargo Hard Top w/windows RHD.
65 RN 60 to 65 RN 62	WV8765 R2600	n/a to n/a	3	Station Wagon RHD.
97 RN 95 to 97 RN 97	WV8765 R2717	n/a to n/a	3	Cargo Hard Top w/windows RHD.
23 RN 02 to 23 RN 20	WV8765 R2724	931-01818C to n/a	19	Station Wagon RHD.
35 RN 87 to 36 RN 18	WV8765 R2893	931-51290C to n/a	32	Station Wagon RHD.
10 RN 24 to 10 RN 26	030-79-1	931-12391D to 931-12574D	3	Station Wagon RHD.
10 RN 28	030-79-1	931-15147D	1	EOD Station Wagon RHD.
12 RN 88 to 12 RN 92	029-80-1 = R3445	127692 to 127727	5	Cargo Hard Top w/windows RHD..
06 RN 30 to 06 RN 33	R3440	127739 to 127833	4	Cargo Hard Top w/windows RHD
19 RN 48 to 19 RN 56	R3510	142089 to 142117	9	Cargo Hard Top w/windows RHD.
04 RN 98	n/a	144414	1	Cargo Hard Top w/windows w/Winch RHD.
12 RN 55 to 12 RN 58	035-81-1	148976 to 148980	4	Cargo RHD.
04 RN 08	n/a	172891	1	Ambulance RHD.
96 RN 64 to 96 RN 65	n/a	172900 to n/a	2	Ambulance RHD.
05 RN 26 to 05 RN 28	n/a	n/a to 192465	3	Ambulance RHD.

Pictured at the War and Peace Show in 2000, by which time it had entered preservation, 64 KC 63 is a rare survivor of a VPK-equipped 109 Series 3. The vehicle operated in Northern Ireland, and like so many vehicles that operated in that theatre, it carries the confidential telephone number of the security forces. The near-vertical bar on the left of the windscreen is a wire-cutter, designed to protect a crew member who was using the roof hatch at the rear. (JT)

LAND ROVER CHASSIS CODES

Land Rover used two different types of chassis numbering system during the production of the Series 3 models. The earlier type was a continuation of that used on previous models. This began with a three-digit identifying prefix, which indicated the model type, steering position and other factors. Neither the model-year nor the calendar-year of manufacture was indicated. The ones relevant to the Series 3 109 models are shown below. The three-figure prefix was followed by a five-figure serial number that began at 00001 for each separate sequence, and this in turn was followed by a suffix letter. The suffix letter indicated major changes in the vehicle's specification that affected servicing.

The later type was introduced on 1 November 1979, and was slightly modified a year later. These later numbers are VIN (Vehicle Identification Number) types that meet the requirements of the International Standards Organisation (ISO) that were issued in two related documents, ISO3779 and ISO3780. Note that some vehicles may have been issued with VINs before 1 November 1979, and some built shortly after that date may still have had the earlier style of chassis number.

Note that the Land Rover model-year began in September and continued until the end of the following July, leaving August clear for the works' annual holiday and for preparing the assembly lines to take new models. A Land Rover built in the 1974 model-year could therefore have been built at any time between September 1973 and July 1974.

(a) Chassis number prefixes

911	RHD, four-cylinder petrol
914	LHD, four-cylinder petrol
916	RHD, diesel
931	RHD, four-cylinder petrol Station Wagon
934	LHD, four-cylinder petrol Station Wagon
942	RHD export specification, six-cylinder petrol
949	LHD, six-cylinder petrol Station Wagon

(b) VIN prefixes

The prefix code used from 1 November 1979 had eight characters. From 1 November 1980, a further three letters were added to identify the country of origin and manufacturer, so making an 11-digit prefix. In each case, a six-digit serial number followed. A 1979-1980 VIN might then read

LBCAG1AA-123456

and one issued after November 1980 might read

SALLBCAG1AA-123456.

Note that the hyphen is not present on the VIN plate and is used here only for clarity.

The relevant prefix codes were as follows:

SAL	(From 1980 only) Built in UK by British Leyland, Land Rover division
LB	Land Rover Series III
C	109-inch wheelbase
A	Utility body (soft top, truck cab or hard top)
	M = Station Wagon
G	Four-cylinder diesel engine
	H = four-cylinder petrol engine
	V = 3.5-litre V8 petrol engine
1	RHD with four-speed manual gearbox
	2 = LHD with four-speed manual gearbox
A	(Variant code used on all 109s; this position would later be used to identify model-year)
A	Assembled at Solihull factory

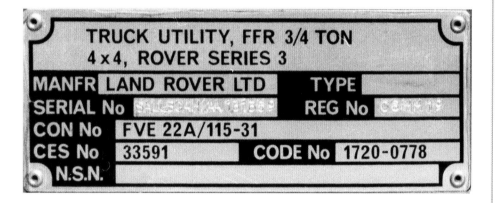

This was the plate from 06 HH 19, an FFR model. The VIN is hard to read in this picture, but the whole 17-digit number just fits into the box. (GF)

A Series 3 109 tows the standard military Sankey 1-ton trailer. Trailers always had their own serial numbers and did not take on the "registration" of the towing vehicle in the way that UK civilian trailers did. (GF)

ARMY SERIAL NUMBERS

The system used for vehicle serial numbers changed during the service life of the Series 3 109. Before 1982, the Army, Royal Navy and RAF all had separate serial number systems. From 1982, a new unified or "tri-service" series was used, and this was allocated to all classes of vehicle as the contracts were placed. This tri-service series in effect carried on from the sequence initiated for Army serials.

The serial numbers allocated by the Army before 1982, and under the tri-service system that followed, gave a clue to the date of the vehicle. Serial letters indicated the financial year in which the vehicle was purchased (which is not necessarily the same as the calendar year in which it was delivered). Those relevant to the Rover Series 3 109 models are shown below.

As before, serial sequences began at 0001 (e.g. 00 FL 01) and ran to 9999 (e.g. 99 FL 99). There was not necessarily any correlation between chassis number order and military serial number within batches.

BT	No date association; the BT series included vehicles purchased individually and second-hand; see also Chapter 13
FL	1971-1972
FM	1972-1973
GB	1973-1974
GF	1974-1975
GJ	1975-1976
GN	1976-1977
GT	1977-1978
GX	1977-1978 (overspill series after GT reached 9999)
HF	1978-1979
HG	1979-1980
HH	1980-1981
HJ	1981-1982
KA	1982 (Tri-service series)
KB	1983 (Tri-service series)
KC	1984 (Tri-service series)
KD	1985 (Tri-service series)
SP	No date association; the SP series was for Special Projects vehicles used for research and development and was allocated from mid-1967 until around 2002. See also Chapter 13.
XB	Berlin Brigade allocation; no date association.
XC	Berlin Brigade allocation; no date association.
XH	Berlin Brigade allocation; no date association.
XK	Berlin Brigade Tri-Service allocation from 1982.

ASSET CODES

1040-0778	Ambulance, 2/4 stretcher, 4x4, Rover Series 3
1153-0778	Car, Utility, EOD, ¾ ton, 4x4, Rover Series 3 (Petrol)
1155-0778	Car, Utility, ¾ ton, 4x4, Rover Series 3
1155-1778	Car, Utility, ¾ Tonne, 4x4, 12 seater, w/trailer atts, Rover Series 3
1155-2778	Car, Utility, ¾ Tonne, 4x4, w/trailer atts, Rover Series 3 (Petrol)
1155-3778	Car, Utility, ¾ ton, 4x4, Tropical, Rover Series 3
1155-4778	Car, Utility, ¾ Tonne, 4x4, 12 seater, w/trailer atts, Rover Series 3 (Petrol)
1155-5778	Car, Utility, ¾ ton, 4x4, LHD, Rover Series 3
1155-6778	Car, Utility, ¾ Tonne, 4x4, 12 seater, LHD, w/trailer atts, Rover Series 3
1155-7778	Car, Utility, ¾ Tonne, 4x4, LHD, w/trailer atts, Rover Series 3 (Petrol)
1155-8778	Car, Utility, ¾ ton, 4x4, Tropical, LHD, Rover Series 3 (P)
1155-9778	Car, Utility, ¾ Tonne, 4x4, 12 seater, w/trailer atts, LHD, Rover Series 3 (Petrol)
1161-5778	Car, Utility, SAAS, ¾ Tonne, 4x4, LHD, w/trailer atts, Rover Series 3 (Petrol)
1683-0778	Truck, Caravan, Commanders, 1 berth, ¾ Tonne, 4x4, LHD, Land Rover Series 3
1683-6778	Truck, Caravan, Commanders, 1 berth, ¾ Tonne, 4x4, Land Rover Series 3
1705-0778	Truck, Utility, ¾ Tonne, 4x4, 24v 90A, Rover Series 3
1709-1778	Truck, Utility, ¾ ton, 4x4, winterised, Rover Series 3
1710-0778	Truck, Utility, ¾ ton, 4x4, Rover Series 3
1710-1778	Truck, Utility, ¾ ton, 4x4, Rover Series 3
1710-2778	Truck, Utility, ¾ ton, 4x4, Plain Hard Top, Rover Series 3
1710-3778	Truck, Utility, CL, ¾ ton, w/Windows, Series 3, Diesel, Rover
1710-4778	Truck, Utility, ¾ ton, 4x4, Plain Hard Top, Rover Series 3
1710-5778	Truck, Utility, ¾ ton, 4x4, LHD, Rover Series 3
1710-6778	Truck, Utility, ¾ ton, 4x4, LHD, Rover Series 3
1710-9778	Truck, Utility, ¾ ton, 4x4, Plain Hard Top, LHD, Rover Series 3
1711-0778	Truck, Utility, CL, ¾ ton, Rover Series 3
1711-1778	Truck, Utility, CL, ¾ ton, 4x4, Plain Hard Top, Rover Series 3
1711-3778	Truck, Utility, CL, ¾ ton, 4x4, Hard Top w/windows, Rover Series 3 (Diesel)
1711-4778	Truck, Utility, CL, ¾ ton, 4x4, Hard Top w/windows and trailer atts, Rover Series 3 (Petrol)
1711-5778	Truck, Utility, CL, ¾ ton, LHD, Rover Series 3
1712-0778	Truck, Utility, Cargo/2 stretcher (MDJR), ¾ ton, 4x4, Rover Series 3
1714-3778	Truck, Utility, CL, ¾ Tonne, 4x4, Hard Top w/windows, Rover Series 3 (Diesel)
1714-4778	Truck, Utility, CL, ¾ Tonne, 4x4, Hard Top w/windows, w/trailer atts, Rover Series 3 (P)
1717-2778	Truck, Utility, ¾ ton, 4x4, Hard Top, Rover Series 3
1717-4778	Truck, Utility, ¾ Tonne, 4x4, Hard Top, w/side windows, Rover Series 3
1717-9778	Truck, Utility, ¾ Tonne, 4x4, LHD, Hard Top, w/side windows, Rover Series 3
1718-0778	Truck, Utility, FFR, ¾ ton, 4x4, Fitted For FACE, Rover Series 3
1719-2778	Truck, Utility, MDJR Control, ¾ Tonne, 4x4, 24v, Rover Series 3
1720-0778	Truck, Utility, FFR, ¾ Tonne, 4x4, Rover Series 3
1720-2778	Truck, Utility, Survey Computing RA, ¾ ton, 4x4, Rover Series 3
1720-3778	Truck, Utility, Survey Computing, RA, Hard Top, ¾ Tonne, 4x4, Rover Series 3
1720-5778	Truck, Utility, FFR, ¾ Tonne, 4x4, LHD, Rover Series 3
1720-6778	Truck, Utility, FFR, ¾ Tonne, 4x4, LHD, Plain Hard Top, Rover Series 3
1721-0778	Truck, Utility, FFR, ¾ ton, 4x4, winterised, Rover Series 3
1730-0778	Truck, Utility, WOMBAT, ¾ ton, 4x4, Rover Series 3
1810-0778	Truck, Firefighting, Airfield Crash Rescue, 1 ton, 4x4, Rover Series 3
1810-5778	Truck, Firefighting, Airfield Crash Rescue, 1 ton, 4x4, LHD, Rover Series 3

TECHNICAL SPECIFICATIONS, SERIES 3 109 MODELS

ENGINES:

Four-cylinder petrol
2286cc (90.47mm x 88.9mm) four-cylinder with overhead valves and single Zenith 36 IV carburettor. 7.0:1 compression ratio. 77bhp at 4250rpm and 124 lb ft at 2500rpm.

Six-cylinder petrol
2625cc (77.8mm x 92.1mm) six-cylinder with overhead inlet and side exhaust valves; single Zenith 175 CD-2S carburettor. 7.8:1 compression ratio. 85bhp at 4500rpm and 132 lb ft at 1500rpm.

V8-cylinder petrol
3528cc (88.9mm x 71.1mm) V8-cylinder with pushrod OHV and two Zenith-Stromberg CD carburettors. 8.13:1 compression ratio. 91bhp at 3500rpm and 166 lb ft at 2000rpm.

Diesel
2286cc (90.47mm x 88.9mm) four-cylinder with overhead valves and indirect injection. 23:1 compression ratio. 56.2bhp at 4000rpm and 101 lb ft at 1800rpm.

TRANSMISSION:

Selectable four-wheel drive with four-cylinder engines; permanent four-wheel drive with V8 engine.

Four-cylinder/Six cylinder/Diesel models
Four-speed main gearbox; ratios 3.60:1, 2.22:1, 1.50:1, 1.00:1, reverse 3.02:1. Synchromesh on all four forward gears. Two-speed transfer gearbox; ratios 1.148:1 (High) and 2.350:1 (Low). Axle ratio: 4.7:1

V8 Models
Four-speed main gearbox; ratios 4.069:1, 2.448:1, 1.505:1, 1.000:1, reverse 3.664:1. Synchromesh on all four forward gears. Two-speed transfer gearbox; ratios 1.336:1 (High) and 3.320:1 (Low) Axle ratio: 3.54:1

SUSPENSION, STEERING AND BRAKES:

Semi-elliptic leaf springs all round. Recirculating-ball steering with 15:1 ratio.Drum brakes on all four wheels, 11in x 2.25in; separate drum-type transmission parking brake.

UNLADEN WEIGHT:

109in (minimum):   3294 lb (1494kg) with petrol engine (civilian models)

ELECTRICAL SYSTEM:

12-volt with dynamo and negative earth; FFR models with 24-volt negative-earth system and 90-amp generator.

PERFORMANCE:

2¼ -litre petrol engine:

0-50mph:	29secs
Maximum:	58mph approx (93.3km/h)
Fuel consumption:	19 mpg approx

2.6-litre petrol engine:

0-50mph:	17secs
Maximum:	70mph approx (112.6km/h)
Fuel consumption:	15 mpg approx

3.5-litre V8 petrol engine

0-50mph:	15.9 sec
Maximum:	85mph (136 km/h)
Fuel consumption:	14mpg

DIMENSIONS:

Overall length:	175in (4445mm)
Wheelbase:	109in (2769mm)
Overall width:	64in (1626mm)
Unladen height:	81in (2057mm) maximum
Track:	51.5in (1308mm)

03 GT 87 started life as a GS Cargo vehicle but was converted in service to review specification. The rear view shows the "traffic-light" system of commands for the driver. (Historics auctioneers)

CHAPTER 10:
THE SERIES 3 HALF-TON

By the early 1970s, the 88-inch Lightweight had become the standard short-wheelbase Land Rover for all three British armed services. Although several older commercial-pattern short-wheelbase models were still in service, and although purchases of such vehicles continued in small quantities and for special rôles (see Chapter 11), mainstream short-wheelbase buys were of the Lightweight.

Deliveries of the final Series IIA or Rover 1 models continued into 1972 to fulfil existing contracts, but from April 1972 new Lightweights were built to Series III specification. The MoD knew them as Series 3 Half-Ton types, using the Arabic numeral that the department favoured. The first examples were delivered to military depots in May 1972.

The Series III version of the Half-Ton was very much an evolution of the earlier Series IIA type, adding to the existing specification many of the new features associated with Series III models. Unlike other Series III Land Rovers, it retained the central instrument panel of the Series IIA, but it did incorporate Series III mechanical improvements such as the all-synchromesh gearbox and larger diameter (9.5-inch) clutch plate. The top section of the bulkhead was also different from the Rover 1 type (although the two types were interchangeable), with different windscreen hinges. An alternator replaced the dynamo on 12-volt models, the horn and headlight dipswitch were now on a steering column stalk, there was a hazard warning light system, and a key-start ignition replaced the earlier push-button starter switch. There were other, minor differences.

Rover built around 15,000 Series III Half-Ton models, and of these just under 11,000 of them entered service with the British armed forces while some 4000 were sold to overseas military authorities. Most were delivered as 12-volt GS or

New Half-Tons in the FM serial range await delivery to their units at Ashchurch Vehicle Depot in November 1974. 72 FM 99 was receipted in April 1974 and issued to its first unit in January 1975. (FMW)

This group of late Half-Tons was photographed in United Nations white livery in storage at RAF Akrotiri, Cyprus. (GF)

This eye-catching and very non-standard colour scheme was applied to 46 FL 57 when the vehicle was used by the Royal Hampshire Regiment's Recruitment and Information Team and was seen at Aldershot Army Days in June 1980. (GF)

24 HF 31 is typical of how many Half-Tons looked in service. Clearly visible here is the cut-out in the bonnet side for the co-axial cable used when an aerial tuner was mounted to the front wing. The vehicle is "HQ5" of 7 Squadron RCT – note the fluorescent "7" on the top of the passenger's windscreen. (FMW)

Many of the later Series 3 Half-Tons seem to have been used without the additional front quarter-bumpers. This one has been fitted with a NATO hitch on the front bumper. It is from the KB series of tri-service serials and is in use with an Enhanced Shore Support (ESS) unit of HMS Intrepid at Portsmouth Navy Days in 1987. (FMW)

05 KD 12 is one of the last Half-Tons, and is again lacking the front quarter-bumpers. The Land Rover badge on the grille is a plastic type that was not introduced until the late 1980s – after this vehicle was built. The vehicle had probably been drawn from Ashchurch for the International Air Tattoo in July 1985. (GF)

24-volt FFR types, although there were also some 24-volt types that were not used as radio vehicles (see below). All were delivered with soft tops, and there were of course both LHD and RHD types. The final British examples were built in 1984, and were delivered during 1985. Between 1972 and 1982, orders were placed by all three branches of the British armed forces and the vehicles delivered were given appro-

priate serial numbers. After 1982, new orders were placed on a tri-service basis; new Half-Tons went into a shared vehicle pool and all carried serial numbers that continued on from the former Army system.

The vast majority of British military Series 3 Lightweights had the 2¼-litre petrol engine, but a small number of fairly late examples for the RAF had 2¼-litre diesels and were used for tasks where spark suppression was important. Early Series 3 Half-Tons were delivered with Dunlop Trakgrip T29A tyres, although later deliveries had Goodyear Hi-Miler Xtra Grip types, and others were also fitted in service.

By the time the Series 3 Half-Ton began to enter service, the original rationale for the Lightweight design was no longer valid. Larger transport aircraft meant that the saving of four inches in width over a standard commercial 88-inch Land Rover was no longer critical, and heavy-lift helicopters meant that there was no longer a need to strip vehicles in order to save weight for heliporting operations. One result was that Series 3 Half-Tons were only rarely seen in fully stripped-down form – although a partial stripdown was often necessary for low-profile operations. Another was that the original requirement for short half-shafts with flat drive flanges was relaxed, and at some point during production standard half-shafts and flanges became the norm; these were recognisable by their conical ends that protruded through the wheel centres.

Nevertheless, Series 3 Half-Tons were usually partially stripped when they were to be air-dropped from a Hercules C-130 transport aircraft, as was quite common in the Parachute Regiment. In such cases, they would be stacked in pairs on an MSP (Medium Stressed Pallet), which would be despatched from the aircraft over the Drop Zone and would parachute gently to earth to be retrieved by the waiting troops.

There was a high degree of commonality between the Rover 1 and the Series 3 Half-Ton models, and as a result military workshops would sometimes cannibalise unserviceable vehicles to keep others going. It was therefore not uncommon for Series 3 types to be fitted with Rover 1 parts, and vice versa, where circumstances demanded. After being struck off, vehicles would be sold on to civilian owners with whatever hybrid specification they had acquired.

Army Series 3 Half-Ton deliveries

The majority of the Series 3 Half-Tons delivered to the British armed forces entered service with the Army, although the

Complete with standard Sankey trailer painted in matching white, 48 FL 64 was seen on exercise in Scandinavia. The markings show it had been issued to the Royal Marines Aviation Squadron. (Royal Marines via Terry Gander)

The Dexion equipment racking in the rear is clearly visible in these pictures of 45 GF 13. Note the rear reflectors, which are much larger than those on 13 FM 30 (see page 154). The vehicle was photographed at Chester. (GF)

post-1982 tri-service arrangements make it difficult to be precise about numbers after that date.

Note also that the Royal Marines used a mixture of vehicles which were funded by the Army (and wore Army serials) and some funded by the Royal Navy (with RN serials).

Bronze Green paint was standard on Series 3 Half-Tons delivered to the Army until mid-way through the second quarter of 1979. From May 1979, Army deliveries were in IRR Green ("NATO Green") paint. This IRR Green was often supplemented by patches of IRR Black applied by individual units.

RAF Series 3 Half-Ton deliveries
The RAF continued to take quantities of Series 3 Half-Tons with their own distinctive serials right up until the 1982

Looking very smart when brand-new in RAF Blue livery was 75 AM 51. (Land Rover)

Typical of the later RAF deliveries was this one in the KD series, seen wearing high-visibility yellow stripes on its otherwise green paint. The vehicle was in preservation when pictured. (JT)

Many RAF Half-Tons were fitted with hardtops, and 47 AJ 21 was fairly typical. Note the black-out canvas folded back across the cab roof. (GF)

change to tri-service numbers. In the beginning, vehicles for the RAF were supplied in RAF Blue-Grey, but from late 1979, all deliveries switched to NATO IRR Green; the first such Lightweight recorded left the Rover factory at Solihull on 16 November 1979.

Royal Navy Series 3 Half-Ton deliveries
Although full details of the Royal Navy Series 3 Lightweights are not currently available, it is clear that a good number entered service. The majority were right-hand-drive Cargo types with the 12-volt specification and a soft top; of these, at least one was carried aboard HMS Bulwark as the ship's official vehicle. There were also FFR 24-volt examples, and a quantity of 24-volt Helicopter Servicing vehicles too.

Variations and workshop conversions
As some of these variations and conversions affected vehicles belonging to more than one arm of the services, all of them are discussed together here.

Clansman
When Series 3 Half-Ton deliveries began in the early 1970s, the standard military radio system was still Larkspur. However, this was gradually replaced from 1978 by the Clansman system, which required different cable assemblies and connectors. New FFR Lightweights were supplied to the new specification, and older FFR models in service during the 1980s were modified if they remained in use as radio vehicles.

Cuthbertson models
Four Series 3 Half-Ton models in service with the RAF were fitted with Cuthbertson track units, and replaced the six similarly-equipped Rover Mk 6 models that had been in service with EOD units since 1961 (see Chapter 4). These conversions may have been carried out as early as August 1973, although the vehicles did not actually enter service until

Several Series 3 Half-Tons were given swamp tyres ("bog cogs") for use in the Falklands. (Left – Land Rover; above – TMB)

Glider recovery

Like the earlier Rover 1s, some Series 3 Half-Tons used by the RAF saw service at gliding schools. These were painted yellow to enhance visibility (although the tilts remained khaki) and normally had a rotating orange beacon on the roof. Some had transparent windows inserted into the roof of the tilt to give the crew a view above the vehicle. Like the Rover 1 types, the Series 3 Half-Tons used in this way were given new Asset Codes with prefix 1614, but this was used only on paperwork and the vehicles retained their original data plates.

Hard tops and Station Wagons

No Series 3 Half-Tons were delivered with hard tops when new, although several were retro-fitted with one in service. Some vehicles were also fitted with window hard tops (with a fixed window in each side panel) and a small number with Station Wagon tops (with sliding windows in each side panel). A few vehicles had tropical roofs, a second-skin roof separated from hard top or Station Wagon top by an air gap that helped reduce interior temperatures.

Typical reasons for fitting a hard top or Station Wagon roof were to improve vehicle security against theft or intrusion, to enable work to be carried out inside the back body without displaying any light, or to raise interior temperatures (e.g. on winterised vehicles; see below).

Most hard tops and Station Wagons were also fitted with a Station Wagon-type side-hinged tail door, but it was common for RAF examples to retain the standard drop-down tailgate and to have above this a top-hinged hatch with a window. Note that the back body of the Half-Ton was narrower than that of the standard commercial 88-inch Land Rover and that the hard tops and Station Wagon sides and roof were adapted commercial-pattern types. This is why Lightweights with fixed-roof bodies displayed a slight overhang of the upper panels on each side.

1975. They had a unique Asset Code of 1616-0778; serials were 53 AM 84, 54 AM 02, 54 AM 04 and one other that is not known.

The Cuthbertson Half-Tons served for a few months at Leconfield and Bicester. At the end of 1975, the two flights became part of the RAF Armament Support Unit (RAFASUPU) at Wittering as the Explosive Ordnance Disposal (EOD) Squadron, comprising No 1 and No 2 EOD Units. RAFASUPU was renamed 5131 EOD Squadron on 1 June 1995, and today is based at RAF Marham.

Flotation tyres conversion

In the early 1980s, a small number of Lightweights (including 93 KA 19, 93 KA 64, 93 KA 66 and 22 KB 66) were converted for use on marshy terrain in the Falkland Islands. The work was done by Gloster Saro Ltd at Hucclecote, and the vehicles were fitted with 15.5-inch wide multi-spoke wheels that carried ultra-wide low-pressure tyres. Wing extensions were added to cover these, and the spare wheel was carried ahead of the radiator on a modified front bumper with a supporting box welded to it. A steering damper and heavy-duty sump guard were also fitted, and the exhaust was re-routed through the left-hand front wing extension and terminated at roof height.

71 AM 56 was one of the RAF vehicles specially adapted as a helicopter servicing vehicle. The servicing platform folded down onto the roof for travelling. (TMB)

Helicopter starting vehicles

The RAF's 230 Squadron was required to deploy its Puma helicopters away from their normal operating base, and this led to the creation of a special version of the Series 3 Half-Ton. This had a 24-volt 90 amp electrical system which was capable of starting the helicopter from cold; the system was used purely for this and the vehicles were not configured as FFR types. The first batch of these vehicles was ordered in the 1973-1974 Financial Year; otherwise the earliest trace is in MVEE photographs dating from summer 1976. It is also clear that 10 of the final Series 3 Half-Ton deliveries in 1985 had this specification.

The Helicopter Starting vehicles had special Asset Codes of 1618-0783 (RHD types) and 1618-5783 (LHD types). They were fitted with strengthened hard tops with a platform on the roof where ground crews could stand to service the helicopters.

The RAF took no chances that the helicopter servicing vehicles might be unserviceable in cold climates. These pictures show the massive extra heater blower and associated ducting. (TMB)

The RAF took no chances that the helicopter servicing vehicles might be unserviceable in cold climates. These pictures show the massive extra heater blower and associated ducting. (TMB)

A small number of Half-Tons were specially prepared as ceremonial vehicles by the Honourable Artillery Company. This one is shown in preservation, and appears to be additional to those listed in the text. (GF)

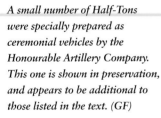

Honourable Artillery Company (HAC) ceremonial vehicles

In 1998, five Series 3 Half-Ton models were transferred from the Royal Green Jackets to the Honourable Artillery Company, where they were specially prepared for use as ceremonial vehicles. Based at the Tower of London, these vehicles carried a gun crew and towed a 25-pounder field gun, which was used for such things as firing a salute on Royal birthdays. Other functions included appearances at the annual Lord Mayor's parade in London.

The five vehicles all had gloss Bronze Green paintwork set off by chromed front bumpers and rear bumperettes (the latter with black side sections). The bumpers incorporated round-headed coach bolts instead of the standard type, to give a neater effect after chroming. The vehicles always operated without soft tops or hood sticks, and had white spare wheel covers and white upholstery. Axle ends and wheel nuts were painted white, and the HAC coat of arms was carried on each door, while a large placard on the front bumper displayed the name of the parent unit.

The five vehicles were 23 HF 82, 24 HF 07, 47 HG 58, 49 HG 62 and 84 KB 48, the last listed being the Commander's vehicle. They remained in service until 1998, when they were replaced by similarly prepared Steyr Daimler Puch gun tractors.

Linelayers

Like the Rover 1, the Series 3 Half-Ton was sometimes used to carry a Linelaying Kit. However, the use of landlines for communication was declining by the time of the Series 3 models, and probably relatively few examples were equipped with the kit.

Position and Azimuth Determining System (PADS)

The Position and Azimuth Determining System entered service in the 1980s and was an electronic unit made by Ferranti. Mark Cook explains (in The Half-Ton Military Land Rover) that it was housed in a small container that could be mounted in the back of a Half-Ton Land Rover, and was used in support of FACE (the Field Artillery Computer System) by Royal Artillery units. The carrying vehicle was often a 24-volt Series 3 Half-Ton.

Para Reconnaissance vehicles

A special conversion for recce units attached to the Parachute Regiment was created by 10 Airborne Workshop, REME, which was attached to 16 Airborne Brigade. Probably around eight vehicles were converted, all of them from Series 3 FFR Half-Tons. Although there was a core specification, each of the vehicles was individually configured to suit the requirements of its crew and their mission. As unit conversions, they did not attract a special Asset Code.

The vehicles carried a four-man crew, with two in the front and two on inward-facing seats in the rear. Some of them had a grab rail around the back body, located in the sockets for the tilt frame. A common characteristic was an expanded metal basket on the bonnet top, used for carrying camo nets and the like. This displaced the spare wheel, which was mounted on a sturdy bracket attached to the bulkhead that allowed the wheel to sit flat against the body side. Some vehicles had a wheel on each side, while others, possibly early versions, had the wheel jutting out from the front bumper, Pink Panther-style.

When the spare was mounted alongside the bulkhead, the doors had to be left off, and the gaps were filled with outrigged jerrycan holders. Typically, folding "shelves" were added on the outside of the back body to carry the crew's Bergens, and then a larger folding shelf above the rear cross-member for carrying additional kit. Some vehicles had a pintle mount in the rear to carry a General Purpose Machine Gun (GPMG) with a 360-degree arc of fire for self-defence. Among the later developments was the addition of a rollover bar, which was actually a cut-down 101 One-Tonne item. Some of the Para recce Half-Tons may have had a special mesh grille.

These vehicles were eventually replaced by specially modified versions of the Land Rover Defender 90.

Red Arrows Support

A small number of Half-Tons, probably mainly Series 3s, were used as support vehicles by the RAF Red Arrows aerial display team. Two of the final batch of 24-volt vehicles were so allocated. Their primary role was to tow support and servicing trailers, but they were often used as aircraft tugs as well.

Some of the Red Arrows vehicles had LHD. All were equipped with hard tops and orange rotating beacons on the roof, and were painted in red with white roof, bumpers, and side stripes. The side stripes on most vehicles carried the Royal Air Force name in black.

REME vehicles

Series 3 Half-Tons allocated to REME Light Aid detachments were typically fitted with a hard top and a front-mounted winch. A rigid tow bar would be carried on the roof, which would sometimes also have an expanded metal basket for carrying additional equipment, and a rotating amber beacon.

The line-layer was a rare variant of the Series 3 Half-Ton. Here an example from the School of Signals at Blandford Forum is seen in use at Middle Wallop in July 1988. (FMW)

05 KD 65 was pictured during use by the Red Arrows display team of the RAF. It has an unusual window hardtop configuration and was the last RHD Lightweight built. (GF)

Just one VPK-equipped Series 3 Half-Ton has been faithfully preserved, by Mark Cook of the EMLRA. (JT)

Vehicle Protection Kit (VPK)

16 HG 76 is seen with 42 Squadron RCT based at Ward Barracks, Bulford. It has been winterized, including the addition of a hardtop for its role with ACE Mobile Force on NATO's northern and southern flanks. (FMW)

As happened with the Rover 1 version of the Half-Ton, Series 3 Half-Tons serving in Northern Ireland were often fitted with the VPK that gave a degree of armoured protection during the civil unrest of the 1970s. Typically, they would also be given Aeon rubber spring assisters at the rear. The last VPK Lightweights were not withdrawn until 1994.

There is more information about the Vehicle Protection Kit itself in Chapter 5.

Winterisation kit

For cold-climate use, Series 3 Half-Tons could be fitted with a Winterisation kit, which was a standard unit modification. Vehicles so modified were given new Asset Codes prefixed 1613 (Anti-Spark), 1619 (GS), 1626 (FFR) and 1624 (24v 90A) but retained their original data plates. These kits were typically fitted to vehicles deployed to Arctic areas, and users included the units of 3 Commando Brigade as well as those units attached to the ACE Mobile Force (AMF).

Winterised Series 3 Half-Tons were often (but not invariably) fitted with hard tops and had rubber floor mats and sheets of a high-density micro-cellular insulating material called Plasterzote on the inside surfaces of the back body. Window blinds and a radiator blind were also usually fitted, and in some cases an inter-vehicle battery slave starter socket was added in the front of the passenger's side seatbox.

The central item of the kit was a large heater manufactured by CJ Williams Ltd and fitted into the centre seat position in the cab. It was fed with hot coolant from the engine through a hose that ran through the bulkhead at floor level alongside the transmission tunnel. A red-painted on-off control was fitted close to the bulkhead, usually on a simple right-angled bracket that ran above the hose. Heat was distributed through four large-diameter hoses, two directed at the windscreen and two into the back body.

On FFR vehicles, the battery box was removed from between the seats and the two batteries were relocated into lockers in the rear wheel-arches, one on either side. On GS vehicles, the single battery was relocated in the rear load bed.

74 FM 93 is an FFR vehicle that has been adapted to carry a PA system for a display at Bovington Open Day in June 1981. (GF)

SUMMARY OF SERIES 3 HALF-TON DELIVERIES, 1972-1985

Lists cover vehicles ordered under contracts, and do not include vehicles transferred in from other services or elsewhere.

Chassis suffix letter codes are given where available. For brevity, the tables show only the serial numbers (and not the prefix code) of vehicles built with VIN numbers.

Note that there were special procurement arrangements for the Berlin Brigade. These are explained more fully in Chapter 9.

ARMY AND TRI-SERVICE PURCHASES

Serials	Contract	Chassis Nos	Total	Remarks
45 FL 36 to 51 FL 39	WV10787	951-00003A to 951-00708A	604	Cargo RHD.
51 FL 40 to 54 FL 54	WV10787	954-00067A to 954-00397A	315	Cargo LHD.
54 FL 55 to 56 FL 94	WV10775	951-00153A to 951-01022A	240	FFR RHD.
56 FL 95 to 58 FL 77	WV107756	954-00217A to 954-00700A	183	FFR LHD.
08 FM 57 to 17 FM 17	WV11139	951-01359A to 951-03035A	861	FFR RHD.
17 FM 18 to 18 FM 77	WV11139	954-00781A to 954-01096A	160	FFR LHD.
19 FM 20 to 26 FM 13	WV11140	951-01059A to 951-02555A	694	Cargo RHD.
67 FM 75 to 69 FM 59	WV11140	951-02556A to 951-02917A	185	Cargo RHD.
69 FM 60 to 70 FM 24	WV11140	954-00867A to 954-00932A	65	Cargo LHD.
72 FM 90 to 75 FM 19	WV11139	951-03036A to 951-03265A	220	FFR RHD
75 FM 20 to 75 FM 39	WV11139	954-01092A to 954-01121A	20	FFR LHD.
31 GB 08 to 33 GB 61	WV11404	951-03379A to 951-03362A	254	FFR RHD.
33 GB 62 to 34 GB 11	WV11404	954-01143A to 954-01192A	50	FFR LHD.
02 GF 39 to 03 GF 38	WV11581	951-03680A to 951-03777A	100	Cargo RHD.
03 GF 39 to 04 GF 38	WV11581	951-01305A to 951-01404A	100	Cargo LHD.
42 GF 78 to 45 GF 67	WV11706	951-03985A to 951-04430A	290	FFR RHD. 45 GF 02 (951-04258) is known to have worn serial 43 GF 02 in error.
45 GF 68 to 46 GF 34	WV11706	954-01457A to 954-01687A	67	FFR LHD.
52 GF 20 to 54 GF 57	WV11733	951-03837A to 951-04175A	238	Cargo RHD.
54 GF 58 to 56 GF 57	WV11733	954-01414A to 954-01668A	200	Cargo LHD.
62 GF 31 to 62 GF 52	WV11733	954-01659A to 954-01704A	22	Cargo LHD.
26 GJ 94 to 27 GJ 53	WV11916	951-04453A to 951-04512C	60	FFR RHD.
27 GJ 54 to 28 GJ 02	WV11916	954-02410A to 954-02458A	49	FFR LHD.
01 GN 62 to 01 GN 85	WV12085	951-04563A to 951-04607A	24	FFR RHD.
01 GN 86 to 02 GN 11	WV12085	954-02470A to 954-02495A	26	FFR LHD.
08 GT 70 to 09 GT 89	FVE 22A/39	951-04747A to 951-04866A	120	Cargo RHD.
09 GT 90 to 10 GT 19	FVE 22A/39	954-03285A to 954-03313A	30	Cargo LHD.
26 GT 85 to 28 GT 43	FVE 22A/48	954-03360A to 954-03518A	159	FFR LHD.
08 GX 69 to 10 GX 16	FVE 22A/70	951-04867A to 951-05030A	148	Cargo RHD.
17 HF 55 to 21 HF 06	FVE 22A/87	951-05338A to 951-05689A	352	FFR RHD.
21 HF 07 to 21 HF 46	FVE 22A/87	954-04447A to 954-04466A	20	FFR LHD.
21 HF 47 to 24 HF 46	FVE 22A/87	951-05303A to 951-05337A	300	Cargo RHD.
24 HF 47 to 26 HF 63	FVE 22A/87	954-04230A to 954-04446A	217	Cargo LHD.
15 HG 39 to 15 HG 81	FVE 22A/95	951-05785A to 100184	43	Cargo RHD.
15 HG 82 to 16 HG 39	FVE 22A/95	100217 to 100625	58	Cargo LHD.
16 HG 40 to 16 HG 84	FVE 22A/95	951-05690A to 951-05733A	45	FFR RHD.
16 HG 85 to 17 HG 16	FVE 22A/95	954-04487A to 954-04518A	32	FFR LHD.
45 HG 57 to 47 HG 36	FVE 22A/115	113565 to 115297	180	Cargo LHD.
47 HG 37 to 51 HG 26	FVE 22A/115	115298 to 125031	390	Cargo RHD.
51 HG 27 to 52 HG 16	FVE 22A/115	130602 to 132190	90	FFR LHD.
52 HG 17 to 57 HG 39	FVE 22A/115	130601 to 130600	523	FFR LHD.
05 HH 38 to 05 HH 76	FVE 22A/115	132882 to 132929	39	FFR RHD.

ARMY AND TRI-SERVICE PURCHASES (continued)

Serials	Contract	Chassis Nos	Total	Remarks
16 KA 92 to 17 KA 39	FVE 21B/229	171963 to 172991	48	Cargo RHD.
17 KA 40 to 17 KA 46	FVE 21B/229	169686 to 169730	7	Cargo Anti-Spark Diesel RHD; to RAF.
17 KA 47 and 17 KA 48	FVE 21B/229	169681 and 169734	2	Cargo Anti-Spark Diesel LHD; to RAF.
17 KA 49	FVE 21B/229	171964	1	FFR RHD.
83 KA 52 to 84 KA 38	FVE 21B/244	174415 to 175549	87	Cargo RHD.
84 KA 39 to 85 KA 51	FVE 21B/244	176217 to 181022	113	Cargo LHD.
91 KA 96 to 93 KA 04	FVE 21B/244	n/a to 182618	109	Cargo LHD.
93 KA 05 to 93 KA 88	FVE 21B/244	184478 to n/a	84	Cargo RHD.
22 KB 54 to 22 KB 79	FVE 21B/244	186581 to 186606	25	Cargo RHD.
23 KB 07 to 23 KB 15	FVE 21B/244	186607 to 186615	9	Cargo RHD.
23 KB 22	FVE 21B/244	187335	1	Cargo 24v 90A RHD; to RN.
23 KB 23 to 23 KB 41	FVE 21B/244	n/a to 186634	19	Cargo RHD.
26 KB 60 to 26 KB 61	FVE 21B/229	187266 and 187275	2	Cargo Anti-Spark Diesel RHD; to RAF.
26 KB 62 to 26 KB 73	FVE 21B/229	187479 to 187759	12	Cargo Anti-Spark Diesel LHD; to RAF.
26 KB 74 to 26 KB 75	FVE 21B/229	187287 and 187296	2	Cargo Anti-Spark Diesel LHD; to RAF.
29 KB 72 to 29 KB 73	FVE 21B/244	n/a and 187337	2	FFR LHD.
30 KB 30 to 30 KB 39	FVE 21B/244	192197 to 192206	10	FFR LHD.
55 KB 86 to 58 KB 35	FVE 22A/225	196934 to 200971	250	Cargo RHD.
73 KB 57 to 73 KB 58	FVE 22A/227	206039 and 206040	2	FFR RHD; for Royal Navy but the History Card for 73 KB 58 was not issued to the RN.
84 KB 26 to 84 KB 47	FVE 22A/240	206041 to 206062	22	FFR LHD.
84 KB 48 to 85 KB 31	FVE 22A/240	204231 to 207692	84	Cargo RHD.
40 KC 33 to 41 KC 32	FVE 22A/251	218757 to 227353	100	Cargo LHD.
41 KC 33 to 41 KC 82	FVE 22A/251	217748 to 227346	50	Cargo RHD.
42 KC 44 to 44 KC 43	FVE 22A/251	220023 to 224514	100	FFR RHD.
44 KC 44 to 44 KC 93	FVE 22A/251	220490 to 226477	50	FFR LHD.
44 KC 95	FVE 22A/251	220022	1	FFR RHD.
04 KD 51 to 04 KD 75	FVE 22A/251	224986 to 226210	25	Cargo Anti-Spark Diesel LHD; to RAF.
04 KD 76 to 05 KD 01	FVE 22A/251	224972 to 226039	26	Cargo Anti-Spark Diesel RHD; to RAF.
05 KD 02 to 05 KD 11	FVE 22A/251	227355 to 229361	10	Cargo 24v 90A LHD; to RAF.
05 KD 12 to 05 KD 65	FVE 22A/251	226501 to 227354	10	Cargo 24v 90A RHD; to RAF.

Total 9036

13 FM 30 of Petroleum Depot, West Moors was pictured next to a slightly newer Series 3 109 hardtop of 10 Ordnance Support Battalion at Devizes. The OEP 220 oil recommendation is just visible in white on the rear differential. (GF)

THE SERIES 3 HALF-TON

RAF PURCHASES

Serials	Contract	Chassis Nos	Total	Remarks
53 AM 52 to 55 AM 29	WV10828	951-00714A to 951-00935A	178	Cargo RHD.
55 AM 30 to 55 AM 59	WV10828	954-00701A to 954-00493A	30	Cargo LHD.
55 AM 60 to 55 AM 80	WV10828	951-01024A to 951-01044A	21	Cargo RHD.
59 AM 20 to 59 AM 94	WV11131	951-01209A to 951-01282A	75	Cargo 24v 90A RHD.
59 AM 95 to 60 AM 00	WV11131	951-01721A to 951-01723A	6	FFR RHD.
60 AM 01 to 60 AM 20	WV11131	954-00752A to 954-00763A	20	Cargo 24v 90A LHD.
60 AM 20 to 60 AM 28	WV11131	954-00844A to 954-00847A	9	FFR LHD.
61 AM 04 to 62 AM 64	WV11147	951-01284A to 951-01481A	161	Cargo RHD.
62 AM 65 to 62 AM 99	WV11147	954-00866A to 954-00801A	35	Cargo LHD.
71 AM 29 to 71 AM 64	WV11430	951-03674A to 951-03578A	36	Cargo 24v 90A RHD.
71 AM 65 to 71 AM 68	WV11430	954-01194A to 954-01193A	4	FFR LHD.
71 AM 69 to 72 AM 68	WV11439	951-03278A to 951-03376A	100	Cargo RHD.
72 AM 69 to 72 AM 80	WV11439	954-01129A to 954-01140A	12	Cargo LHD.
75 AM 46 to 76 AM 40	WV11700	951-03780A to 951-03872A	95	Cargo RHD.
76 AM 41 to 76 AM 45	WV11700	954-01409A to 954-01413A	5	Cargo LHD.
76 AM 50 to 76 AM 75	WV11701	951-03959A to 951-03948A	26	Cargo 24v 90A RHD.
76 AM 76	WV11701	954-01456A	1	Cargo 24v 90A LHD.
77 AM 20 to 77 AM 64	WV11872	951-04513A to 951-04557A	45	Cargo RHD.
77 AM 65 to 77 AM 74	WV11872	954-02459A to 954-02468A	10	Cargo LHD.
29 AJ 83 to 29 AJ 92	WV11876	951-04442A to 951-04451A	10	Cargo 24v 90A RHD.
29 AJ 93 to 29 AJ 96	WV11876	954-01930A to 954-01933A	4	Cargo 24v 90A LHD.
88 AM 13 to 88 AM 60	FVE 22A/22	951-04611A to 951-04658A	48	Cargo RHD.
88 AM 61 to 88 AM 86	FVE 22A/22	954-03148A to 954-03253A	26	Cargo LHD.
30 AJ 88 to 31 AJ 00	FVE 22A/40	951-04659A to 951-04671A	75	Cargo 24v 90A RHD.
31 AJ 01 to 31 AJ 11	FVE 22A/24	954-03254A to 954-03264A	11	Cargo 24v 90A LHD.
31 AJ 90 to 32 AJ 64	FVE 22A/40	951-04672A to 951-04746A	75	Cargo RHD.
32 AJ 71 to 33 AJ 15	FVE 22A/40	954-03315A to 954-03339A	45	Cargo LHD.
39 AJ 82 to 40 AJ 31	FVE 22A/94	951-05735A to 951-05784A	50	Cargo RHD.
40 AJ 32 to 40 AJ 52	FVE 22A/94	100186 to 100216	21	Cargo LHD.
43 AJ 25 to 43 AJ 27	FVE 22A/115	132191 to 132194	3	Cargo 24v 90A RHD.
43 AJ 69 to 43 AJ 83	FVE 22A/115	128277 to 128294	15	Cargo LHD.
43 AJ 84 to 45 AJ 08	FVE 22A/115	128311 to 129765	125	Cargo RHD.
47 AJ 08 to 47 AJ 16	FVE 22A/115	128296 to 128306	9	Cargo LHD.
47 AJ 17 to 47 AJ 70	FVE 22A/115	131457 to 131523	54	Cargo RHD.
49 AJ 15 to 49 AJ 16	FVE 22A/115	128307 to 128308	2	Cargo LHD.
48 AJ 09 to 48 AJ 16	FVE 22A/115	131524 to 132341	8	Cargo RHD.
		Total	1450	

Pictured next to a 101 One-Tonne at the British Army Equipment Exhibition (BAEE) in June 1976, 45 GF 66 displays the side-mounted aerial of an FFR vehicle. (GF)

155

ROYAL NAVY

The following list is possibly incomplete but gives some idea of Royal Navy purchases.

Serials	Contract	Chassis Nos	Total	Remarks
00 RN 96	n/a	951-04575A	6	Cargo RHD.
01 RN 50 to 01 RN 54	n/a	951-04578A to 951-04582A	5	FFR RHD.
02 RN 17	WV12040	951-04558A	5	Cargo RHD.
03 RN 20 to 03 RN 26	006-74-1	951-03488A to 951-03494A	7	Cargo RHD.
04 RN 14	020-77-1	951-04591A	1	FFR RHD.
10 RN 00 and 10 RN 01	FVE 22A/115	129708 and 129709	2	RHD Cargo.
10 RN 49 to 10 RN 50	WV11290	951-03052A & 951-03139A	2	FFR RHD; to Army later.
13 RN 36	n/a	951-04584A	1	RHD.
15 RN 06	n/a	n/a	1	RHD, HMS Bulwark.
15 RN 35 to 15 RN 40	FVE 22A/115	132195 to 132200	6	RHD FFR.
17 RN 96	FVE 22A/18	951-04610A	1	Cargo RHD.
34 RN 71, 34 RN 90, 34 RN 92	FVE 22A/78	951-05033A to 951-05035A	3	RHD Cargo.
40 RN 94 to 40 RN 97	035-72-1	951-01045A to 951-01048A	4	Cargo RHD.
41 RN 00 to 41 RN 09	036-72-1	951-01049A to 951-01058A	10	FFR RHD.
48 RN 95, 48 RN 98, 48 RN 74	009-78-1	951-04924A to 951-04428A	10	RHD 24v 90A Helicopter Starting known.
49 RN 02, 49 RN 39	044-75-1	951-04431A, 951-04433A	7	FFR RHD.
63 RN 66 to 63 RN 68	037-74-1	951-03677A to 951-03679A	3	Cargo RHD.
64 RN 32, 64 RN 33, n/a, 64 RN 00, n/a, 64 RN 18, 64 RN 96	001-78-1	951-04917A to 951-04923A	7	FFR RHD.
66 RN 24	002-76-1	951-04441A	13	FFR RHD.
79 RN 65	024-75-1	951-04176A	1	Cargo RHD.
89 RN 96 and 89 RN 99		951-05036A and 951-05037A	2	RHD FFR.
98 RN 23, 98 RN 29, 98 RN 30	FVE 21B/229	179768, 187333, 187334	3	RHD Cargo.

Total 100

Total should be seen as approximate.

This Half-Ton from the HG batch has an aerial tuner base on the wing and carries the windscreen blackout canvas associated with units that had an arctic role. Alongside is a CL 88in model, with the yellow high-visibility stripe broken by a red-painted filler cap to indicate that it has a petrol engine. Both vehicles belong to the Army School of Mechanical Transport at Leconfield. (FMW)

BERLIN SENÄT

Serials	Contract	Chassis Nos	Total	Remarks
21 XC 40 to 21 XC 59	-	954-00594A to 954-00608A	20	LHD FFR.
04 XC 39 to 04 KC 93	-	954-00743A to 954-00724A	55	LHD FFR.
04 XC 94 to 04 XC 99	-	954-00934A to 954-00937A	6	LHD Cargo.
05 XC 37 to 05 XC 40	-	n/a to 954-01205A	4	LHD Cargo.
05 XC 32 to 05 XC 35	-	954-01220A to n/a	4	LHD Cargo.
05 XC 36	-	n/a	1	LHD Cargo.
05 XC 41 and 05 XC 42	-	n/a	2	LHD Cargo.
05 XC 43 and 05 XC 44	-	n/a	2	LHD Cargo.
05 XC 45 to 05 XC 47	-	n/a	3	LHD Cargo.
05 XC 48	-	n/a	1	LHD Cargo.
05 XC 49 to 05 XC 60	-	n/a	12	LHD Cargo.
05 XC 61 to 05 XC 73	-	954-01231A to 954-01405A	13	LHD FFR.
57 XB 36 to 57 XB 43	-	954-02402 to 954-02409	8	LHD FFR.
43 XB 85 to 43 XB 95	-	954-03541A to 954-03535A	11	LHD FFR.
61 XB 62 to 61 XB 72	-	114233 to 144238	11	LHD FFR.
59 XB 45 and 59 XB 46	-	114247 and 114248	2	LHD Cargo.
61 XB 79 to 61 XB 83	-	114249 to 114244	5	LHD Cargo.
30 XC 48	-	124758	1	LHD Cargo.
29 XC 16 to 29 XC 28	-	143845 to 143847	13	LHD Cargo.
28 XC 25	-	143854	1	LHD Cargo.
30 XC 67	-	166319	1	LHD FFR.
30 XC 71 to 30 XC 75	-	166320 to 166324	5	LHD FFR.
01 XK 69 to 01 XK 77	-	210615 to 210620	9	LHD FFR.
03 XK 33 and 03 XK 34	-	22502 and 220021	2	LHD FFR.
		Total	**192**	

ASSET CODES

Asset Codes followed the system introduced by the British armed forces around 1960. The NSN is the NATO Stock Number.

Asset Code	NSN Code	Type	Notes
1613-2778		Truck, Utility (Winterised), ½ Tonne, 4x4, Anti-Spark, Rover Series 3	RHD
1614-0778		Truck, Utility, ½ Tonne, 4x4, Glider Recovery, Rover Series 3	RHD
1616-0778	(None)	Truck, Utility, ½ Tonne, 4x4 Rover Series 3, with Full Track Conversion	RHD Cuthbertson (RAF only)
1618-0783	2320-99-893-2973	Truck, Utility, ½ Tonne, 24 volt 90 amp, 4x4 Rover Series 3	RHD
1618-5783	2320-99-893-2974	Truck, Utility, ½ Tonne, 24 volt 90 amp, 4x4 Rover Series 3	LHD
1619-0778		Truck, Utility (Winterised), ½ Tonne, 4x4, Rover Series 3	RHD
1620-0778	2320-99-893-2845	Truck, Utility, ½ Tonne, 4x4 Rover Series 3	RHD
1620-5778	2320-99-893-2846	Truck, Utility, ½ tonne, 4x4 Rover Series 3	LHD
1624-0778		Truck, Utility (Winterised), ½ Tonne, 24 volt 90 amp, 4x4, Rover Series 3	
1625-0778	2320-99-893-2847	Truck, Utility, FFR, ½ Tonne, 4x4 Rover Series 3	RHD
1625-5778	2320-99-893-2848	Truck, Utility, FFR, ½ Tonne, 4x4 Rover Series 3	LHD
1626-0778		Truck, Utility, FFR (Winterised), ½ Tonne, 4x4, Land Rover Series 3	RHD

The Series 3 Half-Ton could be prepared for deep-water wading. This example was pictured boarding a landing-craft during trials at ATTURM, in Instow. The engine breather tube is actually held by the solider standing on the passenger's seat. (ATTURM, via Richard de Roos Collection)

45 FL 46 was an early Series 3 Half-Ton which had already seen its fair share of abuse by the time this picture was taken. Note the poor fit at the bottom of the driver's door. (GF)

74 FM 69 displays an unusual camouflage scheme along with its twin tuner boxes for the radio aerials on the front wings. The vehicle was photographed at Larkhill Artillery Day in June 1977 and shows a Battery Commander's vehicle of 29 Commando Regiment Royal Artillery which had an arctic role. (GF)

LAND ROVER CHASSIS CODES

At the start of this period, all Land Rovers had a three-digit identifying prefix in the chassis code, which indicated the model type, steering position and other factors. Neither the model-year nor the calendar-year of manufacture was indicated. The ones relevant to the Series 3 Half-Ton models are shown below. The three-figure prefix was followed by a five-figure serial number that began at 00001 for each separate sequence, and this in turn was followed by a suffix letter. In the case of the Half-Ton, the suffix letter was always A.

Note that the Land Rover model-year began in September and continued until the end of the following July, leaving August clear for the works' annual holiday and for preparing the assembly lines to take new models. A Land Rover built in the 1976 model-year could therefore have been built at any time between September 1975 and July 1976.

951   Home market, petrol
954   LHD, petrol

From November 1, 1979, the Land Rover chassis numbering system changed to conform to internationally-agreed VIN (Vehicle Identification Number) code standards. It is probable that some vehicles built in October 1979 also had these codes. Those used for the first year (i.e. 1980 model-year) had 14 characters and began with the letters LB. From November 1, 1980, three further characters (SAL) were added to the prefix, making 17 characters in all. A single sequential serial numbering system was used for all types.
Example (later type):
SALLBAAG1AA-123456.

This breaks down as follows:
SAL   Manufacturer code (then British Leyland)
LB   Land Rover Series III
A   88-inch wheelbase
A   Utility body (soft top, truck cab or hard top)
G   2.25-litre diesel engine
        H = 2.25-litre four-cylinder petrol engine
1   RHD with 4-speed manual gearbox
        2 = LHD with 4-speed manual gearbox
A   Used for all models up to 1985
A   Assembled at Solihull factory

These pictures show two different types of vehicle identification plate. The larger one was on 43 GF 02 (951-04258A) and the smaller one on 48 HG 61, which was one of the 1980 models with the "short" VINs – in this case LBBAH1AA-119863. (GF)

TECHNICAL SPECIFICATIONS, SERIES 3 HALF-TON MODELS

ENGINES:
Petrol:
2286cc (90.47mm x 88.9mm) four-cylinder with pushrod OHV and Solex carburettor. 8:1 CR. 77bhp at 4250rpm and 124 lb ft at 2500rpm.

Diesel:
2286cc (90.47mm x 88.9mm) four-cylinder with pushrod OHV and indirect injection. 23:1CR. 62bhp at 4000rpm and 103 lb ft at 1800rpm.

TRANSMISSION:
Selectable four-wheel drive.Four-speed main gearbox with synchromesh on all forward gears; ratios 3.6:1, 2.22:1, 1.512:1, 1.0:1, reverse 3.0:1. Two-speed transfer gearbox; ratios 1.148:1 (High) and 2.4:1 (Low) Axle ratio: 4.7:1

SUSPENSION, STEERING AND BRAKES:
Semi-elliptic leaf springs all round. Recirculating-ball steering with 15.6:1 ratio. Drum brakes all round and separate drum-type transmission parking brake.

ELECTRICAL SYSTEM:
12-volt with alternator, or 24-volt with 90-amp alternator.

TRANSMISSION:
Selectable four-wheel drive.Four-speed main gearbox with synchromesh on all forward gears; ratios 3.6:1, 2.22:1, 1.512:1, 1.0:1, reverse 3.0:1. Two-speed transfer gearbox; ratios 1.148:1 (High) and 2.4:1 (Low) Axle ratio: 4.7:1

UNLADEN WEIGHT:
12-volt GS soft top   3210 lb (1456kg), 2660 lb (1206.5kg) when stripped

PERFORMANCE (PETROL MODELS):
0-50mph:	21 secs approximately
Maximum:	65mph (105km/h)
Fuel consumption:	15-18 mpg

DIMENSIONS:
Overall length:	144in (3650mm)
Wheelbase:	88in (2235mm)
Overall width:	60in (1520mm)
Unladen height:	77in (1950mm) – GS soft top
Track:	51.5in (1310mm)
Ground clearance:	8.5in (210mm)

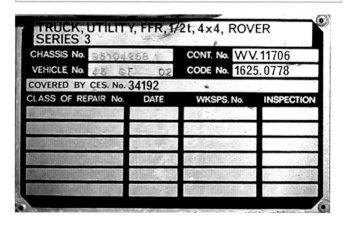

ARMY SERIAL NUMBERS

The serial numbers allocated by the Army gave a clue to the date of the vehicle, although those issued by the RAF and Royal Navy did not. In this period, serial letters indicated the financial year in which the vehicle was purchased (which is not necessarily the same as the calendar year in which it was delivered). Those relevant to the Rover Series 3 Half-Ton models are shown below.

As before, serial sequences began at 0001 (e.g. 00 FL 01) and ran to 9999 (eg 99 FL 99). There was not necessarily any correlation between chassis number order and military serial number within batches.

Note that Berlin serial letters were allocated in no particular sequence. Suitable gaps were found in the existing "X" registers. To coincide with the introduction of tri-service allocation with KA for the rest of the Army, XK was used.

FL	1971-1972	HH	1980-1981	KC	8 December 1983
FM	1972-1973	HJ	1981-1982		(tri-service unified
GB	1973-1974	KA	December 1981 (tri-		series)
GF	1974-1975		service unified series);	KD	19 July 1984 (tri-
GJ	1975-1976		once 99 KA 99 was		service unified series)
GN	1976-1977		reached, 00 KB 01	XB	Berlin Brigade
GT	1977-1978		followed immediately.	XC	Berlin Brigade
GX	1977-1978	KB	10 August 1982 (tri-	XK	Berlin Brigade
HF	1978-1979		service unified series)		
HG	1979-1980				

CHAPTER 11:
THE SERIES III 88

The short-wheelbase Series III models bought by the Army were to CL specification because the Lightweight had assumed the short-wheelbase GS and FFR rôles. 27 FL 13 is a Station Wagon, and has a civilian specification even down to the contrasting colour on the roof – although it does have military-specification towing rings on the front bumper and the civilian option of a bonnet locking hasp. (GF)

Initially, with the advent of the Lightweight, the Army bought only small quantities of the 88-inch vehicle in civilian Commercial (CL) form. Purchases between 1966 and 1972 were never more than 44 in a single Financial Year. As the table at the end of this chapter makes clear, there were two principal rôles for the Series 3 88-inch chassis with the forces – the Station Wagon and the CL Cargo. The Station Wagon and CL cargo were essentially the civilian model with a few military additions such as a fire extinguisher and, of course, a data plate as well as an appropriate military colour scheme.

The Station Wagon was used by the Services Attaché and Advisor Service (SAAS) and also in small volumes by some specific units of the Army. These units included Postal and Courier units of the Royal Engineers responsible for delivering mail in the field, and various Procurement Executive experimental establishments. One LHD batch (64 FM 99 to 65 FM 06) delivered to BAOR was recoded as CL Cargo as it seems to have been mistakenly coded as a Station Wagon in the first place! There were few units that needed the Station Wagon in BAOR although they were used by some Headquarters units.

The CL Cargo was initially bought in small numbers in Series IIA form but as the Series 3 entered service the vehicle began to be used by Driver Training units. These included 3 Training Regiment, Royal Engineers at Minley, 12 Regiment, Royal Corps of Transport (RCT) at Aldershot and 8 Signal Regiment, Royal Corps of Signals (RCS) at Catterick. Many of these Driver Training vehicles were subsequently transferred to the Army School of Transport at Leconfield when it formed in late spring 1977. Some TA units with a Home Defence rôle – that is to say in the event of the Cold War turning "hot" their rôle would have been to defend and support the home base – were equipped with CL Land Rovers and also CL 4-Tonne Trucks.

A number were issued to 58 Squadron RCT in Cyprus, which had a rôle operating a Military Training Wing (MTW) that provided vehicles to units deployed to the Sovereign Base Areas to undergo training. In addition, a number of RCT

This slightly later Series III 88 was pictured in service with the Military Police in Cyprus. Note the blue rotating beacon on a stalk attached to the rear body side, and that the side mirrors were by this stage attached to the top door hinge. (GF)

23 HG 70 has a yellow stripe on each flank, marking it out as belonging to the Army School of Mechanical Transport at Leconfield. The yellow stripes were used because Leconfield was still an active airbase. (RLC)

Line-laying vehicles were quite rare by the time 17 GF 34 entered service. The base vehicle is a CL specification Series 3 88-inch. (GF)

"garrison transport units" (GTUs) had them. The GTUs provided drivers and vehicles to support units with no, or insufficient, vehicles of their own to meet their transport tasks. They included 40 Squadron at Catterick, 41 Squadron at Aldershot, 43 Squadron at Shorncliffe, 44 Squadron at Camberley and 45 Squadron at Arborfield, and 410 Troop at Edinburgh, 416 Troop at Preston and 417 Troop at York.

The RAF made use of the Series 3 88-inch in "Anti-Spark" form, and these were diesel-engined cargo versions with a hard top body and a front towing eye. They were used for general transport duties around airfields, and were described as "anti-spark" because they did not have the ignition system of a petrol-engined vehicle. This meant that there was less likelihood of the vehicle creating a fire risk when operating around aircraft, where there are often fuel spillages and leaks.

The Royal Navy has always preferred diesel-engined vehicles because of their reduced fire hazard, and this service also took small numbers of Series 3 88s with diesel engines. Some provided transport for officers on some of the larger ships when in foreign ports and were part of "Enhanced Shore Support". The larger vessels were capable of carrying them as

94 AM 09 and 94 AM 13 were typical of later RAF Series III 88 models. Both were again window hardtops with a semi-military specification. The yellow side stripes and amber rotating beacon on the roof were intended to make these vehicles more easily visible on airfields. (GF)

The Royal Navy usually carried two Land Rovers aboard each of its capital ships. These two Series III 88s belonged to the aircraft carrier HMS Ark Royal, although the boards proclaiming the fact were somewhat worse for wear when this picture was taken. Note the yellow fuel filler caps, so painted to remind users that these had diesel engines. (GF)

As usual, the RAF ordered window hardtop models. 60 AM 96 has a semi-military specification, with FV-pattern headlamp fittings and a front towing jaw, but no towing eyes on the bumper. The side filler cap is also a feature of the civilian specification. (GF)

deck cargo or, in the case of an aircraft carrier, below deck. Others were used around dockyards as part of the "Motor Transport Operational Pools". They were invariably painted Royal Blue and where appropriate carried the ship's crest on the radiator grille and the ship's name in white on the doors.

Both the petrol and diesel engines in these CL models were four-cylinder types, and both originally had three main bearings and were known to Rover as 2¼-litre types. From late 1981, both were re-engineered with five main bearings and, despite retaining the earlier bore and stroke dimensions, were rebranded as 2.3-litre types.

41 GT 03 seems to have been bulled-up for this picture. The regimental markings are for to the Army School of Mechanical Transport at Leconfield but the flagpole base on the wing suggests that this vehicle was for the use of a senior officer. (GF)

HMS Bristol was the Royal Navy's last steam-powered ship and the only example of a Type 82 destroyer ever built. This Land Rover was carried aboard and shows how the name-boards looked when at their best. The silver headlamp surrounds were part of the standard civilian specification from August 1980. (GF)

18 GF 95 was a LHD Series III 88 that was converted to a review vehicle and used by the Military Police. Note the road tyres visible in these pictures. It was one of the last Series IIIs to remain in service. (R Dawson)

ARMY SERIAL NUMBERS

The serial numbers allocated by the Army gave a clue to the date of the vehicle, although those issued by the RAF and Royal Navy did not. In this period, serial letters indicated the financial year in which the vehicle was purchased (which is not necessarily the same as the calendar year in which it was delivered). Those relevant to the Rover Series 3 88-inch CL models are shown below.

As before, serial sequences began at 0001 (e.g. 00 FL 01) and ran to 9999 (eg 99 FL 99). There was not necessarily any correlation between chassis number order and military serial number within batches.

FL	1971-1972	once 99 KA 99 was
FM	1972-1973	reached, 00 KB 01
GB	1973-1974	followed immediately.
GF	1974-1975	
GJ	1975-1976	KB 10 August 1982
GN	1976-1977	(tri-service unified
GT	1977-1978	series)
HF	1978-1979	
HG	1979-1980	KC 8 December 1983
HH	1980-1981	(tri-service unified
HJ	1981-1982	series)
KA	December 1981	KD 19 July 1984
	(tri-service unified	(tri-service unified
	series);	series)

This line-up of late Series III 88s was seen at Akrotiri while they were in storage. The nearest vehicle had previously belonged to the Sovereign Base Police who police the base areas in Cyprus. (GF)

LAND ROVER CHASSIS CODES

At the start of this period, all Land Rovers had a three-digit identifying prefix in the chassis code, which indicated the model type, steering position and other factors. Neither the model-year nor the calendar-year of manufacture was indicated. The ones relevant to the Series 3 88 CL models are shown below. The three-figure prefix was followed by a five-figure serial number that began at 00001 for each separate sequence, and this in turn was followed by a suffix letter that indicated changes of significance in servicing the vehicle.

Note that the Land Rover model-year began in September and continued until the end of the following July, leaving August clear for the works' annual holiday and for preparing the assembly lines to take new models. A Land Rover built in the 1976 model-year could therefore have been built at any time between September 1975 and July 1976.

901	Home market, petrol
904	LHD, petrol
906	Home market, diesel
909	LHD, diesel
921	Home market, petrol, Station Wagon
924	LHD, petrol, Station Wagon

From November 1, 1979, the Land Rover chassis numbering system changed to conform to internationally-agreed VIN (Vehicle Identification Number) code standards. It is probable that some vehicles built in October 1979 also had these codes. Those used for the first year (i.e. 1980 model-year) had 14 characters and began with the letters LB. From November 1, 1980, three further characters (SAL) were added to the prefix, making 17 characters in all. A single sequential serial numbering system was used for all types. Example (later type): SALLBAAG1AA-123456.
This breaks down as follows:

SAL	Manufacturer code (then British Leyland)
LB	Land Rover Series III
A	88-inch wheelbase
A	Utility body (soft top, truck cab or hard top) B = Station Wagon
G	2.25-litre or 2.3-litre diesel engine H = 2.25-litre or 2.3-litre four-cylinder petrol engine
1	RHD with 4-speed manual gearbox 2 = LHD with 4-speed manual gearbox
A	Used for all models up to 1985
A	Assembled at Solihull factory

ASSET CODES

Asset Codes followed the system introduced by the British armed forces around 1960. NSN codes are not available for these vehicle types.

1150-0778	Car, Utility, ¼ ton, 4x4, Rover Series 3
1150-1778	Car, Utility, ¼ Tonne, 4x4, w/tlr attachments, Rover Series 3 (Petrol)
1150-6778	Car, Utility, ¼ Tonne, 4x4, LHD, w/tlr attachments, Rover Series 3 (Petrol)
1151-0778	Car, Utility, SAAS, ¼ Tonne, 4x4, Rover
1615-3778	Truck, Utility, CL, ½ ton, 4x4, Rover Series 3
1621-0778	Truck, Utility, CL, ½ Tonne, 4x4, Rover Series 3
1621-1778	Truck, Utility, CL, ½ Tonne, 4x4, Hard Top, Land Rover Series 3 (Petrol)
1621-2778	Truck, Utility, CL, ½ Tonne, 4x4, w/trailer atts, Rover Series 3
1621-5778	Truck, Utility, CL, ½ ton, 4x4, LHD, w/trailer atts, Rover Series 3 (Petrol)

SUMMARY OF SERIES 3 88-INCH CL DELIVERIES, 1972-1985

Lists cover vehicles ordered under contracts, and do not include vehicles transferred in from other services or elsewhere.
Chassis suffix letter codes are given where available. For brevity, the tables show only the serial numbers (and not the prefix code) of vehicles built with VIN numbers.

ARMY AND TRI-SERVICE

Serials	Contract	Chassis Nos	Total	Remarks
26 FL 98 to 27 FL 20	WV8765 R2183	921-00087A to 921-00108A	23	Station Wagon RHD.
56 FM 86 to 57 FM 15	WV8765 R2383	901-08130A to 901-08151A	30	CL Cargo RHD.
57 FM 16 to 57 FM 17	WV8765 R2383	906-04371A to 906-04372A	2	CL Cargo RHD Diesel
57 FM 19 to 57 FM 22	WV8765 R2392	901-06931A to 901-06827A	4	CL Cargo RHD.
64 FM 99 to 65 FM 06	WV8765 R2416	904-04103A to 904-04102A	8	Station Wagon LHD. These soft tops were mistakenly coded as Station Wagons (1150-6778). This was corrected in November 1978.
01 GB 64 to 02 GB 83	WV8765 R2417	901-08125A to 901-08317A	120	CL Cargo RHD.
02 GB 84 to 03 GB 13	WV8765 R2417	904-05002A to 904-05119A	30	CL Cargo LHD.
05 GB 49 to 05 GB 52	WV8765 R2474	901-07257A to 901-07260A	4	CL Cargo RHD.
06 GB 05	WV8765 R2431	921-00481A	1	Station Wagon RHD; to British Defence Liaison Staff, Australia.
41 GB 45	WV8765 R2608	924-03578A	1	Station Wagon LHD; to Defence Attaché, Sofia.
42 GB 26	WV8765 R2609	921-00738A	1	Station Wagon RHD; to Defence Attaché, Beirut.
42 GB 27 to 43 GB 02	WV8765 R2594	901-10711A to 901-10656A	76	CL Cargo RHD.
00 GF 03	WV8765 R2654	921-00739A	1	Station Wagon RHD; to Defence Attaché, Kathmandu.
16 GF 54 to 18 GF 55	WV8765 R2732	901-11425 to 901-15190A	202	CL Cargo RHD.
18 GF 56 to 19 GF 21	WV8765 R2732	904-09039A to 904-15217A	66	CL Cargo LHD.
46 GF 41	WV8765 R2790	924-19203A	1	Station Wagon LHD; to Defence Attaché, Bucharest.
46 GF 50	WV8765 R2800	924-19197A	1	Station Wagon LHD; to Services Attaché, Cairo.
66 GJ 85 to 67 GJ 13	WV8765 R2931	901-30966A to 901-32548A	29	CL Cargo RHD.
67 GJ 14	WV8765 R2931	906-17126	1	CL Cargo RHD Diesel.
00 GN 01	WV8765 R2940	924-34973A	1	Station Wagon LHD; to Services Attaché, Helsinki.
06 GN 54 to 09 GN 53	WV8765 R2993	901-37932A to 901-44055A	300	CL Cargo RHD.
01 GT 48 to 02 GT 56	WV8765 R3122	901-45940A to 901-53529A	109	CL Cargo RHD.
02 GT 57 to 03 GT 17	WV8765 R3122	904-48098A to 904-54785A	61	CL Cargo LHD.
40 GT 05 to 42 GT 16	FVE 22A/44 R3180	901-49635A to 901-53595A	212	CL Cargo RHD.
42 GT 17 to 42 GT 57	FVE 22A/44 R3180	904-52582A to 904-54807A	41	CL Cargo LHD.
11 HF 67 to 11 HF 70	FVE 22A/44 R3304	924-51353A to 924-51500A	4	Station Wagon LHD.
11 HF 71 to 11 HF 73	FVE 22A/44 R3304	921-55363A to 921-55304A	3	Station Wagon RHD.
17 HF 03	FVE 22A/44	924-51353A	1	Station Wagon LHD; to Services Attaché, Cairo.
45 HF 24	FVE 22A/44	924-55840A	1	Station Wagon LHD; to Defence Attaché, Sofia.
45 HF 76 to 46 HF 10	FVE 22A/44 R3352	904-56627A to 101068	35	CL Cargo LHD.
23 HG 02 to 24 HG 19	FVE 22A/44 R3398	108382 to 125830	118	CL Cargo RHD.
24 HG 20 to 24 HG 36	FVE 22A/44 R3398	122270 to 127239	17	CL Cargo LHD.
04 HH 08 to 04 HH 27	FVE 22A/44 R3459	128037 to 131189	20	CL Cargo RHD.
04 HJ 04	FVE 22A/140	157698	1	Station Wagon LHD; to Service Attaché, Damascus.
10 KA 54 to 12 KA 16	FVE 22A/140 R3526	158451 to 159238	163	CL Cargo RHD.
20 KA 26	FVE 22A/140 LR3564	172658	1	Station Wagon LHD; for Services Attaché, Warsaw.
25 KA 81 to 25 KA 93	FVE 22A/140 LR3568	175122 to 177237	13	CL Cargo LHD.
21 KB 46 to 21 KB 47	FVE 22A/140 LR3602	185333 and 185323	2	Station Wagon RHD.
21 KB 48	FVE 22A/140 LR3602	184780	1	Station Wagon LHD.

ARMY AND TRI-SERVICE PURCHASES (continued)

Serials	Contract	Chassis Nos	Total	Remarks
27 KB 21	FVE 22A/140 LR3628	186255	1	Station Wagon LHD; to Services Attaché, Helsinki.
29 KB 74 to 29 KB 81	FVE 22A/140 LR3626	187786 to 187797	8	CL Cargo RHD Diesel; to RN.
50 KB 08 to 50 KB 15	FVE 22A/140 LR3674	196853 to 197538	8	CL Cargo RHD Diesel; Blue; to RN.
87 KB 78 to 88 KB 14	FVE 22A/140 LR3760	210884 to 211631	37	CL Cargo RHD; to RAF.
88 KB 15 to 88 KB 24	FVE 22A/140 LR3760	211634 to 211826	10	CL Cargo LHD; to RAF.
81 KC 35 to 81 KC 52	FVE 22A/251	222682 to 223912	18	CL Cargo LHD.
81 KC 53 to 81 KC 87	FVE 22A/251	221974 to 224654	36	CL Cargo RHD.
81 KC 88 to 81 KC 93	FVE 22A/251	223723 to 224669	6	CL Cargo RHD.
81 KC 94 to 81 KC 96	FVE 22A/251	222460 to 222703	3	CL Cargo RHD.
00 KD 33	FVE 22A/140 LR5033	226411	1	CL Cargo RHD; to RN.
00 KD 34 to 00 KD 35	FVE 22A/140 LR5015	226224 to 226229	2	CL Cargo RHD Diesel; to RN.
18 KD 63 to 18 KD 65	FVE 22A/140 LR5015	n/a	3	CL Cargo RHD Diesel; to RN.
		Total	**1838**	

RAF PURCHASES

Serials	Contract	Chassis Nos	Total	Remarks
57 AM 75 to 57 AM 84	WV10788	906-02995A to 906-03069A	10	Cargo RHD Anti-Spark Diesel.
60 AM 85 to 60 AM 97	WV11088	906-04939A to 906-04982B	13	Cargo RHD Anti-Spark Diesel.
60 AM 98	WV11088	909-01558A	1	Cargo RHD CL Diesel.
69 AM 29 to 69 AM 51	WV11369	906-06541 to 906-06578	23	Cargo RHD Anti-Spark Diesel.
69 AM 52 to 69 AM 55	WV11369	909-02524 to 909-02530	4	Cargo LHD Anti-Spark Diesel.
75 AM 25 to 75 AM 28	WV11369	906-10873 to 906-10882	4	Cargo RHD Anti-Spark Diesel.
75 AM 29 to 75 AM 34	WV11369	909-13363 to 909-13376	6	Cargo LHD Anti-Spark Diesel.
77 AM 07 to 77 AM 14	WV11715	906-11875A to 906-13361A	8	Cargo RHD Anti-Spark Diesel.
77 AM 15 to 77 AM 18	WV11715	909-13378A to 909-13385A	4	Cargo LHD Anti-Spark Diesel.
80 AM 99 to 81 AM 10	WV12011	906-23586 to 906-23644	12	Cargo RHD Anti-Spark Diesel.
81 AM 11 to 81 AM 16	WV12011	909-23672A to 909-23715A	6	Cargo LHD Anti-Spark Diesel.
86 AM 59 to 86 AM 76	FVE 22A/20	909-23724A to 909-23869A	18	Cargo LHD Anti-Spark Diesel.
90 AM 21 to 90 AM 23	FVE 22A/35	906-23656A to 906-23662A	3	Cargo RHD Anti-Spark Diesel.
90 AM 24 to 90 AM 29	FVE 22A/35	909-23869A to 909-24820A	6	Cargo LHD Anti-Spark Diesel.
94 AM 09 to 94 AM 14	FVE 22A/35	906-24833A to 906-24857	6	Cargo RHD Anti-Spark Diesel.
94 AM 15 to 94 AM 16	FVE 22A/35	909-24828 to 909-24831	2	Cargo LHD Anti-Spark Diesel.
48 AJ 68 to 48 AJ 94	FVE 22A/115	125628 to 135316	27	Cargo RHD Anti-Spark Diesel.
48 AJ 95 to 49 AJ 11	FVE 22A/115	132709 to 134973	17	Cargo LHD Anti-Spark Diesel.
52 AJ 44 to 52 AJ 64	FVE 21B/173	147578 to 148234	21	Cargo RHD Anti-Spark Diesel.
52 AJ 65 to 52 AJ 67	FVE 21B/173	148377 to 148393	3	Cargo LHD Anti-Spark Diesel.
		Total	**194**	

ROYAL NAVY

The following list is incomplete but gives some idea of Royal Navy purchases.

Royal Navy contract numbers sometimes have the format nnn-mm-p, where mm is the two-digit financial year, nnn is the number within that year and p is a suffix (usually 1). An example is 057-73-1, which is the 57th contract of the 1973 Fiscal Year. Note, however, that others were drawn on warrants from "rolling contracts" and the official records show only the warrant, such as R3509, and not the rolling contract number.

Serials	Contract	Chassis Nos	Total	Remarks
03 RN 02 to 03 RN 04	057-73-1	906 series	3	CL RHD Diesel.
36 RN 85 to 37 RN 00	n/a	901 series	6	CL RHD.
15 RN 28 to 15 RN 31	101-74-1	901-11414A to 901-11417A	4	CL RHD Petrol.
21 RN 68 to 21 RN 82	WV8765 R2115	n/a	15	CL RHD.
79 RN 47 to 79 RN 49	WV8765 R2951	901-34383A to n/a	3	CL RHD.
03 RN 16 to 03 RN 19 R3509		143621 to 145557	4	CL RHD Diesel.
96 RN 67	n/a	179171	1	CL RHD Diesel.
97 RN 74 to 97 RN 80	n/a	181638 to 181660	7	CL RHD Petrol.
			Total 43	

TECHNICAL SPECIFICATIONS, SERIES 3 88-INCH CL MODELS

ENGINES:
Petrol:
2286cc (90.47mm x 88.9mm) four-cylinder with pushrod OHV and Solex carburettor. 8:1 compression ratio. 77bhp at 4250rpm and 124 lb ft at 2500rpm.

Diesel:
2286cc (90.47mm x 88.9mm) four-cylinder with overhead valves and indirect injection. 23:1 compression ratio. 62bhp at 4000rpm and 103 lb ft at 1800rpm.

TRANSMISSION:
Selectable four-wheel drive.
Four-speed main gearbox with synchromesh on all forward gears; ratios 3.6:1, 2.22:1, 1.512:1, 1.0:1, reverse 3.0:1. Two-speed transfer gearbox; ratios 1.148:1 (High) and 2.4:1 (Low). Axle ratio: 4.7:1

SUSPENSION, STEERING AND BRAKES:
Semi-elliptic leaf springs all round.
Recirculating-ball steering with 15.6:1 ratio .
Drum brakes all round and separate drum-type transmission parking brake.

UNLADEN WEIGHT:
CL soft top   3210 lb (1456kg)

ELECTRICAL SYSTEM:
12-volt with alternator, or 24-volt with 90-amp alternator.

PERFORMANCE:
0-50mph:	21 secs approximately
Maximum:	65mph (105km/h)
Fuel consumption:	15-18 mpg

DIMENSIONS:
Overall length:	144in (3650mm)
Wheelbase:	88in (2235mm)
Overall width:	64in (1626mm)
Unladen height:	81in (2057mm) maximum
Track:	51.5in (1310mm)

CHAPTER 12:
THE ONE-TONNE FORWARD CONTROL MODELS

There were two main drivers behind the development of the Land Rover 101 1-Tonne in the 1960s. The first was a desire for a logistic vehicle of greater capacity than the ¾ ton Land Rover and less than the Bedford 3-ton (later 4-ton) truck, and the second was a realisation that the ¾-ton Land Rover was too small as a tractor for the next generation of towed Field Gun (which became the 105mm Light Gun). Another important factor was that the vehicle should be airportable because it would equip the brigades of the Strategic Reserve, which still had commitments all over the globe, in the event of unrest in the remnants of the Empire and the Commonwealth.

As Chapter 7 shows, the military authorities had taken an interest in Forward Control designs from 1963, looking at different variants capable of carrying a 30cwt payload. However, neither purpose-built nor standard production models from Land Rover met the requirement satisfactorily. An alternative option, again submitted for consideration by Land Rover, was a normal-control model with a one ton payload and a more powerful engine than was then used in British military models. This incorporated a power take-off system designed by FVRDE that was intended to provide the gun carriage of the new Light Gun with a driven axle and so give greater mobility in rough terrain. At the time, the new Light Gun was not ready, and so tests of this experimental vehicle went ahead with a powered-axle trailer capable of carrying a further ton of cargo.

There were two of these prototype Land Rovers, larger and sturdier than the production models and on a slightly longer wheelbase of 110 inches. They were submitted for evaluation in autumn 1966 and one was displayed at the SMMT-FVRDE exhibition in October that year, when it was described as a "private venture experimental model" and as a "Truck, Cargo (Rover ¾ ton for Power Trailers)". Although one of the prototypes was also shown at Aldershot Army Day in June 1967, the project did not prosper. By that stage, FVRDE had already drawn up an outline and made full-size mock-ups of the forward-control vehicle it wanted, and was in discussions with Rover about its development and production. For more details of the 110-inch prototypes, see Chapter 13.

Contract WV7791 for five engineering prototypes was issued on 16 January 1968, and the vehicles were delivered to FVRDE for trials over the next 11 months. Their chassis numbers (101/FC/2 to 101/FC/6) reflected their prototype

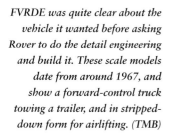

FVRDE was quite clear about the vehicle it wanted before asking Rover to do the detail engineering and build it. These scale models date from around 1967, and show a forward-control truck towing a trailer, and in stripped-down form for airlifting. (TMB)

Even the ambulance variant had already been "designed". Here is the scale model. (TMB)

This full-size wooden model was used to test the proposed dimensions for load space. (TMB)

status and the fact that their wheelbase was 101 inches. All were powered by the same 110bhp six-cylinder 3-litre petrol engine that had been used in the earlier 110-inch Gun Tractor prototypes, and all had the same selectable four-wheel drive system used on production Land Rovers of the time.

A General Specification of Requirement document, GSR3463, followed in June 1968. This recognised that there were 16 types of vehicle from around the world that might meet the requirement for which the new 101-inch Land Rover had been designed. In practice, the only manufacturer prepared to put up a rival to the new Land Rover when comparative trials began in 1971 was Volvo, who submitted versions of their C303.

Meanwhile, Rover had begun production of a new and more powerful engine, a 3.5-litre light-alloy V8 bought in from the Buick division of General Motors in the USA. Initial production was all for Rover saloons, but as production built up it became clear that there would be enough for the 101 as well. In addition, work at Rover on the forthcoming Range Rover (which would be announced in 1970) had led to a new design of gearbox that was drawn up to be shared with the 101. Not only stronger than earlier types, this was arranged with an integral transfer gearbox to give permanent four-wheel drive and used a centre differential to avoid axle wind-up.

Two six-cylinder 101 prototypes retained at Rover were given the new V8 engine and drivetrain in late 1968 and early 1969, and then three more V8 prototypes were built in late 1970 and early 1971. There were further evolutions of the basic design in this period, and trials of the contenders for GSR3463 began in spring 1971. Two V8-engined 101s were pitched head to head with two Volvos, and on 3 December 1971 Rover was awarded a contract for 25 pre-production vehicles, 15 of them with 12-volt electrical systems and 10

with 24-volt systems. The vehicles were built between summer 1972 and early 1973, and were delivered to FVRDE for further trials.

Full production began in February 1975 and the original contract was amended to include a large quantity of production vehicles. By this time, the Army had begun to use metric payload ratings, and the new forward-control Land Rover, developed with a one-ton rating, was reclassified as a 1-Tonne type. Examples were now scheduled for delivery to all three services, and the RAF vehicles would carry their own distinctive serial numbers but the Royal Marines 101s would be numbered in the Army series. Probably only one 101 ever carried an RN number, and that was almost certainly a trials prototype on temporary loan to the Royal Navy.

In the meantime, four specially-built production-standard vehicles assembled in late 1974 went on an expedition across

The first engineering prototypes were much more brutal in appearance than the production models, and had the Rover six-cylinder engine. This was the first one delivered to FVRDE, in fact prototype number 2.(TMB)

The One-Tonne was intended as an artillery tractor. One of the prototypes is seen here with an ammunition limber trailer and the new 105mm gun. Hitching all three together would have made for a long and unwieldy vehicle train. (Land Rover)

One of the late prototypes, by now with the V8 engine, shows how the vehicle was designed to be stripped for air lifting operations. There are some differences between this vehicle and the eventual production type. (TMB)

A gun crew de-busses from a One-Tonne to get its weapon ready for action. This is 60 FL 32 – one of the pre-production examples – in use by the Royal School of Artillery at Artillery Day in July 1973. (GF)

the Sahara Desert, led by RAF Squadron Leader Tom Sheppard. Some of the pre-production vehicles had been delivered for trials with powered-axle trailers, but the trials had not gone smoothly: in some circumstances, the powered trailer could push the 101 tractor vehicle over, and FVRDE was having doubts about the system. The Sahara expedition, which took two prototype one-ton trailers with it, helped confirm the decision not to go ahead with the powered-axle system. The 105mm Light Gun was built without it.

Although 12-volt GS and 24-volt FFR trucks were always the most numerous versions of the 1-Tonne, there were several other types as well. The most striking were the ambulance and box-body versions, the latter often known as Signals-body types. Some were built on freshly-supplied chassis, and others were converted from existing soft top GS or FFR types. A total of 2342 101 1-Tonne Land Rovers was delivered to the MoD, in addition to the original prototypes. Deliveries were completed in 1978, although many vehicles remained in store until required in the early 1980s.

The 12-volt GS types

As the 101s were delivered, 26 Regular Infantry Battalions based in the UK were each equipped with 7 RHD GS vehicles and one GS with winch vehicle. The 20 Territorial Army Infantry Battalions with NATO roles received 10 RHD GS vehicles. The 1-Tonne was used to equip Support Company in these battalions, carrying the MILAN Anti-Tank Guided Weapon and the 81mm Mortar. The three Royal Artillery Light Regiments in the UK (supporting 6 Field Force, 7 Field Force and the Commando Brigade) received 18 RHD GS with winch as 105mm Light Gun Tractors and 18 GS vehicles Limber vehicles with notionally a Tractor and Limber for each of three batteries of six guns.

In BAOR, 13 Infantry Battalions were each equipped with 4 LHD GS vehicles in early 1978 and two battalions were equipped as the UK wheeled battalions – 12 LHD GS vehicles went to the Nuclear Convoy Escort Battalion (1 Battalion The Royal Scots) and eight to the 5 Field Force wheeled Infantry Battalion in BAOR. There were 18 LHD GS with winch Tractors and 18 LHD GS Limbers issued to 5 Field Force Light Gun Field Regiment (7 Regiment, The Royal Horse Artillery).

It was not uncommon to see a One-Tonne gun tractor without its tilt, particularly when used in a display. This one is from 29 Commando Regiment, Royal Artillery and was pictured in July 1984. (GF)

The gun crew gets to work once the One-Tonne Land Rover has towed the weapon into position. (FMW)

The 24-volt FFR types

The FFR versions of the 101 1-Tonne had their own chassis number sequences, as explained below. Their 24-volt electrical systems were intended to power radios and related equipment, and they were built both with and without winch.

The FFR vehicles without winch were used in two rôles. One was as Royal Artillery Command Posts to equip field regiments, providing two per battery to house the Field Artillery Computer Equipment (FACE). The other was as a Royal Armoured Corps Quartermaster's vehicle at both regimental and squadron level in Armoured and Recce Regiments. Only one UK Artillery Regiment was ever fully equipped – 47 Regiment at Lille Barracks, Colchester – and received six. Three RAC regiments received five – 3 RTR (glossary) at Bhurtpore Barracks, Tidworth, the Life Guards at Combermere Barracks, Windsor and 9/12 Lancers at Assaye Barracks, Tidworth. A further 33 RHD FFR vehicles

This pre-production One-Tonne GS with Winch was pictured with some of its contemporaries at a Larkhill Artillery Day in July 1974. (GF)

This black-on-IRR Green camouflage was fairly typical of the One-Tonnes retained in the UK as part of the Strategic Reserve. 73 FL 76 is "B" Sub of one of the batteries of from 29 Commando Regiment, Royal Artillery. (FMW)

58 AM 38 was numerically the first RAF One-Tonne, and was a RHD 24-volt FFR model for the RAF Regiment. (GF)

were converted to Signals body by Marshalls of Cambridge, but many of the rest remained in storage until the 1980s.

The winch-equipped FFR vehicles were primarily intended to equip regiments training and equipping with the Rapier surface-to-air missile in 1977, and each regiment received 36 vehicles. The LHD vehicles equipped 12 LAD Regiment (based at Napier Barracks, Dortmund) and 22 LAD Regiment, each of which took around 36. After completion of training in the UK, 22 LAD Regiment moved with its LHD vehicles to Dortmund. The RHD examples equipped the UK Rapier Regiment – initially 16 LAD Regiment – based at Rapier Barracks, Kirton in Lindsey. In addition, each RAF Regiment Low Level Air Defence (LLAD) Squadron was equipped in the same way as a Royal Artillery Battery.

Some FFR vehicles were converted to carry the Automatic Test Equipment (ATE) for the Rapiers. There were 26 of these, seven being issued to Engineering Flights of RAF Rapier units while each Rapier Regiment REME Light Aid Detachment (LAD) had six units. The REME vehicles were issued two to each Forward Repair Team (FRT) attached to each battery.

SPECIAL VARIANTS

From the beginning, FVRDE had envisaged a number of rôles for the new forward-control Land Rover, and many of these had been illustrated by scale models long before the detail design of the vehicle began. Other variants were created as the need arose in service.

Ambulance

A front-line ambulance was included in the initial plans for the 1-Tonne model. After the initial contracts for GS and FFR trucks had been placed, contract WV12074 in March 1976

Pictured when new by Marshall's, who built the body, this ambulance shows the panels on roof and sides that could be folded over the red cross markings to improve concealment. (MCE)

The twin rear doors of the ambulance are in evidence here, and the side panel has been folded down to conceal the cross marking. Note how this vehicle has been fitted with additional red rear fog guard lamps. (GF)

The ambulance body was configured to take four stretchers, or two stretchers plus seated casualties. This one was pictured during some thermal insulation tests under lights at FVRDE. (TMB)

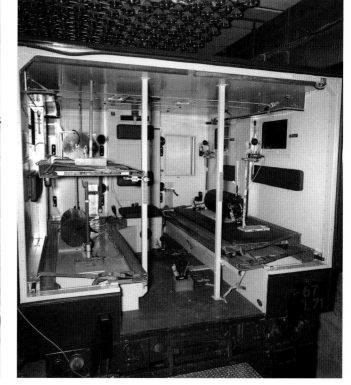

called for well over 500 chassis-cab versions of the 101. (The exact quantity is the subject of some dispute, and the contract was amended several times.) Nevertheless, no contract was placed for the ambulance bodies until December 1979, when Marshall's of Cambridge were asked for a purpose-designed ambulance body to go onto these chassis. In the mean time, the chassis-cabs intended to receive ambulance bodies were allocated chassis-cab serials (such as 77 CC 43) and placed in storage.

Amendments to the original ambulance contract saw many of the planned RAF orders either cancelled or turned over to the Army before deliveries were made. Bizarrely, although the ambulance bodies for 69 chassis were cancelled, 17 LHD GS vehicles were taken from storage in May 1980, stripped down to chassis-cab condition at 93 Vehicle Depot Workshop, REME, and given ambulance bodies.

The ambulance variants of the 101 began to enter service in 1981, and eventually totalled 450 vehicles (plus two prototypes). There were examples with both RHD and LHD. Approximately 22 entered service bearing RAF serials, although the RAF also took a number after 1982 that carried tri-service serials.

Armoured variants

FVRDE sketches from the mid-1970s show a proposed armoured logistics vehicle. The basic idea was turned into a full-size wooden mock-up, but the idea went no further. Possibly related was a project to create an armoured vehicle for use in riot situations such as were being encountered in Northern Ireland. A vehicle was converted, probably at 34 Central Workshops at Donnington, but no quantity production followed.

Challenger

Three 101s were converted by 10 Airborne Workshops REME by the addition of a small 1-Tonne crane. Their purpose was apparently as logistics vehicles, but the loads from the crane caused chassis cracking. These vehicles were locally named Challenger types.

Electronic Repair Workshop

10 Airborne Workshops created a single Electronic Repair Workshop by mounting a tall box body with Luton head to a 101 GS. This was probably used only for a short time before being replaced by a Signals-bodied vehicle.

FACE vehicle

Several 101s were used to carry FACE – Field Artillery Computer Equipment. This artillery survey and fire control system was deployed alongside a gun battery. Typically, a gun battery that used 101 tractors would have its FACE in a 101 too; the vehicle appeared from the outside to be a standard GS type.

69 FL 31 was one of the unit-converted Challenger vehicles. This picture shows the metal cab, the crane arm with work light on the jib, and the stabiliser under the body side. The vehicle was modified in this way for use with 10 Field Workshop who used it from 1983 until 1998, when it was given to the REME Museum. (FMW)

FRT recovery vehicle

10 Airborne Workshops built four recovery vehicles in the late 1980s for the Brigade's Forward Repair Team (FRT). These had a Dixon Bate Tuckaway vehicle recovery crane, which folded out over the rear cross-member and could be swung back into the vehicle for stowage. The first two cracked their chassis under the additional strains, and the second pair were built as replacements for them.

This was the REME FRT vehicle, with a Dixon-Bate Tuckaway recovery crane mounted at the rear. (GF)

Rapier missiles stowed aboard an RAF One-Tonne. The Rapier vehicles lost their rear grab-handles, because these interfered with stowage of the missiles in the back body. (101 FCC&R)

Rapier tractors

The 101 was designated as a tractor for the Rapier surface-to-air missile system very early on. The first Rapier tractors were delivered to the British Army in January 1975, and deliveries continued at a fairly constant rate until mid-1977. The vehicles were based on standard production 101s and in the beginning were converted by the British Aircraft Corporation (BAC) at Stevenage before onward

81 AM 36 was an RAF Rapier tractor, and was pictured here to show the equipment it carried. The large boxes house the Rapier missiles. (101 FCC&R)

delivery to their end-users. Some later vehicles – notably those used by RAF 6 Wing (see below) – were converted by 18 Command Workshops at Bovington.

The RAF Regiment also had Rapiers and each RAF Regi-

Many One-Tonnes became Rapier missile tractors. This example, 74 FL 84, was seen during evaluation at FVRDE. The small wheels on the trailer unit belong to the portable generator carried at the back. (TMB)

The so-called Signals-bodied One-Tonnes were mainly used for signals work but a small number were used for other purposes. Note the ladder at the rear and the special roof stowage box. (TMB)

71 FL 01 was an Intercept Complex vehicle, based on a Signals-body 24-volt One-Tonne. It served with 14 Signal Regiment, and was pictured here in preservation. (GF)

ment squadron had six Rapier units, normally divided into three flights ("A", "B" and "C"). In all six squadrons (63, 37, 26, 16, 27 and 48 in that order) were equipped with eight vehicles. Each squadron received a further eight vehicles in 1978. Three further squadrons (66, 19, 20) were funded by the United States Air Force (USAF) to provided air defence for their airfields in the UK. 66 and 19 Squadrons had three flights, although 20 only had two. These units equipped in 1984.

Signals body

A box-body version of the 101 had been in the plan since very early in the 101 project. After a first design by Cammell Laird was rejected, the MoD turned to Marshall's of Cambridge for the volume contract. Around 100 vehicles were built (the total is in dispute).

Though generally known as the Signals body or Radio body, the Marshall's box-body was not intended exclusively for Signals use. In fact a dozen examples were on the 12-volt

The Intercept Complex vehicles used a standard Signals body but the spare wheel was mounted in front of the grille to increase internal space. 72 FL 70 is seen here with its trailer, specially rigged to carry a large mast aerial. Note the distinctive panel of electrical connections behind the ladder. (TMB)

The Vampire was a special signals-intercept variant of the One-Tonne. Note the aerial mast carried diagonally across the roof, and the long arm of the Sperry GPS system projecting ahead of the cab. (TMB)

The rear of the Vampire body was quite different from the Signals type; note the ladder on the left and the large cable reel in the centre. The end of the mast aerial can be seen on the roof. This vehicle tows a special trailer associated with the rôle. (JT)

chassis, made up of all seven RAF vehicles and five belonging to the army. Although some of the 24-volt 101s did become communications vehicles, many appear to have been used by REME units as radio and electronics repair vehicles. Around 25 were used as Intercept Complex vehicles with the Vampire electronic warfare units (see below). A few saw service as command posts.

Vampire

The Vampire was a special hard-body version of the 101 used for electronic warfare purposes. About 18 are thought to have been built. They had a completely different design of body from the Signals vehicles, and each vehicle towed a specially equipped Sankey trailer that contained aerials and other equipment. Their rôle was to intercept enemy communications and to pass the material back to an Intercept Complex behind the front line for processing.

Winterised and waterproofed

A Winterisation Kit, also known as a Cold Weather Kit, was developed early on and was fitted to those 101s used in cold climates. A semi-permanent Waterproofing installation was also developed at ATTURM (Amphibious Trials and Training Unit, Royal Marines) at Instow in Devon, and this became available for issue to units in May 1980. The waterproofing kit was regularly found on vehicles allocated to Royal Marines units, and 29 Commando Regiment RA was one unit which employed waterproofed 101s as gun tractors. The vehicles were used for deep-water wading during amphibious landings, and were also carried under Sea King helicopters for air-mobile operations.

The One-Tonne was designed with air transportation and air-dropping in mind. This example was pictured after a safe landing aboard a Medium Stressed Platform (MSP), with the parachute still billowing in the background. The Light Gun can just be seen underneath the vehicle. (FMW)

When no air-drop was in the plan, multiple vehicles might be carried like this inside a transport aircraft. (Copyright unknown)

A One-Tonne is seen here in service as a gun tractor with 19 Field Regiment, Royal Artillery. 37 AJ 04 was originally 67 FL 48 but was transferred for service with the RAF Regiment. After vehicles were issued on a tri-service basis it was used by the Royal Artillery. (FMW)

ARMY SERIAL NUMBERS

The serial numbers allocated by the Army gave a clue to the date of the vehicle, although those issued by the RAF and Royal Navy did not. In this period, serial letters indicated the financial year in which the vehicle was purchased (which is not necessarily the same as the calendar year in which it was delivered). Those relevant to the 1-Tonne models are shown below.

As before, serial sequences began at 0001 (e.g. 00 FL 01) and ran to 9999 (eg 99 FL 99). There was not necessarily any correlation between chassis number order and military serial number within batches.

FL	1971-1972	SP	No date association; the SP series was for Special Projects vehicles used for research and development and was allocated from mid-1967 until around 2002. (See Chapter 13)
GJ	1975-1976		
KB	1983 (tri-service unified series)		
KJ	1989 (tri-service unified series)		
		XB	Berlin Brigade – not date related
		XH	Berlin Brigade – not date related

An all-over white scheme was applied to this FFR vehicle and its Sankey trailer before deployment overseas on a United Nations mission. The unit is 7 Regiment, Royal Horse Artillery and the location is Air Mounting Centre at South Cerney. (GF)

In this case, the gun displayed behind an Army One-Tonne is a 105mm Light Gun. This is the Land Rover stand at British Army Equipment Exhibition in June 1976. (GF)

LAND ROVER CHASSIS CODES

All Land Rovers in this period had a three-digit identifying prefix in the chassis code, which indicated the model type, steering position and other factors. Neither the model-year nor the calendar-year of manufacture was indicated. The ones relevant to the Rover 1-Tonne models are shown below. The three-figure prefix was followed by a five-figure serial number that began at 00001 for each separate sequence, and this in turn was followed by a suffix letter. In the case of the 1-Tonne, the suffix letter was always A.

Note that the Land Rover model-year began in September and continued until the end of the following July, leaving August clear for the works' annual holiday and for preparing the assembly lines to take new models. A Land Rover built in the 1976 model-year could therefore have been built at any time between September 1975 and July 1976.

956	RHD 12-volt	959	LHD 12-volt
961	RHD 24-volt	964	LHD 24-volt

ASSET CODES

1043-9100	Ambulance, Crash Rescue, 2/4 stretcher, 4x4, LHD, Rover FV19010
1053-2750	Ambulance, 4 stretcher, 4x4, Tropical, Rover
1053-6750	Ambulance, 4 stretcher, 4x4, Tropical, LHD, Rover
1054-0750	Ambulance, 4 stretcher, 4x4, Rover FV19009
1054-5750	Ambulance, 4 stretcher, 4x4, LHD, Rover FV19010
1825-0750	Truck, General Service, w/winch, 1 Tonne, 4x4, Rover
1825-5750	Truck, General Service, w/winch, 1 Tonne, 4x4, LHD, Rover
1826-0750	Truck, General Service, 12v, w/winch, Radar Tracking, Rapier, 1 Tonne, 4x4, Rover
1826-5750	Truck, General Service, 12v, w/winch, Radar Tracking, Rapier, 1 Tonne, 4x4, LHD, Rover
1830-0750	Truck, General Service, FFR, w/winch, 1 Tonne, 4x4, Rover
1830-5750	Truck, General Service, FFR, w/winch, 1 Tonne, 4x4, LHD, Rover
1831-0750	Truck, General Service, 24v, Signals, w/winch, 1 Tonne, 4x4, Land Rover
1832-0750	Truck, General Service, FFR, w/winch, 1 Tonne, 4x4, Rover
1832-5750	Truck, General Service, FFR, w/winch, 1 Tonne, 4x4, LHD, Rover
1833-0750	Truck, GS, 24v, w/winch, Launcher Towing, Rapier, 1 Tonne, 4x4, Land Rover
1833-5750	Truck, GS, 24v, w/winch, Launcher Towing, Rapier, 1 Tonne, 4x4, LHD, Land Rover
1834-0750	Truck, General Service, 24v, Signals, 1 Tonne, 4x4, Land Rover
1834-5750	Truck, General Service, 24v, Signals, 1 Tonne, 4x4, LHD, Land Rover
1835-0750	Truck, General Service, 24v, Signals (Winterised), 1 Tonne, 4x4, Rover
1836-0750	Truck, General Service, 12v, Signals, 1 Tonne, 4x4, Rover
1840-0750	Truck, General Service, 1 Tonne, 4x4, Rover
1840-1750	Truck, General Service, 1 Tonne, 4x4, with trailer drive, Rover
1840-5750	Truck, General Service, 1 Tonne, 4x4, LHD, Rover
1841-0750	Truck, General Service, 1 Tonne, 4x4, Rover (Winterised)
1850-0750	Truck, General Service, FFR, 1 Tonne, 4x4, Rover
1850-5750	Truck, General Service, FFR, 1 Tonne, 4x4, LHD, Rover
1851-0750	Truck, General Service, 24v, FACE, 1 Tonne, 4x4, Rover
1852-4100	Intercept Complex, Electronic Warfare, Truck Mounted, 1 Tonne, Rover
3646-0750	Automatic Test Equipment, FRTV, Truck Mounted, Field Standard 1B, Rapier, 1 Tonne, 4x4, Rover
3646-1750	Automatic Test Equipment, FRTV, Truck Mounted, Field Standard 1A, Rapier, 1 Tonne, 4x4, Rover
3646-5750	Automatic Test Equipment, FRTV, Truck Mounted, Field Standard 1B, Rapier, 1 Tonne, 4x4, LHD, Rover
3664-9300	Mobile VHF Direction System (Vampire), Truck-mounted, UK/VLD 581 Tech Services, 4x4, 1 ton, w/winch, LHD, Rover)

SUMMARY OF ONE-TONNE MODEL DELIVERIES, 1974-1978

ARMY

Serials	Contract	Chassis Nos	Total	Remarks
01 SP 13 to 01 SP 17	WV7791	101/FC/2 to 101/FC/6	5	Engineering prototypes. Contract dated 16 January 1968.
03 SP 67		956-00001A	1	Later 54 BT 06.
03 SP 68		956-00004A	1	
03 SP 69		964-00004A	1	Later 54 BT 07.
03 SP 70		956-00005A	1	Later 77 FL 29.
03 SP 71		964-00005A	1	Later 54 BT 08.
03 SP 72		959-00002A	1	Probably later 54 BT 11.
03 SP 78		961-00001A	1	This chassis number is also recorded as 04 SP 07.
04 SP 08		964-00007A	1	FFR; Powered Axle Trials.
05 SP 10 and 05 SP 11		961-00010A and 961-00019A	2	Powered Axle Trailer.
see details below	WV9615	see details below	1748	Contract dated 3 December 1971. Cargo, Cargo with winch, FFR and FFR with winch types.
60 FL 32 to 60 FL 38	WV9615	956-00007A to 956-00021A	7	Pre-Production GS RHD.
60 FL 39 to 67 FL 49	WV9615	956-00605A to 956-00951A	718	Cargo GS RHD.
67 FL 50 and 67 FL 51	WV9615	959-00410A and 959-00344A	2	FFR w/Winch LHD.
67 FL 52	WV9615	959-00010A	1	GS w/Winch LHD.
67 FL 53 to 68 FL 38	WV9615	959-00003A to 959-00180A	84	Cargo GS LHD.
68 FL 40 to 68 FL 46	WV9615	961-00006A to 961-00012A	6	Pre-Production FFR RHD; 961-00010A (68 FL 44) was converted to LHD and became 05 SP 10.
68 FL 44	WV9615	964-00006A	1	FFR LHD; see details above.
68 FL 47 to 69 FL 39	WV9615	961-00024A to 961-00158A	93	FFR RHD; many were converted to Signals Body (see details below).
69 FL 40 to 69 FL 82	WV9615	956-00952A to 956-00839A	43	Cargo GS RHD (originally to have been FFR).
69 FL 83 to 70 FL 72	WV9615	959-00248A to 959-00385A	90	Cargo GS LHD.
70 FL 83 to 70 FL 85	WV9615	956-00008A to 956-00015A	3	Pre-Production GS w/Winch RHD.
71 FL 40 to 71 FL 67	WV9615	959-00181A to 959-00388A	28	GS w/Winch LHD.
71 FL 68 to 72 FL 78	WV9615	964-00009A to 964-00156A	111	FFR LHD; many were converted to Signals Body (see details below).
72 FL 79 to 74 FL 10	WV9615	956-00017A to 956-00969A	132	GS w/Winch RHD.
74 FL 11 and 74 FL 12	WV9615	961-00004A and 961-00005A	2	Pre-Production FFR w/Winch RHD.
74 FL 13 to 74 FL 73	WV9615	956-00970A to 956-00872A	61	GS w/Winch RHD.
74 FL 81 to 75 FL 30	WV9615	961-00020A to 961-00169A	50	FFR w/Winch RHD.
75 FL 31 to 75 FL 38	WV9615	959-00389A to 959-00396A	8	GS w/Winch LHD.
75 FL 39 to 76 FL 50	WV9615	964-00042A to 964-00363A	112	FFR w/Winch LHD.
76 FL 51 to 76 FL 63	WV9615	959-00397A to 959-00409A	13	GS w/Winch LHD.
76 FL 64 to 76 FL 66	WV9615	956-00022A to 956-00024A	3	GS Powered Axle.
76 FL 67 to 77 FL 06	WV9615	959-00011A to 959-00174A	40	GS w/Winch LHD.
71 GJ 51 to 72 GJ 99 and 73 GJ 01 to 73 GJ 34	WV12074	956-01004A to 956-01192A	183	Contract dated 26 March 1976. Chassis-cabs for Ambulance RHD. 73 GJ 00 was cancelled.
73 GJ 35 to 73 GJ 52	WV12074	956-01196A to 956-01074A	18	Chassis-cabs for Ambulance Tropical RHD.
73 GJ 53 and 73 GJ 54	WV12074	-	-	see 31 KB 97 and 31 KB 98 below.
73 GJ 55 to 73 GJ 57	WV12074	956-01205A to 956-01055A	3	Chassis-cabs for Ambulance RHD.
73 GJ 65 to 75 GJ 14	WV12074	959-00414A to 959-00439A	150	Chassis-cabs for Ambulance LHD.
75 GJ 17 to 75 GJ 34	WV12074	964-00448A to 964-00465A	18	FFR LHD.

ARMY (continued)

Serials	Contract	Chassis Nos	Total	Remarks
75 GJ 50 to 76 GJ 02	WV12074	956-01251A to 959-01293A	53	Chassis-cabs for Ambulance RHD. (Originally for RAF).
	FVE21A/27		-	Contract placed in early 1977 with Marshall's for Signals bodies.
	FVE21A/156		450	Contract placed in December 1979 with Marshall's for ambulance bodies. Of 519 planned, 450 were built; contract amended to include 69 "pattern" GS bodies for remaining chassis.
31 KB 97 to 31 KB 98	WV12074	959-00491A to 959-00430A	2	Chassis-cabs for Ambulance Tropical LHD; originally to have been 73 GJ 53 and 73 GJ 54.
42 KB 59 to 42 KB 68	FVE 22A/209	959-00116A to 959-00128A	10	Cargo GS RHD; diverted from BAE contract for Abu Dhabi.
18 KJ 35	No contract recorded	956-01229A	1	Cargo GS RHD; built from chassis-cab.
18 KJ 43	No contract recorded	956-01001A	1	Cargo GS RHD; built from chassis-cab.
34 KJ 79 and 34 KJ 80	No contract recorded	956-01277A and 956-01061A	2	Cargo GS RHD; built from chassis-cab.
34 KJ 95	No contract recorded	956-01212A	1	Cargo GS RHD; built from chassis-cab.
48 KJ 49 and 48 KJ 50	No contract recorded	956-01046A and 956-01237A	2	Cargo GS RHD; built from chassis-cab.
55 KJ 69 and 55 KJ 70	No contract recorded	956-01035A and 956-01269A	2	Cargo GS w/Winch RHD; built from chassis-cab.

RAF

Serials	Contract	Chassis Nos	Total	Remarks
58 AM 38 to 58 AM 46	WV9615	961-00112A to 961-00116A	9	FFR w/Winch RHD.
58 AM 47 and 58 AM 48	WV9615	956-00815A and 956-00816A	2	Cargo GS w/Winch RHD.
58 AM 49 to 58 AM 54	WV9615	959-00345A to 959-00350A	6	Cargo GS w/Winch LHD.
81 AM 31 to 81 AM 33	WV9615	959-00351A to 959-00353A	3	Cargo GS w/Winch LHD.
81 AM 35 to 81 AM 43	WV9615	956-00840A to 956-00848A	9	Cargo GS w/Winch RHD.
81 AM 44 to 81 AM 76	WV9615	959-00320A to 959-00298A	33	Cargo GS w/Winch LHD.
81 AM 77 to 81 AM 80	WV9615	959-00159A to 959-00162A	4	FFR RHD.
81 AM 81 and 81 AM 82	WV12074	956-01264A and 956-01007A	2	Chassis-cabs for Ambulance RHD; both to Army without RAF issue.
82 AM 37 to 82 AM 41	WV12074	959-00412A to 959-00534A	5	Chassis-cabs for Ambulance LHD.
83 AM 76 to 83 AM 80.	FVE 22A/5	964-00443A to 964-00447A	5	Signals LHD.
00 AM 72 to 01 AM 06	FVE 21A/230	956-01210A to 956-01087A	35	Rapier Launcher Tractor 24v w/Winch RHD.
01 AM 07 to 01 AM 41	FVE 21A/230	956-01125A to 956-01076A	35	Rapier Radar Tractor 12v w/Winch RHD.

ROYAL NAVY

Serials	Contract	Chassis Nos	Total	Remarks
73 RN 00	n/a	n/a	1	It is not known if this vehicle was ex-Army or purchased for the RN.

TECHNICAL SPECIFICATIONS, 101 1-TONNE PRODUCTION MODELS

ENGINE:
3528cc (88.9mm x 71.1mm) V8 petrol, with pushrod OHV and two Zenith 175 CD 2S carburettors. 8.5:1 compression ratio. 128bhp at 5000rpm and 185 lb ft at 2500rpm.

TRANSMISSION:
Permanent four-wheel drive with vacuum-lockable centre differential. Four-speed type main gearbox; ratios 4.069:1, 2.448:1, 1.505:1, 1.000:1, reverse 3.665:1. Synchromesh on all four forward gears. Integral two-speed transfer gearbox; ratios 1.174:1 (High) and 3.321:1 (Low)
Axle ratio: 5.571:1

SUSPENSION, STEERING AND BRAKES:
Semi-elliptic taper-leaf springs all round. Front anti-roll bar. Recirculating-ball steering with 23.3:1 ratio.
Drum brakes on all four wheels, with vacuum servo and pressure-apportioning valve in the rear hydraulic line; 11 x 3in at the front, 11 x 2.25in at the rear; separate drum-type transmission parking brake.

ELECTRICAL SYSTEM:
12-volt with 34-amp alternator and negative earth; FFR models with 24-volt negative-earth system and 90-amp generator.

UNLADEN WEIGHT:
(These weights are for vehicles with coolant, oil, and 24 gallons of fuel)
4242 lb (1924kg) for 12-volt GS soft top models
3500 lb (1580kg) when fully stripped for airporting operations
4259 lb (1940kg) for 24-volt GS soft top models

DIMENSIONS:
Overall length:	170.5in (4330mm) fully equipped 166in (4217mm), stripped
Wheelbase:	101in (2565mm)
Overall width:	72.5in (1842mm)
Unladen height:	90in (2283mm) over canvas tilt 84in (2138mm) to top of windscreen
Front track:	60in (1524mm)
Rear track:	61in (1549mm)

PERFORMANCE:
0-50mph:	21 secs approximately
Maximum:	65mph (105km/h)
Fuel consumption:	15-18 mpg

The canvas tilt sometimes concealed a hard body of one sort or another. 69 FL 29 is a Quartermaster Sergeant's Stores Vehicle, and 69 FL 22 contains FACE equipment. (GF/FCC&R)

CHAPTER 13:

BEYOND THE MAINSTREAM

We made the decision in writing the book to try to avoid cluttering the main tables in with details of small volumes of vehicles associated with inter-service transfers, other non-contract acquisitions and prototypes. In practice, we have included some details in the tables and text where it seemed to make sense to do so. This chapter attempts to document these vehicles so that the book is complete in its coverage of vehicles wearing service registrations – as far as is possible.

Captured vehicles: CV serials

Captured vehicles in conflicts after the Falklands were given "CV" serials. No Land Rovers were captured in the Falklands from the Argentineans since they used the Mercedes Geländewagen. However, one Land Rover is known to have been captured in Iraq during the first Gulf War in 1991.

Chassis-cabs: CC serials

From around 1975, when chassis-cabs were purchased from manufacturers in advance of the body being fitted, these chassis-cabs were held in Vehicle Depots. They were given serials commencing at 40 CC 01 to aid stock control. The most numerous Land Rovers wearing such serials were Land Rover 101s waiting to become Ambulances and Range Rovers waiting to become TACR-2s. This practice was followed until the system changed around 1993; from that date, contracts were placed with the body manufacturer, who was then required to obtain the appropriate chassis as part of the tendering process.

Former attaché vehicles: BT serials

Naval Attachés, Military Attachés and Air Attachés at overseas embassies were provided with vehicles by their parent service, and in the beginning those vehicles wore the registration mark of the relevant service. From the formation of the Services Attaché and Adviser Service (SAAS) in July 1972 until tri-service standardisation in late 1981, all vehicles were provided by the Army. All attaché vehicles existing in July 1972 were transferred to the Army and given BT serials.

Former MoS vehicles: EP serials

After the Ministry of Defence was formed, it absorbed the remaining Ministry of Supply defence establishments in 1966 and so a number of vehicles that had previously worn Central

London Local Vehicle Licensing Office (LVLO) registrations were given new serials. Armour was given serials in late ED, plant in late EW and soft-skin vehicles commenced at 50 EP 00. Included in these transfers were a large number of civilian Land Rovers as well as one or two more unusual types.

Military sales vehicles: MS serials

Vehicles intended for sale overseas were given military sales registrations commencing at 00 MS 01. The MS serials were mainly given to armoured vehicles, although certain Land Rovers which were to be driven by Army personnel or shown at UK Military Trade Shows also received them. The only example it is possible to quote is 56 MS 07, which was a Hotspur 6x6 Command Vehicle.

MPBW vehicles: MW, PB and AZ serials

The Ministry of Public Buildings and Works (MPBW) used serials commencing at 00 PB 01 and 00 MW 01 when supporting barracks overseas. RAF Stations were supported by vehicles wearing AZ and some vehicles are listed below. Only one Land Rover is known in the PB and MW series, although it is possible there were more as no complete records of any of these MPBW series are known to survive. This practice continued until the MPBW became the Property Services Agency as part of The Department of the Environment in 1972, and subsequently until the PSA was turned into a commercial entity in 1992.

00 SP 53 was a long-wheelbase Mk 11 that was used in early trials with the Rapier missile system. It is seen here in preservation. (JT)

38 BT 28 is an ex-Royal Navy 109 which has been fitted with a truck cab. It was previously 97 RN 98 and was transferred for use with the Trials section of the Royal School of Artillery, Larkhill, where it was photographed in July 1984. (GF)

NAAFI vehicles: BZ serials

In 1956, a number of vehicles from the NAAFI (Navy, Army and Air Force Institute) were impressed for the Suez Emergency and were given serials in the BZ series. Two Land Rovers that had previously been with the NAAFI – probably in Cyprus – were given such serials but they were returned to the NAAFI in February 1957.

Prototype vehicles: BT, SP, WA and WB serials

Prototypes were initially allocated serials in BT, but after the spring of 1967 all new prototypes were given "Special Project" (SP) registrations and several vehicles were transferred to the new series. After tri-service standardisation, two new series were introduced (WA and WB), and these were used by the experimental establishments.

Transfers: YA to ZC serials and BT serials

Numerous vehicles were transferred between the services over the years. Such transfers took place as a result of unit closures overseas. So, for example, although an Army unit might close, if the RAF continued to operate in that location then the Army vehicle fleet would be transferred to the RAF. Where the location of the transfer is documented we have included this in the tables. A good example of a transfer is the closure of RN Sydenham in Northern Ireland, when much of the fleet was transferred to the RAF (29 AJ 25 to 29 AJ 38) on 6 November 1973. (In this example, though, no Land Rovers were involved.) Later, some transfers were made at Depots when shortages of vehicles for one service arose and there were adequate stocks for another service. These transfers ceased once tri-service standardisation was introduced at the end of 1981.

The Royal Navy used large numbers of transferred vehi-

03 SP 70 was a 101 One-Tonne that was stripped to its chassis and then built up as a mock-up of the proposed ambulance. The body is quite convincing, but is actually made of wood. (TMB)

This Shorts publicity picture shows two of the Shorland armoured cars on Series IIA chassis after transfer from the RUC to the UDR and re-serialling as 27 BT 50 and 27 BT 51. The transfer took place in 1971. (Shorts)

These two plates were found on a vehicle that was transferred from the Army to the Royal Navy in or about 1955. 04 BC 25 was a vehicle from the first large Army batch, and the plate is typical of those used by the Army; it shows the contract, chassis number and War Department number. Note the limited designation on this early vehicle – "Land Rover 4x4". Later designations would grow more complex! The larger brass plate was attached under the bonnet when 04 BC 25 became 38 RN 24. Note how the record of major overhauls was stamped into the plate. (Andrew Stevens)

cles, although a lack of records has meant we can only include a sample.

Early transfers, YA to ZC serials

From 1949, transfers were given registrations at end of the YA to ZC series that had been used to bring mainly wartime vehicles in to the new system. The vehicles from the regiments of the Malay Army were transferred in 1952 when the Malayan Emergency led to the formation of Federation Regiments under British auspices. The Land Rover 80-inch vehicles transferred are documented in Chapter 1. There were other transfers into the YJ series although the origins of these vehicles are not recorded.

The Welfare series seems to have appeared as both "WL" and "WEL". Here 01 WEL 09 is seen at Dhekelia Garrison Fete in May 1984. (GF)

Transfers into BT serials

The Army registered some of its transfers in a special series that used the BT letter pair, and the first examples were allocated around 1957. Initially the series was split according to different theatres (00 BT 01 onwards for FARELF (Far Eastern Land Forces), 10 BT 01 for MELF (Middle East Land Forces), and so on, but this system was eventually abandoned. In addition the BT series was also used for vehicles loaned by military vehicle manufacturers and which needed to carry a military registration for Road Traffic Act purposes.

Welfare vehicles: WL and WEL serials

Welfare organisations that supported British Forces overseas had their own transport that wore "WL" or "WEL" plates to allow them to operate as military vehicles. These organisations included the Church Army, YMCA, Garrison Saddle Clubs and WRVS. At least one in Cyprus was a Land Rover, although there may have been many more!

SPECIAL TRIALS VEHICLES

As noted above, many vehicles trialled by FVRDE were allocated serials in the BT and SP series. Some of these vehicles had special characteristics not described in earlier chapters of this book, and some notes on representative vehicles are included here, in date order for ease of reference.

1962: The Land Rover hovercraft

At the 1962 SMMT-FVRDE exhibition, FVRDE demonstrated a 109-inch Land Rover that had been converted to function as a hovercraft. This was clearly part of the same line of thinking that had already produced the APGP (see Chapter 5). The vehicle carried registration number UXM 154, from one of the blocks allocated to FVRDE, and

The War Department became interested in the possibilities of hover-craft at the start of the 1960s, and at the 1962 SMMT/FVRDE exhibition demonstrated this experimental machine. It was not listed in the exhibition catalogue, however. It always carried one of FVRDE's civilian number-plates. (Above and below – unknown sources)

The auxiliary engine in the back powered the fans for the air cushion, and had been borrowed from a sports car of the time. (Unknown via PW)

according to Commercial Motor magazine had been built by ROF Woolwich. It had a second engine mounted in the load bed to power the fans that created the air cushion on which the vehicle rode; this engine seems to have been a twin-carburettor Triumph sports car unit.

William Suttie notes (in The Tank Story, 2015) that film still exists showing that the Land Rover hovercraft was trialled against a conventional Land Rover and that it demonstrated problems when crossing rolling terrain and in steering on a side slope. At about the same time, the Vickers factory at South Marston was experimenting with its Hovertruck, a Land Rover conversion that was similar in

concept but different in execution. There does not appear to have been any cross-fertilisation between the two projects, and both were abandoned.

1965: The 110-inch gun tractor prototypes

The early story of the 110 gun tractor is in Chapter 12. In April 1970, FVRDE borrowed the two 110-inch prototypes back from the Rover Company and allocated them serials 02 SP 52 (with Wing Number 7360) and 02 SP 53 (with Wing Number 7341).

The two vehicles were fitted with Goodyear Terra-Tires and were put through trials on Hankley Common, near

This 110-inch gun tractor was returned to Rover and regained its civilian registration number. (Land Rover)

The Laird Centaur was an interesting attempt to combine high mobility and high payload with Land Rover elements. The number 06 SP 17 later reappeared on a Centaur with a coil-sprung Land Rover front end. (TMB)

Aldershot, in each case towing a powered-axle trailer that also had these high-flotation tyres. The trailers carried serials 02 SP 00 and 02 SP 01. These trials may have been associated with Malayan interest in a 101 with powered-axle trailer and Terra-Tires, and may have been carried out mainly to assist the Rover Company.

1978: Laird Centaur

Laird (Anglesey) Ltd was formed in 1968 and opened a factory at Fryars in Llanfaes, Anglesey, converting and maintaining Catalina flying boats and launching them on to Fryars Bay. The company later moved into other military

The two 110-inch gun tractors were borrowed back for trials with Terra-Tires. (TMB)

hardware and civilian vehicles. Laird contracts included amphibious and other marine craft, tanks, radar equipment, bridges, trackways, buses, tankers, containers, railway wagons, and refuse collection vehicles.

Laird developed the Centaur – a half-tracked Land Rover – as a "multi-purpose military vehicle system". It had a Land Rover bonnet and cab and then an extended cargo body over a tracked chassis based on CVR (T) components. The rear cargo body was 16 inches wider than the bonnet, so the doors were angled outwards to meet the cargo body sides. Eight prototypes are known; the six early prototypes were based on the leaf-sprung Stage 1 V8 Land Rover and the last two on the coil-sprung One Ten. Both types weighed around 4 tonnes unladen, were capable of carrying a further 3 Tonnes and had a maximum speed of 50 mph.

Development started in 1977 and the engineering model was ready in April 1978. This was in time for the British Army Equipment Exhibition (BAEE) of June 1978, for which it was given serial 48 BT 07.

The prototypes had the 156bhp Range Rover version of the 3.5-litre V8 engine; standard Stage 1 V8 Land Rovers had a 91bhp version. The first three Centaurs had RHD, the next three LHD, and all started life with soft-top bodywork. The manufacturers envisaged several uses for this vehicle, including M40 Recoilless Rifle portee, armoured personnel carrier, ammunition carrier, ambulance, command car, bomb disposal vehicle, 105mm gun Tractor and missile (Swingfire, MILAN or TOW) platform.

There is great confusion over registrations as some Centaurs were given fake serials (19 LA 78, 65 FL 73) and

Hotspur's 139-inh 6x6 chassis was the basis of 28 KB 70, a Hi-Line Command Vehicle. It did not enter British military service, but was given a military serial for a Defence Sales Tour. (Hotspur)

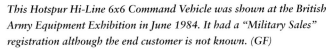

This Hotspur Hi-Line 6x6 Command Vehicle was shown at the British Army Equipment Exhibition in June 1984. It had a "Military Sales" registration although the end customer is not known. (GF)

serials were transferred between prototypes. In addition it is believed the first prototype was fitted with a 110-style front-end in 1983 prior to a Libyan Sales Tour.

The Centaur failed to attract orders and the project was brought to an end in 1985 although it still rated a mention at BAEE in June 1986.

1983: Hotspur & SMC

SMC Engineering of Bristol was one of several companies that developed three-axle conversions of the Land Rover in the late 1970s to give a greater payload of 2000kg with six-wheel drive. The SMC conversion was marketed as a Sandringham 6, and to expand its sales potential into the military world, SMC appears to have licensed production to Hotspur Armoured Products in Neath, south Wales. Hotspur already produced a range of Internal Security products including riot shields, batons and security posts, and its specialised steel was used in the Hotspur armoured Land Rover that was used by the Royal Ulster Constabulary in the late 1970s.

Under the banner of Hotspur Cars Ltd, Hotspur built the Sandringham 6 with either a 125-inch wheelbase (as the S6) or a 139-inch wheelbase (as the S6E). All the known production models were based on the Stage 1 V8 Land Rover, and military versions incorporated Hotspur armour. Only two are known to have worn British Army serials, and neither was intended for service with the UK Army. They were 28 KB 70 and 56 MS 07, and both were S6E Hi-Line 6x6 Command Vehicles. 28 KB 70 was given a serial for an overseas Defence

Sales Tour in December 1982, while 56 MS 07 was obviously intended for an overseas customer as it wore a "Military Sales" serial and was shown at the British Army Equipment Exhibition (BAEE) in 1984. A Hi-Line also turned up at the Cardiff Searchlight Tattoo in 1981, rigged as a Personnel Carrier with firing ports in the rear compartment.

1985: Townley 6x6

In May 1985, a single three-axle conversion of the 109-inch Land Rover was taken into the SP series. 06 SP 61 had started military life as a Stage 1 V8 Land Rover with the Royal Artillery Sales Team in May 1982, but in 1985 was sent to Townley Cross-Country Vehicles (a Land Rover franchised dealership specialising in conversion work) in Bexleyheath, Kent for conversion to a 6x6 vehicle. It was described on the Army vehicle register as "LR109 V8 modified to 6x6 tractor by Townley" and in practice was supposedly used for light recovery duties.

It's not often that you find a 109 trying to tow a hovercraft! During the trials of the SRN6 on Browndown beach, it seems it got trapped on the gorse on the low dunes. 58 EP 36, which had originally born civilian registration 630 ELM, is attempting to pull it out. (TMB)

SUMMARY OF NON-MAINSTREAM VEHICLE DELIVERIES AND TRANSFERS, 1974-1978

ARMY

Serials	Source	Chassis Nos	Total	Remarks
04 BT 02	Ex Trade	n/a	1	Sandringham 6x6; for British Army Equipment Exhibition 1980
04 BT 03	Ex Trade	n/a	1	109 Tactical Command Post; for BAEE 1980
04 BT 05	Ex Trade	n/a	1	109 V8
04 BT 37	Ex Trade	n/a	1	Townley 6x6 V8
04 BT 64	Ex Trade	n/a	1	SMC FC82; for BAEE 1986
04 BT 65	Ex Trade	n/a	1	Sandringham 6x6; for BAEE 1986
04 BT 66	Ex Trade	n/a	1	Shorland S515; for BAEE 1986
10 BT 60	Ex 34 AA 19	1610-3416		
10 BT 61	Ex 34 AA 15	1610-3395		
10 BT 62	Ex 36 AA 25	2610-0749		
10 BT 63	Ex 34 AA 81	1610-3673		
10 BT 64	Ex 34 AA 89	1610-3691		
10 BT 65	Ex 35 AA 22	2610-0521		
10 BT 66	Ex 35 AA 38	2610-0557		
10 BT 67	Ex 35 AA 47	2610-0586		
10 BT 68	Ex 36 AA 25	2610-0749		
10 BT 69	Ex 37 AA 03	2610-0914		
10 BT 70	Ex 37 AA 07	2610-0928		
10 BT 71	Ex 37 AA 13	2610-0934		
10 BT 72	Ex 37 AA 16	2610-0937		
10 BT 73	Ex 37 AA 37	2610-0984		
10 BT 74	Ex 37 AA 43	2610-1004		
10 BT 75	Ex 40 AA 50	2610-1921		
10 BT 76	Ex 40 AA 52	2610-1923		
10 BT 77	Ex 40 AA 65	2610-2070		
10 BT 78	Ex 44 AA 43	3610-2326		
10 BT 79	Ex 45 AA 92	3610-2796		
10 BT 80	Ex 46 AA 09	3610-2843		
10 BT 81	Ex 46 AA 37	3610-2926		
10 BT 82	Ex 46 AA 43	3610-2932		
10 BT 83	Ex 46 AA 58	3610-2984		
10 BT 84	Ex 50 AA 32	4710-1059		
10 BT 85	Ex 50 AA 33	4710-1060		
10 BT 86	Ex 50 AA 39	4710-1066		
10 BT 87	Ex 50 AA 51	4710-1106		
10 BT 88	Ex 50 AA 67	4710-1128		
10 BT 89	Ex 50 AA 70	4710-1131		
10 BT 90	Ex 50 AA 72	4710-1143		
10 BT 91	Ex 50 AA 75	4710-1146		
10 BT 92	Ex 50 AA 76	4710-1147		
10 BT 93	Ex 50 AA 77	4710-1148		
10 BT 94	Ex 50 AA 84	4710-1167		
10 BT 95	Ex 51 AA 00	4710-1207		
10 BT 96	Ex 51 AA 18	4710-1222		
10 BT 97	Ex 35 AA 22	2610-0521		
10 BT 98	Ex 51 AA 24	4710-1226		
10 BT 99	Ex 51 AA 35	4710-1277		
11 BT 00	Ex 63 AA 26	1706-03803		
11 BT 01	Ex 35 AA 38	2610-0557		
11 BT 02	Ex 36 AA 48	2610-0789		

There were prolonged trials of Rapier before it entered service, and it was originally to be towed by the 109. 00 SP 51 was displayed at Farnborough Air Show in 1967. (RES)

04 BT 66 was a Shorland S515 Armoured Patrol Vehicle. It was given an army registration for the 1986 British Army Equipment Exhibition at Aldershot. (GF)

ARMY

Serials	Source	Chassis Nos	Total	Remarks
11 BT 03	Ex 56 AA 50	5710-1502		
11 BT 04	Ex 56 AA 51	5710-1564		
11 BT 05	Ex 56 AA 55	5710-1625		
11 BT 06	Ex 56 AA 75	5710-1921		
11 BT 07	Ex 62 AA 91	1706-02832		
11 BT 08	Ex 62 AA 92	1706-02832		
11 BT 09	Ex 62 AA 93	1706-02777		
11 BT 10	Ex 62 AA 95	1706-02720		
11 BT 11	Ex 62 AA 96	1706-02867		
11 BT 12	Ex 62 AA 97	1706-02865		
11 BT 13	Ex 62 AA 99	1706-02862		
11 BT 14	Ex 63 AA 02	1706-02859		
11 BT 15	Ex 63 AA 07	1706-02650		
11 BT 16	Ex 63 AA 08	1706-02864		
11 BT 17	Ex 63 AA 11	1706-02763		
11 BT 18	Ex 63 AA 13	1706-02861	59	80 and 86 Cargo; transferred from RAF in December 1957. Note that the records show 10 BT 62 and 10 BT 68 with the same chassis number.
12 BT 92	Ex 56 AV 45	n/a	1	80 Cargo
12 BT 95	Ex civilian registration	n/a	1	"Land Rover - Civilian"
13 BT 30 to 13 BT 37	n/a	n/a	1	86 Cargo LHD; origin not known
13 BT 38	Ex 61 AA 21	1706-01083		
13 BT 39	Ex 42 AA 46	3610-0862	1	86 Cargo; transferred to Army Air Corps at Middle Wallop in July 1958
13 BT 59	Ex Allied Land Forces,	36130751		
13 BT 60	Central Europe	36130909		
13 BT 61		36130746		
13 BT 62		36130886		
13 BT 63		36100883		
13 BT 64		36130765		
13 BT 65		36130863		
13 BT 66		36130865		
13 BT 67		36130885		
13 BT 68		36130910		
13 BT 69		36130884	11	86 Cargo; transferred at MoS Hassworth in December 1960
13 BT 72	Ex 38 RN 22	06100244		
13 BT 73	Ex 21 RN 81	26100546		
13 BT 74	Ex 61 RN 81	36103792		
13 BT 75	Ex 42 RN 43	270600614		
13 BT 76	Ex 42 RN 44	270600615		
13 BT 77	Ex 43 RN 10	270600818		
13 BT 78	Ex 43 RN 11	270600819		
13 BT 79	Ex 43 RN 12	270600820	8	86 Cargo; transferred in May 1959 when 42 Commando RM was reduced to a Training Cadre; only first two transfers made, others cancelled.
14 BT 66	Ex OAH 963	3610-2284	1	80 Cargo fitted mobile conveyor; for BAOR trials.
15 BT 11	Ex 47 BR 39	1706-02298		
15 BT 12	Ex 47 BR 22	1706-02256	2	86 Cargo; reason for transfer internally not known; 15 BT 12 cancelled.
15 BT 18	Ex Trade	1510-00213	1	109 Cargo WOMBAT Portee Prototype; later to 00 SP 27
15 BT 24 to 15 BT 84	Ex Kings African Rifles	1420-01647 rest n/a	1	88 Cargo

ARMY

Serials	Source	Chassis Nos	Total	Remarks
15 BT 85 to 16 BT 48	Ex Kings African Rifles	n/a	68	109 Cargo Mk 7
16 BT 71	Ex Trade	1510-20514	1	109 Cargo LHD; Local purchase in Leopoldville, Congo
16 BT 79	Ex KGL752	1420-0572	1	88 Cargo Mk 6; transferred by Kenyan Government to War Department.
16 BT 80	Ex URS 906	1520-03546		
16 BT 81	Ex URT 812	1520-03633	2	109 Cargo Mk 7; transferred by Kenyan Government to War Department.
17 BT 10	Ex URN 897	n/a	1	88 Cargo Mk 6; transferred by Kenyan Government to War Department.
17 BT 11 to 17 BT 30	Ex New Zealand	3616-1523 rest n/a	20	88 Cargo Mk 6
18 BT 10	Ex 72 AA 93	1410-03934		
18 BT 11	Ex 68 AA 10	1410-01337		
18 BT 12	Ex 68 AA 74	1410-01437		
18 BT 13	Ex 68 AA 70	1410-01433		
18 BT 14	Ex 73 AA 70	1410-04157		
18 BT 15	Ex 69 AA 27	1410-01526		
18 BT 16	Ex 68 AA 07	1410-01334	7	88 Cargo Mk 6; transferred in December 1961
18 BT 38 to 18 BT 57	n/a	n/a	1	"Land Rover"; exact type and origin not known
20 BT 18	n/a	1128-01467		88 Cargo RHD
20 BT 19	n/a	1420-00685		
20 BT 20		1420-00684		
20 BT 21		1420-00679		
20 BT 22		1420-00681		
20 BT 23		1420-01070		
20 BT 24		1420-00789		
20 BT 25		1420-00790		
20 BT 26		1420-00791	8	88 Cargo Mk 6
20 BT 32	Ex 5907 HB	n/a	1	"Land Rover"; Exact type not known; for trip to Africa by Army Kinema Corporation, towing caravan
20 BT 36	n/a	n/a	1	"Land Rover"; exact type not known; possibly for trials with Powered Axle Trailer at School of Artillery, Larkhill
20 BT 39	Ex 08 RN 08	2410-7939A	1	88 FFR Mk 8
20 BT 90	Ex Trade	LW2		
20 BT 91	Ex Trade	LW3	2	Prototype Lightweight; see also Chapter 8
21 BT 29	Ex Trade	286-00352C	1	1 ton, Forward Control, Cargo, LWB, Petrol 2286cc Series IIA; prototype; see also Chapter 7
21 BT 38	Ex 68 AA 97	1410-01476	1	88 Cargo Mk 6; transferred after closure of Airfield Construction Branch, RAF at Waterbeach in March 1966
21 BT 84	Ex Trade	244-26934C		
21 BT 85	Ex Trade	241-25945C	2	Lightweight Prototype LHD and RHD; see also Chapter 8
21 BT 92	Ex –	241-25521C		
21 BT 93	Ex –	244-27323C		
21 BT 94	Ex –	241-26991C		
21 BT 95	Ex –	241-27158C	4	Lightweight Prototype LHD and RHD; built from 88 Series IIA
22 BT 25	Ex Trade	330-00019A		
22 BT 26	Ex Trade	330-00016A	2	110 FC Cargo Series IIB; prototypes for trials in February 1967; see also Chapter 7
22 BT 85	Ex G 18556	254-02594A	1	109 Cargo Series IIA Petrol; transferred from civilian registration at Gibraltar in 1967

ARMY

Serials	Source	Chassis Nos	Total	Remarks
22 BT 86	Ex G 23484	279-03234A	1	109 Cargo Series IIA Diesel; transferred from civilian registration at Gibraltar in 1967
22 BT 87	Ex G 18896	254-03444A	1	109 Cargo Series IIA Petrol; transferred from civilian registration at Gibraltar in 1967
22 BT 88	Ex G 23585	279-03235A	1	109 Cargo Series IIA Diesel; transferred from civilian registration at Gibraltar in 1967
23 BT 42	Ex 08 RN 06	24107939A		
23 BT 43	Ex 08 RN 07	24107938A		
23 BT 44	Ex 08 RN 09	24107940A		
23 BT 45	Ex 51 RN 01	24114739	4	88 FFR Mk8; transferred in August 1967
23 BT 56	Ex UXW 506	n/a	1	Land Rover; fitted with Sperry/Chobham navigator
24 BT 23	n/a	253-10675J		
24 BT 24		253-10661J		
24 BT 25		253-10662J	3	109 Cargo
24 BT 36	Ex 82 AA 43	241-10374	1	88 Cargo Mk 6; transferred in the Persian Gulf, May 1968
24 BT 47	Ex 31 EL 90	254-07520B	1	109 Cargo LHD Mk 9; allocated for Exercise in BAOR September 1968
24 BT 48	Ex 74 EL 63	244-18204B	1	88 Cargo LHD Mk 8; allocated for Exercise in BAOR September 1968
24 BT 52	Ex 83 AA 06	261-00998B	1	109 Cargo Mk 9/2; transferred in Athens June 1968
24 BT 53	Ex 82 AA 43	241-10374	1	88 Cargo Mk 6; note duplication with 24 BT 36.
25 BT 80	Ex 36 AM 42	251-16888		
25 BT 81	Ex 36 AM 43	251-16890		
25 BT 82	Ex 90 AA 29	251-10101		
25 BT 83	Ex 99 AA 10	251-15510		
25 BT 84	Ex 88 AA 57	241-25166		
25 BT 85	Ex 88 AA 56	241-25160		
25 BT 86	Ex 99 AA 11	251-15514		
25 BT 87	Ex 86 AA 58	251-08300		
25 BT 88	Ex 36 AM 58	251-16914	9	109 Cargo 24v 90A Series IIA; transferred at Tangmere in March 1970 from Tactical Signals Wing, RAF
26 BT 65	Ex 94 AA 06	271-08290	1	88 Cargo Diesel; transferred at RA Range, Hebrides in April 1970
26 BT 82	Ex 99 AA 87	236-01281		
26 BT 83	Ex 99 AA 89	236-01283		
26 BT 84	Ex 99 AA 95	236-01289		
26 BT 85	Ex 99 AA 96	236-01290	4	Lightweight FFR; transferred by Near East Air Force, August 1970
27 BT 06	Ex 99 AA 33	241-22265	1	88 FFR Mk 8; transferred at RAF Benson in January 1971
27 BT 07	Ex 90 AA 70	241-27090		88 24v Helicopter Starting Mk 6; transferred at RAF Benson in January 1971
27 BT 48	Ex 40 AM 78	251-18542	1	109 FFR RHD; transferred in July 1971
27 BT 50	Ex AOI 4051	252-17430C		
27 BT 51	Ex AOI 4056	252-17211C	2	Shorland; transferred ex-Royal Ulster Constabulary, to Ulster Defence Regiment in July 1971
27 BT 62	Ex 1960 TZ	252-15489C		
27 BT 63	Ex 1443 PZ	252-13250C		
27 BT 64	Ex 577 PZ	252-15498C		
27 BT 65	Ex 6078 TZ	252-15498C		
27 BT 66	Ex 8281 PZ	252-13287C		

ARMY

Serials	Source	Chassis Nos	Total	Remarks
27 BT 67	Ex AOI 4053	252-17260C		
27 BT 68	Ex 3547 PZ	252-13275C		
27 BT 69	Ex AOI 4054	252-17429C		
27 BT 70	Ex 8780 PZ	252-15492C		
27 BT 71	Ex 9551 OZ	252-13228C		
27 BT 72	Ex 3339 OZ	252-13313C		
27 BT 73	Ex AOI 4056	252-19472D		
27 BT 74	Ex AOI 4052	252-10424B	13	Shorland; transferred ex-Royal Ulster Constabulary, to Ulster Defence Regiment in July 1971
28 BT 22	Ex 89 AA 52	241-25715	1	88 Cargo Series IIA; transferred in Persian Gulf October 1971
28 BT 25	Ex 83 AA 03	251-05232B	1	109 Station Wagon Mk9/2; transferred in Persian Gulf, October 1971
28 BT 27	Ex 89 AA 93	241-25833		
28 BT 28	Ex 89 AA 66	241-25765		
28 BT 29	Ex 89 AA 63	241-25754	3	88 Cargo Series IIA; transferred in Persian Gulf October 1971
28 BT 39	Ex 47 AA 25	251-01878		
28 BT 40	Ex 47 AA 26	251-01879	2	109 Field Ambulance Series IIA; transferred in Persian Gulf, December 1971
28 BT 81	Ex 88 AA 43	241-25104	1	88 Cargo Series IIA; transferred to Military Attaché Teheran in February 1972
29 BT 54	Ex 95 AA 47	261-02270	1	109 Station Wagon Tropical Mk 11; transferred in June 1972
29 BT 55	Ex 51 RN 11	261-02098	1	109 Station Wagon Series IIA; transferred in June 1972
29 BT 89	Ex 96 AA 83	244-32729	1	88 Cargo Series IIA LHD; transferred from Air Attaché (?) Baghdad to Defence Attaché Dubai in June 1972
29 BT 99	Ex 39 AA 83	251-02133A	1	109 Fire tender RHD Mk 9; transferred from Joint Warfare Establishment, RAF Upavon, to 22 Squadron RCT in July 1972
30 BT 07	ex EJJ 339J	254-36752H		109 Station Wagon LHD; transferred to Defence Attaché, Istanbul from Commonwealth War Graves Commission in July 1972
30 BT 21	Ex 40 AM 58	353-01212G	1	109 6-cyl Station Wagon LHD Mk 11; transferred at Ankara on formation of SAAS
30 BT 24	Ex 43 AM 62	264-17181		
30 BT 25	Ex 28 AM 34	264-15492G	2	109 Station Wagon Mk 11; transferred at UK Professional Military Development Programme (UKPMD) Ankara on formation of SAAS
30 BT 26	Ex 43 AM 61	318-075206	1	88 Station Wagon Mk 10 LHD; transferred at UKPMD Ankara on formation of SAAS
30 BT 34	Ex 98 AA 80	251-14311	1	109 Cargo Series IIA; transferred at Djakarta on formation of SAAS
30 BT 40	Ex 40 AM 43	264-16195G	1	109 Station Wagon Mk 11; transferred at Jeddah on formation of SAAS
30 BT 44	Ex 03 AM 43	264-11606D	1	109 Station Wagon Tropical Mk 9/2 LHD; transferred at Manila on formation of SAAS
30 BT 57	Ex 99 AA 83	254-18119	1	109 Cargo Series IIA LHD; transferred at Saigon on formation of SAAS
30 BT 70	Ex 41 AM 79	251-18805	1	109 Cargo Series IIA; transferred at Islamabad on formation of SAAS

ARMY

Serials	Source	Chassis Nos	Total	Remarks
30 BT 73	Ex 48 AM 32	949-00101	1	109 6-cyl Station Wagon Series 3 LHD; transferred at Teheran on formation of SAAS
30 BT 74	Ex 90 AA 27	244-26933	1	88 Cargo Series IIA LHD; transferred at Teheran on formation of SAAS
30 BT 79	Ex 01 RN 66	261-02377D	1	109 Cargo Series IIA hardtop; transferred at Djakarta on formation of SAAS
30 BT 82	Ex 03 RN 07	264-10742D	1	109 Station Wagon Mk 11 LHD; transferred at Ankara on formation of SAAS
30 BT 83	Ex 04 RN 18	n/a	1	109 6-cyl Station Wagon Series 3 LHD; transferred at Ankara on formation of SAAS
30 BT 92	Ex 00 RN 71	353-01037G	1	109 6-cyl Station Wagon Mk 11 LHD; transferred at Caracas on formation of SAAS
31 BT 17	Ex 07 RN 52	264-18236H	1	109 Station Wagon Series IIA LHD; transferred at Freetown on formation of SAAS
31 BT 45	Ex 04 RN 18	949-00468B	1	109 6-cyl Station Wagon Series 3 LHD
31 BT 53	Ex 99 AA 16	318-05056F	1	88 Station Wagon Mk 10; transferred at Belgrade on formation of SAAS
31 BT 54	Ex 83 AA 10	254-09046B	1	109 Cargo Series IIA LHD; transferred at Warsaw on formation of SAAS
31 BT 76	Ex 00 RN 55	n/a	1	107 Fire tender RHD; transferred in October 1972
32 BT 29	Ex 87 AA 17	251-07932	1	109 Station Wagon Mk 9/2 RHD; transferred British Honduras
32 BT 49	Ex Trade	n/a	1	109 Station Wagon; transferred in Malta after local purchase
32 BT 55	Ex FXC 861L	901-05350A		
32 BT 56	Ex DXC 959L	901-03667A	2	88 CL Cargo Series 3 Hard Top RHD; transferred in May 1973
32 BT 71	Ex 55 AM 58	954-00493A	1	Lightweight Cargo Series 3 LHD; transferred in June 1973
33 BT 00	Ex Trade	n/a		Shorland Trooper
33 BT 69	Ex 10 RN 49	951-03052A		
33 BT 70	Ex 10 RN 50	951-03139A	2	Lightweight FFR Series 3 RHD; transferred at CVD Hilton in May 1974
35 BT 11	n/a	n/a	1	109 Station Wagon; a temporary allocation for movement from docks in May 1975
35 BT 92	Ex 50 RN 80	n/a	1	109 Station Wagon RHD; transferred in Hong Kong in April 1975
35 BT 99	Ex 21 RN 75	n/a		
36 BT 00	Ex 21 RN 78	n/a	2	88 CL Cargo; transferred in Hong Kong April 1975
36 BT 01	Ex 96 RN 84	n/a	1	109 CL Cargo Series IIA; transferred in Hong Kong in April 1975
36 BT 79	Ex 91 AA 18	251-12052	1	109 Fire tender Mk9 RHD
36 BT 91	Ex 46 RN 44	241-20947B	1	88 CL Cargo Series IIA
37 BT 02	Ex 05 AG 50	330-00179D	1	110 FC Fire Tender RHD; transferred at Akrotiri ; see also Chapter 7
37 BT 70	Ex 61 AM 04	951-01284A		
37 BT 71	Ex 61 AM 09	951-01495A		
37 BT 72	Ex 62 AM 45	951-01472A	3	Lightweight Cargo RHD Series 3; transferred from RAF Selarang to Hong Kong
37 BT 73	Ex 75 AM 22	253-34060G		
37 BT 74	Ex 75 AM 23	253-29764G		
37 BT 75	Ex 75 AM 24	253-29758G	3	109 Cargo GS Series 2A (Australian pattern); transferred from RAF Tengah to Hong Kong in December 1975

ARMY

Serials	Source	Chassis Nos	Total	Remarks
37 BT 76	Ex 60 AM 45	911-03317B		
37 BT 77	Ex 60 AM 82	911-03389B	2	109 Cargo GS Series 3; transferred from RAF Tengah to Hong Kong in December 1975
38 BT 27	Ex 97 RN 93	911-17386C		
38 BT 28	Ex 97 RN 94	911-17388C		
38 BT 29	Ex 97 RN 95	911-17391C		
38 BT 30	Ex 97 RN 96	911-17868C		
38 BT 31	Ex 97 RN 97	911-17871C	5	109 CL Cargo Hard Top w/Windows; transferred December 1975
40 BT 78	Ex 59 AM 23	951-01211A		
40 BT 79	Ex 59 AM 25	951-01219A		
40 BT 80	Ex 59 AM 32	951-01220A		
40 BT 81	Ex 59 AM 40	951-01222A		
40 BT 82	Ex 59 AM 45	951-01235A		
40 BT 83	Ex 59 AM 58	951-01248A	6	Lightweight 24V 90A RHD; transferred to Headquarters and Signal Squadron, Hong Kong in July 1976
40 BT 84	Ex 60 AM 71	911-03329A	1	109 Cargo Series 3; transferred to Headquarters and Signal Squadron, Hong Kong in July 1976
42 BT 75	Ex 92 AA 86	251-13038	1	109 Airfield Crash Rescue Ambulance RHD; transferred in February 1977
42 BT 76	Ex 62 AM 19	951-01455A		
42 BT 77	Ex 62 AM 23	951-01451A	2	Lightweight Cargo Series 3; transferred in February 1977
42 BT 78	Ex 60 AM 43	911-03325B	1	109 Cargo Series 3; transferred in February 1977
43 BT 37	Ex PUV 640F	251-14297D	1	109 Recovery Series 2A; transferred in May 1977
46 BT 15	Local Purchase	934-69296C		
46 BT 16	Local Purchase	932-91742C	2	109 Station Wagon (Grey with White Roof); for 262 Signal Squadron, RCS, Cyprus
46 BT 17	Ex 87 AA 53	251-11701		
46 BT 18	Ex 87 AA 71	251-11771	2	109 Field Ambulance Mk9; transferred at Ashchurch in March 1978
46 BT 58	Ex 57 RN 81	251-17555G	1	109 CL Cargo Hard Top w/windows Series IIA; transferred in Hong Kong in March 1978
46 BT 93	Ex 54 AM 44	951-00850A	1	Lightweight Cargo Series 3; transferred in Hong Kong in March 1978
46 BT 94	Ex 41 AM 83	n/a		
46 BT 95	Ex 41 AM 84	n/a	2	109 Cargo Hard Top Series IIA; transferred in Hong Kong in March 1978
47 BT 14	Ex 54 AM 54	951-00860A	1	Lightweight Cargo Series 3; transferred in March 1978
47 BT 52	Ex 39 AM 86	251-19561G	1	109 Airfield Crash Rescue Ambulance RHD; transferred in Hong Kong in April 1978
47 BT 93	Ex 87 AA 51	251-11692	1	109 Field Ambulance Mk9; transferred in Cyprus in June 1978
48 BT 00	Ex Trade	n/a	1	Shorts SB301; for transport to and from British Army Equipment Exhibition (BAEE) in June 1978
48 BT 04	Ex Trade	n/a	1	109 Armoured; for transport to and from BAEE in June 1978
48 BT 07	Ex Trade	n/a	1	Laird Centaur; for transport to and from BAEE in June 1978
49 BT 13	Ex 65 RN 62	931-01763C		
49 BT 14	Ex 36 RN 18	931-51374C		
49 BT 15	Ex 48 RN 42	931-68799C	3	109 Station Wagon Series 3; transferred in December 1978
50 BT 37	Ex 39 AA 57	1511-01059		

ARMY

Serials	Source	Chassis Nos	Total	Remarks
50 BT 38	Ex 39 AA 88	251-02144	2	109 Fire Tender Mk 9; transferred at Singapore in September 1971
50 BT 59	Ex 87 AA 24	251-08538		
50 BT 60	Ex 87 AA 30	251-08547		
50 BT 61	Ex 87 AA 32	251-08550	3	109 Station Wagon Mk 9/2; transferred at Singapore in July 1972
50 BT 62	Ex 86 AA 55	251-08256		
50 BT 63	Ex 91 AA 16	251-11857	2	109 Cargo 24v 90A Series IIA; transferred in Singapore in July 1972
50 BT 77	Ex 07 RN 07	n/a		
50 BT 78	Ex 08 RN 80	n/a	2	107 Fire Tender ; transferred in Singapore in July 1972
54 BT 04	Ex 00 SP 59	251-12758	1	109 Cargo Mk 9; Rapier Tractor prototype; transferred in January 1980
54 BT 06	Ex 03 SP 67	956-00001A	1	101 Cargo; transferred in January 1980
54 BT 08	Ex 03 SP 71	964-00005A	1	101 FFR LHD; transferred in January 1980
54 BT 09	Ex 00 SP 53	251-12784D	1	109 FFR Mk 9; Rapier Tractor prototype; transferred in January 1980
54 BT 11	Ex 03 SP 72	959-00002A	1	101 Cargo LHD; transferred in January 1980
54 BT 25	Ex 10 RN 94	911-59028C		
54 BT 26	Ex 10 RN 96	911-59030C		
54 BT 27	Ex 10 RN 97	911-59031C	3	Type n/a; transferred in Northern Ireland in January 1980
56 BT 83	Ex 72 RN 99	901-34374		
56 BT 84	Ex 79 RN 41	901-34375		
56 BT 85	Ex 79 RN 42	901-34377		
56 BT 86	Ex 79 RN 43	901-34379		
56 BT 87	Ex 79 RN 44	901-34380	5	88 CL Cargo Series 3; transferred in Hong Kong in July 1980
59 BT 76	Ex 81 AM 81	956-01264A		
59 BT 77	Ex 81 AM 82	956-01007A	2	101 Field Ambulance; transferred at Ashchurch in August 1981
60 BT 67	Ex 23 RN 01	931-01817C	1	109 Station Wagon Series 3; transferred at RAF Akrotiri November 1981
63 BT 12	Ex KA 964	901-462441 (sic)	1	88 Station Wagon Series 3; transferred in Cyprus from civil registration in September 1982
00 BZ 01	Ex LR 6842	1736-03863		
00 BZ 02	Ex LR 6483	1736-03851	2	86 Cargo LHD; ex-NAAFI during Suez Emergency 1956
01 CV 22	Ex Iraq	228885		109 Cargo Series 3 V8
50 EP 03	Ex CYY 687C	251-03850B		109 Forward Control (FC) Fire Tender; transferred at OESD Yardley in December 1965
50 EP 04	Ex UXM 74	1419-01178		88 Fire Tender; transferred at OESD Yardley in December 1965
50 EP 07	Ex UXM 9	1418-01343		88 Fire Tender; transferred at OESD Pontrilas in December 1965
50 EP 09	Ex CYY 686C	2510-3852B		109 FC Fire Tender; transferred at OESD Pontrilas in December 1965
50 EP 11	Ex NGY 983	1571-02285		88 Fire Tender; transferred at OESD Ulnes Walton in December 1965
50 EP 28	Ex CYY 688C	251-03855B		109 FC Fire Tender; transferred at CAD (?) Longtown in December 1965
50 EP 30	Ex RGX 616	8706-00062		107 Station Wagon; transferred at CAD Longtown in December 1965

ARMY

Serials	Source	Chassis Nos	Total	Remarks
50 EP 32	Ex CYY 689C	251-03857B		109 FC Fire Tender; transferred at CAD Longtown in December 1965
50 EP 35	Ex NGY 984	5710-5453		86 Fire Tender; transferred at CAD Longtown in December 1965
50 EP 37	Ex ALF 215B	251-05404B		109 Utility; transferred at CAD Longtown in December 1965
50 EP 40	Ex NGY 998	5710-4603		86 Fire Tender; transferred at OS&DD Rotherwas
50 EP 46	Ex RGX 635	1117-01381		88 Fire Tender; transferred at OSD Marsworth
50 EP 59	Ex 613 ELM	251-02813		
50 EP 60	Ex 125 DYE	251-02198A		
50 EP 61	Ex 353 ALR	n/a		109 Utility; transferred at P&EE Lavington 1966
50 EP 72	Ex NGY 715	4710-2542		86 Fire Tender; transferred at P&EE Inchterf
50 EP 97	Ex 354 ALR	1411-01838		
50 EP 98	Ex 615 ELM	241-10018B		
50 EP 99	Ex 622 ELM	241-10019B		
51 EP 00	Ex 482 ALR	n/a		
51 EP 01	Ex 29 DYE	241-04980		
51 EP 02	Ex 47 DYE	241-05535		
51 EP 03	Ex 105 DYE	241-06415C		
51 EP 04	Ex 154 DYE	241-07815C		
51 EP 05	Ex 544 FUW	241-03402B		
51 EP 06	Ex 545 FUW	241-03403B		
51 EP 07	Ex 546 FUW	241-03404B		88 Station Wagon; transferred at P&EE Shoeburyness in July 1966
51 EP 09	Ex YUV 843	1510-01339		
51 EP 10	Ex PGK 624	n/a		
51 EP 11	Ex YUV 844	1510-01340		
51 EP 12	Ex 106 DYE	251-02169		
51 EP 13	Ex CYY 706C	251-06695		109 Station Wagon; transferred at P&EE Shoeburyness in July 1966
52 EP 12	Ex CYY 719C	241-19101B		88 Cargo; transferred at P&EE Pendine in January 1965
53 EP 05	Ex 505 FUW	241-00931B	1	88 Cargo; transferred at MGO South Midlands Region
53 EP 27	Ex CYY 718C	241-20365B		
53 EP 34	Ex 535 FUW	n/a		
53 EP 35	Ex 536 FUW	241-13143B		
53 EP 37	Ex 537 FUW	241-13144B		
53 EP 38	Ex 127 BXR	1511-01500		
53 EP 47	Ex 538 FUW	241-13145B		
53 EP 49	Ex ALF 221B	241-14340B		
53 EP 53	Ex 195 DYE	241-08856B		
53 EP 55	Ex 196 DYE	241-08857B		88 Station Wagon; transferred at P&EE Eskmeals in August 1966
53 EP 56	Ex 288 BXR	251-00413A		109 Station Wagon; transferred at P&EE Eskmeals in August 1966
53 EP 66	Ex 120 BXR	276-00588		109 Station Wagon Diesel; transferred at P&EE Eskmeals
53 EP 67	Ex ALF 240B	241-16862B		
53 EP 68	Ex 82 DYE	n/a		88 Station Wagon; transferred at P&EE Eskmeals in August 1966
54 EP 11	Ex 118 DYE	241-06417C		
54 EP 12	Ex 119 DYE	241-06419C		
54 EP 13	Ex 508 FUW	241-09288		88 Station Wagon; transferred at RARDE Fort

ARMY

Serials	Source	Chassis Nos	Total	Remarks
				Halstead
54 EP 14	Ex YWV 822	1410-04006		88 Cargo; transferred at RARDE Fort Halstead
54 EP 15	Ex 15 DYE	251-00760		109 Cargo; transferred at RARDE Potton Island
54 EP 16	Ex 509 FUW	241-10929B		
54 EP 17	Ex 510 FUW	241-10930B		88 Cargo; transferred at RARDE Langhurst
54 EP 58	Ex PGK 959	5710-5895		88 Fire Tender; transferred at RARDE Potton Island
54 EP 59	Ex PGK 957	2710-5893		107 Fire Tender; transferred at RARDE Potton Island
54 EP 60	Ex RGX 786	1117-03434		
54 EP 61	Ex 511 FUW	251-03140B		109 Fire Tender; transferred at RARDE Langhurst
55 EP 79	Ex 616 ELM	241-09917B		88 Station Wagon; transferred at MEXE (?) Christchurch in August 1966
56 EP 03	Ex ALF 225B	241-16379E		88 Fire Tender; transferred at MEXE Christchurch in August 1966
56 EP 04	Ex RGX 274	1706-02875		86 Fire Tender; transferred at MEXE Christchurch in August 1966
56 EP 72	Ex PGK 955	5710-4601		86 Fire Tender; transferred at Chemical Defence Experimental Establishment (CDEE), Nacekuke
56 EP 89	Ex 63 DYE	241-05644A		
56 EP 90	Ex 64 DYE	241-05646A		
56 EP 91	Ex 65 DYE	241-05647A		88 Station Wagon; transferred at CDEE Porton Down in August 1966
57 EP 02	Ex RGX 903	n/a		
57 EP 03	Ex RGX 904	n/a		
57 EP 04	Ex UXM 228	n/a		
57 EP 05	Ex UXM 229	n/a		
57 EP 06	Ex UXM 332	1410-00354		
57 EP 07	Ex 165 BXR	n/a		
57 EP 08	Ex 166 BXR	n/a		
57 EP 09	Ex 66 DYE	241-05706		
57 EP 10	Ex 95 DYE	n/a		
57 EP 11	Ex 646 ELM	241-10569		
57 EP 12	Ex 525 FUW	n/a		88 Cargo CL Hard Top; transferred at CDEE Porton Down in August 1966
57 EP 13	Ex 408 ALR	1511-00869		
57 EP 14	Ex 626 ELM	251-02964		
57 EP 15	Ex 647 ELM	251-03030		
57 EP 16	Ex ALF 248B	251-06384		
57 EP 17	Ex ALF 249B	251-06385		
57 EP 18	Ex ALF 250B	251-06386		
57 EP 19	Ex ALF 899B	251-06387		
57 EP 20	Ex ALF 908B	251-06388		
57 EP 21	Ex ALF 909B	251-06389		109 Cargo CL Hard Top; transferred at CDEE Porton Down in August 1966
57 EP 23	Ex NGY 982	5710-2284		86 Fire Tender; transferred at CDEE Porton Down in August 1966
57 EP 86	Ex 472 ALR	1611-00119		109 Station Wagon; transferred at Inspectorate of Fighting Vehicles and Mechanical Equipment (IFVME), Pinehurst in August 1966
57 EP 95	Ex 96 DYE	241-06158		88 Cargo w/Winch; transferred at IFVME Pinehurst in August 1966
58 EP 22	Ex 249 BXR	241-01200		
58 EP 23	Ex 542 CYE	n/a		
58 EP 24	Ex 238 BXR	241-00488		88 Cargo; transferred at FVRDE Chertsey

ARMY

Serials	Source	Chassis Nos	Total	Remarks
58 EP 27	Ex 462 ALR	1411-03357		
58 EP 28	Ex YUV 855	1410-04125		88 Cargo; transferred at FVRDE Chertsey in September 1966
58 EP 35	Ex YUV 906	1561-00121		109 Cargo Truck Cab; transferred at FVRDE Chertsey in September 1966
58 EP 36	Ex 630 ELM	1611-0056		109 Station Wagon; transferred at FVRDE Chertsey in September 1966
59 EP 18	Ex NGY 469	5710-4649		88 Station Wagon; transferred at Inspectorate of Ammunition (IoA), Woolwich
59 EP 19	Ex 490 ALR	1511-01429		88 Station Wagon; transferred at IoA Woolwich
60 EP 23	Ex NGY 999	n/a		86 Fire Tender; transferred at FVRDE Chertsey
60 EP 28	Ex CYY 724C	261-01206		109 Station Wagon; transferred at FVRDE Chertsey
60 EP 33	Ex CYY 678C	241-17897B		88 Cargo; transferred at FVRDE Chertsey
60 EP 47	Ex -	1611-00060		109 Cargo; transferred at FVRDE Chertsey
60 EP 48	Ex 365 ALR	1610-00053		
60 EP 49	Ex UXM 299	1619-00003		109 Station Wagon; transferred at FVRDE Chertsey
60 EP 66	Ex 01 SP 69	251-15777F		
60 EP 67	Ex 01 SP 70	251-15786F		109 Cargo; transferred at FVRDE Chertsey
60 EP 69	Ex 00 SP 47	335-00011A		110 FC Cargo; transferred at FVRDE Chertsey; see also Chapter 7
60 EP 78	Ex 00 SP 13	241-25512C		
60 EP 79	Ex 00 SP 14	244-26934C		
60 EP 80	Ex 00 SP 18	241-27158C		
60 EP 81	Ex 00 SP 16	244-27323C		Lightweight Prototypes RHD and LHD; transferred at FVRDE Chertsey; see also Chapter 8
60 EP 82	Ex 02 SP 55	251-17676B		109 1-Tonne Cargo
60 EP 83	Ex 01 SP 71	251-15787F		
60 EP 84	Ex 01 SP 72	251-15788F		109 Cargo; transferred at FVRDE Chertsey
60 EP 85	Ex 02 SP 83	251-04265B		109 FFR; transferred at FVRDE Chertsey
60 EP 86	Ex 01 SP 68	251-15785F		109 Cargo; transferred at FVRDE Chertsey
57 FJ 22	Ex 00 SP 51	251-12768D		109 FFR Mk 11; as Rapier Tractor; transferred in October 1972
77 FL 28	Ex 03 SP 72	959-00002A		
77 FL 29	Ex 03 SP 70	956-00005A		101 Cargo LHD & RHD; 77 FL 28 "not used"; transferred in August 1977
28 KB 60	Ex Trade	125189		109 Station Wagon V8; for Defence Sales Tour in December 1982
28 KB 70	Ex Trade	102505		Hotspur S6E Hi-Line 6x6 Command Vehicle; for Defence Sales Tour in December 1982
29 KB 71	Ex Trade	158849		109; for Defence Sales Tour in November 1982
30 KB 23	-	171484	1	109 Station Wagon Tropical Series 3 LHD; transferred after local purchase by SAAS in Jeddah in December 1982
31 KB 68	-	934-87166C		109 Electronic Warfare; for Defence Sales Tour in February 1983
65 KB 80	-	175011	1	109 Station Wagon Tropical Series 3 LHD; transferred after local purchase by SAAS in Riyadh in June 1983
65 KB 82	Ex 36 KA 69	175209	1	109 Station Wagon Series 3; transferred in Kenya in June 1983 to avoid confusion with local army registrations
73 KB 67	-	537198	1	109 Station Wagon; transferred after local purchase by SAAS in Pretoria in August 1983
07 KC 36	-	180242	1	109 CL Cargo hardtop w/windows; transferred after local purchase by RAF High Wycombe in March 1983

ARMY

Serials	Source	Chassis Nos	Total	Remarks
65 KC 52	08 KA 07	158858		
65 KC 53	09 KA 91	159131		
65 KC 54	09 KA 93	159135		
65 KC 55	10 KA 00	159152		
65 KC 56	10 KA 32	159562		
65 KC 57	37 KA 68	175219		
65 KC 58	37 KA 79	175244		
65 KC 59	37 KA 81	175253		
65 KC 60	38 KA 10	175759	9	109 CL Cargo Series 3; transferred in Kenya in June 1984 to avoid confusion with local army registrations
67 KC 10	-	540649	1	109 Station Wagon Tropical Series 3; transferred after local purchase by SAAS in Pretoria in August 1983
36 KH 09	Local Purchase for PSA	183807		
36 KH 10		182936		
36 KH 11		214918		
36 KH 12		183829		Lightweight Cargo Series 3 Diesel; for Property Services Agency in Falklands Islands in October 1988
05 PB 98	n/a	230489		109 Station Wagon Series 3; for Property Services Agency
00 SP 13	Ex 21 BT 92	241-25512C		
00 SP 14	Ex 21 BT 84	244-26934C		
00 SP 15	Ex 21 BT 85	241-25945C		
00 SP 16	Ex 21 BT 93	244-27323C		
00 SP 17	Ex 21 BT 94	241-26991C		
00 SP 18	Ex 21 BT 95	241-27158C	6	Lightweight Prototype LHD and RHD; see also Chapter 8
00 SP 25	Ex 463 ALR	n/a		109 Station Wagon; transferred at Fort Halstead
00 SP 26	Ex 20 EL 17	251-03863B	1	109 Station Wagon Mk9; transferred at Fort Halstead
00 SP 27	Ex 15 BT 18	1510-00213		
00 SP 28	Ex 18 DE 75	1510-01033		
00 SP 29	Ex 18 DE 82	1510-01040	3	109 Cargo Mk 7 – converted to WOMBAT Portee; transferred at Fort Halstead
00 SP 30	Ex 02 DM 86	251-00300A	1	109 Cargo Mk 9
00 SP 47	WV7110	335-00011A	1	110 FC for Trucial Oman Scouts; see also Chapter 7; later to 60 EP 69
00 SP 49	WV7135	251-12760D		
00 SP 50		251-12764D		
00 SP 51		251-12768D		
00 SP 52		251-12772D		
00 SP 53		251-12784D	5	109 FFR; as Rapier Tractors 00 SP 51 later to 57 FJ 22; 00 SP 53 later to 54 BT 09
00 SP 54	WV7135	251-13107		
00 SP 55		251-13113		
00 SP 56		251-13114		
00 SP 57		251-13116		
00 SP 58		251-13098		
00 SP 59		251-12758	6	109 Cargo Mk 11; as Rapier Re-supply to 49 FJ 67 to 49 FJ 71
00 SP 64	Ex 04 ET 83	251-12559D	1	109 FFR Mk 11
01 SP 49	Ex 47 FG 08	251-13736D	1	109 Cargo Mk 9 w/400 c/s Power Supply
01 SP 62	Ex 87 EL 59	241-14984B	1	88 FFR Mk 8
01 SP 64	Ex 51 DM 20	251-01773A	1	88 FFR Mk 8
01 SP 65	Ex 29 ES 59	251-12121C	1	109 FFR Mk 9

ARMY

Serials	Source	Chassis Nos	Total	Remarks
01 SP 68	n/a	251-15785F		
01 SP 69		251-15777F		
01 SP 70		251-15786F		
01 SP 71		251-15787F		
01 SP 72		251-15788F	5	109 Cargo Mk 11
01 SP 90	Ex 18 DM 93	251-00536A		109 Cargo
02 SP 29	n/a	n/a		109 FFR
02 SP 32	Ex 641 ELM and	310-00004and 310-00003		
and 02 SP 33	Ex 640 ELM		2	109 APGP
02 SP 36	n/a	286-00302B		109 FC with screw propulsion system; see also Chapter 7
02 SP 52	Ex Trade	n/a		
02 SP 53		n/a	2	109 1 ton
02 SP 54	n/a	n/a		
02 SP 55	n/a	251-17676B	2	109 Cargo
02 SP 72	n/a	n/a	1	110 FC
02 SP 83	Ex 30 EL 86	251-04265B	1	109 FFR Mk 9
03 SP 26	n/a	223-00019C	1	Rover 1 ton Cargo; for Oman
03 SP 32	n/a	223-00021C	1	Rover 1 ton Cargo; for Oman
03 SP 67	Ex Trade	956-00001A		
03 SP 68		956-00004A		
03 SP 69		964-00004A		
03 SP 70		956-00005A		
03 SP 71		964-00005A		
03 SP 72		959-00002A	6	101 various; Pre-Production (see Chapter 12)
03 SP 77	Ex VXC 754K	101/FC/8C		101 Prototype
03 SP 78	Ex Trade	961-00001A		101 FFR Pre-Production
04 SP 13	Ex 48 ER 33	251-11754C	1	109 Cargo Mk 9
04 SP 14	Ex 74 EN 88	241-23095B	1	88 Cargo Mk 8
04 SP 16	n/a	1611-00060	1	109 Cargo Mk 7
04 SP 41	Ex 30 FJ 28	251-19298G		
04 SP 44	Ex 38 FG 11	236-00580A		
04 SP 45	Ex 62 FK 23	n/a		
04 SP 46	Ex 30 FG 24	251-14876D		
04 SP 47	Ex 41 FL 23	911-02567B		
04 SP 48	Ex 37 FM 23	911-03441B		
04 SP 49	Ex 38 FM 16	911-03681B		
04 SP 50	Ex 39 FM 70	911-03978B		
04 SP 51	Ex 41 FM 19	911-04374B		
04 SP 52	Ex 41 FM 56	911-04744B		
04 SP 53	Ex 65 FM 72	911-05195B		
04 SP 54	Ex 66 FM 66	911-05335B		
04 SP 55	Ex 66 FM 74	911-05351B		
04 SP 56	Ex 54 FM 90	911-04647B		Various vehicles at MVEE re-serialled for "Special
04 SP 59	Ex 68 FL 41	961-00007A	17	Projects" – all reverted to their original identities later
05 SP 18	Ex 19 FM 74	951-01114A	1	Lightweight Cargo Series 3
05 SP 35	Ex 78 FM 93	911-05534B		
05 SP 36	Ex 50 GF 83	911-27537C	1	109 FFR Series 3
05 SP 37	Ex 33 GB 22	951-03635A	1	Lightweight FFR Series 3
05 SP 38	Ex 27 GB 76	931-01445B	1	109 Station Wagon Series 3
05 SP 61	Ex Trade	911-006061C	1	109; for Defence Sales Tour
06 SP 33	Ex Trade	n/a	1	SMC Sandringham 6x6
06 SP 61	Ex Trade	102348		Townley 6x6
00 WA 07	n/a	n/a	1	Lightweight Series IIA

ARMY

Serials	Source	Chassis Nos	Total	Remarks
00 WA 08	Ex n/a	n/a		
00 WA 09	Ex 60 EP 83	251-15787F		
00 WA 10	Ex 60 EP 86	251-15785F		
00 WA 11	Ex 60 EP 66	251-15777F		109 Cargo Hard Top Series IIA
00 WA 24	n/a			
00 WA 25	n/a			Lightweight Series 3
00 WA 28	n/a	n/a		109 Cargo Series IIA
00 WA 80	n/a	n/a		109 Cargo fitted VPK
01 WEL 09	n/a	n/a		109 Station Wagon Series 3; Cyprus
90 YJ 28	n/a	1616-0737		
90 YJ 29	n/a	1616-0703		
90 YJ 30	n/a	1616-0707		
90 YJ 31	n/a	1616-0698		
90 YJ 32	n/a	1616-0706		
90 YJ 33	n/a	0611-4889		
90 YJ 34	n/a	1616-0708		
90 YJ 35	n/a	1616-0702		
90 YJ 36	n/a	1616-0713		
90 YJ 37	n/a	1616-0705		
90 YJ 38	n/a	1616-0710		
90 YJ 39	n/a	1616-0699		
90 YJ 40	n/a	1616-0700		
90 YJ 41	n/a	1616-0711		
90 YJ 42	n/a	1616-0701		
90 YJ 43	n/a	1616-0736		
90 YJ 44	n/a	1616-0704		
90 YJ 45	n/a	1616-0709		
90 YJ 46	n/a	1616-0735		
90 YJ 47	Ex M6279788	86-0758		
90 YJ 48	Ex 34 AA 68	1610-8440		
90 YJ 49	Ex MLM 823	2610-8978		
90 YJ 51	Ex KYW 542	0611-2757		80 Cargo; origins n/a
90 YJ 55	Ex C14556	1613-5014		
90 YJ 56	Ex C9563	1613-5012		80 Cargo LHD
90 YJ 57	Ex C17251	4723-0210		107 LHD

Largely unmodified from its civilian specification, this long-wheelbase model – probably a Series II – was used for WOMBAT trias by FVRDE. It carries an FVRDE "wing number" (5866) but otherwise remains unidentified. (TMB)

59 BT 77 started life as 81 AM 82 and was originally intended for service with the RAF Regiment. Proving surplus to RAF requirements it was transferred to the Army and issued to 220 Field Ambulance, RAMC and is shown here at Aldershot Army Day in June 1982. (GF)

RAF

Serials	Source	Chassis Nos	Total	Remarks
05 AA 13	Ex 89 BR 29	1117-00838	1	88 Cargo
08 AA 43	Ex 46 DM 91	241-05132		
08 AA 44	Ex 44 DM 03	241-03736		
08 AA 45	Ex 46 DM 52	241-04969		
08 AA 46	Ex 48 DM 11	241-05705		
08 AA 47	Ex 48 DM 31	241-05764	5	88 FFR for Helicopter Starting; transferred at 389 MU at Seletar in April 1968
08 AA 65	Ex 17 DM 64	241-03540		
08 AA 66	Ex 17 DM 64	241-03540		
08 AA 67	Ex 54 EK 48	241-09829		
08 AA 68	Ex 31 EK 84	241-08302		
08 AA 69	Ex 85 EL 29	241-14490		
08 AA 70	Ex 54 EK 60	241-09860		
08 AA 71	Ex 61 EK 62	241-12069		
08 AA 72	Ex 53 EK 28	241-09415		
08 AA 73	Ex 54 EK 52	241-09844		
08 AA 74	Ex 64 EL 04	241-16217		
08 AA 75	Ex 54 EK 01	241-09567		
08 AA 76	Ex 85 EL 07	241-14435		
08 AA 77	Ex 57 EK 84	241-11168		
08 AA 78	Ex 53 EK 58	241-09512		
08 AA 79	Ex 33 EK 02	241-09057		
08 AA 80	Ex 59 EK 59	241-11587	16	88 Cargo; transferred at 389 MU in Seletar in May 1969. Both 08 AA 65 and 08 AA 66 are shown as having chassis number 241-03540; 08 AA 79 is recorded with chassis number 242-09057.
08 AA 81	Ex 67 EN 22	241-18980		
08 AA 82	Ex 68 EN 36	241-19214		
08 AA 83	Ex 69 EN 41	241-19458		
08 AA 84	Ex 69 EN 43	241-19431		
08 AA 85	Ex 69 EN 52	241-19445		
08 AA 86	Ex 69 EN 59	241-19425		
08 AA 87	Ex 69 EN 64	241-19593		
08 AA 88	Ex 69 EN 80	241-19588		
08 AA 89	Ex 69 EN 84	241-19563		
08 AA 90	Ex 69 EN 85	241-19564		
08 AA 91	Ex 70 EN 59	241-19656		
08 AA 92	Ex 70 EN 70	241-19632		
08 AA 93	Ex 71 EN 27	241-19755		
08 AA 94	Ex 71 EN 30	241-19758	14	88 Cargo; transferred at 389 MU in Seletar in May 1969
12 AA 99	Ex 62 EK 47	241-12305B		
13 AA 00	Ex 83 EL 46	241-14039B	2	88 FFR; transferred at RAF Kai Tak
24 AA 34	Ex RN	1511-01036	1	109 Station Wagon; at Ascension Island
47 AA 33	Ex 05 RN 56	244-16909B	1	88 Cargo LHD; ex Naval Attaché, Belgrade in June 1969
47 AA 34	Ex 74745	264-05661	1	109 Station Wagon LHD; ex Marconi in Teheran
47 AA 36	Ex 23 FJ 86	251-17998G	1	109 FFR; transferred in February 1970
62 AA 89	Ex 49 BR 14	1706-02838		
62 AA 90	Ex 49 BR 13	1706-02837		
62 AA 91	Ex 49 BR 08	1706-02832		
62 AA 92	Ex 49 BR 07	1706-02810		
62 AA 93	Ex 48 BR 94	1706-02777		

RAF

Serials	Source	Chassis Nos	Total	Remarks
62 AA 94	Ex 48 BR 76	1706-02739		
62 AA 95	Ex 48 BR 70	1706-02720		
62 AA 96	Ex 49 BR 25	1706-02867		
62 AA 97	Ex 49 BR 23	1706-02865		
62 AA 98	Ex 49 BR 21	1706-02863		
62 AA 99	Ex 49 BR 20	1706-02862		
63 AA 00	Ex 49 BR 34	1706-02913		
63 AA 01	Ex 49 BR 18	1706-02860		
63 AA 02	Ex 49 BR 17	1706-02859		
63 AA 03	Ex 49 BR 16	1706-02840		
63 AA 04	Ex 49 BR 24	1706-02866		
63 AA 05	Ex 49 BR 15	1706-02859		
63 AA 06	Ex 49 BR 27	1706-02906		
63 AA 07	Ex 48 BR 43	1706-02650		
63 AA 08	Ex 49 BR 22	1706-02864		
63 AA 09	Ex 49 BR 30	1706-02909		
63 AA 10	Ex 49 BR 32	1706-02911		
63 AA 11	Ex 48 BR 87	1706-02763		
63 AA 12	Ex 49 BR 33	1706-02912		
63 AA 13	Ex 49 BR 19	1706-02861	25	86 Cargo Mk 3. 62 AA 90 was struck off to the Army
64 AA 30	Ex 26 BS 45	1117-02310	1	86 Cargo (fitted with Radio)
65 AA 53	Ex 09 BH 28	2610-2974	1	80 Cargo
66 AA 05	Ex 15 BH 83	2610-4364	1	80 Cargo
82 AA 18	Ex 07 RN 70	264-09000	1	109 Station Wagon LHD; ex Naval Attaché, Teheran in August 1969
87 AA 18	Ex 01 RN 21	1511-01035	1	109 Cargo
95 AA 44	Ex 47 DM 76	241-05420		
95 AA 45	Ex 47 DM 54	241-05372	2	88 FFR; transferred July 1967
99 AA 12	Ex Army	251-08592		
99 AA 13	Ex 97 EN 22	251-07994		
99 AA 14	Ex 96 EN 88	251-07380		
99 AA 15	Ex 97 EN 12	251-07911	4	109 FFR; transferred Persian Gulf February 1968
99 AA 17	Ex 11 ER 91	241-24194		
99 AA 18	Ex 13 ER 23	241-24721		
99 AA 19	Ex 60 ER 43	241-25774		
99 AA 20	Ex 11 ER 10	241-23819		
99 AA 21	Ex 12 ER 44	241-24409		
99 AA 22	Ex 13 ER 40	241-24770		
99 AA 23	Ex 12 ER 88	241-24556		
99 AA 24	Ex 12 ER 97	241-24597		
99 AA 25	Ex 11 ER 98	241-24231		
99 AA 26	Ex 12 ER 99	241-24600		
99 AA 27	Ex 86 EN 40	241-21310		
99 AA 28	Ex 85 EN 13	241-20581		
99 AA 29	Ex 88 EN 44	241-22954		
99 AA 30	Ex 84 EN 54	241-20324		
99 AA 31	Ex 86 EN 43	241-21324		
99 AA 32	Ex 94 EL 60	241-17747		
99 AA 33	Ex 87 EN 10	241-22265		
99 AA 34	Ex 88 EN 35	241-22902		
99 AA 35	Ex 88 EN 61	241-22853		
99 AA 36	Ex 89 EN 16	241-23615		
99 AA 37	Ex 92 EN 39	241-21633		
99 AA 38	Ex 13 ER 25	241-24725		

00 WA 80 was a Series 3 109-inch model fitted with a VPK for potential use in Northern Ireland. It was used for trials at FVRDE and was presented to the Aldershot Military Museum in 1994. These conversions were familiarly known as "Piglets", after the armoured Humber 1-ton "Pig" that they were intended to replace. (JT)

RAF

Serials	Source	Chassis Nos	Total	Remarks
99 AA 39	Ex 59 ER 46	241-25021		
99 AA 40	Ex 59 ER 88	241-25327		
99 AA 41	Ex 60 ER 87	241-26324	25	88 FFR
99 AA 98	Ex 84 EL 67	241-14363C		
99 AA 99	Ex 61 EK 13	241-11955B	2	88 FFR
06 AF 41	Ex 88 ER 77	244-28019C		
06 AF 42	Ex 88 ER 81	244-27880C		
06 AF 43	Ex 79 EN 73	244-21777B		
06 AF 44	Ex 87 ER 79	244-27349C		
06 AF 45	Ex 86 ER 67	244-26939C		
06 AF 46	Ex 87 ER 79	244-27349C		
06 AF 47	Ex 87 ER 79	244-27349C	7	88 Cargo LHD; transferred at Ashchurch in June 1980. Note that 87 ER 79 is shown against 06 AF 44, 06 AF 46 and 06 AF 47!
06 AF 54	Ex 48 XB 83	914-93458C	1	109 Station Wagon; transferred at RAF Gatow in October 1980
11 AF 17	Ex 29 XC 16	143845	1	Lightweight Series 3 Cargo LHD
24 AJ 58	Ex 69 EN 12	241-19298B		
24 AJ 59	Ex 77 EN 93	244-21018B		
24 AJ 60	Ex 80 EN 56	244-23289B	3	88 Cargo LHD
24 AJ 61	Ex 45 ER 06	251-10142C	1	109 Cargo RHD
24 AJ 62	Ex 93 EN 60	254-11329B	1	109 Cargo LHD
25 AJ 48	Ex 57 EK 77	241-11150B	1	88 FFR; transferred at RAF Kai Tak
26 AJ 50	Ex 07 EM 90	251-05626B	1	109 Cargo; transferred at RAF Tengah
26 AJ 56	Ex 18 ER 00	251-08981B		
26 AJ 57	Ex 18 ER 48	251-09122B	2	109 FFR; transferred at RAF Tengah
28 AJ 60	Ex n/a	254-22013D		
28 AJ 61	Ex n/a	254-22011D	2	109 Cargo LHD; transferred at RAF Masirah in May 1973
33 AJ 22	Ex 73 FL 85	956-00757A	1	101 Cargo w/winch. Later stuck off to 49 AS 56.
33 AJ 23	Ex 53 GJ 94	915-56477C		
33 AJ 24	Ex 53 GJ 56	911-57038C	2	109 FFR; transferred at Vehicle Depot, Hilton in September 1977
35 AJ 52	Ex 69 FL 78	956-00894A		
35 AJ 53	Ex 67 FL 17	956-00803A		
35 AJ 54	Ex 69 FL 46	956-00897A		
35 AJ 55	Ex 67 FL 38	956-00940A		
35 AJ 56	Ex 69 FL 73	956-00889A		
35 AJ 57	Ex 69 FL 50	956-00901A		
35 AJ 58	Ex 67 FL 33	956-00935A		
35 AJ 59	Ex 67 FL 14	956-00827A		
35 AJ 60	Ex 66 FL 93	956-00788A		
35 AJ 61	Ex 67 FL 29	956-00822A		
35 AJ 62	Ex 62 FL 77	956-00304A		
35 AJ 63	Ex 67 FL 09	956-00804A		
35 AJ 64	Ex 66 FL 70	956-00765A		
35 AJ 65	Ex 66 FL 83	956-00778A		
35 AJ 66	Ex 69 FL 60	956-00876A		
35 AJ 67	Ex 67 FL 44	956-00946A		
35 AJ 68	Ex 69 FL 76	956-00892A		
35 AJ 69	Ex 67 FL 43	956-00945A	18	101 Cargo; transferred at Vehicle Depot, Ashchurch in August 1978
37 AJ 06	Ex 70 FL 50	959-00313A		

RAF

Serials	Source	Chassis Nos	Total	Remarks
37 AJ 07	Ex 68 FL 13	959-00141A	2	101 Cargo LHD; transferred at Vehicle Depot, Hilton in October 1978
49 AJ 18	Ex 57 XB 54	954-02391A	1	Lightweight Series 3 Cargo LHD; transferred at RAF Gatow in February 1981
03 AM 43	Ex 90 RN 06	264-11606D	1	109 Station Wagon Tropical LHD; transferred ex Naval Attaché, Manila February 1971. Struck off to 30 BT 44 in July 1972.
06 AM 91	Ex 11 EM 13	251-05294B	1	109 Cargo; transferred in Malta May 1971
40 AM 38	Ex 69 EN 47	241-18318		
40 AM 39	Ex 67 EL 42	241-17616B		
40 AM 40	Ex n/a	n/a		
40 AM 41	Ex 68 EL 84	241-18134B		
40 AM 42	Ex 62 EN 63	241-18774B	5	88 Cargo; transferred at RAF Masirah in November 1969
43 AM 09	Ex 31 FG 02	251-15114D	1	109 Cargo
47 AM 98	Ex 78 ER 57	241-28599C		
47 AM 99	Ex 71 EN 53	241-19477B	2	88 Cargo
48 AM 00	Ex 58 EK 88	244-18204B	1	88 FFR LHD
53 AM 44	Ex 63 FK 50	251-21647	1	109 Cargo; transferred at Vehicle Depot Ashchurch in June 1972
55 AM 81	Ex 75 EN 22	241-23062		
55 AM 82	Ex 74 EK 23	241-12333		
55 AM 83	Ex 60 ER 06	241-25449		
55 AM 84	Ex 12 ER 64	241-24444		
55 AM 85	Ex 84 EL 65	241-14356		
55 AM 86	Ex 85 EL 63	241-14507	6	88 Cargo
55 AM 88	Ex 51 RN 08	261-02095	1	109 Station Wagon; transferred at RN Lossiemouth in October 1972
57 AM 70	Ex 83 EN 99	241-21296B		
57 AM 71	Ex 62 EL 13	241-14781B	2	88 Cargo mineplated; transferred at RAF Masirah in November 1971
60 AM 99	Ex 14 DM 33	241-01443A	1	88 FFR; transferred at RAF Hullavington in February 1973
66 AM 23	Ex 62 EN 35	241-18710B	1	88 Cargo; transferred at RAF Salalah in June 1973
75 AM 22	Local Purchase	253-34060G		
75 AM 23		253-29764G		
75 AM 24		253-29758G	3	109 Cargo Series IIA (Australian pattern); for RAF Tengah
76 AM 46	Ex 59 FH 24	251-16371G		
76 AM 47	Ex 58 FH 70	251-16249G		
76 AM 48	Ex 58 FH 69	251-16293G	3	109 Cargo converted to Rapier Forward Repair Team Vehicle; transferred at Stores Depot, Old Dalby
78 AM 38	Ex 58 FH 95	251-16325G	1	109 Cargo
80 AM 74	Ex 58 FH 82	251-16310G	1	109 Cargo
86 AM 80	Ex 53 XB 90	934-00884A	1	109 Station Wagon LHD; transferred at RAF Gatow in April 1977
94 AM 01	Ex 76 FL 77	959-00021A	1	101 Cargo w/Winch LHD; transferred at RAF Leuchars in October 1977
94 AM 48	Ex 72 FL 79	956-00017A	1	101 Cargo w/Winch. Photographic evidence suggests the plate was printed as 94 AV 48.
97 AM 23	Ex 17 XG 28	254-31703G	1	109 FFR LHD; transferred at RAF Gatow in October 1978
99 AM 13	Ex 27 XH 42	914-80642C	1	109 Station Wagon LHD; transferred at RAF Gatow in February 1979

RAF

Serials	Source	Chassis Nos	Total	Remarks
49 AS 53	Ex 48 ER 57	n/a		
49 AS 54	Ex 58 FH 76	251-12051C	1	109 Cargo; converted as Rapier Automatic Test Equipment
49 AS 55	Ex 76 FL 95	959-00163A	1	101 Cargo w/Winch; converted to Rapier ATE (?) and transferred at RAF Laarbruch in March 1979
49 AS 56	Ex 27 EK 30	261-00017	1	109 Sensitivity Test
49 AS 62	Ex 73 FL 88	956-00760A	1	101 Cargo w/Winch; converted to Rapier ATE
49 AS 66	Ex 73 FL 50	956-00646A	1	101 Cargo w/Winch; converted to Rapier ATE
50 AS 06	Ex 73 FL 70	956-00742A		
50 AS 07	Ex 76 FL 52	956-00398A	2	101 Cargo w/Winch; converted to Rapier ATE
50 AS 96	Ex 73 FL 98	956-00814A		
50 AS 97	Ex 71 FL 41	956-00171A	2	101 Cargo w/Winch; converted to Rapier ATE
94 AV 39	Ex 60 FL 72	956-00066A		
94 AV 40	Ex 60 FL 92	956-00094A		
94 AV 41	Ex 60 FL 94	956-00096A		
94 AV 42	Ex 61 FL 22	956-00122A		
94 AV 43	Ex 61 FL 37	956-00137A		
94 AV 44	Ex 61 FL 39	956-00139A		
94 AV 45	Ex 61 FL 44	956-00171A	7	101 Cargo
20 AZ 51 to 20 AZ 60	n/a	n/a	10	109 Cargo Hard Top w/windows LHD; for MPBW
21 AZ 47	n/a	n/a	1	109 Cargo Hard Top w/windows LHD; for MPBW Gibraltar
24 AZ 23	n/a	n/a	1	88 Cargo Hard Top w/windows LHD; for MPBW Gibraltar

ROYAL NAVY

This list is incomplete because no full record of Navy vehicles exists.

Serials	Source	Chassis Nos	Total	Remarks
07 RN 38	Ex 22 DM 17	241-01854A		
07 RN 39	Ex 23 DM 95	241-02339A	2	88 Cargo Mk 8/2
18 RN 07	Ex 72 FG 88	236-00118A		
18 RN 08	Ex 38 FG 39	236-00602A		
18 RN 09	Ex 38 FG 10	236-00581A		
18 RN 10	Ex 40 FG 73	236-00902A		
18 RN 11	Ex 41 FG 23	236-00952A	5	Lightweight Cargo Series IIA; transferred in September 1972
20 RN 96	Ex 60 ER 21	241-25620C	1	88 FFR Mk 8
38 RN 24	Ex 04 BC 25	0610-3934		80 Mk 1; probably transferred 1955
54 RN 00	Ex 16 FM 80	951-02998A	1	Lightweight Cargo Series 3; transferred in June 1974
62 RN 34	Ex 09 FM 97	951-01585A		
62 RN 35	Ex 10 FM 45	951-01078A	2	Lightweight FFR Series 3; transferred in December 1980
67 RN 79	Ex 75 FM 13	951-03259A	1	Lightweight FFR Series 3; transferred in December 1980

LAND ROVER PURCHASES BY ARMY BY FY

Does not include "Special Project Vehicles" or Transfers (e.g. ex RAF).
Excludes all coil-sprung models, ie Ninety, One Ten and Range Rover except as noted below.

FY	SWB	LWB	FC	LW	101	Total
before 49	20					20
49/50 (BC)	1911					1911
50/51 00 BD 01 to 49 BD 99	600					600
51/52 50 BD 00 to 99 BJ 99	1900					1900
52/53 00 BK 01 to 99 BM 99	-					0
53/54 00 BN 01 to 02 BP 95	-					0
54/55 02 BP 96 to 28 BR 00	4646					4646
55/56 28 BR 01 to 23 BS 54	1000	20				1020
56/57 23 BS 55 to 68 BS 00	600					600
57/58 (CE)	675					675
58/59 (CL)	275	70				345
59/60 (DE)		42				42
60/61 (DL)	585	6				591
61/62 (DM)	2850	748				3598
62/63 (EK)	3631	28				3659
63/64 (EL/EM)	3187	2667				5854
64/65 (EN/EP)	3127	2106				5233
65/66 (ER/ES)	2706	2319				5025
66/67 (ET)	0	585				585
67/68 (FG)	2	1151	10	1148		2291
68/69 (FH)	21	695	5	191		912
69/70 (FJ)	18	1689	2	38		1747
70/71 (FK)	24	2153	41	1279		3497
71/72 (FL)	23	917		1342	1569	3851
72/73 (FM)	44	2424		2205		4673
73/74 (GB)	233	559		304		1096
74/75 (GF)	323	1410		1017		2750
75/76 (GJ)	30	1004		109	396	1539
76/77 (GN)	301	1197		50		1548
77/78 (GT/GX)	571	2484		309		3364
78/79 (HF)	43	679		909		1631
79/80 (HG)	135	1893		1852		3880
80/81 (HH)	20	213		39		272
81/82 (HJ and to 22 KA 00)[1][2]	165	661		58		884
82/83 (to 45 KB 48)	26	1761		477	12	2291[3]
83/84 (to 40 KC 15)	55	1103		358		1523[4]
84/85 (to 97 KD 20)	75	1474		516		2065
Totals	29,822	32,058	58	12,201	1977[5]	

[1] After the introduction of KA all vehicles were acquired on a tri-service basis (so were no longer just for the Army) and also all vehicles held by the three services became part of a pool and were issued to all three services.
[2] The ERMs associated with the end of the Financial Year are approximations.
[3] Includes 12 "Stage 2" 110 Validation vehicles and 3 110 Station Wagons.
[4] Includes 4 DPV SAS Validation, 1 110 Station Wagon and 2 Sandringhams.
[5] Note that 10 further 101s were made from spare Chassis Cabs - 18 KJ 35, 18 KJ 43, 33 KJ 71, 34 KJ 79, 34 KJ 80, 34 KJ 95, 48 KJ 49, 48 KJ 50, 55 KJ 69 and 55 KJ 70.

GLOSSARY

AC	Alternating Current		LHD	Left Hand Drive
ACE	Allied Commander Europe		MDJR	Mountain, Desert and Jungle Rescue
ACRT	Airfield Crash Rescue Truck		MELF	Middle East Land Forces
AFFF	Aqueous Film-Forming Foam		MEXE	Military Engineering Experimental Establishment at Christchurch
AMF	ACE Mobile Force			
Ammo	Ammunition		MGO	Master General of the Ordnance
APGP	Air-Portable General Purpose		MILAN	Missile d'Infanterie Léger Antichar (French), and in English – Light anti-tank infantry missile
Atts	Attachments – as in "trailer attachments"			
ATTURM	Amphibious Trials & Training Unit RM		MOBAT	Mobile BAT
BAEE	British Army Equipment Exhibition		MoS	Ministry of Supply
BAOR	British Army of the Rhine		MPBW	Ministry of Public Buildings and Works
BAT	Battalion Anti-Tank – a weapon used by the British Army		MSP	Medium Stressed Platform
Bergen	British Army rucksack		MTDE	Motor Transport Development Establishment
BDLS	British Defence Liaison Staff		MU	Maintenance Unit
BMIHT	British Motor Industry Heritage Trust, which preserves the surviving records of some British vehicle manufacturers including Land Rover		MVEE	Military Vehicles Experimental Establishment – successor to FVRDE and MEXE
			MY	Model Year
BRIXMIS	British Commanders'-in-Chief Mission to the Soviet Forces in Germany		NAAFI	Navy, Army and Air Force Institute
			NATO	North Atlantic Treaty Organisation
Camo	Camouflage – often a reference to black on IRR green European Theatre camouflage		PA	Public Address
			PSA	Property Services Agency
CAD	Central Ammunition Depot		P&EE	Proof & Experimental Establishment
CDEE	Chemical Defence Experimental Establishment		OHV	Overhead Valve
CKD	Completely Knocked Down (ie a kit of parts to assemble a vehicle overseas)		OS&DD	Ordnance Storage & Distribution Depot
			OSD	Ordnance Storage Depot
CL	Commercial class of wheeled vehicles		RARDE	Royal Armament Research & Development Establishment
CONBAT	A conversion of the L4 MOBAT or L2 BAT, designated L7		Recce	Reconnaissance
CT	Combat class of wheeled vehicles		REME	Royal Electrical and Mechanical Engineers
EOD	Explosive Ordnance Disposal		RHD	Right Hand Drive
ESS	Enhanced Shore Support		RLC	Royal Logistic Corps
EW & EW/Y	Electronic Warfare and Interception		RM	Royal Marines
FACE	Field Artillery Computer Equipment		RNAS	Royal Naval Air Service
FARELF	Far-Eastern Land Forces		ROF	Royal Ordnance Factory
FC	Forward Control		RTR	Royal Tank Regiment
FFR	Fitted For Radio		SAGW	Surface-to-Air Guided Weapon
FFW	Fitted For Wireless		SAAS	Services Attaché and Adviser Service
FV	Fighting Vehicle, as in "FV pattern headlights"		SAS	Special Air Service
FVRDE	Fighting Vehicles Research and Development Establishment, Chertsey		Senät	The executive body governing Berlin
			SMMT	Society of Motor Manufacturers and Traders
GCHQ	Government Communications Headquarters		SP	Special Project – as used in Army registration series eg 01 SP 14
GPMG	General Purpose Machine Gun		TA	Territorial Army
GRP	Glass Reinforced Plastic		TACR	Truck Airfield Crash Rescue
GS	General Service class of wheeled vehicles		TOW	Tube-launched, Optically tracked, Wire-guided anti-tank missile
GTU	Garrison Transport Unit			
IFS	Independent Front Suspension		VPK	Vehicle Protection Kit
IFVME	Inspectorate of Fighting Vehicles and Mechanical Equipment		WOMBAT	Weapon Of AluminiuM – Battalion Anti-Tank
IoA	Inspectorate of Ammunition		WD	War Department
IRR	Infra-Red Reflecting		WO	War Office